Walking in Baltimore

WALKING IN BALTIMORE

An Intimate Guide to the Old City

FRANK R. SHIVERS JR.

Frank R. Shivers Jr.

The Johns Hopkins University Press
Baltimore & London

© 1995 The Johns Hopkins University Press
All rights reserved. Published 1995
Printed in the United States of America on acid-free paper
04 03 02 01 00 99 98 97 96   5 4 3 2

The Johns Hopkins University Press
2715 North Charles Street
Baltimore, Maryland 21218-4319
The Johns Hopkins Press Ltd., London

Library of Congress Cataloging-in-Publication Data

Shivers, Frank R., 1924–
    Walking in Baltimore : an intimate guide to the Old City / by
Frank R. Shivers Jr.
       p.   cm.
    ISBN 0-8018-4872-5 (acid-free paper). — ISBN 0-8018-4868-7
(pbk. : acid-free paper)
    1. Baltimore (Md.)—Guidebooks.   2. Walking—Maryland—
Baltimore—Guidebooks.   I. Title.
F189.B13S46   1995
917.52'60443—dc20   94-40575

A catalog record for this book is available from the British Library.

Illustration sources: Pages i, xv, Charles Norton; vii, 138, 141, 188,
Jean Louis Bouët; 2, 5, 6, 7, 12, 14, 15, 23, 46, 61, 91, 187, 206, 259,
Library of Congress; 6, 13, 98, 111, 167, Enoch Pratt Free Library; 8,
The Peale Museum, Baltimore City Life Museums; 9, 11, author's
collection; 16, Margaret Littlehales Shivers; 17, Pride of Baltimore,
Inc.; 95, Eubie Blake Cultural Center/Maryland Historical Society; 99,
Jewish Historical Society of Maryland, Inc.; 134, Maryland Historical
Society; 235, George Wend; 238, The Walters Art Gallery, Baltimore;
253, 257, Alan Mason Chesney Archives, The Johns Hopkins Medical
Institutions; 260, The Baltimore Museum of Art: The Cone Collec-
tion, formed by Dr. Claribel Cone and Miss Etta Cone as Baltimore,
Maryland, BMA 1950.300; 276, Margaret Warner Deford; 281,
National Portrait Gallery.

All other photographs by Lisa Frances Davis. Walking tour maps by
William L. Nelson, after drafts by Rodney Clough.

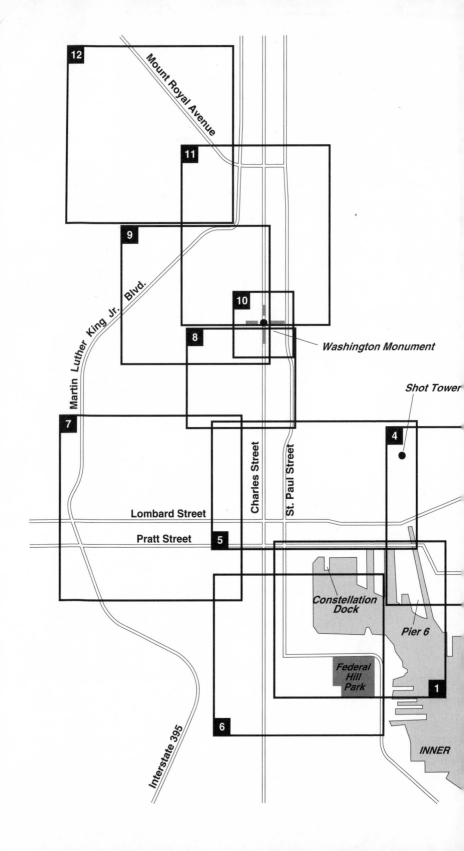

Washington Monument

Shot Tower

Charles Street

St. Paul Street

Martin Luther King Jr. Blvd.

Mount Royal Avenue

Lombard Street

Pratt Street

Constellation Dock

Pier 6

Federal Hill Park

Interstate 395

INNER

12

11

9

10

8

7

4

5

6

1

Broadway

0   .25   .50   .75   1 Mile

3

*Patterson
Park*

Eastern Avenue

2

HARBOR

A few years back, one of the *Sunpapers* published a picture to announce the coming of spring. It showed a street cleaner, looking very grumpy and grimy, doggedly pushing his broom, while directly above him that Mount Vernon Place statue of a little sprite was dancing away on one toe. I don't know why this should sum up Baltimore for me, but it does—perhaps because it combines blue-collar grittiness with a capacity for enjoyment that I think abounds in Baltimore.

Anne Tyler, letter to the author (1982, the year she published *Dinner at the Homesick Restaurant;* reprinted with permission)

Contents

Preface

This cozy semi-major city [Baltimore] exercises a powerful gravitational force . . . on its two leading literary residents, Anne Tyler and John Barth [who exhibit, as did H. L. Mencken], a sense of happy insulation, of brimming sufficiency in an exemplary province.

Critic John Updike, writing with a touch of irony in the *New Yorker* about Baltimoreans' passion for Baltimore (1991)

My own life in the exemplary province of Baltimore goes back only a generation. When my wife and I moved here from Cincinnati, we knew the city only as an obstacle for interstate drivers. Not for nothing was Baltimore called the ingrown toenail of the East Coast. Arriving here after a trip abroad, we thought we had come to another foreign country. People even talked a different language—Baltimorese—or puzzled us with strong Southern accents. Daily we barked our shins against local ways. Our 1860s house had real grandeur, but why were baseboards painted black? And why when we asked for window screens did the landlady say that screens only keep out the air?

The whole backward place looked like one of Italy's old cities—grand but shabby. Like them, it was hard to know. Maybe that was because Baltimoreans act slowly; they change their opinions only once a generation. No wonder another newcomer, Mrs. Alexander Smith Cochran, facing a perverse, old-fashioned town, cried for a year.

But Baltimore, like most delicious things, turned out to be an acquired taste. First, we began to find our way around. We learned that Maryland Avenue changed its name—twice. We even found addresses midst Old Town's snarl of tiny streets. Next, we discovered Baltimore history, were charmed, and wanted to know more. For instance, how did it happen that such a staid place figured in so many romantic pairings—those of Poe, the Duchess of Windsor, Blaze Starr, F. Scott Fitzgerald, Gertrude Stein, Prince Bonaparte, Russell Baker? Although we didn't find the answer to that and many other questions, we became converted Baltimoreans. "The more you know," wrote philosopher George Santayana, "the more beautiful everything becomes."

We made our greatest discovery when we found Baltimore's character hidden in neighborhoods and homes.

So we bought a Civil War rowhouse on Bolton Hill and settled down. "You soon learn in Baltimore that caring for an old house is one form of caring for Baltimore," wrote author Jonathan Yardley, another newcomer.

Now, so that you too can get to know Baltimore, I propose guiding you through twelve special districts. I have laid out a simple structure. You get your bearings in Tour 1 and then can choose among the ten walks that fall naturally into pairs. Each pair covers adjacent districts that have something interesting in common. Then comes a climactic tour. If you set aside a full morning and afternoon, with a decent Baltimore lunch between, you can well manage a pair of tours in a day, without hurrying.

All tours begin and end at Constellation Dock in the Inner Harbor. Sadly enough, as this book goes to press the old frigate herself, bowed and leaky, has been overdue for a trip away from her hometown to undergo repairs, so you may have to come back another time to see her. In any case, from Constellation Dock the tours fan out through areas easily reached by water-taxi or public transportation. Visiting districts that were settled before 1900 will take you back to Baltimore's heyday. Everywhere you will see how Baltimoreans have used urban space, what they have thought and still think handsome, and how they have hated pretension. Their rowhouses reflect a fear of being garish or overbearing. From funky Fells Point to classic Mount Vernon, Baltimore is nothing if not a city of contrasts.

Before you put on your walking shoes, study the pictures freshly taken by Lisa Frances Davis. Then, as you walk, listen to the witnesses tell of how things used to be. Their experiences enrich yours.

Now that the Inner Harbor, sparkling with newness, lures the once-disdainful traveler, 17 million people come to Baltimore each year. They—and you—can choose a tour and, book in hand, begin.

Note: For anyone wanting an introduction to Baltimore but with only a couple of hours to spare, take one of these three tours:

Tour 1 Harbor Promenade—a walk around the world-famous Inner Harbor and up on Federal Hill for a bird's-eye picture of the city

Tour 10 Mount Vernon Place and Washington Place— "the most imposing site to be found in any American city," reported an 1896 magazine, and a century later

still grand with the Washington Monument (1814)
towering over Baltimore's cultural parlor

PUBLISHER'S NOTE

This book is intended as a guide for those who
would explore historic Baltimore on foot. Unfortunately,
as is true in most large American cities, not every neighborhood provides the setting for safe, quiet strolling.
Readers who carry this book afield are reminded to
exercise the caution and good judgment appropriate
in urban areas and to consider driving when walking
seems unwise.

Walking in Baltimore

Introduction to Baltimore

Baltimore has ranked high as a special place for people as diverse as the Duchess of Windsor and John Waters, Henry Louis Mencken and Edgar Allan Poe, Eubie Blake and Cole Porter. "Baltimore is a great, colorful city with great, colorful characters," observed Barry Levinson, the native Baltimorean filmmaker. "It's a rich and fertile place and we're happy to put it up on film" (and one must accordingly see *Diner, Avalon,* and *Tin Men*).

You may locate the specialness yourself by walking through the streets. Places you will visit, Tony Hiss of the *New Yorker* said, "still anchor understandings of what it means to be a Baltimorean." Old street names that you will encounter do that, too. Their sources range from French priests (Tessier) to the idol of homesick Englishmen (Shakespeare), from world-roaming sailors (Boyle, Hull) to a New England entrepreneur (Peabody), from English peers who defended the rights of colonists (Pratt, Granby) to Revolutionary battles (Lexington, Saratoga). The name Water Street tells of settlement along a river arm of the Chesapeake Bay. And the word "hill" in so many spots reveals the town's siting, where tidewater meets the piedmont.

No place name points to the important fact of Baltimore's being "the tip of the South and the toe of the North" (as poet Ogden Nash wrote). The city lies below the Mason-Dixon Line. During the Civil War, some Baltimoreans fought for the Union, others for the Confederacy. In any event, Southern influence was perhaps what one observer detected when he said, "Baltimoreans are inclined to regard yesterday as more important and more divine than tomorrow."

Baltimore, as home, is one of the most delightful cities in the world. Situated about the centre of the Atlantic coast, at the head of the Great Mediterranean Sea of America, it is equally removed from the intense cold of northern latitudes, and the blinding heat of our more tropical sisters of the South. An equable climate, soft, balmy, salubrious, and almost entirely free from the dense fogs which are the horror of the generality of cities adjacent to the seaboard, gives to it that healthy mean, which is seldom present along any of the water courses of this country or Europe.

George W. Howard, *Baltimore, The Monumental City* (1873)

Pedestrians crossing open drains at Baltimore and Liberty streets, 1856. Cathedral dome in background.

Other influences entered the town via ships bringing immigrant families who gave Baltimore what columnist George F. Will called its rough tweed. You can especially feel it in the waterside districts of Canton and Federal Hill. It may be responsible for a point Anne Tyler raised —the Baltimorean's large capacity for enjoyment.

You will doubtless find other reasons in the following facts and time line.

FACTS

Baltimore: pronounced BAWL-tih-mohr (or Bawlamer by the natives), largest city in Maryland, metropolis of the Chesapeake Bay, with a population of 740,000 in 85 square miles. Its metropolitan area of 2,364 square miles holds a population of 2,500,000.

Altitude: 20 feet above sea level to 512 feet

Latitude: 39°12′

Climate: Average precipitation, 44 inches; average annual snowfall, 21.7 inches; days of rain or snow, 115; clear days, 105

Government: Mayor and Council (four-year term)

Founded: Chartered 1729; incorporated as a city 1797

City seal: The Battle Monument

City flag: The Battle Monument on a field of gold or orange and black diagonal stripes, colors deriving from the arms of the original seventeenth-century proprietors of Maryland, the Calverts, Lords Baltimore. The official state bird, the Baltimore Oriole, also displays these colors. The local baseball team uses the name of the bird and the Calverts' colors.

TIME LINE

The empty century, 1609–1729

Abroad during these years the Taj Mahal is completed, John Milton writes *Paradise Lost,* and Pompeii is unearthed.

1609 Capt. John Smith explores the Inner Harbor and makes note of Federal Hill.

1632 King Charles I grants Maryland charter to Cecil Calvert, second Lord Baltimore.

1634 First Calvert settlers arrive, buy land from Indians, and build Fort St. Mary's City.

1649 Maryland legislators pass an act of religious toleration, permitting all forms of Christian worship.

1661 Survey completed for David Jones of 380 acres along Jones Falls at present Front Street.

Baltimore's beginnings looked unpromising. Ironically, the Indian name for its river, Patapsco, meant a backwater. And the names Smith and Jones, discoverers of the site, lack glamor. Hereabouts tobacco planters tilled the land that originally Charles I had granted to the Calverts, Lords Baltimore, proprietors of Maryland.

The opening gate, 1729–1800

Abroad during this time, Jonathan Swift publishes *Gulliver's Travels,* Handel conducts his *Messiah,* and the British Museum opens.

1729 Baltimore-Town receives charter and is laid out.

1730 Estimated population of Maryland is 90,000.

1732 Jonestown (now Old Town) is laid out.

1756 Mount Clare Plantation is established.

1763 Fells Point is laid out.

1763 The first public produce market opens.

1776–77 The Continental Congress meets in Baltimore, after having fled the British in Philadelphia.

1797 Baltimore leaders obtain city incorporation.

Go to Mount Clare (now in Carroll Park) to learn what the terrain looked like before the town grew. At Mount Clare, one of the prominent Carrolls—Charles Carroll, Barrister—with others established an iron foundry and built the mansion that you can visit. Downriver from Mount Clare three settlements were founded and slowly prospered: Fells Point became the deep-water port and ship building center, Jones Town (now part of Old Town) developed as a kind of suburb of Fells Point, and Baltimore-Town soon attracted businessmen and fashion. By the end of the eighteenth century, the three had merged.

The first big promoter of the city, Dr. John Stevenson, instituted shipping wheat and flour abroad. That proved a smart move because abundant grain grew nearby, waterpower from piedmont streams turned mill wheels, and shipbuilding became a major industry. In addition, a site on the Great Eastern Road between Philadelphia and the South complemented its water road. Voyaging up the Chesapeake brought ships 100 miles nearer the interior of the continent than other cities.

The Baltimore of 1780, seen through the eyes of a visitor, was "so conceited, so bustling and debonaire, growing up like a chubby boy, with his dumpling cheeks and short, grinning face, fat and mischievous, and bursting incontinently out of his clothes." The rising town attracted immigrants by the boatload. Leadership arrived with merchants from Northern Ireland. They were said to be of the Venetian stamp because of their wealth and civic pride. These men sometimes married into families of the landed gentry. Whether they did or not, they together formed what to some observers was an aristocracy of talent. Together they built the village into a city.

A delegate to the Continental Congress, Samuel Adams, reported that "we have done more important business here in six weeks than we have done, or I believe should have been done, in Philadelphia in six months." Another delegate, however, wrote home, "If you desire to keep out of the damndest hole on earth, come not here."

Associated with the merchants was John Eager Howard, who served as an officer with the Maryland Line throughout the Revolution. As inheritor from his mother of most of Baltimore, he oversaw development. As promoter he gave land for public use, headed the commission to lay out streets, and generally pushed the city ahead.

Born on Baltimore Street, John Pendleton Kennedy remembered 1800 Baltimore as having "passed out of the village phase, but it had not got out of the village peculiarities. . . . Society had a more aristocratic air than now—not because the educated and wealthy assumed

Dined in Baltimore. This is the principal trading town of Maryland. It is regularly laid out and tolerably well built, but the situation is exceedingly inconvenient. Ships can't come within a mile of the town to a place called Fells Point when they are sent upon flats to town.

Nicholas Creswell's journal (1774–77)

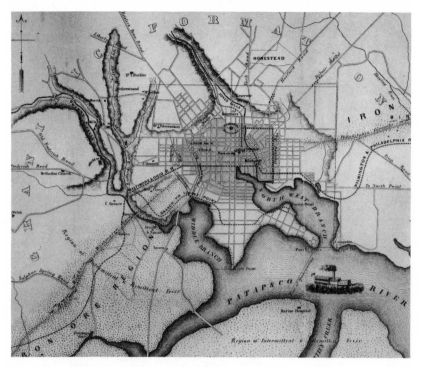

more, but because the community itself had a better appreciation of personal worth, and voluntarily gave it the healthful privilege of taking the lead in the direction of manners and in the conducting of public affairs." And, he added, "How sadly we have retrograded in these perfections ever since!"

Locations of frequent outbreaks of fevers, 1851; also note the expansion of the city away from the Inner Harbor.

Enterprising crossroads, 1800–1861

Abroad, a potato famine in Ireland and a revolution on the continent propel thousands to leave home. Louis Braille develops a new form of writing. Jane Austen publishes *Pride and Prejudice,* and Charles Darwin, *On the Origin of Species.*

1800–1815 Baltimore shipyards produce 122 Baltimore Clippers for privateering.

1807 A medical school is founded, around which will develop the University of Maryland.

1808 Mother Elizabeth Anne Seton opens academy for young women.

1813 First steamboat, *Chesapeake,* appears in the bay.

1814 Battle of Baltimore.

1816 Adjacent land is annexed and new streets are laid out, under the aegis of John Eager Howard, chief landowner.

Aerial view of Baltimore from the north, with the harbor in the distance and the Washington Monument dominant in the foreground.

1817 First gas streetlight in the world is lit on Holliday Street.

1828 Baltimore & Ohio Railroad is founded.

1830 Population of 80,625 makes Baltimore the second largest American city (after New York).

1830 Peter Cooper and local investors open the first industrial park in America on the Canton plantation.

1832 *Ann McKim,* first of Baltimore's Clipper ships, is launched.

1833 Resident writer Edgar Allan Poe receives his first public recognition by winning a $50 prize for "Ms. Found in a Bottle."

1838 Frederick Douglass escapes from slavery by train from Baltimore.

1849 Edgar Allan Poe dies in a Broadway hospital and is buried in a cemetery plot with grandparents Poe on Greene and Fayette streets.

1860 Druid Hill Park opens (still the largest city park).

1861 Civil War's first blood is shed, on Pratt Street, when a Baltimore mob attacks Massachusetts volunteers.

1863 President Lincoln delivers the "Liberty Address" at Maryland Institute and spends the night as a guest of William Albert on Mount Vernon Place.

Baltimore became a nest of pirates in British eyes when shipping was raided for Baltimoreans' profit. Raiders were fast schooners called Baltimore Clippers. Appropriately, the War of 1812 culminated in a British attack on Baltimore, September 12–13, 1814. Citizens, with some outside help, defeated the enemy. Thus Baltimore remained the only major American city never occupied by foreign forces. A Marylander, Francis Scott Key, witnessed the attack and celebrated victory in a poem, "The Star-Spangled Banner." Postwar Baltimoreans made the town the peppiest in the Union. Its clipper schooners threaded trade routes everywhere, carrying cargoes of wheat and flour from the back country.

To reach farther and farther west, citizens evolved a railroad, the Baltimore & Ohio (B&O). Philip Thomas borrowed the idea from England, and Peter Cooper, investor and inventor, helped make it work. So did inventor Ross Winans and financiers Johns Hopkins and John Work Garrett.

Commerce and money may have been the sea on which Baltimore floated, but civilizing tides lifted it to notice everywhere. Edgar Allan Poe, for example, scion

Pre–Civil War slave buildings near Pratt and Howard streets, where slaves were lodged before sale.

8

Rectory of Old St. Paul's Episcopal Church (*left*), where the Poetry Society of Maryland met. Johns Hopkins's mansion is on the right.

of a local family, achieved his first public recognition in Baltimore. Here he found himself (and was found) as a writer. And another resident, Mother Elizabeth Seton, began her founding of the American parochial school when she moved to Paca Street. Other innovators were the artists in the Peale family. Rembrandt Peale not only painted, but also built the first museum building in the country. After being the first person anywhere to light a street with gas light, he formed the first company to light a city.

Civilizing influences came with notable architecture. Luckily, the city attracted three architects of genius who created landmarks: Benjamin Henry Latrobe's Cathedral, Robert Mills's Washington Monument, and Maximilien Godefroy's Unitarian Church and his Battle Monument. The classic restraint embodied in those works influenced builders of rowhouses. They thus gave Baltimore its logo —refined and restrained style in red-brick rows with white-marble trim. Baltimore County quarries yielded the white marble.

The town needed civilizing. Slaves were declining in numbers (one slave who had learned to read and write in Baltimore, Frederick Douglass, went on to become a heroic statesman and reformer), but free blacks, a relatively large group, suffered discrimination. Violent rioting gave Baltimore the name of Mob Town. In 1812 a mob broke into jail to kill or maim men whose political opinions offended. Violence erupted again in 1835, when

Francis Scott Key
Monument, with
Altamont Hotel, c. 1915

popular anger over a bank closing led to several sacked
houses, including the mayor's.

One mayor, on April 19, 1861, confronted and tried
to appease a pro-Confederate crowd but failed to prevent shedding of the first blood in the Civil War. Southern sympathizers that day attacked Massachusetts troops
moving through the city to defend Washington. Soon
afterward, Baltimore was occupied by Union troops,
who stayed longer even than did troops in New Orleans.
An English newspaperman, William Howard Russell,
called wartime Baltimore "the Warsaw of the United
States."

Foundry and melting pot, 1861–1904

Abroad pogroms in Russia and Poland send thousands into exile. The French build the Eiffel Tower and
develop the first popular form of photography. Dosto-
yevsky publishes *Crime and Punishment,* and Charles
Dickens, *Great Expectations.*

1866 Peabody Institute opens.
1870 Pimlico Race Course opens.
1876 Johns Hopkins University opens.

There is a city for you—
mere rabble. I am not
surprised at their tarring
and feathering, maiming
and murdering: ashamed I
am that I am a native of
the state.

Anne Royall (1828)

1877 Employees of B&O Railroad strike along line, riot in Baltimore, to institute biggest labor strike in U.S. history.

1886 Streets are renumbered, with Charles Street as the new divider between east and west (replacing Calvert Street).

1887 Chesapeake oyster harvesting and canning peaks.

1889 Enoch Pratt Free Library opens.

1889 Johns Hopkins Hospital opens.

1899 Henrietta Szold opens school for immigrant children.

After the Civil War, Baltimore became the "Poor House of the Confederacy." Virginians and others came here seeking to recoup their fortunes. Since some of them brought a love of education and cultural expression, they raised the tone of the town. European immigrants also arrived. Women and children, as well as men, worked in factories turning out canned tomatoes, pianos, straw hats, umbrellas, and trains.

A German immigrant named Ottmar Mergenthaler invented the linotype. Russian Jews worked in sweatshops making clothes. And some jobs went to freed slaves drifting north, mostly in domestic service and other menial work. In time off work, newcomers took what pleasures they could in new parks, church socials, and clubs. By the end of the century, streetcar lines wove together all parts of town and extended to waterside resorts where people could try to escape the awful subtropical heat. Everyone sampled the finfish and shellfish pulled from the bay.

Four rich men endowed institutions that made them known outside their city. George Peabody gave the first cultural center—a public library, an art gallery, a conservatory of music, and space for the Maryland Historical Society's collections.

Enoch Pratt paid for the first public circulating library and branch libraries. William and Henry Walters, father and son, paid for 5,000 years of the world's art. To house the collections, Henry built a palatial gallery, which he willed with the collections to the citizens of Baltimore.

Johns Hopkins founded a university (one that stressed graduate scholarship) and a hospital (to which a medical school was later added). His gifts are credited with moving American medical training and all scholar-

I eat, drink, and sleep Russians. In fact, the Russian business so absorbs my thoughts that I have gone back to my early girlish longing to be a man. I am sure that if I were one I could mature plans of great benefit to them.

Henrietta Szold, founder of a night school for immigrant Russian Jews in Old Town (letter, October 31, 1891)

ship into the modern world. Hopkins physicians such as
William Osler Baltimoreans practically deified.

Mount Royal Station,
B&O Railroad, c. 1900

*Noon and a long afternoon of the Queen City of
the Patapsco, 1904–1960*
Abroad, two world wars, the Holocaust, and the
atomic bomb make people very familiar with tragedy.
Leaders of culture are excited by a Paris exhibit of paintings by Les Fauves (the Wild Beasts, including Matisse).
George Orwell publishes *Animal Farm*.

1904 Fire destroys most of downtown, including more
than 1,500 structures and 2,500 businesses, from
Hopkins Place to Jones Falls and from the harbor to
Lexington Street—seventy blocks of ruins.
1909 Walters Art Gallery is built (bequeathed to city,
1931).
1909 The Back River sewage treatment plant opens to
provide the first proper sewers in the city.
1914 Babe Ruth pitches for International League Orioles.
1914 The Baltimore Museum of Art is incorporated and
exhibits in Miss Mary Garrett's mansion on Mount
Vernon Place.
1916 H. L. Mencken publishes first book of *Prejudices*.

Official inspection of
oyster takes, Long Wharf,
Inner Harbor, 1914

1918 City's final annexation of county districts.

1931 Dashiell Hammett publishes *The Glass Key,* a murder mystery based on Baltimore's political corruption.

1935 University of Maryland School of Law opens to African Americans after NAACP attorney Thurgood Marshall brings suit.

1958 Baltimore Colts win the National Football League championship.

1958 Greater Baltimore Committee announces plans for Charles Center.

The Big Fire cleared out much of the city's downtown architecture. Although repairing the damage brought little improvement to ancient street patterns, businessmen rebuilt offices rapidly. Baltimore continued to be the sinful seaport where H. L. Mencken said you could get "earfuls and eyefuls of instruction in a hundred giddy arcana, none of them taught in school."

Steamboats spun a cobweb connecting towns around the bay. In summer, Baltimoreans voyaged to Chesapeake resorts on both shores. So polluted was the Inner Harbor in 1912 that the water stained white hulls of ships a foul yellow. Officials of the Pennsylvania Railroad ordered their steamboats repainted a deep Pennsylvania Railroad red.

The advent of automobiles perhaps enlarged the romance attached to horses. Contests at Pimlico Race Track supported innumerable bookmakers. The Preakness, inaugurated in the 1870s, became the second race of the Triple Crown. The horsy set gradually gave up its winter townhouses to live in the valleys miles to the north.

Lexington Street, Pascault Row, c. 1920

No city outside of Boston, Cleveland Amory said, set such store by family pride as oldtime Baltimoreans did. One of them, Wallis Warfield, later Duchess of Windsor, believed her own pedigree certainly as fine as that of Lady Elizabeth Bowes-Lyon, who became queen instead of the Baltimorean after King Edward VIII's abdication in 1936.

Intellectual females also found a place, although a more tenuous one than that of girls who came out at the Bachelor's Cotillon. Women of high caliber, such as M. Carey Thomas, Gertrude Stein, the Cone sisters, and Edith Hamilton, managed to achieve a good deal despite living in Baltimore.

As for literary males, four or five grew up around Union Square. H. L. Mencken became, some say, the conscience of intellectual America in the 1920s. Dashiell Hammett made his mark as founder of the hard-boiled school of detective fiction. Russell Baker, who lived and worked in Baltimore as a young man, later earned a reputation as humorist and memoirist.

World War II war
workers David Marlin
and Walter Shired,
Bethlehem Fairfield
Shipyards, May 1943

New York's Harlem Renaissance of the 1920s set a
standard Baltimore tried to match. Black entertainers
with local roots—Eubie Blake, Billie Holliday, Cab
Calloway among them—made national reputations.
Pennsylvania Avenue theaters and clubs attracted white
patrons as well as black into the 1940s.

Early suburbs followed streetcar lines and spread
into surrounding counties after cars became cheap. But
Baltimoreans entered the motor age with characteristic
reluctance, and so they built only one expressway before
1970. Citizen pressure later forced bureaucrats to tunnel
interstate I-95 under the harbor instead of knifing right
through the heart of the old city.

During two world wars, settled Baltimoreans noted
the arrival of thousands of newcomers, many of them
from rural areas. Housing war workers posed serious
challenges, and many old neighborhoods, badly over-
crowded, declined.

*The scrubbed-clean face of preservation and
renewal in key places, 1960–95*
Abroad the Cold War's terrors are mitigated once
by three English Nobel laureates discovering the

Overheated dog and man
on steps, July 1938; mortar
lines are painted on bricks
of rowhouse façade.

structure of DNA. Graham Greene publishes *A Burnt Out Case*.

1966 Baltimore Orioles win the World Series in four games.

1968 Riots follow the murder of Martin Luther King Jr.

1971 Inner Harbor redevelopment begins.

1975 Pope Paul VI canonizes Mother Elizabeth Anne Seton.

1976 Tall ships from around the world sail into Inner Harbor for U.S. bicentennial and attract huge crowds.

1976 Maryland Science Center opens.

1979 Baltimore Convention Center opens.

1980 The Rouse Company's Harborplace opens.

1981 The National Aquarium at Baltimore opens.

1982 Barry Levinson writes and directs *Diner*.

1982 Russell Baker publishes *Growing Up* and wins Pulitzer Prize.

1983 Baltimore Orioles win the World Series.

1985 Anne Tyler publishes *The Accidental Tourist* and wins Pulitzer Prize.

1986 Clarence "Du" Burns, president of the Baltimore City Council, becomes Baltimore's first African-

Bolton Common

American mayor, succeeding William Donald Schaefer, who became governor of Maryland.

1987 Kurt Schmoke wins election as mayor—the city's first African American to be so honored.

1992 Oriole Park at Camden Yards opens.

1992 Baltimore and Washington, D.C., officially join as Washington-Baltimore Consolidated Metropolitan Statistical Area of six million, fourth largest metropolitan area.

1993 Christopher Columbus Center of Marine Research and Exploration opens.

Much of Baltimore had been preserved. As late as the 1990s, most nineteenth-century streetscapes were still intact. Landmark structures like the Shot Tower and the Flag House had been cared for. Solid buildings like the B&O Mount Royal Station (it houses a library and studios for the Maryland Institute College of Art) have been recycled. Whole streetscapes have survived through "homesteading," a plan by which one buys a house shell for one dollar. "Shopsteading" has followed.

Renewal of downtown began in 1958 with the thirty-three acres of Charles Center. It gave Baltimore a New York look with a new hotel, parking, two theaters, apartments, shops, numerous offices. Then eighty-five more acres were revived all around the Inner Harbor. Today millions go there each year, partly for the series of concerts, shows, and festivals open to sky and water (and

A big city is not a number of people. It's a set of attitudes and values. Higher education, arts, sports—that's what makes Baltimore a big city.

Robert Keller, president of the Greater Baltimore Committee (February 11, 1992)

Baltimore has the frowzy, out-of-the-elbow, forlorn air of a third-rate boarding house.

H. L. Mencken, *Evening Sun* (April 18, 1910)

mostly free), and partly just to enjoy the sights and people-watch.

Pride of Baltimore II

The city is the front office of civilization still, as H. L. Mencken said, but Baltimore's front office is changing.

Inner Harbor Promenade and Vistas from Federal Hill Park

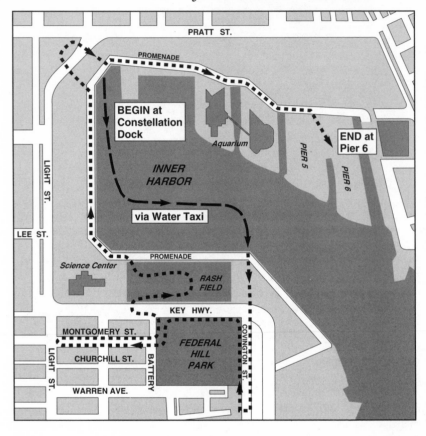

- "The welcoming city of Oz," as a visitor called the Inner Harbor, with a waterfront that is fun to visit and a view of the old port worthy of San Francisco
- The heart of the heart of the city for visitors, with the National Aquarium, Science Center, proposed Sports Center USA, and Christopher Columbus Center for Marine Research and Exploration
- The world's tallest pentagonal office building and other high-profile structures by internationally known architects
- One of the earliest waterside festival market-places—brainchild of James Rouse, native Marylander
- Historic ships, including the first ship in the U.S.

Navy and the last submarine to sink a Japanese ship in World War II

A hundred miles up the Chesapeake Bay from the ocean, at the fall line of the Patapsco River, sparkles the carnival-like Inner Harbor. Every prospect pleases. Here waterfront and what amounts to a pleasure lake look like Tivoli Gardens in Copenhagen. And Federal Hill elevates you for views of city, port, and saltwater like San Francisco's.

The Inner Harbor, though, is no foreign place: it introduces the comfortable balance that makes Baltimore Baltimore. You will see a natural hill on the south side balanced by manmade high-rises on the north. Here this city integrates North with South, new with old. Although comfort and attractiveness count, no one knows for sure why natives and visitors alike find happiness in the Inner Harbor. Just notice how many couples of all stripes stroll along holding hands.

Because this rim of water looks too new and maybe a bit glitzy, it's a good idea to connect it with the rest of the city and link it with shaping forces of the past. For the place has a long, long history. You are not in a sudden metropolis, like Houston, or a new town, like James Rouse's Columbia, Maryland, so recently farmland.

Planners now worry that the Promenade could be anywhere at all because it lacks obvious evidence of what is special about Baltimore. So new images may be in place by the time you arrive: horse racing at the Preakness Stakes, Civil War battlefields, what has been called the "beauty and easy charm of the Eastern Shore." And everywhere you may see reminders of good times at old-home crab feasts—the image of the Atlantic blue crab.

HISTORY

Named by Indians, the Patapsco River lured its first European mapmaker, Capt. John Smith, to Baltimore harbor in 1608. What he saw did not excite him. He described the red clay of our Federal Hill ("resembling bole Armoniac"), but didn't foresee a major port below that hill. Not until a century and a quarter later did surveyors lay out Baltimore-Town across the river from the hill.

"White sails to white sails" sums up the rest of Inner Harbor history. In the eighteenth century, white-sailed ships, built here, carried flour to the Caribbean and Europe. Now in front of you spread white sails of pleasure boats.

Baltimore visitors in 1880 all agreed, often with lubricious gloats and gurgles, (a) that its indigenous victualry was unsurpassed in the Republic, (b) that its native Caucasian females of all ages up to thirty-five were of incomparable pulchritude, and as amiable as they were lovely, and (c) that its home life was spacious, charming, full of creature comforts, and highly conducive to the facile and orderly propagation of the species.

H. L. Mencken, *Happy Days* (1940)

No major city, with the possible exception of Boston, has more inventively transformed its once-declining waterfront into a civic asset. There's more in store too, and the talents of some of those involved bode well.

Benjamin Forgey, *Washington Post* (December 29, 1990)

Inner Harbor/Aquarium

"There's no real separating the past from the present in a town such as ours," wrote *Evening Sun* columnist Jacques Kelly. In Baltimore you will find persistence of colonial street patterns and street names. Calvert Street, for example, has run north from the water ever since 1729 when Maryland's proprietary Calvert family ran the show. Another early name, Light Street, played wittily on the name of eighteenth-century landowner Capt. Darby Lux: *lux* is Latin for "light."

Here at the Inner Harbor you face a knot of commercial routes, both land and sea. From colonial tobacco wharves to today's Harborplace and Promenade, this riverside has pumped money lavishly.

Wars have brought prosperity and trouble. In the American Revolution, the town prospered as it remained one of the few ports not occupied by the British. In the War of 1812, Baltimore Clippers raided treasure from enemy cargo ships. "Wealth by stealth," to quote a chronicler. In 1814 Baltimoreans faced pillage and fire by Redcoats, who had just whipped Napoleon and burned Washington. "A near-run thing" is how the Duke of

Wellington described the Battle of Baltimore.

The Civil War also brought trouble. Since President Lincoln needed Maryland as shield to protect the national capital, Union troops on May 13, 1861, seized Federal Hill and trained guns on a city of divided loyalties. After the war, steamboats bustled below this hill. And harborside canneries here and farther east furnished oysters and peaches in such abundance that Baltimore became the canning capital of the world.

After the Civil War, the Baltimore and Bremen Line and the Allan Line instituted the first regular transatlantic passenger steamship service. Just out of sight on that right-hand shore, Baltimore's counterpart of Ellis Island's structures admitted more than 700,000 immigrants. In the nineteenth century, a crossing took a month or more. Often a deck of only 200 feet was allotted for 700 to 1,000 passengers. "In Hamburg David and I bought two sacks of straw [for beds]," recalled Heinrich Moller in 1860.

Steamboats and canneries are no more. In the 1960s rotting timbers of their old piers disappeared under fill for the Promenade in front of Harborplace. Today that market and other Inner Harbor magnets attract more visitors annually than does Disney World. "It's not [important] how many people live in a city," said James Rouse, developer of Harborplace, "it's how many people use it."

TOUR

Starting point: Constellation Dock, Inner Harbor
Length of tour: Two hours
Snacks and rest stops: Harborplace, Gallery at Harborplace, Chart House, Rusty Scupper
Transportation: Water-taxi

Begin your tour by boarding a water-taxi from its Constellation Dock landing, next to Harborplace Amphitheater at the south end of Calvert Street. You will be heading across the river to Federal Hill. While your taxi threads its way among tiny paddleboats, look back at the glittering shore. That vista shows the awakening of what a visitor in 1950 had called "the chief dead lady of East Coast cities."

Look ahead of you at Federal Hill. Its grassy softness balances the hardness of skyscrapers behind you. The water skirting the hill gives gentle permanence. *Debark at Landing 4 (Rusty Scupper). Cross Key Highway and walk along Covington Street. At the first intersection,*

Lounger on Constellation
Dock with water view

*Grindall Street, turn right and immediately take the steps
going up on the right. At the top, proceed straight ahead
along a path to Warren Avenue.* Pause there to look at
rowhouses, a park, and a long water view.

*For people who don't want to climb steps, take a water-
taxi voyage around the harbor and land at the Science
Center. Walk to the left of the building and turn left along
the Key Highway sidewalk. Cross to Battery Avenue (it
passes the western edge of the hill). Go one block to Warren
Avenue, turn left, and walk until you come to a driveway
into the park. Turn left onto a path flanked by a water
fountain and sundial.* Too much shade inhibits the latter,
a sixty-year-old memorial to Yankee soldiers.

At the top of Federal Hill, pause to look around. You
will see playground swings and picnic tables, handy for
nearby residents. The park marks the northern boundary
of the Federal Hill Historic District, twenty blocks of
nineteenth-century working-class rows. Rehabilitated
homes edge the park. New residents easily walk downtown or commute the forty miles to Washington on

Captain Joshua Barney: Baltimore naval hero

Near Federal Hill Park runs Barney Street, honoring Capt. Joshua Barney, naval hero of the American Revolution and the War of 1812. He supplied his hometown with a heroic image of its own vigor and audacity. Off the British coast he recorded in the *Chasseur*'s log such successes as "July 31, seized brig *Nymph*. Took and burnt the *Princess Royal*. August 1, Took and manned ship *Kitty*. August 2, Took and burnt brig *Fame,* brig *Devonshire,* schooner *Squid*."

When in 1788 the whole city turned out to celebrate ratification of the new federal Constitution, Barney stole the show. Ascending Federal Hill on a wagon drawn by four horses, the captain stood on the deck of a miniature ship. Fifteen feet long, the fully rigged ship sported three masts. Once it was anchored on the hilltop, Barney fired a salute from its brass cannon.

After the party, Barney sailed this miniature ship, *The Federalist,* down the Chesapeake and up the Potomac River to Mount Vernon. There he presented it to George Washington "in the name of the merchants and shipmasters of Baltimore, as a memorial of their gratitude, respect, and veneration for the great achiever of their country's liberty and independence." Washington was perplexed as to what to do with "that beautiful curiosity" (his phrase). Luckily for him, a storm destroyed it.

freeways or train. That is why real estate—especially with a water view—costs the earth.

You will be circumnavigating the edge of the park hill. From this starting point, you face the first of three vistas giving an overview of districts to be toured with this guide.

What you see jumbles Baltimore's history. Behind you in the middle of the park, for example, shipowners used to pay a watchman to man a thirty-foot wooden tower (now demolished). Built in 1795, it was shaped like a Dutch windmill, with a gallery at the top—the whole surmounted by a flagpole. On it, the watchman raised a merchant's flag to signal the sighting of a returning vessel.

In the nineteenth century, industrialists mined Federal Hill itself. Its clay formed the now admired Bennett "Rebecca pitchers." The hill's sand supplied the glass factory belonging to a son of John Frederick Amelung, creator of prized Amelung glass. So much mining—and erosion—damaged the hill.

*Begin with the eastern vista, down a long lake-like river
stretching out of sight to the Chesapeake Bay.* Far out on
the right-hand shore, railroad tracks weave their way to
Locust Point grain elevators, coal depots, and docks.

Look to the right toward the ten-story Domino Sugar
sign of 1922, said to be one of the largest neon signs anywhere. Next to it a tall white building stores 6 million
pounds of sugar—one day's production. "If the raw
product [molasses] is being unloaded from a ship's
hold," wrote columnist Jacques Kelly, "the harbor will
smell like cotton candy." Other odors sometimes blend
in, noted another writer with a sensitive nose—"decay-
ing fish, tankage, decomposed animal matter, sulfuric
acid, sludge, rendered bones . . . cocoa-bean hulls and
so-called 'trace odors.'"

You are facing east toward Fort McHenry, where this
Northwest Branch of the Patapsco River meets Middle
Branch. (Read about the fort, now a national park, in
Tour 6.) Off to the far right, look for the arch of Francis
Scott Key Bridge, whose heavy traffic bypasses the city.
It is named for the poet of "The Star-Spangled Banner,"
who witnessed "the bombs bursting in air" from a ship
anchored near the bridge site. Near the bridge, notice
tall cranes for loading container ships.

You may see an exotic sight as well. "Out of the mist
comes riding a clipper ship with the effortless speed of
an albatross," wrote historian Samuel Eliot Morison
about a tall ship such as you may be lucky enough to
spot sailing in from the Chesapeake. Tall ships have been
visiting this port since the 1976 Bicentennial celebration
attracted an international fleet of sail.

In the water within this eastern vista the first successful submarine submerged (1897), when inventor
Simon Lake launched his *Argonaut* to run along the river
bottom on big wheels. From there he held an under-
water-to-land telephone conversation with the mayor.
Then the *Argonaut* voyaged to Norfolk—mostly under-
water. When it surfaced downriver, a lone fisherman
fled in terror.

To the east, the vista extends on the left-hand shore
beyond Fort McHenry toward Sparrows Point and Bethlehem Steel's chief plant. In 1900 the company boasted
owning the largest steel plant on tidewater in the world.

Nearer, and to the right of where you are standing,
rises the first tower of a planned 1,490-unit condo-
minium community, HarborView (1993). The top four
floors of the seventeen-story structure are divided into
twelve penthouse apartments at prices ranging from

$750,000 to $1.5 million. "If the truth be known," said architect Richard Burns, "we had to convince Richard [Swirnow, the developer] that . . . people weren't going to buy a building that looked like a machine in the sky. [He] would have wanted an all-glass building with wrap-around balconies on every floor, not unlike something you'd see in Miami Beach." With an eight-sided beacon at top, the tower at night looks like a lighthouse—an extraordinarily bright one.

To the left and across the river, another huge development will be coming into place. When finished, the twenty-odd acres of cleared land may retain ten acres for park and hold a million square feet of office space and 400 houses. You can imagine how protective city-lovers feel about this intrusion on such a prominent slice of waterfront. Until recently, the tip nearest you contained a chrome processing plant that had polluted so heavily that owner Allied Chemical has paid $100 million to clean and cap the site. On the right shore, cruise ships will embark passengers—if plans work out.

Behind this cleared site, the church steeples of Canton and Fells Point survive from the era when the Roman Catholic archdiocese provided each national group of immigrants with a church. Look on the horizon for the copper domes of the new St. Michael's Ukrainian Catholic Church in Canton. Canton survives as a rowhouse neighborhood built around an early industrial park. Space inside several old factories has been converted to modern apartments (*Tour 3*).

Nearer to the water, note old brick warehouses of Fells Point. Over there you face a rarity, an eighteenth-century port town in the heart of a big, modern city (*Tour 2*). There, early nineteenth-century shipbuilders built the Baltimore Clipper. "A beautiful vessel," wrote English traveler Edward J. Trelawney, "[it] looked and moved like an Arab horse in the desert and was as obedient to command."

Look left of Fells Point to the north and find a hill topped by the complex of Johns Hopkins Medical Institutions—mostly red brick. The hospital's original dome (1879) is overshadowed by newer, less memorable buildings. Every year a national poll of physicians places Hopkins at the top for quality.

Lower your eye to the shoreline again. There, new construction is always beginning. All along the shore, commercial ships used to congregate. For instance, the Merchants and Miners Transportation Company's coast-wise ships docked there. Founded in 1852 when Baltimore was a tanning center, this line hauled tanned leather to Boston and brought back finished shoes and other leather merchandise. "Cargo was handled through sideports similar to those on Noah's ark," said retired employee J. Frederick Douty. "From the north came canned goods, chocolates, machinery, shoes and soap. From the south came fruit, raw wool in big bags, lumber and stinking bundles of uncured hides."

If you look to the right of the four smokestacks of the Power Plant, you will find the next major hump, Scarlett Place. Its apartments surmount the old Scarlett Seed Company headquarters building in what critics see as an awkward attempt to preserve a landmark. The new suffocates the old. Project architects called it an image of an Italian hill town, meant to link thematically the new apartments with old Little Italy, a segment of rowhoused streets to the right of Scarlett Place. "A 15-story brick wall," said architect Richard Burns. "It's very unfriendly. It's like a fortress."

Next, to the left behind a tent, find the white Christopher Columbus Center for Marine Research and Exploration. Find the glass pyramids of the Marine Mammal Pavilion and the National Aquarium at Baltimore. You will be walking past them later. On the horizon, Memorial Stadium is just visible. There the Baltimore Colts created football mania so intense that removal of the team to Indianapolis still pains fans. There, too, the Baltimore Orioles played for pennants and World Series victories.

Now walk left along the edge of the hill to the corner where you face downtown skyscrapers. By your side stands a monument to Col. George Armistead, "the gallant defender of Fort McHenry near this city during the bombardment by the British Fleet 13 and 14 of September 1814" (so reads the now much blurred inscription). "This tight precise block of stone is unworthy of the brave and dauntless men who withstood the fire of that hostile fleet," a sentimental Baltimorean complained. Next to it is a statue of Gen. Sam Smith, organizer of the town's defense at the time. If his name had been something more striking than Smith, he might be better remembered. In Smith's funeral procession, Pres. Martin Van Buren rode in an open barouche with the governor and mayor.

As you look across the harbor (moving your eyes nearer to the *Constellation*), you can see skyscrapers in pale colors. Most of them were built by banks to advertise their prominence. To the right of that mountain

range, you can just see the white dome of City Hall (1875) topped with a gold hat.

USF *Constellation,* oyster boat *Minnie V,* and tourists

Since it isn't possible to give a note for each building in your downtown view, wait for discussion of some prominent structures—mostly banks—in Tour 5. From up here you can see, just left of the row of tall banks, what can be thought of as a giant gateway. The right gatepost is formed by the gray-blue-green World Trade Center. It rises 423 feet above the water, the tallest pentagon anywhere when built. "That shape prevents the tower from walling off views of the city from the water as a rectangular building would," said an out-of-town architectural critic. "The transparency of the glass base combined with its pale coloring keep the building from overwhelming its neighbors." The World Trade Center resembles a beacon for passersby.

As a left-hand gatepost the gold-tinted, forty-story United States Fidelity and Guarantee (USF&G) headquarters aligns with the right-hand post of the World Trade Center. For these tall buildings, city leaders chose designs by nationally known out-of-town architects; I. M. Pei did the World Trade Center and Vlastimil Koubek, the USF&G. They hoped that the architects' prestige would rub off on this city.

In between those towers, seen as two quite narrow gateposts, there appears what can be imagined as a very wide gate, the white tower of the IBM Building. Its tiara at top has raised hackles: "part erector set, part jungle gym, part skeletal cornice piece, part Mohawk warrior/ urban punk-rocker hairdo" is how the *Sun* architectural critic saw it.

Midway along this northern rim, notice what could be a Civil War cannon aimed at those skyscrapers. It remains from sixty guns deployed in the 1861 seizure of this promontory by Union troops. They made part of an occupying army ordered to keep secessionists from forcing Baltimore and its border state, Maryland, into the Confederacy.

Now turn to your left to survey the western vista. You are looking at the beginning of the Piedmont hills that eventually build up to the Allegheny Mountains. In your near view, you scan rows and rows of nineteenth-century rowhouses. "Baltimore appeared to my eyes," wrote an English visitor a century ago, "as a formal red brick place enveloped in dullness." Today residents of those old brick rows find them anything but dull.

On that side of the hill the vista encompasses the rehabilitated south end of the B&O Railroad freight warehouse. Above it are the lights of Oriole Park at Camden Yards. That set of preserved and new buildings opened in 1992 to cheers (*Tour 7*). Look for a pair of gold-capped towers on the Church of the Lord Jesus Christ in Otterbein (*Tour 6*). It adjoins old rows of nationally known "dollar houses" sold by lot in the 1970s to restorers for $1 apiece.

Now that you have completed walking three sides of the hill, you are ready to descend. Leave the park at Warren

> There are few American cities in which one could so immediately locate oneself were one to be led blindfolded into minor streets. . . . It has street after street of neat [red brick] houses . . . bound together by the white cornice at the top and by the recurrent white marble steps.
>
> Henry-Russell Hitchcock (1953)

Avenue, turn right at Battery Avenue to go downhill. At Montgomery Street turn left, amble along two blocks of restored early rows. (For a full tour of these streets, take Tour 4.) *Then return to Battery Avenue and descend to Key Highway and cross to the park on the east—right side—of the red-brick Science Center.* You are walking where shipyard workers built wooden ships bound for Brazil's coffee ports.

Descend to the waterside Promenade next to the carousel, turn right, and proceed eastward until you see a flower garden on the right surrounding what looks like the mast of a sailing vessel. That pole centers the *Pride of Baltimore* memorial. Its location may have changed by the time you arrive. In 1976 builders reproduced a nine-teenth-century Baltimore Clipper to sail the globe adver-tising Baltimore. A decade later, the *Pride of Baltimore* was caught near Bermuda in the kind of storm—a micro-burst—that early sailors rightly feared. When she sank, the captain and three of the crew drowned. Experts blamed the loss partly on the builders' fidelity to the original design and absence of up-to-date safety equip-ment. No wonder the Baltimore Clipper had been called "a wild and skittery thoroughbred of a sailing ship."

Today you may be lucky enough to see the *Pride of Baltimore II* (1988). Although it looks like *Pride I,* it is 50 percent larger. Key alterations in design and equipment supposedly ensure a safe voyage for its crew of twelve (the 1813 Clipper *Chasseur* carried fifty-five).

Rash Field remembers Joseph Rash, a man from out of town who while vice-president of Safeway Stores in the 1950s headed the city's Park Board. It used to be said that outsiders like Rash pumped the civic and cultural life blood of Baltimore. Rash Field began as sports space for nearby Southern High School and now serves kids flying kites. Kite-flyers give a wide berth to festive flower gardens surrounding the *Pride* memorial.

Return to the Promenade from Rash Field, turn left, and stay on it past the Maryland Science Center. Most likely you have already seen Imax shows on a sixty-foot screen inside, particularly if you have had children in tow. Attractions often show nature's violence—earth-quakes, fires, volcanoes. The rest of the Science Center (685-5225) focuses on human achievement, including the Davis Planetarium.

Within a hundred yards or so of the Science Center are scattered a half dozen sculptures. There is no telling where they will be when you are walking along the Har-bor Promenade. One reason is a $7-million reorganizing

and freshening of Rash Field and the west shore. Here
you have a list given with the original locations:

In front of the waterside entrance to the Science Center:
Easy Landing (1967), by Kenneth Snelson. "A force
diagram in space" is Snelson's description of the construction (made of stainless steel, compression tubes,
and tension cables).

To the immediate right (facing the water): *Yuai Tachigata*
(1984)—lantern and garden stones of granite. "Good
will for our friends and a strong bond of friendship
from generation to generation" is the translation
from Japanese. The whole arrangement came as a gift
from Baltimore's sister city, Kawasaki, Japan.

About twenty paces beyond the lantern (going east away
from the Science Center): a children's playground
(1976) created by Jacques Smolens, who had once
been a tree surgeon. For this sculpture he selected
nine white ash and white oak trees that were doomed.
He cut them and, after they had weathered, carved
on the site what has been called a "family" with
nautical themes.

Farther away also (near the police building on the west
shore): *King Penguin* (1956) by Grace Turnbull,
carved from Vermont green marble. Turnbull made it
for the American headquarters of Penguin Books,
then in Baltimore.

*Now walk the Promenade toward downtown sky-
scrapers.* You are strolling where, at Light Street wharves,
steamboats tied up and crowds gathered. A century and
a half ago sewage and industrial waste polluted this shallow harbor. A local gadfly, Dr. Thomas Buckler, urged
city fathers to level Federal Hill and fill in the Inner
Harbor. Baltimore would thus rid itself of a cesspool and
also add building lots. Merchants, however, needed
wharves and Federal Hill's signal tower.

Both before and after the Civil War, steamboats at
Light Street wharves knitted together Maryland and Virginia ports. "The stately *Three Rivers* nosed into incredi-
bly small creeks," wrote novelist John Dos Passos, who
traveled on it as a boy, "[with] roustabouts laughing and
singing as they . . . rolled bags of wheat or barley up the
gangplank." Through the 1950s, voyagers to Norfolk
down the Chesapeake breakfasted on Southern corn
cakes—"thin, lacy, brown."

Smaller, less elegant steamboats such as one called the
Maggie nosed into the Choptank and other rivers around
the bay. "The gents' cabin, scarcely separate from the

engine, held three tiers of bunks and no air," recalled one unhappy, mid-nineteenth-century passenger. "There was no way to wash, and toilets were just little boxes stuck out over the water inside the paddle box."

You are now at the northwest corner of the Inner Harbor. Around you are the two green-roofed pavilions of Harborplace. Walk along the Promenade to watch people. Today it is hard to believe how opposed some Baltimoreans were to developing Harborplace. South Baltimoreans feared loss of low real estate taxes and a sense of community. Their fears became fact, to some extent, because tax assessments on nearby renovated houses soared.

Some North Baltimoreans wanted to retain an open grassy space that had replaced mouldering wharves and empty warehouses. "Down by the wharves the houses did lean upon one another for support," wrote Letitia Stockett in 1928, "but there was color and there was flavor and there was a goodly smell . . . the tang of tar and salt water and, most potent of all, guano—that rich Baltimorean reek that delighted the hardy nostril, and made the returning excursionist know that he was near-ing port." The aroma of spices from the Light Street McCormick factory (now demolished) also delighted nostrils. "[The] mystic, rich, and heady blend of cloves, cinnamon, nutmeg, and pepper . . . helped define Balti-more," recalled columnist Gilbert Sandler. "It was a little sniff of heaven."

Now you have a chance to buy a snack and sit. *Go inside the Light Street Pavilion of Harborplace* to find restrooms as well as a variety of foods and drinks. "Maryland is always well fed," wrote H. L. Mencken more than half seriously, "hence the beauty of its women and noble presence and flashing eyes of its men."

On the second floor, find the exit to the Skywalk (the side away from the water). Stop at McKeldin Fountain. If you go during a heavy rainstorm, you could easily imagine that you were climbing under Niagara Falls. "The cascade is symbolic of Maryland, its waterways and their relation to Chesapeake Bay and the sea," said designer Thomas A. Todd. "The planters on top of vari-ous concrete 'hills' or promontories are symbolic of the green of Maryland." This fountain takes its name from Theodore Roosevelt McKeldin, a native of nearby South Baltimore who in the mid-twentieth century twice served as Baltimore's mayor—once before he was elected governor of Maryland and again afterward. In office, he gloried in Charles Center and planned Inner Harbor

["Emma Giles"] is a lovely little vessel, all resplen-dent with mirrors, inkblack walnut frames picked out with gold, and with an "elegant saloon" furnished with red plush settees and chairs. . . . Oh, those mar-velous sails when one was ten! There are few sounds in life as thrilling as the splash of the great ropes in the water."

Letitia Stockett, *Baltimore: A Not Too Serious History* (1928)

James Rouse: Creator of Harborplace

Flowers and cheers engulfed developer James Rouse and Gov. William Donald Schaefer when they sailed up to Constellation Dock and jumped ashore to celebrate the tenth birthday of adjacent Harborplace. Both men cheered back; they had been midwives to the rebirth of the Inner Harbor.

For years Rouse, from Easton on the Eastern Shore, and Schaefer, from Baltimore, had worked in downtown. In 1980 Rouse opened Harborplace. Behind its development, according to a cover story in *Time,* lay Rouse's long experience in building shopping centers nationwide. True, the proliferation of suburban malls had all but destroyed shopping in downtowns. But Rouse lamented the loss. "We have lived so long with grim, congested, worn-out cities," he said, " . . . that we have subconsciously come to accept them as inevitable and unavoidable."

So he countered fatalism by putting money and brains to work in Boston (in rebuilding the Quincy Market) and here, envisioning downtown malls that might prove magnets for suburbanites and tourists. To the task he took a unique and highly optimistic approach to urban problems. "Cities can be beautiful, humane, and truly responsive to the needs and yearnings of our people." With this stated goal in mind, Rouse since 1980 has gone on to convert other American downtowns and waterfronts and to also spearhead a program for housing the poor.

Harborplace's designers, Benjamin Thompson Associates of Cambridge, Massachusetts, took care to make the two structures low and of glass so that they would not block the landsmen's views of the water or vistas from the water. You might want to go out on a second-floor porch in Harborplace to view a kaleidoscope of cheerful strollers, paddleboaters, sailors.

developments. "The Inner Harbor should be a diverse and exciting public place," asserted his city planners, "where a balance of day and night attractions and amenities are readily available." McKeldin's dream has taken shape: today 17 million people throng here every year.

McKeldin and planners also kept an image of this city's long history. That explains why walking here differs from a stroll through Dallas or most other big cities: Baltimoreans hang on to relics of their past. Evidence: the old Navy frigate docked here. For another example, take a detour across the bridge over Pratt Street from the Pratt Street Pavilion to the Gallery at Harborplace: exhibits help you imagine eighteenth-century Cheapside Wharf located where you are walking. In the entrance corridor you will see why archaeologists raced bulldozers digging the shopping center's foundation. They unearthed a rich record of the city's world trade—coconuts, delft porcelain, coins from six different countries, and

Prussian dolls. Today, you may feel that you are in a
summer resort: even native Baltimoreans feel like
tourists here.

*Descend to the Promenade and walk past the outdoor
amphitheater to the Pratt Street Pavilion.* Pause in the
open space to look left across Pratt Street at the bright
sculpture *Red Buoyant* (1978) by Mary Ann E. Mears.
"I made it curvilinear and bright red to reflect the movement of people and traffic and to contrast with the geo-
metric building. The piece also evokes waves and water
—and my feeling that Baltimore is an alive, energetic
city." Behind the sculpture is the entrance to the IBM
Building, designed by Pietro Belluschi, one of the internationally known architects brought here to glamorize
the Inner Harbor.

Anchored on the left is the U.S. frigate *Constellation*
with a rather ungainly-looking shop and ticket office
(539-1797). This oldest ship in the American Navy (*Tour
3*) cost $314,202 and had these statistics: length, 64';
beam, 40'6"; weight, 1,278 tons. Experts say that not
much of its structure is original. Still, the ship gives visitors an idea of what early warships were like. Nicknamed "Yankee Race Horse" by the French, she sailed
with 340 officers and men.

In 1799 the *Constellation* and her thirty-six guns defeated a man-of-war reported to have been the fastest
ship in the French Navy, *L'Insurgente.* Approaching the
enemy, the *Constellation*'s captain, "grim and silent,"
according to a witness, maneuvered parallel with the
French ship and let go a broadside of twenty-four heavy
guns at once. Soon *L'Insurgente,* "half her guns unwork-
able, the masts and rigging shattered, and seventy casualties aboard, could no longer offer effective resistance."
That was a first for the U.S. Navy. Today the *Constellation*'s guns can still fire salutes, which makes the whole
vessel shake alarmingly.

*Before the Aquarium you next skirt the World Trade
Center* (837-4515). Entrance is on the far side. For a view
quite different from Federal Hill's, ride a sleek elevator
to the twenty-first floor. From the Top of the World you
see for miles. You can also study exhibits showing Baltimore's growth. Other displays come from Baltimore's
sister cities—Genoa, Rotterdam, and Kawasaki.

Once back on terra firma, walk behind the building.
Open space to the north of the World Trade Center,
Sondheim Plaza, offers praise for Mayor Schaefer's right-
hand man, Walter Sondheim Jr., "who dreamed the
dreams earlier and made them happen sooner."

When you leave the World Trade Center, walk toward the glass pyramids of the Aquarium. On the left, just past the World Trade Center, stands a mammoth sculpture by Mark de Suvero (1980), *Under Sky/One Family.* The title comes from a Chinese proverb. Sunny noontimes, people like to rest next to it and children play in the wheel, a souvenir of Baltimore's industrial past.

You will come upon a small fleet of disparate ships collected for the Maritime Museum afloat (396-3854). You can board three, veterans all. The first, the lightship *Chesapeake,* once guarded entrances to East Coast ports. The second ship, the U.S. Coast Guard cutter *Taney* (pronounced TAWN-y), bears the name of U.S. Supreme Court Chief Justice Roger Brooke Taney, a Marylander (*Tour 10*). It may be the only warship now afloat that survived the attack on Pearl Harbor. Another survivor of World War II, the submarine USS *Torsk,* allows you to experience how confined life is for submariners. Service on this sub began the naval career of Ens. Jimmy Carter. The 1945 crew sank three Japanese ships on the very last day of the war. So you have here, side by side, two ships that bracket America's part in World War II.

Next to these ships on Pier 3 is the National Aquarium at Baltimore (576-3800). When it failed to open as promised on July 4, 1981, then-mayor William Donald Schaefer carried out a threat to don a striped Victorian swimsuit and straw hat and take a dip in the completed seal pool. Seen on national television, that publicity stunt did the trick: when the Aquarium opened, crowds lined up at the doors. Now summer crowds enliven the plaza facing Pratt Street. They come inside to see fish of all species and sizes, a 200,000-gallon shark-tank, an Atlantic Ocean coral reef five levels deep, a feeder stream to the Chesapeake Bay, a children's cove, a fifty-foot tile mural entitled *Swim Along,* and much more.

Seen from the outside, three huge glass triangles sparkle from solid bases. Inside one triangle, there steams a rain forest replete with birds and snakes. Another glass triangle admits brilliant light to the tank where sea lions disport themselves. Since 1991 a Marine Mammal Pavilion has offered a dolphin show, further reason for millions of tourists to come in. To explore more of the natural world, someday you may go to Baltimore's 150-acre zoo, only thirty blocks north.

Go to the left of the main entrance to the National Aquarium at Baltimore, cross over a footbridge, turn right past the Chart House, and veer diagonally toward the pyra-

mid of the Mammal Pavilion. Notice at the right end of the façade a plaque announcing the time capsule hidden there. In front of the entrance you can sit on the steps above a pool that is usually called *The Dolphin Fountain* (1991). In it romp five dolphins. Sculptor Leonard Streckfus shaped them from recycled common objects easily identified—a shoe tree, tricycle parts, a golf bag.

You are strolling along the Promenade as though you were on a seaside boardwalk. Like a huge, four-stack ship, the Power Plant looms over Pier 3. An entrepreneur wants to convert this 1901 industrial building to a $32-million sports museum and entertainment complex, Sports Center USA. It will add to the illusion that you are in a resort. (Formerly, machinery here produced power for streetcars.)

This conversion, if accomplished, will replace sections of brick with glass, so that passersby can see some of what is going on inside, and so that fee-paying sports lovers inside can look at both downtown skyscrapers and the Outer Harbor. After you complete this walk, you may want to come back to explore what is going on overhead in Sports Center USA.

As you proceed past Pier 5, you will notice a Chesapeake Bay lighthouse on stilts. Brought from lower down the Chesapeake at Seven-Foot Knoll, it lends nautical flavor to a restaurant-hotel. It is said that the wooden box suspended below the light once housed livestock for the lighthouse-keeper's larder.

Your walk ends here on Pier 6. Next door, across a small bridge, you can come to the Christopher Columbus Center for Marine Research and Exploration, for which ground was broken on October 12, 1992. Spanning piers 4, 5, and 6, this center includes research laboratories and a conference center. For visitors, the exhibition hall may interest most. In it the Smithsonian Institution is providing historic artifacts from its vast attic, items collected since 1846. Here, with Smithsonian advisers, planners have set up an education program for urban schools. "A lot of things that inner-city kids pride themselves on—creativity, toughness and curiosity—are exactly the things that make researchers great," said Columbus Center president Stanley Heuisler.

Politicians and planners hope that this $160-million investment will make Baltimore a world center for biotechnology, and thus a place "with a high-tech economy founded on life sciences." Their plan divides the center in two: the Center for Marine Archaeology goes

in for deep-water exploration, and the Center for
Marine Biotechnology researches marine molecular
genetics and molecular biology.

Farther into the harbor, a white tent shelters concert-
goers and performers on summer nights. Then music
wafts over the harbor.

Although the music is pleasant and although some of
this stern science may be presented as fun, it is far different from life on this shoreline a century ago. "The old
Baltimore had a saucy and picturesque personality," recalled H. L. Mencken. "The dance-halls that then flourished in the regions along the harbor would shock [the
police] to death today and they'd be horrified by some
of the old-time saloons." Mencken concluded that the
town was "unlike any other American city." For the present you may settle for an ice cream cone at the Ben and
Jerry's dispensary located on Harrison's Pier 5 plaza. A
water-taxi landing on Pier 6 gives the option of cruising
back to Constellation Dock or of strolling and people-
watching along the Promenade.

Baltimore *is* permissiveness. The pleasures of the flesh, the table, the
bottle, and the purse are tolerated with a civilized understanding of
the subtleties of moral questions that would have been perfectly
comprehensible to Edwardian Londoners. Gross and overt indul-
gence, however, is frowned upon. The gunned corpses that litter
New Jersey are not part of Baltimore life. That sort of thing is a vice.
Baltimore does not like vice. Vice leads to cruelty and suffering, and
what's more, is in bad taste. Sin is something else. Baltimore toler-
ates sin. Sin is the human condition.

Russell Baker, New York Times (1973)

Quiet Inner Harbor
morning

Fells Point

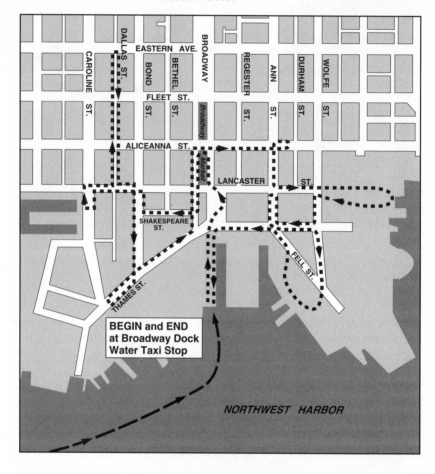

EASTERN AVE.

CAROLINE ST.

DALLAS ST.

BROADWAY

BOND ST.

BETHEL ST.

FLEET ST.

REGESTER ST.

ANN ST.

DURHAM ST.

WOLFE ST.

Broadway

ALICEANNA ST.

Market

LANCASTER ST.

SHAKESPEARE ST.

FELL ST.

THAMES ST.

BEGIN and END
at Broadway Dock
Water Taxi Stop

NORTHWEST HARBOR

COME HERE FOR:

- "Mardi Gras in Red Square"
- Places filmed as sets by our contemporary filmmakers John Waters and Barry Levinson, natives of Baltimore
- Sites made famous in *My Bondage and My Freedom* and other writings by nineteenth-century author-reformer Frederick Douglass
- One of America's largest groups of eighteenth- and early nineteenth-century buildings
- Maritime flavor provided by marinas and working tugboats in Baltimore's original deep-water port

Approach Fells Point from the water (water-taxis available). The scene from your boat may look like an old European river town, with ragged rooflines of warehouses, shops, and houses, but don't be fooled: here you will learn how far funkiness can go and still be Baltimore. "The trashiest town anywhere," says filmmaker John Waters.

After dark, Fells Point has a racy waterfront. "Weekend nights often resemble Mardi Gras," says a reporter. "Too many yuppies. Too many bars. Too many BMWs. Impossible to park. All true. But that's on the weekend and at night. [The place] is working waterfront and Greenwich Village with a dash of Georgetown and a little Colonial Williamsburg on the side." The Point's many eighteenth- and nineteenth-century working-class residences and shops qualified it for the National Register of Historic Places. No other whole community in the country had previously merited such an honor.

Bars still abound here, as always in a sailors' port of call. "Drinks are cheap," said John Waters, a regular here in 1982. "If you ever make the mistake of leaving a tip on the bar, the bar maid panics and chases after you, yelling, 'Hon, you left a quarter.'" Today a tip is probably expected, and the clientele is likely to give a significant one without flinching.

Through the work of Waters and word-of-mouth, the charms of Fells Point became well known—but not ruined. Evidence: another filmmaker with Baltimore roots, Barry Levinson, chose Fells Point for filming his television series *Homicide,* about his hometown detectives. "When I would sit down to write these pieces, Baltimore and its characters and its rhythms just made sense to me." He added, "I don't find it any different from a writer who wrote about his particular region, whether it was William Faulkner or Tennessee Williams or whoever."

Baltimore is multifarious, 39 has the attractive dirt of a fishing town, the nightmare horizons of a great industrial town; it is very old, sordid, traditional, and proud. It despises no sort of traffic that can be conceived of.

Christina Stead, *The Man Who Loved Children* (1930)

Over all, and penetrating all, is a mist from the Bay, and in the dusk comes the hoot of a tug nuzzling through the twilight. Always there are the thoughts of ships.

Letitia Stockett, *Baltimore: A Not Too Serious History* (1928)

HISTORY

Before colonists arrived from England, Fells Point's marshy hook reached out into a tidal river, the Patapsco. Its shore provided just one of many harbors around Chesapeake Bay. Not until the nineteenth century did Baltimore surge ahead as the major harbor.

In 1730 an English ship's carpenter named William Fell, a Quaker, bought the marshy hook and named it Fells Prospect. That was nine years before the laying out of streets in Baltimore-Town (*see Tour 5*) and 100 years after the founding of Boston.

Fortunately for the shipbuilding Fell family, the river here ran deep enough to dock large eighteenth-century ships. In 1763 William Fell's son Edward laid out streets. "Here lived captains, petty officers, and thousands of sailors," recalled a purchaser of one of the first Fells

Point lots. "Tar and pitch were predominant. Rope walks abounded; joiner workshops, shipsmiths and forges were sandwiched between sailors' boarding houses and ship chandlers' stores."

Because some ships carried yellow fever, epidemics sometimes caused panicked residents to flee, temporarily, to the hill above town. "An interest stronger than love of life . . . anchors all [Fells Pointers] who believe the promises of fortune rather than the threats of inexorable death," wrote Moreau de Saint Mery, a visitor in 1794.

That was the year Joseph Despeaux, a refugee carpenter from a slave revolt in Saint Dominique, established a shipyard here. With him came slaves skilled in shipbuilding. By then shipbuilders here and on the Eastern Shore of Maryland had developed the prototype of the Baltimore Clipper, a superb merchant sailing design that soon made the city's reputation.

Before and after the era of Baltimore Clippers, Fells Point served as a busy port of call for the world's sailors. Their legendary raffishness gave the Point a notoriety like that of Marseilles or Port Said. "Here ships land their cargoes," reported a visitor in 1798, "and here their crews wait not even for the twilight to fly to the polluted arms of the white, the black, and yellow harlot."

After the Civil War, shipping gave way to manufacturing. All along the waterfront workers canned Chesapeake oysters and the fruits and vegetables from fertile farms around the bay. Factory workers in Fells Point and Canton made the cans, too. "Those were the good old days for the ones who never lived it," wryly recalled Mary Ljek Eber, a canner sixty years ago. "I was making 25 cents an hour, but you had nothing because you came home and gave your mother everything you made."

By 1920 clothing manufacturing employed one-quarter of the city's workforce. Fells Point workers sewed and lived in officially licensed "dwellings and tenements"— sweatshops.

Today's streetscapes, churches, and bars look much as they did then. H&S Bakery on Eastern Avenue continues to spread the fragrance of baking bread for blocks. And heavy trucks still thunder along Wolfe Street going to and from Arundel Corporation's concrete plant.

. . . a beautiful sharp built schooner, evidently intended for warlike purposes. . . . The Baltimore shipbuilders particularly excel in the construction of such vessels and it was their astonishing fleetness of sailing which enabled the privateers to pick up so many of our merchantmen during the last war. They are very low in the water, and broad in the beam; the masts are sloped very much backwards, and they sail exceedingly close to the wind.

John M. Duncan, *Travels through Part of the United States and Canada in 1818 and 1819* (1820)

TOUR

Starting point: Constellation Dock in the Inner Harbor
and then Broadway Dock in Fells Point

Length of walk: One and a half hours on foot

Boats at dock

Snacks and restrooms: Broadway Market and the numerous restaurants

Transportation: You are embarking on a waterfront tour and should arrive by boat—your own, if possible— or a water-taxi. A seat in a water-taxi will give you a front-row view of the Inner Harbor. Water-taxis run regularly from downtown—either Constellation Dock, which is the starting point of all these tours, or the Science Center.

If you want to walk along the Harbor Promenade from Constellation Dock, take the path going east past the National Aquarium and follow route signs. Count on walking a mile or so. Should you choose to drive, take Pratt Street to President Street and there turn right and go two blocks to Eastern Avenue. Turn left and drive eleven blocks to Broadway. Turn right and look for a parking place near the foot of Broadway. Public parking lots are open to the right, a block west on Thames Street.

Begin your tour by walking away from Broadway Dock inland across Thames Street into the open plaza. Once there, walk to the right where at the corner you will find an official historic marker on a pole. When you read about Baltimore Clippers and Fells Point's past, doubt the date given. Next, look around the plaza. When its designers recently erected massive, pink-marble blocks, some local people called the plaza Red Square. For surely, they said,

Lenin had abandoned a Moscow tomb for reburial in a grander, pink-marble tomb here.

From the historic marker, cross Broadway and turn left to walk along the sidewalk away from the water. You will see old houses and shops, many sparkling after rehabilitation. Look on your right at numbers 813–815, the Port Mission. Although ships' running lights no longer adorn the shopfront, a cast-iron façade of 1881 survives. Over the years the mission served as a haven for sailors. It hosted a rowdy group that (according to an observer) was often preyed upon by bartenders, boardinghouse crimps, and prostitutes. Some sailors resented the mission's proselytizing its brand of religion, as well as its condescending attitude.

At the end of this block, at 801, now popular Jimmy's Restaurant, stood a pre-Revolutionary clockmaker's shop. If you own a tall clock signed "P. Belsner," it came from here—and your fortune is made. Today, local entrepreneurs make money from a mixing of tourists, bar-hopping college students, and equally diverse residents, such as young preservationists and pursuers of a laid-back 1960s way of looking at things, and a U.S. senator.

"Every eccentric from the South wanted to go North," said John Waters about World War II. "They ran out of gas in Baltimore and decided to stay." Some of them stayed in Fells Point. They give it a funkiness now. Strange how a reputation lingers, long after the very different reality has come about through a spoiling of what gave the place its original attraction. "We're treated as something chic, as something quaint to come to," complained Sen. Barbara Mikulski. "I live in a real neighborhood with real people who raise real families."

Walk to the end of the plaza to the entrance of the Broadway Market's South Shed. Here at the foot of Broadway, a market predated the 1797 incorporation of Baltimore City itself. A 1784 market building anchored outdoor market stalls. Stall renters sold fresh-dug potatoes, spring lamb, strawberries, and other comestibles. Look in the curbing of Broadway next to the Port Mission for numbers marking each stall.

Go inside the market for a fresh croissant and a panorama of fresh fish, oranges, apples, and carrots. Aisles usually fill around lunchtime and on Saturdays—and always have. "Saturday afternoon is a splendid time for a visit," wrote Letitia Stockett in 1928. "The flaring lamps throw strange lights and shadows upon the dark foreign faces of Edward Fell's modern neighbors." Today

Back in those days, at the foot of Broadway they had this market that reached all the way up Thames Street. They used to sell dressed pigs, hairless. . . . I can remember my dad buying several of these pigs every fall of the year. . . . And he'd bring this pig down the basement and cut it up and salt it down and cover it with salt in a barrel. . . . I'd say four times a week we ate sauerkraut and pork. I ate so damn much of the sauerkraut and pork meat by the time I was 14 I couldn't even look at sauerkraut.

Baltimore Neighborhood
Heritage Project (1979)

you may meet well-known artists, such as Grace Harti-
gan, just in from nearby studios.

*Walk straight through the market's South Shed and exit
into Aliceanna Street. Turn left immediately and then left
again and walk down the side of the market.* At 734 Broadway, corner of Lancaster Street, you will find a popular
restaurant, Bertha's, whose mussels are advertised both
abroad and around town on bumper stickers, "Eat
Bertha's Mussels." The place has the feel of an English
pub, and in fact does serve an English tea. Bertha's carries
on a tradition of drinking and eating near the harbor.

*Continue walking south to Shakespeare Street and
turn right.* How many other American towns have an
eighteenth-century byway named for Shakespeare? The
Fell family must have suffered from the common
eighteenth-century affliction of "bardolatry," a passion
for the bard of Avon. A memorial stone for William Fell
(died in 1746), his son Edward (died in 1776), and for
his brother Edward Fell (died in 1743) rests behind a
fence at 1607, near where the Fell family lived.

As you stroll along this one narrow block of Shakespeare Street, you enter a world of 200 years ago. But
don't be fooled: this street never before looked as tidy,
as pretty. Residents have cleaned façades, duplicated
worn-out windows, and applied historically authentic
colors to doors. For instance, restorations of 1621 and
1611 Shakespeare Street have received awards.

Pause at 1600, the oldest and most unusual-looking
house in this block. Contrast its brick work and roofline
with that of less-old neighbors. Built in 1770, it originally
carried a ground rent paid in shillings to Ann Bond Fell,
Edward Fell's widow. As an erring Quaker, she had been
"read out of meeting" (excommunicated) for having
"gone contrary to the principles of Friends as appears by
the woman's books." No one knows what incendiary

"Mother" Geier died yesterday and the heart of the waterfront was sad. . . . A robust, white-haired,
laughing woman who came to this country thirty-six years ago, Mrs. Paulina L. Geier ran Geier's
restaurant with her husband, August Geier. It was nothing for a man fresh from a ship, and broke
from the night before, to roll into Mother Geier's, confess empty pockets and eat her substantial
grub. . . . And the seamen—with little money as a result of the [1936] strike—are going to send
Mother Geier a blanket of roses and lilies and a floral cross. Skimming quickly through his list, Fred
(Blacky) Nassar pointed proudly to the names and contributions collected . . . $40. "See that, Old
John gave $5; old John Swain, he's about 80 and he's a ship's carpenter who's on strike. He had 50
cents this afternoon. He played two-horse parley; won $25 and gave me $5."

Baltimore Sun (November 25, 1936)

reading led to her downfall. Husband Edward had been
kicked out, too, for having married her, a cousin.

Even today some owners rent the ground under the
houses they buy. That is an old Baltimore custom, introduced to make buying a house cheaper: you buy only
the house and rent the land under the house. For generations, income from ground rents has supported many
a Baltimorean.

Shakespeare Street, like so much of the original physical fabric of Fells Point, endures partly because twenty-
three people in 1967 formed the Society for the Preservation of Fells Point and Federal Hill. Just before that
meeting, Lucretia Fisher had bought an eighteenth-
century house facing the water. "You can get a beautiful
building near the harbor for practically nothing," she
said to a Thames Street neighbor. "Very quietly he told
me, 'That's where the East-West Expressway is going to
take out the whole block.'"

Fisher and other society members led—and won—
a fight to stop the road. Today the society adds to its
treasury and to the gaiety of the Point by putting on an
October Fells Point Fun Festival. Two hundred thousand celebrants typically attend.

*At the Bond Street corner of Shakespeare Street, turn
right into the 700 block, and walk one block to Lancaster
Street. Turn left at Lancaster Street and walk in the direction of downtown Baltimore's skyline.* Much of the land
cleared in the mid-twentieth century may still be empty
when you walk here. The city owns part, and so does
Allied/Signal and Constellation Properties, of the Baltimore Gas and Electric Company. By the time you come
here, you may see on the Allied/Signal segment a part of
an extensive development—twenty-odd acres of offices
and residences.

*Stop at Caroline Street, the boundary of Fells Point
Historic District.* This street name makes three named
for women (Ann and Aliceanna are the others). Caroline
Calvert Eden, wife of the last colonial Maryland governor, Sir Robert Eden, topped the social pyramid. The
Edens bequeathed two street names in Baltimore (Caroline and Eden), and the name of Caroline County and
its county seat, Denton (the E of Edenton has since disappeared) on the Eastern Shore of Maryland. "A hearty,
rattling young dog of an officer" remains as Governor
Eden's recorded image.

All along the mostly empty path, you will trample
historic ghosts. First settlers called this place the Hook
because it hooks out into the harbor. Here they lived

crowded lives turned seaward. Later, canneries were
built. Nearby once rose a young mountain of oyster
shells from an oyster canning plant. "I remember my
mother shucked oysters for Langrell's," says 80-year-old
Helen Sadowski. "It was cold and they wore rags around
their shoes to keep warm—all bundled up and all day
shucking. That was hard work, babe, but it was easy to
get work in them days."

Turn left on Caroline Street and approach the water.
Nearby, plans call for the building of Frederick Douglass
Marine Railway (for launching boats). Not far from
here, after the Civil War, fifteen black men raised
$10,000 to create a completely equipped marine railway
and shipyard, the Chesapeake Marine Railway and Dry
Dock Company. They employed 300 black workers.
One of the organizers, Isaac Myers, led the company for
eighteen successful years. Earlier, as a ship's caulker, he
had formed the first African-American labor union here.
"If citizenship means anything at all," affirmed Myers,
"it means the freedom of labor, as broad and as universal
as the freedom of the ballot."

Walk to the right of the sign to see "The Living
Classrooms Foundation and Maritime Institute." It
offers training in wooden boat building, skipjack
restoration, and ship repair. Here you are looking at
old City Dock. *Turn away from the water, and return to
Caroline and Lancaster streets.*

*Walk along Lancaster Street to Dallas Street, formerly
Strawberry Alley,* an important street for African-
American and religious history. To see why, you may
want to make a loop left up three blocks north and
back. At Dallas and Fleet streets stand five rowhouses
built as an investment by Frederick Douglass many
years after escaping slavery. As an ironist, he must have
savored the pleasure of owning property in the very
place where he once was considered owned property.
The original plaque on one house reads Douglass Terrace. Some houses have newly cleaned façades; others
wear Formstone faces. "It's a slice of Baltimore life,"
wrote an old-time reporter, "with a little trash blowing
around but a great deal more pride of place."

What makes the site of these 1890s houses even more
historic was that Douglass used foundations of Strawberry Alley Chapel. That oldest Methodist church in
Baltimore stood on land bought in 1773 by Francis
Asbury, the first American Methodist bishop. Both
whites and blacks worshiped there until 1802, when the
church was given to blacks and renamed Dallas Street

Frederick Douglass: Baltimore slave

Abroad, Douglass may well be the best-known American after Abraham Lincoln. At home, his account of growing up as a slave in Baltimore and on Maryland's Eastern Shore, the *Narrative of the Life of Frederick Douglass* (1845), remains a classic. Much of the book treats his life in Fells Point. When you walk past any of several Douglass landmarks here, look back to this sketch to help fix him in mind.

"Going to live in Baltimore laid the foundation," he wrote, "opened the gateway, to all my subsequent prosperity." He had been born a plantation slave across Chesapeake Bay from Baltimore in Talbot County, on the Eastern Shore of Maryland. Although his white father has not been identified, the boy did fare better than most slaves. His "tall and finely proportioned," "remarkably sedate and dignified" mother was separated from him early and died before he was seven. "I am quite willing, and even happy, to attribute any love of letters I possess . . . *not* to my admitted Anglo-Saxon paternity, but to the native genius of my sable, unprotected, and uncultivated mother—a woman, who belonged to a race whose mental endowments it is, at present, fashionable to hold in disparagement and contempt." He was sent at age seven to live with his master's brother in Fells Point. "I had resided but a short time in Baltimore," Douglass later wrote, "before I observed a marked difference in the treatment of slaves, from that which I had witnessed in the country. A city slave . . . is much better fed and clothed, and enjoys privileges altogether unknown to the slave on the plantation."

This city gave Douglass the vital privilege of learning to read. When his master, Hugh Auld, discovered his wife, Sophia, teaching a slave, he put a stop to reading lessons. "If you give a nigger an inch, he will take an ell. Learning will spoil the best nigger in the world." "Very well," thought Douglass, "knowledge unfits a child to be a slave."

Many a night have I been wakened in Philpotts-street, Baltimore, by the passing-by, at midnight, of hundreds of slaves, carrying their chains and fetters and uttering cries and howlings, almost enough to startle the dead. They were going to the market to work in cotton or sugar, going off to be killed in the space of five or six years, in the swamps of Alabama, Georgia, and Louisiana.

Frederick Douglass, speech at Sheffield, England (September 11, 1846)

In his late teens Douglass was sent back to rural Talbot County on the Eastern Shore for an ordeal of physical work and punishment. Soon returned to Baltimore, he caulked ships alongside white men, who deeply resented black competition for jobs. He had to turn over his earnings to his master. By then his imposing physique and rich baritone voice, writes historian Benjamin Quarles, gave him "the initial advantage of looking like a person destined for prominence."

No fewer than fifty white men stood by and saw this brutal and shameful outrage committed [a shipyard attack on Douglass with bricks, fists, and feet], and not a man of them all interposed a single word of mercy. There were four against one, and that one's face was beaten and battered most horribly, and no one said, "That is enough," but some cried out, "Kill him! kill him! kill the damned nigger! knock his brains out! he struck a white person!" I mention this inhuman outcry to show the character of the men and the spirit of the times at Gardiner's shipyard, and, indeed, in Baltimore generally, in 1836.

Frederick Douglass, *Life and Times of Frederick Douglass* (1881)

In 1838 he escaped from slavery on a train from Baltimore. In New York he married a free black woman from Baltimore, Anna Murray, and after they had settled in New England he began to prove himself a powerful champion of abolition. "In listening to him," said a contemporary, "your whole soul is fired, every nerve strung—every faculty you possess ready to perform at a moment's bidding."

"Physically, Douglass was a commanding person," wrote W. E. B. Du Bois, "over six feet in height, with brown skin, frizzly hair, leonine head, strong constitution, and a fine voice." In 1884 critics blamed him for choosing a white woman as his second wife. "He laughingly remarked that he was quite impartial," said Du Bois; his first wife "was the color of my mother, and the second, the color of my father."

Methodist Episcopal Church. If you are interested in learning the history of Baltimore Methodists, drive twenty-odd blocks north to a museum in Lovely Lane Methodist Church, 2200 St. Paul Street (889-1512).

Return to Lancaster Street and progress eastward; you are passing houses that were sweatshops of 1900. For example, a 1904 report of Maryland Industrial Statistics gives typical statistics (this set concerns 1738 Thames Street):

No. of hours of labor required—10

No. of families in house—4

No. of persons in families—12

No. of rooms in house—8

country of origin—Russia

Continue along Lancaster Street from Dallas Street and when you reach Bond Street, turn right. You will be strolling down two recently refurbished blocks. Bond

Street is broad enough to have had train tracks down its center during the Point's industrial period. Recent removal of track, re-laying of cobblestone paving, and planting of new trees completes an image of old times.

Notice how residents care for old ornamental details and add their own. If you care about such things, look at the wood construction of the front of 809, including a slanted cellar door in the sidewalk. A neon tugboat lights the door at 821.

Across the street, you see why experts admire the old local bricks and bricklayers; in just one block is a chance to compare three patterns of brickwork. At 830, 832, and 834, you see *Flemish bond*—a pattern of bricks with the long side (called stretchers) and short side (called headers) laid alternately in each horizontal row. At 828, examine *English bond*—a full row of headers alternating with a full row of stretchers. At 824, look for *running bond,* a pattern of bricks all laid lengthwise with staggered mortar joints. Finally, at 736, you find a fourth pattern, *common bond,* which is like running bond except that a row of headers was inserted every sixth row. To complete the range of Baltimoreans' attention to brick, look at the end house to the right of 826. Its façade, painted burgundy red with each mortar joint painted white, makes the façade look fresh.

Walk to the southern end of the block to 854 Bond Street, where you are seeing what is said to be the only surviving eighteenth-century coffeehouse on the East Coast, the 1772 London Coffee House. The structure has held on to life tenaciously, although abandoned for years. Let's hope that it is still standing when you look for it. Here and in other coffeehouses, sea captains, landowners, news gatherers, and town leaders met three years before the Declaration of Independence, to declare "brave and manly opposition" to British tyranny.

Adjacent to the coffeehouse, George Wells oversaw building the frigate *Virginia* (1773) for the new American Navy of the Continental Congress. His shipyard was just across the street. The derelict structure at 1532–1534 Thames Street, probably an eighteenth-century inn, has cried for help year after year. *With it behind you, loop west one block to Caroline Street and walk fifty yards farther in order to look diagonally to the left at a round-cornered dark cube of a warehouse.* Round corners eased horse-drawn wagons around corners. It is the sole remnant of mid-nineteenth-century Chase's Wharf, destination of West Indian coffee and sugar.

At Chase's Wharf on Sunday, April 14, 1861, Baltimoreans dramatized their divided sympathies in the brand-new Civil War. A secessionist flag flew from the mizzen topmast of a Richmond barque, *Fanny Crenshaw*. Soon other vessels ran up the American flag. Before long (so goes the chronicle) a crowd, belonging mostly to East Baltimore, assembled at the wharf, expressing emphatic disapproval of the secession flag, and then, going on board, had it lowered. Back up went the flag, on the owners' orders, this time protected by the police force. That happened just two days after Confederate guns fired on Fort Sumter and began the Civil War.

As you turn the corner to the left from Bond Street into the angled 1600 block of Thames Street, you enter the part of Fells Point that originally was called Fell's Street. That name was appropriate because William Fell's eighteenth-century mansion stood nearby until demolished. The stepped-back houses on the left look like the pleats of an accordion.

One of those houses, now a bar at 1626, The Horse You Came In On, inspired a novel with that title by mystery writer Martha Grimes. "The only reason part of this book is set in Baltimore is that I saw this pub sign," she said. "I knew I would have to figure out some way to get Jury and Melrose [suave Scotland Yard detective and aristocratic sidekick] to come over [from their usual London habitat], purely on the basis of the name of this pub."

A mythical old salt gave a name to the Admiral Fell Inn at the far corner of the left hand side (888 S. Broadway). Real sailors—as many as 50,000 in all—have slept here. They lodged in rooms so tiny that the Anchorage Hotel was nicknamed "The Doghouse," and cost 35 cents a night. That was between 1892 and 1930, when the Women's Auxiliary of the Port Mission ran a boardinghouse, later managed by the YMCA. Now the building is a colonialized bed and breakfast retreat costing $135 a night.

Another building with a long history of hospitality stands at 1645, now the Admiral's Cup.

As you walk along this north side of the block, look at 1638–1640 Thames Street, a restored cast-iron storefront of fluted Corinthian columns and pilasters. You can see why cast-iron appealed to shopkeepers: it was tough, handsome, and cheap. This example from 1862 originally invited customers into the grocery and ship's chandlery of Henry G. Tyark Deetjen.

Across the street, in rehabilitated buildings near Broadway, you will find gift shops that you may want to patronize before you leave Fells Point. In them, recent

---

Despite the obvious quaintness in danger of sliding into chic, Fells Point was a genuine period piece. Left to itself for over two hundred years, it was evidently becoming trendy, but it still kept the appearance of its eighteenth-century origins. It had about it a pleasant sort of scruffiness that the galleries and shops hadn't managed to glamorize or suppress.

Martha Grimes, *The Horse You Came In On* (1993)

English visitors found favorite souvenirs of America. Adjacent Brown's Wharf retains its sharp, angular roof lines of the early nineteenth-century. Converted to a bank, a restaurant, and offices, this old wharf keeps one top loft where ships' sails were dried. The Brown name has been important in Baltimore ever since the first Brown, Alexander, emigrated from Northern Ireland and made money as an importer. His name is carried by a well-known brokerage house headquartered in Baltimore, Alex. Brown and Sons (*Tour 5*).

Alexander's son George built this brick warehouse as part of his overseas commercial empire. "[Brown's] fault of over-diffuseness" bothered English cloth merchant Richard Cobden in 1835, "after a little more tact must have convinced him that his hearer was sufficiently informed." But that fault didn't keep him from making a bundle.

You have now come back to Broadway Plaza and may need a rest. Snacks and meals surround you. *When you are ready to move on, turn away from the water and proceed up the left-hand sidewalk along the 800 block of Broadway.* You will pass on your left the current theater of the Vagabonds, long a stage where local amateurs had fun.

Cross Lancaster Street and with Broadway Market on your right, walk to Aliceanna Street. There you can make a small loop left to a public comfort station (right-hand side of Aliceanna Street next to the Salty Dog). It doesn't offer much in the way of comfort or cleanliness, but it is available and has a drinking fountain outside. *Return to the Broadway corner and continue in this eastward direction along Aliceanna Street.*

In this section of Fells Point you will discover remnants of what one famous son of Baltimore recalled as the "pervasive rowdiness and bawdiness of the town— the general air of devil-may-care freedom—the infinite oddity and extravagance of its daily, and especially nightly, life." In one incident a woman marked her one-hundredth arrest for drunkenness by whisking off all her clothes and smothering the arresting police lieutenant with them. Today this district has straightened up—but only a bit.

Now you near the walk's northern edge. As you walk east along Aliceanna Street, pronounce its name "Alice-ann" or "Alizan," as natives do. Here you may agree with one recent observer's likening this area to Rome— peeling masonry, a plethora of cats, and the smell of fresh bread. The fragrance emanates 'round the clock from H&S Bakery. Special scents on special days. The street

My parents were always very busy people. When they had free lunch on the bar, my father would get up early, go to the wholesale fish market and buy 100 pounds of fish, unscaled. He'd bring them home and clean them. They were both up by 5 o'clock, frying the fish and getting the bar ready for the day. They cooked ham and black bread for the bar—that was served every day. Friday was fish day.

Helen Christopher, daughter of Polish bar owners of what is now the Admiral's Cup, interviewed in 1950, in Elizabeth Fee, *The Baltimore Book* (1991)

John Waters: "Sultan of Sleaze"

In the 1960s and after, Waters gave moviegoers a look at Fells Point eccentrics and seediness. In *Pink Flamingos,* for example, one of his offbeat
Fells Point "stars," named Edith Massey in real life, ran a shop on Broadway called Edith's Shopping Bag. Now Edith and shop have vanished from
the street. Waters lives nearby in Guilford.

In 1981, Waters assures us, he met hillbilly truckdrivers who cruised
Broadway looking for "half-finished sex changes who hang out between
medical appointments at Johns Hopkins Hospital" just a dozen blocks up
Broadway on Washington Hill. Waters himself hangs out in a weird Baltimore. Like H. L. Mencken, he finds the place a circus—but one that, as
critic Stephen Hunter noted, is "crass, tacky, disgusting, tasteless, and
grotesque." "No one ever went broke underestimating the taste of the
American people," said Mencken.

John Waters has exploited Fells Point and other working-class districts
in such films as *Multiple Maniacs* and *Polyester.* "Baltimore has a tradition
of great eccentrics. Any town that gave you Madalyn Murray O'Hair and
Spiro Agnew has to have something going for it," he wrote in *Shock Value.*
"You can look far and wide, but you'll never discover a stranger city with
such extreme style."

Of Waters and his own extreme style, a Washingtonian said, "He's a
gas, but, frankly, we're glad he doesn't live in our neighborhood."

name Aliceanna honors Edward's mother-in-law, Aliceanna Webster Bond (1715–67). Her local fame came from
skill in "medicine and midwifery," which, it was said, she
"administered with freedom and benevolence." Among
her ten children, more than one got into trouble with
fellow Quakers—playing cards or a fiddle, marrying a
Methodist, lending a man a gun. So many ways to err!

As you proceed along Aliceanna Street, you will see a
variety of façades. Many housefronts in Fells Point and
Canton display an overall coating of Formstone. After
World War II, Formstone, manufactured in Baltimore,
covered old brick all over town with a plaster coat.
Shaped to resemble blocks of stone, Formstone is supposed to prevent leaks, to obviate need to repoint brick,
and to provide much-needed insulation.

Some people have objected to this coating on aes-
thetic grounds, although homeowner Bob Eney gave
another reason when a Fells Point neighbor saw him
removing Formstone. "It holds in the dampness. And as
we were pulling it off, you could see the water running
down the walls, and underneath was rusts and roaches—
millions of roaches."

Pause at the corner of Aliceanna and Ann streets; at 1727 is St. Stanislaus Kostka Church Hall. There in 1936 longshoremen of the local International Longshoremen's Association defied national officers and voted to support the merchant seamen's strike. When national president Joseph Ryan came from New York, he found the door locked and 2,000 seamen waiting outside to pelt him with rocks. A poet named Forty Fathoms wrote these commemorative lines:

> In Baltimore town
> the boys are rough.
> Ryan lost his pants
> by an ILA hand
> and clad in fig leaves
> he turned and scrammed.

Around the corner to the right on Ann Street, the St. Stanislaus Kostka complex of religious institutions long made a center for Polish immigrants. Recently, the convent closed after generations of nuns had taught parish school scholars at 900 S. Ann Street. "I was always attracted to the work of the nuns," Sister Juanita Zebron told a reporter. "I remember when this building was filled with nuns. They were always happy and prayerful." In 1994 the vacant convent became an experimental middle school, Mother Seton Academy. Students from poor East Baltimore families receive free tuition and meals in a long-day program.

Immigrants from Prussian Poland came to Baltimore after our Civil War (mostly in the 1880s). Then in the 1890s and just after the turn of the century the Austrian Poles arrived. In the era just before World War I, Russian Poles joined the others and, in turn, were joined during the Cold War by supporters of Solidarity. Even now the Polish National Alliance is a major center for descendants. "The Polish community no longer exists as a spatial entity," says Polish descendant and historian Tom Hollowak, "but a state of mind."

Proceed now along the right-hand sidewalk of Aliceanna Street to Durham Street, a nationally important site for African-American history. Here the seven-year-old slave Frederick Douglass learned rudiments of reading. Even without a historic marker to tell you, anyone who cares about civil rights knows the importance of Douglass's writings. And even though the actual house is gone, other houses around this corner date from his era and doubtless look like it.

From Durham Street retrace your steps along Aliceanna Street back to Ann Street and turn left. Today this street, named, you will recall, for the street-namer's wife, Ann Bond, fits a recent writer's image of Fells Point—"a dowager who's had a face lift and a new wardrobe and is having the time of her life—but carefully." Most houses look as though residents are taking good care of them.

As you stroll in the 700 and 800 blocks of Ann Street, you will note wooden houses at 717 and 719. In early days every householder hung a firebucket out front, each with his name painted on. Today old row-houses in this and adjacent blocks attract newcomers interested in their preservation, including U.S. Sen. Barbara Mikulski, who grew up not very far from Fells Point in Highlandtown (*Tour 4*).

At Lancaster Street, go left one block, turn right on Wolfe Street and walk to Thames Street, in order to see the recycled factory of National Can Company, Thames Point Apartments. Go in the entrance on Thames Street to see a mural of old Fells Point by Kevin B. Raines (1984). Then walk beyond the apartment building to a parking lot for views over the water.

Come back to Ann Street and make a loop to the right to see the oldest Baltimore house. A note on an old plat called this corner "Flower of Baltimore." That fragrant name certainly fits the old-fashioned garden at 812, the Robert Long House (675-6750), a residence and office built in 1765 by Robert Long, a Quaker merchant from Cecil County, Maryland. Although we don't know much about him, he possibly foresaw this city's rapid growth as described only a little later by a Boston poet living 400 miles northward:

> How rich and great, no more a slave to sloth
> She [Baltimore] claims importance from her hasty
>   growth,
> High in renown, her streets and homes arrang'd.
> A group of cabins to a city chang'd . . .

This house had become derelict before restoration by the Society for the Preservation of Fells Point and Federal Hill. Now you can survey the first-floor counting room and living quarters. In summer go through a gate to the right of the house and see hollyhocks and other colonial blossoms—and such herbs as fennel and rosemary. A bench invites you to sit and read. Or you may venture across to 801 Ann Street, where the Wharf Rat Bar serves twenty-seven varieties of beer on draught.

In Baltimore, as in Alexandria and Norfolk, residents named Wolfe Street to commemorate the death of British Gen. James Wolfe, victor in 1759 over the French defenders of Canada. Persistence of such old street names defines the character of Baltimore. "The qualities we lack," wrote a Washingtonian in the *Baltimore City Paper,* "such as a respect for tradition, stability, a sense of community, can be found everywhere in Baltimore." And he added, "Not to mention the cheap beer."

Return to Thames Street, turn left, go one block to Wolfe Street, and walk down Wolfe Street. You will see remnants of commerce now disappearing from Fells Point. For example, at 927 is the cement plant of the Arundel Corporation. Before refrigeration, the site was covered by the ice storage warehouse of the American Ice Company. From it horse-drawn wagons delivered fifty-pound cakes of ice (cut in winter from the Susquehanna River) to overheated Baltimoreans. At 933 S. Wolfe Street a pre–Revolutionary War fortification had guarded Baltimore. Then in 1836 Lord Mott's cannery was built there.

When you reach the foot of South Wolfe Street, you will meet Fell Street and the Promenade. At the water's edge you can also go into the Residences at Henderson's Wharf and ask to see a sample apartment. A model will show how architects turn nineteenth-century warehouse spaces into apartments. The original windows still frame views of Fells Point and the river.

When it was time to pack tomatoes she [my wife] who had come from Italy used to go in the packing house . . . to wash them and clean them. And then after work I used to go there and help her. But I didn't get no credit, you know. Because they worked by the bucket. According to how many buckets you cleaned so I used to throw my tomatoes in her bucket so she could make a little more money.

Frank S. Villella, Baltimore Neighborhood Heritage Project (1979)

From some windows and from Inner Harbor Promenade at Henderson's Wharf, you can look to the left at distant Francis Scott Key Bridge and, to the left of it, Canton. Straight across the water you note structures for transferring coal and grain from trains to ships. Over there for many years also ships delivered raw materials to Procter and Gamble's soap plant.

Take time to explore along the Promenade by walking around the waterside end to the other side of Henderson's Wharf. Look down at the paving to see bricks inscribed with names of contributors to the cost of the Promenade, including Mayor William Donald Schaefer. See if you can find bricks for filmmakers John Waters, Barry Levinson, and Nora Ephron, all of whom filmed nearby.

On your right, as you go along the Promenade, you will walk between new pier housing on the left and Belt's Wharf Warehouses (c. 1855), converted to apartments, on the right. A century ago the coffee fleet unloaded green coffee beans from South America here. Captain Erickson of the *Francis,* one story goes, looked like a sedate, well-dressed businessman ashore, but looked and acted like a pirate at sea. Sometimes he would make a little money on the side by smuggling diamonds and ostrich feathers out of Brazil.

For centuries bowsprits of schooners and brigantines hung over Fell Street. Although the shoreline was extended with debris from the Big Fire of 1904, this street still resembles the Deptford of Dickens's London docks, and indeed Fells Point was once called Deptford Hundred.

When you reach the point on the Promenade where Belt's Wharf ends at a short lane, turn right and walk to Fell Street. Just across that street stands 931, Capt. John Steel's mansion (c. 1788–92). The owner, Mrs. Jean Hepner, often opens it on special tour days. She tells of finding this house being used as a tenement, "its walls festooned with sagging wallpaper." Luckily for her, much of the original carved woodwork remained.

Outside, at the second-floor window over the door at 931, look for a "busybody," an arrangement of three angled mirrors—one looking down to the door and the others facing up and down the sidewalk. A busybody allows someone inside to peer out without being seen.

At the north end of Fell Street, at Thames Street, loop to the right to 1815. What you see is a re-creation of an 1810 residence—pitched roofline, nine-over-six windows on the first floor, and brick entrance steps. Until 1968 this house was two workingmen's houses lacking cellars and not attracting notice.

Named after London's river (yet pronounced so as to rhyme with "names," while using the "th" of "they"), Thames Street looks somewhat foreign, as you saw from your boat. Up close, you may find it unglamorous. If you do, it may be time for refreshment. So why not drop in at Lee's for an ice cream cone, or sip coffee in the Daily Grind Coffee House at 1726 Thames Street? Crowds assemble all along here and around the corner on Broadway to browse in shops, drink, see and be seen. So noisy are some Friday and Saturday nights that residents lucky enough to own boats sail away for the weekend.

At 1730 Thames Street, the Cat's Eye has been a favorite pub of both tugboat workers and nascent Ph.D.s. Its barkeep became a familiar Fells Point character, Jefferson Knapp III. "Mr. Knapp is best remembered as the blasphemous wit who gave away drinks like water," reported the *Sun*'s Rafael Alvarez. "He was an incorrigible prankster, and a slavish scene-maker. To dedicate the Tomb of the Unknown Wino in the Fells Point square," he dressed up like Lincoln (whom he resembled) "to the

I can remember those Polish women that went to work in the morning. Along about 3 o'clock in the morning! They were heading into all these packing houses. And that's how they made both ends meet. They practically worked for nothing. But they were doing a hell of a sight better here than they were doing in Poland, you can bet . . . this was like a heaven compared to Poland for them. And they all said so, too! . . . They shucked oysters right here on Fell Street—steamed oysters.

Baltimore Neighborhood Heritage Project (1979)

Overhanging sign, plus banner with two entrances below

dismay of the then Mayor Schaefer." For Knapp's funeral on September 30, 1992, his friends had an eight-piece brass band flown in from New Orleans. For a New Orleans style send-off, the Treme Brass Band led a procession along Thames Street to the new Broadway pier, from which his ashes were deposited in the harbor.

Across from the Cat's Eye, the interior of the huge Recreation Pier may have been rehabilitated by the time you pass by. Although this building is not generally open to visitors, phone anyway (396-7900). The rehabilitation was part of a deal made with the city by Barry Levinson to use the pier in filming the television series *Homicide*. In 1914 Baltimoreans were proud of having spent $1 million for this pier. Tugboats tie up here, and inside and on a large deck children play. The upper level retains an original ballroom of elaborate plaster work and oak trim, one of the first municipal dancehalls in America.

"Municipal docks are not beautiful," wrote Letitia Stockett, "but there is always the shifting light and shadow upon the water, and the tang of salt air and the wheeling gulls." No question about it—this Point enjoys the power of nostalgia, of romance. It is the only area where the beginnings of Baltimore can be felt.

Recently a young, new resident told me that the

place attracted him because it is romantic. The same reaction stirred observers fifty years ago. In ship chandleries, we are told by an old-timer, there mingled delightful odors of spices, coffee, and "the good clean smell of the oakum which filled the lofts." And sometimes children were startled to see an extremely human figure, "the figure-head of a brave ship which sailed out of Baltimore with its presiding deity to the fore."

To finish within the allotted time, you will have to neglect much of interest uphill from this point. For example, Eastern Avenue, the cross street beyond Aliceanna Street, used to be called the Polish Wall Street because so many Polish immigrants banked there. One block east of Broadway, at South Ann Street, you can wander into a remnant of eccentricity, John's Junk Shop, where you can find preowned Easter finery or a complete set of Baltimore Oriole mugs. Do not go unless you want to get lost in nostalgia. Other shops for antiques and collectibles dot this district, notably on Aliceanna and Fleet streets.

Other suggested later excursions also will take you up Broadway Hill toward the two hospitals, Church Home and Hospital (522-8000), at Fayette Street (where Edgar Allan Poe died), and Johns Hopkins Hospital (and other Hopkins medical institutions), at Orleans Street (955-5000). Two blocks north of Aliceanna Street at Bank Street, nineteenth-century Irish immigrants worshiped at St. Patrick's Roman Catholic Church, and the faithful still do (675-0640). A son of one family became a priest here, later archbishop of Baltimore, and then cardinal—James Gibbons, first of two princes of the church who grew up in Baltimore (*Tour 8*).

Beyond the church and to the right of Broadway, at 1729 E. Pratt Street, you can dine at Olde Obrycki's Crab House, a favorite of New York actors (open only from April to October: 732-6399). At 612–614 S. Wolfe Street stand two wooden houses built about 1750. They interest not only as the earliest, simplest rowhouses in town, but also as rare survivors anywhere on the East Coast of urban wood dwellings.

Now you may be ready to take to the river in a water-taxi. *To find Broadway Dock landing, turn left on Thames Street at Fell Street, and walk past the Municipal Pier to Broadway Dock, and turn left down to the water-taxi landing. From there you will enjoy a short cruise to Canton, subject of Tour 3. Or you can return to Constellation Dock.*

We Baltimoreans let it all hang out—literally. When out-of-towners come here, they see things other cities try to hide, ban through local ordinance or vanquish through social pressure—tattooed midriffs, smiles with brown teeth, bellies the size of beach balls, hairdos from hell, rampant polyester, guys with long sideburns, women in white go-go boots.

Dan Rodricks, *Evening Sun* (c. 1990)

Canton

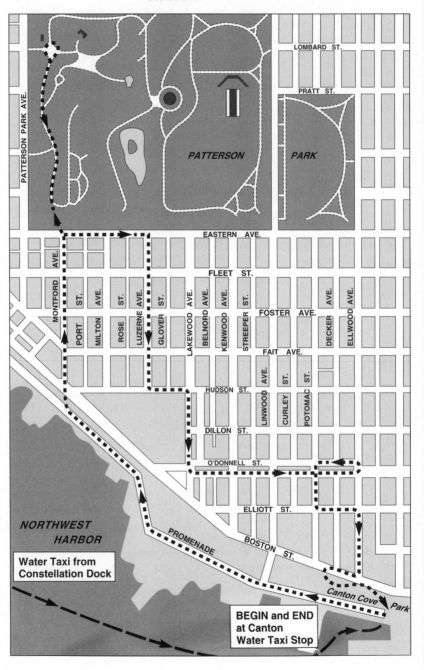

LOMBARD ST.

PRATT ST.

PATTERSON PARK ST.

PATTERSON   PARK

EASTERN   AVE.

FLEET   ST.

FOSTER   AVE.

FAIT   AVE.

MONTFORD   AVE.

PORT ST.

MILTON AVE.

ROSE ST.

LUZERNE AVE.

GLOVER ST.

LAKEWOOD AVE.

BELNORD AVE.

KENWOOD AVE.

STREEPER ST.

LINWOOD AVE.

CURLEY ST.

POTOMAC ST.

DECKER AVE.

ELLWOOD AVE.

HUDSON ST.

DILLON ST.

O'DONNELL   ST.

ELLIOTT   ST.

NORTHWEST HARBOR

PROMENADE

BOSTON ST.

Water Taxi from Constellation Dock

Canton Cove   Park

BEGIN and END at Canton Water Taxi Stop

- ◆ Historic ribbon of water in Canton Cove and around Fort McHenry (1799) with its huge replica of the Star-Spangled Banner waving day and night
- ◆ Sites significant for immigrant men and women, as well as for King George III, Pres. William Henry Harrison, and Gen. Dwight D. Eisenhower
- ◆ Streets associated with Peter Cooper, inventor and investor in America's first huge industrial park
- ◆ Old neighborhood haunts of Sen. Barbara Mikulski, first woman elected to the U.S. Senate on her own without a prominent husband or father
- ◆ Factories converted to expensive residences, in contrast to blocks and blocks of small nineteenth-century rowhouses, whose white-marble steps housewives scrubbed daily to a fare-thee-well.
- ◆ Painted screens, Formstone, corner bars, and other Baltimore neighborhood specialties
- ◆ Two green parks overlooking the water, both featuring memorials of American wars

In the summertime, why everybody used to be setting out on the steps because it used to be hot. Now, people got their houses air-conditioned. Then you used to sit and turn on the radio in your living room, and everybody sat on the steps, listening to the radio— Jack Benny, Fred Allen, The Shadow on Sunday, and Inner Sanctum, and Blue Hawaii. . . . You go in the 800 block of Kenwood Avenue tonight, at one-thirty or two in the morning, and if it ain't some of those Polish women still sitting on the steps, talking, I give you a hundred-dollar bill.

Baltimore Neighborhood Heritage Project (1979)

"It's the water, the pull of the water," says Ted Rouse, a developer of Tindeco Wharf. "There's just nothing like it. The boats, the skyline, even the weather changes here." Flowing past Canton (pronounced CAN-ton), a wide ribbon of water ties Baltimore to the Chesapeake Bay and then the sea.

Here old factory buildings, now converted to pricey housing, attract residents who can't resist a waterside with boats out front. In 1827, this neighborhood was the first large industrial park in America. Today you will walk by what by 1900 had become Cannery Row and blocks of workers' white marble–stepped rowhouses.

Baltimore, oh, Baltimore, you moth-eaten town,
Your brick row houses should all be torn down.
You can't speak English, you speak Baltimorese.
And the stench off the bay is what you call breeze.
You make us pay double for all you can sell,
And after the war you can all go to hell.
The worst of it is that you think you are swell,
You can take it from us, Baltimore, you stink.

Anonymous satire employing the rhythm of the official municipal anthem entitled "Baltimore, Our Baltimore," *Baltimore Sun* (purported to be by one of the horde of World War II factory workers in Canton and other industrial sites of what was called Baltimore's "arsenal of democracy")

Even now, churches show the diverse strands of immigration. The latest addition, the copper domes of St. Michael's Ukrainian Catholic Church, shines above everything.

Canton lacks the historic plaques it deserves. For instance, you pass near Fort Holabird where, early in World War II, the jeep took its first lurches. Here, too, you scan what was "Baptizing Shore" for Baptists both black and white. From the Korean War Memorial, look across the river to the greenery around Fort McHenry—Canton's big front lawn. Spot the fort's out-sized Star-Spangled Banner—fifteen stars and fifteen stripes—flying day and night.

HISTORY

In the eighteenth century, Canton's 3,000-acre plantation produced, among other things, a fine peach brandy. Its distillers were Capt. John O'Donnell, from Limerick, Ireland, and his wife Ellen, daughter of Baltimore's Capt. Thomas Elliott. Their "long low house, with a deep veranda in front," reported a visitor, "had somewhat the appearance of a pucka bungalow" like those O'Donnell had seen in India.

In the early nineteenth century, this site outside city limits drew Baltimoreans as a haven of pleasure. Flat fields were fine for horse races. And riverside beer gardens slaked the thirst of townspeople.

Those havens mostly vanished after 1827 when O'Donnell's son, Columbus, with Baltimore tycoon William Patterson and New Yorker Peter Cooper, incorporated the Canton Company. On 10,000 acres, they planned factories and "such other buildings and improvements as may be deemed necessary, ornamental and convenient." By the Civil War, Canton had developed into a major industrial park. Formation of the Baltimore & Ohio (B&O) Railroad had assured the prosperity of the Canton Company. "Baltimore will rival New York," predicted an English tourist in 1829. "You cannot well say more, for there imagination cannot outstrip their activity."

The flat waterside site proved ideal for industry: a harbor on a fog-free sea lane and an iron ore deposit. For decades Canton bustled with trains and ships, ironworks and sawmills, canneries and bottling plants, fertilizer works and can manufacturing factories.

During World War I, in that same area, the federal government acquired 225 acres from the Canton

Merrylanders [are] great horse-racers and cock-fighters, mighty wrestlers and jumpers, and enormous consumers of hoecake and bacon. They lay claim to be the first inventors of those recondite beverages cock-tail, stone fence and sherry cobblers, and to have discovered the gastronomical merits of terrapins, soft crabs and canvas-back ducks.

Diedrich Knickerbocker (pen name of Washington Irving), *History of New York* (1809)

Peter Cooper: Inventor, entrepreneur

Known to be self-assured and self-possessed, Cooper proved a good choice as partner in buying land and erecting the Canton Iron Works. Evidently, Cooper grasped Canton's potential as manufacturing center, just as he saw a dazzling future of railroads. Looking back in 1855, he wrote John H. B. Latrobe, "Many of the B&O stockholders with whom I was acquainted [in 1830] were seriously considering the propriety of forfeiting their stock, in the belief that the short curves in the road caused it to become an entire failure."

He then persuaded stockholders to hold on to shares. "I'll knock an engine together in six weeks that will pull carriages ten miles an hour." He did that, and so is remembered for inventions used in the first successful American steam locomotive, the Tom Thumb (1830). It made its first trip, according to Cooper's recollection, "on an ascending grade drawing one car with thirty passengers thirteen miles in an hour and twelve minutes." On September 18, 1830, the Tom Thumb raced a horse and would have won but for a leak in the boiler. "My contrivance saved this road [the B&O Railroad] from bankruptcy," Cooper said. In 1836 he traded his interest in the property for B&O stock selling at $45 a share. Soon afterward he sold the stock at $230 a share. Much later, his profits benefited everyone with the founding of Cooper Union and Cooper-Hewitt in New York.

Company for Fort Holabird (1917–70), a laboratory for military equipment. Holabird's engineers introduced, among other things, olive-drab paint, blackout lights for Army vehicles, and a motorcycle fender that won't clog with mud.

"The industrial concerns involved in the jeep's design have engaged in bitter argument about its parentage," wrote chronicler Norman Rukert. "The jeep as it now travels, however, spent its infant years at Holabird with military evaluators seeking flaws." What would General Eisenhower have done without his jeep? Also at that fort in World War II, the Army trained men to serve overseas in the Counter Intelligence Corps. The fort took its name from Gen. Samuel Beckley Holabird of the Quartermaster Corps, U.S. Army.

Street names, as is usual in Baltimore, give a key to a neighborhood. For instance, names of streets leading from Boston Street honor once-great men who ran the Canton Company: Conkling, Baylis, Gwynne, Leakin. Under them the industrial park prospered. After 1872 its growth accelerated when company president Charles J. Baker scoured Europe for skilled mechanics to help develop metalworking plants.

Because immigrant workers and their families put down roots, you touch Baltimore's ethnic fabric here. In it blend European traditions brought over more than a century ago. "We have our tradition, like at Easter we always have lamb on the table," says Dorothy Matthews, whose mother emigrated from a village near Sparta, Greece. "Like the Polish people have ham, we have lamb."

As you pass those white marble steps, you will be surveying miles of nineteenth-century rows that made up a company town, snaking over hills up from the harbor. "The sons and daughters of those blue-collar workers are no longer replacing them in the assembly line," says *Baltimore Sun* columnist Gilbert Sandler. "They are going to the community colleges and becoming dental technicians and lab assistants." And the assembly lines are vanishing faster than laborers can train for other lines of work.

On your walk you will be able to contrast old residents with new. What strikes some observers as a cabin-cruiser invasion threatens to bring a rise in tax assessments for an old blue-collar community. This invasion could rip apart the ethnic fabric.

Although similar culture conflicts bother people elsewhere—not just Canton or Baltimore—the solution may well follow a strong local tradition: "The quintessential spirit of Baltimore," wrote historian Gerald W. Johnson, "[is] an addiction to calm deliberation which may cost a city some opportunities but also saves it from making some costly mistakes."

TOUR

Starting point: Constellation Dock, Inner Harbor; then the Fishing Pier, Boston Street, Canton Light Marina (water-taxi stop 15)

Length of tour: Two hours

Snacks and restrooms: O'Donnell Square restaurants and Enoch Pratt Free Library; Bay Café next to Tindeco

Transportation: Like Canton's nineteenth-century immigrants, come by water. Take a water-taxi from Fells Point. On board the water-taxi you own a first-class theater seat. From your floating chair your vision will blend old landmarks to the south, such as Federal Hill, with brand-new HarborView towers. Smells— sweet, under the huge Domino Sugar sign; . . . tidal, from the Chesapeake Bay—also mark the route if the wind is right and if your voyage touches the taxi stop at the Museum of Industry. Debark at the Canton Cove water-taxi landing.

If you choose not to come by water, you can walk from Fells Point on the Harbor Promenade. Should you come by car, take Eastern Avenue east to Boston Street. Turn right and stay on Boston Street until you reach the parking lot of Canton Cove Park. The tour begins at the Harris Creek bridge adjacent to the Fishing Pier and Anchorage Tower.

Your water-taxi voyage ends at the Harbor Promenade, which begins its seven-mile waterside parade here in Canton Cove. Your walking tour begins at the brick path of the Promenade. You left it in Fells Point if you took that walk, and you will walk segments in other tours.

Go along the Promenade to the right as you face the water to see why new residents flock to Canton— passing ships, downtown towers, and, directly opposite, Fort McHenry's park, like a vast front lawn spread for a Fourth of July picnic under the Star-Spangled Banner.

Here you can survey a tributary of the Chesapeake Bay, the Northwest Branch of the Patapsco River. "A noble arm of the sea" is what a nineteenth-century visitor, Lord Morpeth, called the Chesapeake—America's largest estuary. It has served settlers for almost 400 years as road, food larder, and sink for wastes, and especially now as lure for recreational sailors.

Because some segments of the Promenade are incomplete, it breaks off here and there. When it does, just walk out to Boston Street and look for signs directing you back to the Promenade. As you walk, you will notice tall recycled factories. The first, Lighthouse Point, eight acres in the 2700 block of Boston Street, may be off the drawing boards when you reach what is a proposed mixture of residences with offices, maritime retail shops, and 600 boat slips. What looks like a blue and white striped lighthouse was a chimney on the J. S. Young licorice plant. Its product flavored tobacco.

At 2639 Boston Street, the second factory, now called the Shipyard, rents fifty-six apartments and abuts a private marina of twenty boat slips. Canton Cove was just one of the riverfront shipyard sites in Baltimore. As late as 1875, Thomas Booz and Brother shipyard built wooden schooners for the lumber trade. "Wooden ships for iron men" was a popular motto.

After passing the Shipyard, you come to Canton Fishing Pier, a state-funded pier and park. From the park a pedes-

trian bridge (1991) carries you across the mouth of Harris Creek. When you cross the bridge, look right and imagine a creek deep enough in 1788 to launch the frigate *Constellation,* Baltimore's largest sailing vessel, built chiefly by African Americans. "A fine vessel . . . too much encumbered with wood-work within," said visitor Duc La Rochefoucault-Liancourt.

Now walk past Anchorage Towers (2515 Boston Street). From apartments here, water views on your left are, of course, expensive. Housing here is labeled "upscale," although the rooms inside, some say, look ordinary— even boring. The Tower offers ninety-five apartments, rising up, some neighbors say, out of scale and out of context. Critics complain that it could be Anywhere, USA. Future limiting of heights to sixty feet may retain views for people living and working across Boston Street.

Past Anchorage Towers stretches a brick row of forty-eight low houses, their faces turned toward their marina. Mayor William Donald Schaefer persuaded the owner of the ground, a dealer in lumber, to build residences instead of a lumberyard here because Schaefer had admired just such waterfront housing in Boston.

Imagine crowds of immigrant women in 1900 processing ripe tomatoes and peaches in canneries right here along Boston Street. A relic of those days, a roster of Monarch Cannery (owned by water-taxi captain Ed Kane) notes his grandmother's name, followed by a code mark showing that she was a nursing mother and had to be allowed time and place to nurse her baby.

When you see that you are nearing the end of the Anchorage row, you should cut through between houses and go out to Boston Street. Before you go, it is a good idea to sit down, enjoy the water, and read about the route. *Facing Boston Street, turn right and go to the first street coming in on the left, Montford Avenue, and take it all the way to Patterson Park (four blocks).*

You may wonder why Boston Street, a street in a city in the Upper South, came to be named for Beantown. New Englanders had emigrated to Baltimore when it was the second largest city in the nation after New York. It also stood at the center of population of the United States. "Within the recollection of some of its inhabitants, there were but few houses on its present site," reported an English tourist in 1830. "It now contains a population of 80,000 inhabitants." And the number doubled every decade. Specifically, enterprising New Englanders came to launch the Canton Company's metal-processing plants. They named Boston Street and

---

I was a hog-eye on tomatoes, I could skin 'em fast. I could do the work of two women. We used to have tomato trucks sitting around here, all along Boston Street. The farmers would pick the nice ones off the top and give 'em to you.

Mary Ljek Eber, age 76, *Baltimore Sun* (February 16, 1992)

The odors arising from the souring mass of tomato pulp and skins on the floors, the clouds of steam from the nearby vats, together with the addition of an oppressive and distinguishing odor whose origin could not be determined, produced an environment that was distinctly discredible and called for attention on broader grounds than the health and comfort of employees.

U.S. Bureau of Labor report (1911)

other streets with Massachusetts names—Cambridge, Concord, and Essex.

Immigrants settled in small brick rowhouses, built churches, and formed social clubs and building and loan societies. Everything was an easy walk from the rowhouse door. Often a parent willed the house to a son or daughter. Sometimes, married children simply bought houses in the same block with their parents.

In the twentieth century, jobs opened farther east along the river—at Sparrows Point Bethlehem Steel plant, General Motors, Maryland Dry Dock, and Continental Can. As late as the 1950s, residents here and in adjacent Highlandtown gave Baltimore its reputation as a blue-collar town. "We were the city where people sat out on white steps, drinking National Boh, relaxing after they'd washed the 'payment' [Baltimorese for "pavement"]," says Gilbert Sandler.

Canton's oldest rowhouses line Leakin Street and other streets in the southwestern section of Canton, where you are walking. Many built in the mid-nineteenth century were homes to German and Irish workers. Between 1880 and 1921 those nationalities gave place to newer immigrants from eastern and southern Europe—Russians, Ukrainians, Lithuanians, Poles, Italians, Hungarians, Greeks.

Ethnic settlement spread uphill to the northeast into Highlandtown. There a new Little Italy grew up around Our Lady of Pompeii Church, Greektown settled around St. Nicholas Church, and Polish Americans made Holy Rosary a large, rich parish. Service at Holy Rosary is conducted half in English and half in Polish. Once upon a time, no one could become a communicant until he or she could say the Lord's Prayer in Polish.

As you cross Fait Avenue and Foster Avenue, look up and down rowhoused streets. Most of the rowhouses are narrow, have two stories, and open on an alley in back. In 1979 Mary Kraus Feehley recalled that her mother-in-

Q.: Did you ever hear German spoken at home? *A.:* No, because my mother could not understand nor talk German but my father could. My father went to school to learn German. It was a 3 cent school [at] Kenwood Avenue and Hudson Street. . . . he attended school there on Saturday mornings, see, and they had to pay three cents. I guess that was probably the teacher's salary.

Lloyd Konigkremer, Baltimore Neighborhood Heritage Project (1979)

When I got married in 1930 my husband was working for the Continental Can and for $15 a week. Well, he didn't work very long when he got laid off. The Depression had hit. There was no work, no work for nobody. . . . Back during that time I remember I got pregnant. . . . I went to the clinic in Johns Hopkins Hospital. Then my husband got a job . . . digging a ditch. . . . Trying to get money together to pay the hospital bill to get me out of the hospital. It was about two weeks work digging a ditch.

Ethel Zwick, Baltimore Neighborhood Heritage Project (1979)

Formstone façade

law, widowed, was lucky enough to have her brothers
buy her a house—"$500. For a six-room house. And a
corner house. $500." Today you are surveying hundreds
of those six-room houses.

"A long row of them, to be sure, was somewhat monotonous," said H. L. Mencken, "but it at least escaped
being trashy and annoying." Today some observers are
annoyed with the gray cement called Formstone covering many brick façades. Formstone was a brand name,
coined by Albert Knight in 1937. On the sloping street,
rows of Formstone houses resemble the mottled skin of
a snake.

"There's a penchant in Baltimore for creative illusion.
Formstone is part of a tradition that goes back to the
nineteenth century, when people were making things
look like what they weren't—faux-graining, marbleizing,
sand-painting," said a Kansan newly come to town. "A
certain love of fakery is part of the Baltimore character,"
says *Sun* reporter Carl Schoettler. "Big hair and polyester
have never gone out of fashion."

As you walk along Montford Avenue, spot examples
of creative illusion. You will be approaching the showy,
shiny turnip domes of St. Michael's Ukrainian Catholic
Church (1991). Look for ornamental touches on row-

houses. Houses at 702 and 704 are embellished with
stained glass panels above entrances or first-floor windows. Note the windows at 807 for another example.
The whole front seems to glow with color from what in
East Baltimore has become a popular folk-art form,
painted screens. Each ordinary mesh window screen displays a picture—the most common scene has been a cot-
tage surrounded by trees and showing some clouds and
background hills. "They are a kind of substitute for the
pink flamingos in the front yards of suburbia," says
Elaine Eff, Maryland folklorist. "They are a basic expression of the people, a gift to the streets."

The originator of that scene and of the whole painted
screen vogue was William Anton Oktavec, a Czech immigrant who opened a grocery in 1913. He soon found a
market for the screens that he painted in his spare time.
His first customer, it is said, was a neighbor, Mrs. John
Schott, in the section called Little Bohemia, who wanted
"to keep the bums on the corner from rubbering [peek-
ing] in her windows." Painting the screening made it
hard for passersby to see in, yet permitted the homeowner to see out.

"Ideally," wrote a flippant *Washington Post* columnist,
"a great Baltimore rowhouse should feature a window
shrine, a painted screen (the Matterhorn is preferred), a
stoop sign reading NO LOITERING, and Christmas lights
blinking year round. Plus fluorescent green indoor-out-
door carpet on the stoop in front of the abode. And a
tire (painted white) as a planter."

At this point you are exploring inland to Patterson
Park. Surrounding the park are early twentieth-century
rowhouses of three stories. There you see pale yellow
Roman brick façades and the familiar white marble
steps, many still kept very clean. Years ago Canton

Clad in Mother Hubbard house-wrappers, the housewives of my boyhood appeared right after breakfast, each carrying a pail of water, a
scrub brush, a cake of "Olean" soap, a washrag, and a doormat to
kneel on. They scrubbed the three or four steps and the broader top
landing with demoniac energy, until the mica, spar and quartz glistened to dazzle the eye. All morning and afternoon they screamed
reproaches at letter carriers, bill collectors, and street Arabs hawking
fruits and vegetables, who profaned the white perfection with dusty or
even muddy shoes. Then, just before dinnertime, the stoops would be
scrubbed again.

Fulton Oursler, *Behold the Dreamer!* (1960)

housewives became known for cleanliness: their steps gleamed in the sun.

At the corner of Fleet and Montford streets, look for Harry's Bakery. Nearer the park you can see spotty gentrification: young college graduates, sometimes without much money, long have gravitated here to enjoy what they regard as authentic ethnicity, with a view encompassing a vast lawn. At the corner of Eastern Avenue stands a new landmark, the Ukrainian church. The century-old congregation chose to model their church on one in Kiev. A black iron fence encloses the church complex and its green skirt of a lawn. The copper-domed structure is the latest addition to a set of ethnic churches dominating Canton corners. You saw their steeples from the water-taxi.

Cross Eastern Avenue and rest in the park. Then, climb Hampstead Hill above Eastern Avenue as far as the strange-looking tower of the Patterson Park Observatory (1891), called the Pagoda. There you can view downtown towers as well as Canton Cove. Constellation Dock is not far away, as the crow flies. When you face the hill, you have Butcher's Hill Historic District to the left, and far to the right the various ethnic enclaves of Highlandtown. The walk up the gentle slope takes about ten minutes. Go to the Pagoda for history, and for the view.

The Pagoda's three encircling balconies are crowned with a pagoda-like roof. After one of its periodic refurbishings, it shimmers with its wood painted the original colors, yellow and orange, and with varied-colored glass windows and transoms. "A most substantial and ornamental building," said its designer, Charles H. Latrobe, "commanding a very fine view, especially over the harbor." Two centuries after this district took the name of China's Canton, the Chinese Nationalist government on Taiwan gave marble sculptures called Palace Lions for the entrance to this fake Chinese pagoda.

During the early days of the United States, Thomas Jefferson and other traveling Virginians rode horseback over this hill to the capital, Philadelphia, or New York. Then—a shining moment—just before the 1814 Battle of Baltimore this height became a fort, the main defensive line against troops of King George III in a British land attack on Baltimore. "White and black are all at work together [preparing defensive positions]," wrote a young Baltimore woman. "You'll see a master and his slave digging side by side. There is no distinction whatsoever." Look for swellings in the park's hillside left over

There was a lumber yard near the water . . . a quiet isolated place. . . . On Sunday afternoons many of us would walk there and sit on the water's edge and talk. . . . And we all sang our songs like we used to do in our villages in Ukraine.

Warwara Pise, *The Ukrainians of Maryland* (1979)

from battlements, once occupied by 100 cannons and 12,000 men.

The Pagoda rises on the site of Rodgers' Bastion, so named because at the Battle of Baltimore Cmdr. John Rodgers's naval forces stood ready here to fight the British. Luckily for Rodgers's men, the enemy troops turned tail before charging uphill. They left because their commanding officer had been killed, because attack by water had failed, and, as chronicler Hamilton Owens speculates, possibly because Baltimore's sultry heat was the "sort that always gets Englishmen down and dulls their interest in life."

After you find a commemorative plaque on a cannon (the isolated one on the water side) look next to it for the Star-Spangled Banner Centennial Monument (1914, J. Maxwell Miller). Since schoolchildren helped pay for it, it is right to have two children hold the scroll telling that here "the citizen soldiers of Maryland stood ready to sacrifice their lives in defense of their homes and their country." From here you can see the Francis Scott Key Bridge (distant half-left), honoring the poet of the national anthem. Key had composed the words after having witnessed the British failure to subdue Fort McHenry.

The same hill in 1819 served as campground for 1,000 harborside residents fleeing an epidemic of yellow fever. In the Civil War, Union troops occupied the hill, as they did other hills overlooking the city, in order to prevent trouble from Confederate sympathizers. Here in a temporary hospital, wounded soldiers from the Gettysburg battle received treatment.

Today Patterson Park is said to be the most used park in town. It is also the oldest large park, a gift almost 200 years ago from William Patterson. Later, less generous tycoons sold their estates for use as public parks: Druid Hill (now with zoo and swimming area), and woodland Cylburn.

An Ulsterman by birth, William Patterson grew up in Pennsylvania. In 1778 at age 26, he arrived in Baltimore, soon married Dorcas Spear of the mercantile establishment, and settled down to make money. During the American Revolution he risked his fortune to buy ammunition from France for Washington's army. He risked his life fighting with the First Maryland Cavalry at the Battle of Yorktown. Later Patterson led in organizing the B&O. Of his thirteen children, the youngest, Betsy, brought him international fame and also proved the

Hampstead Hill (Laudenslager's) was white with tents; and trainings were going on: in town, twice a day, for a month before the attack. . . . I remember to have seen [casualties], brought to town, on litters:—a day or two after the battle of North Point; and I think that John Jeppson, Bootmaker, of South Street. was one of them: He, afterwards, died.

Richard Townsend, diary (September 1814)

most troublesome when she married Napoleon's brother (*Tour 11*). In his will he left her only the house where she had been born. "A small spare man, of dark complexion," said a contemporary, John H. B. Latrobe, "with great determination in his quiet look."

Walking away from Patterson Park, go along Eastern Avenue and the park to Luzerne Avenue (past Port Street, Milton Avenue, and Rose Street). Look toward the far park corner for the large monument (by Hans Shuler) honoring Revolutionary War hero Count Casimir Pulaski, a Polish cavalry officer. (It stands near the Eastern and Linwood Avenue corner.) In Baltimore he recruited an independent corps soon known as "Pulaski's Corps." Pulaski was killed in 1779 at the siege of Savannah. He died in the arms of Baltimorean and fellow officer Capt. Paul Bentalou, who took command and retrieved Pulaski's embroidered silk banner, now at the Maryland Historical Society. The bas-relief statue of the count on horseback makes the centerpiece of an annual Polish festival. Make a loop over to see it if you like large-scale battle scenes of men on horseback.

Turn right down Luzerne Avenue. It is namesake of Count de la Luzerne, who fulfilled an eighteenth-century diplomat's dream of making a grand splash. As French minister to the Continental Congress (1779–83), he helped win aid for the Americans. His memorable gesture of friendship was a big party just before the Battle of Yorktown. He appropriated thirty chefs from the French army to prepare for French Comte de Rochambeau and 180 guests a ninety-pound turtle, served in its immense shell. It tasted, a guest said, "sumptuous, spectacular." If he did that before the French-American victory at Yorktown, don't you wonder what he did after it?

Walk four blocks on Luzerne Avenue to Hudson Street. It forms the western boundary of an important industrial site occupied most recently by the American Can Company. When the company ceased operations here in the late 1980s, it left nine acres and sixteen buildings. Only the four-story 1924 "signature" building here at Hudson and Boston streets is protected by a city-approved land use plan.

Turn left on Hudson Street. Nothing remains of a factory that revolutionized warfare: its products made wooden war ships obsolete. On this site during the Civil War, a Massachusetts blacksmith named Horace Abbott manufactured iron plates for the *Monitor*, first ironclad ship in the Union Navy. Called "the cheese box that made history," it fought off the Confederate

encounter of 1862.

Other Baltimore inventors improved canning
machines and processes to make this part of the Patapsco River a center for canning oysters and vegetables.
Small wonder, then, that an English visitor reported seeing "a peculiar sight, a hill composed of hundreds of .
tons of oyster-shells." Inventor Isaac Solomon cut food
cooking time by adding calcium chloride to the water in
order to raise the temperature. Inventor Mark Owings
Shriver produced a steam pressure cooker. In Baltimore,
Thomas Kensett invented the tin can (1825). Cans were
handmade until a Baltimore inventor introduced a
machine to do the job.

*Turn right from Hudson Street into South Lakewood
Avenue.* At 940 S. Lakewood, you pass Indecco Apartments, a prize-winning recycling of a factory (look for
the fading white painted sign on the brick façade). Here
are apartments for elderly people, many of whom have
moved from nearby rowhouses. Go inside, if you like,
to see the transformation from factory to apartments.
Conversions like this one have preserved many other old
Baltimore streetscapes.

*At the end of two blocks you face the eastern boundary
of the American Can Company plant at O'Donnell Street.
Turn left and proceed into O'Donnell Square.* There a park
divides the street in two. Places to eat and drink line
both long sides of the square: Dypski's Turn of the Century Museum Saloon and Phil's Canton Crab House
have been there a while. The green park square occupies
what was a farmers' market (1858).

In the center stands a statue of founder John O'Donnell (by Tylden Street). With hand outstretched, he lords
it over the park. Capt. John O'Donnell, immigrant,
merchant, and planter, displayed an adventurous streak
as broad as his Irish brogue. Long before he immigrated
to Baltimore in 1785, he traded throughout the Far East.
Once he had been captured by Arabs and sold as a slave
(or so we are told). Later, in Baltimore, he owned thirty-
six African-American slaves.

O'Donnell called the place Canton, after the southern Chinese port that made him rich. His ship *Pallas*
imported "an extensive variety of teas, china, silks,
satins, nankeens, etc. etc." That line from a 1785 newspaper attracted the notice of George Washington, who
authorized his agent to buy, "if great bargains are to be
had—my purchases depend entirely on the prices."

Boutiques cater to an influx of outlanders. Yet St.

O'Donnell Square shop
with pedestrian

Casimir's Roman Catholic Church and Father Kolbe
School continue to dominate the water end of the
square. A whole block long, the church spun off from
Polish-American St. Stanislaus in Fells Point. For it and
other churches and recreational clubs, the Canton Company gave land.

Across the green park from St. Casimir's, Messiah
Lutheran Church in strong, gray stone seems a twin
anchor. Next to it, its social hall of 1925, converted by a
private firm, Jubilee, Inc., added in 1993 to investments
in low-income housing for the elderly. *Walk behind the
church to the first branch library built by Enoch Pratt in
1882.* The building has Romanesque arches and a decorated chimney.

Go inside this century-old library. Ask to see pictures
of early librarians, most of whom were women.
"Women are steadier workers and more reliable," said
donor Enoch Pratt. "Besides, they require less wages
than men in the same position." Pratt added, "When a
woman has an extra dollar, it gets spent on gewgaws."
Today Mr. Pratt's library governing board includes eight
women out of a total of twenty-two, and the director is
a woman.

Outside the entrance, read a historic site marker
about how branch libraries were "a somewhat new and
untried experiment." Note that libraries and churches
all over Baltimore helped workers put hard industrial
work—hazardous and monotonous—in perspective.

Another resource was the corner saloon. It is appropriate, then, that O'Donnell Street darts from the square eastward away from the library to Lager Beer Hill. The name tells us that Baltimore breweries operated around Conkling Street, including Helldorfer's, Gunther's, and National. In the 1870s an advertisement headed Globe Distillery, Canton, shows whiskey barrels piled up in layers. Another picture advertises Superior Old Mountain rye whiskey from W. T. Walters & Company. Profits went to enrich the Walters Art Gallery (*Tour 10*).

But you needn't go that far for a drink: just look around O'Donnell Square. *After you have rested in the square, you should walk toward the water down Potomac Street, which exits the square to the right in front of Messiah Lutheran Church.* Appropriately, you can see the river down this street, though it is the Patapsco, not the Potomac. Many Maryland rivers gave names to streets in Thomas Poppleton's 1816 plan enlarging the city. They also proved popular as names of ships.

By now you no doubt have formed impressions of what life has been like in Canton for immigrants and their heirs. After 1870, the Canton Company laid out streets and graded and paved them. Then, 2,500 lots (20 feet by 100 feet) were mapped. In 1888, residents of both districts refused annexation to Baltimore City, partly because saloons in the city were closed on Sunday and those in the county remained open.

When you reach Elliott Street, turn left and walk to Ellwood Street. Elliott Street is namesake of Captain O'Donnell's in-laws. The name "Ellwood" belongs to a series ending with "wood"—Kenwood, Linwood, Lakewood—all from a suburban developer's lexicon. At the corner of Elliott and Potomac streets, you may like to make a loop left to Canton Square's 124 brand-new townhouses. They stand here because 215 old Canton houses were torn down in 1968 for a ramming of I-83 through Canton along the inland side of Boston Street. When plans went forward to build a superhighway through Canton, Southeast Council Against the Road (SCAR) was formed to stop the road. One of the leaders was Barbara Mikulski.

Now walk toward the water, down Ellwood Street past the Canton Harbor Nursing Center, the Greenery, on the right. Opened in 1987, it was created for disabled and handicapped people, as well as senior citizens of moderate income. Notice how second-floor large windows command one of the best views of Fort McHenry and the river. On the left you pass Du Burns Arena, used for

Church going people may raise Cain six other days of the week, but come Sunday they will get themselves together and get dressed and go to Church. Down St. Casimir's Church, you have more Polish down there. Then it's all Irish people around St. Bridget because you had to have a mass in English for the people that weren't Polish. The same way . . . at Sacred Heart Church they had a German mass there. Our Lady of Pompeii Church, that's where you would find your Italian people, naturally.

Baltimore Neighborhood Heritage Project (1979)

Senator Barbara Mikulski: East Baltimore activist and "Queen of the Ethnics"

"Some poor guy didn't have to die for me to get the job [of U.S. senator]," she said. At her swearing-in to political office, Senator Mikulski wore a black scarf hand-embroidered by her great-grandmother, who had come from Poland at 16 without job or money. Barbara Ann (born in 1936) grew up across the street from her family's grocery store and attended the Institute of Notre Dame. She still lives nearby. After St. Agnes College and a degree in social work, she worked for Catholic and city social work agencies. Then she saw red: the city announced plans to push a sixteen-lane highway through Canton, Fells Point, and neighborhoods west.

"We got started with about eight of us meeting seven times a week in groups under different names to create the illusion of power," she said. "We didn't have lots of money. All we had was each other." Even so, by reporting every one of their protest meetings to the powers that be, they helped triumph over the interstate road.

In 1971 she campaigned for a seat on the city council. "I knocked on 15,000 doors that summer, wore out five pair of shoes and got mugged by fourteen Chihuahuas." In 1976 she moved up to the U.S. House of Representatives, and in 1986 to the Senate. "This is not the Montessori day camp," the senator said recently. "This is the United States Senate with someone who's broken the glass ceiling, who has a strong commitment to an agenda and pursues it aggressively. And I don't just preside over things. I make things happen."

indoor soccer and lacrosse. Its name honors an East Baltimore politician, Clarence "Du" Burns. When Mayor William Donald Schaefer was elected governor, Burns served out Schaefer's term and became the first African-American mayor of this city.

When you come to Boston Street, cross over into Canton Cove Park. Go down to the water and choose a bench so you can watch ships and take time to discover in these pages what makes this cove historic. If you didn't pause in O'Donnell Square for refreshment, you can cut diagonally across the park to a waterfront low building next to Tindeco, the Bay Café. Food and restrooms are there.

Before you leave this freshly created Canton Cove Park, think about this shoreline as historic center of good times. The street name of Toone Street nearby, for instance, honors a saloonkeeper. In the first quarter of the nineteenth century, Baltimoreans could catch a breeze and relax at Toone's Pleasure Gardens. For excitement they bet on horses at the nearby Canton Race Track, located at present-day Boston and Clinton streets.

Canton Cove Park

As early as 1823 Martin Potter managed a racecourse in the then-undeveloped flat land near the river. Later, patrons of the track arrived on the steamboat *Relief* from Pratt and Light streets for 12 ½ cents each way.

Even before that era, Baltimoreans came out from town to the inviting freedom and emptiness. "An assemblage of people," reports an onlooker in 1809, "for the purpose of giving expression to political opinion" held a barbecue near where you walk. "The swilling of liquors and the pulling and tearing of the half-raw beef would have done honor to the feast of Abyssinians."

Even more exciting, in 1840, 20,000 Whigs from all over the country gathered at the Canton Race Track to hear speeches by Daniel Webster, Henry Clay, and other famous orators of the day. Afterwards, the crowd nominated William Henry Harrison for president. Thus Canton hosted what is generally considered to have been the very first presidential nominating convention in the United States. The catchy cry, "Tippecanoe and Tyler Too," led Harrison to the White House.

Of course, most of the time the racetrack was patronized by a familiar race crowd, a breed that has long flourished in Maryland. Horses, after all, have been king here longer than in Kentucky. It is no surprise that a Baltimore horse fancier, John S. Skinner, pioneered as the country's first publisher of pedigrees, stud listings, race results, and individual horses' performances.

A later pleasure centered at the water's edge around

Sail to the fort, meet the east India ship. . . . Recid [*sic*] a letter from Genl. Washington. . . . Do little. Lament that I am in Baltimore. . . . Begin my remarks on the English language. . . . Attend the races. Horse-Races, every spring and autumn, are holidays; like Election & Thanksgiving in Connecticut. 7 horses enter the lists, 5 run 3 four mile heats. The Brilliant wins the purse £75.

Journal of Noah Webster, who, when he lived in Baltimore, had already published his grammar and spelling book, but not his famous dictionary (1785)

the curve to the left (at Cardiff Avenue): in 1893 the city
opened the first official city bathing beach. For three cents
a citizen could rent a bathing suit and a bar of soap. Earlier in the nineteenth century the same waters offered
total immersion as part of the baptismal ceremony of
Baptists, black and white. Those Sunday afternoon dunk-
ings caused the place to be called "Baptizing Shore."

Still looking toward Clinton Street, you can see the
site of the B&O ferry slip one block south of Cardiff
Avenue, destination of ferries carrying trains from docks
on Locust Point. From here in Canton, trains headed
north to Philadelphia and Jersey City, the terminal
opposite Manhattan. A rival railroad, the Pennsylvania,
prevented the B&O from going all the way into New
York City.

No such restriction hampered completion of I-95 in
1985. After crossing Locust Point, it ducks under the
harbor and emerges not far from the site of the ferry
terminal. Not only is it the nation's widest vehicular
tunnel, but it also is unique for turning in two directions simultaneously—down and curving (around the
point of Fort McHenry). This tunnel is said to have
been the largest project in the national highway program
by the time it was completed.

Spoil from dredging a trench now forms the base of
Canton Sea Girt container terminal with its three 1,000-
foot-long berths. Sea Girt, the last word in speedy ship-
ping, is supposed to show the way in reviving the port.
You can see its blue tall cranes from the water-taxi.
Other tall cranes in view add to the effect of welcoming
Statues of Liberty—stripped to skeletons and yet still
able to salute.

Today Clinton Street itself may not have such noble
dreams. Its name, though, remembers a national politician, George Clinton. He seems to have been a man of
such impressive physique that he was called Magnus
Apollo. Also he was a friend of Peter Cooper, a founder
of Canton, you will recall.

At the water end of Clinton Street (far left as you face
the water but just out of sight) stood for a long time the
town's quarantine station, called Lazaretto, from the Italian for pesthouse or fever hospital. The isolation of this
point made it ideal as hospital for contagious diseases
brought by ship. Nevertheless, Baltimoreans suffered
epidemic malaria, yellow fever, and cholera. During the
early 1830s an epidemic killed 5 percent of the population. Next to the hospital site stood an early lighthouse,
demolished but recently reproduced. Across the river, to

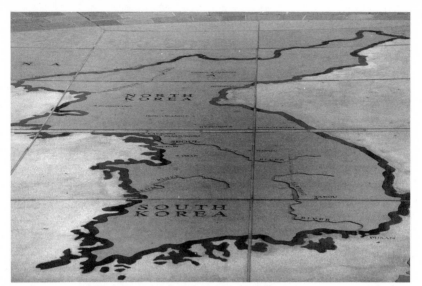

Korean War Memorial

the right of Fort McHenry, is the site of this city's Ellis Island. No historic plaque notes that immigrants entered in numbers second only to New York.

Within your view to the left, you can see outer Canton, the still active commercial port. There in World War II workers fulfilled President Roosevelt's promise, "We must be the great arsenal of democracy." Bethlehem Steel produced 20 million tons of steel. Workers followed three shifts, seven days a week. At the Fairfield operation, Bethlehem Steel workers managed to cut the time to build a Liberty ship from 244 days to 30 days. At Canton's Continental Can plant, 60 percent of the workers were women, and of them 40 percent were black.

A resuscitated Liberty ship, *John W. Brown,* has been anchored for some time at the foot of Clinton Street. Local volunteers restored it recently as one of only two ships of that type still afloat. During World War II, it was built in Baltimore to ferry supplies and troops. Union Shipbuilding Yard launched 384 of these Liberty ships, 74 of the larger Victory ships, and 30 LST landing craft. That was the largest number of ships built by any American shipyard during the war.

Now Korean War veterans visit the Korean War Memorial on the Boston Street edge of Canton Cove Park, a simple memorial circle marked by a ring of flags. In the center is incised a map of Korea, and around the rim of the circle you can read a list of battles fought. When you turn toward the water, you look across to Fort McHenry. That view expands the aura of patriotism.

As you turn away from the memorial, look left to

where the river widens. It is easy to visualize cargo ships pushing down the Chesapeake Bay to the sea. From these waters Clipper ships sailed, and in this harbor Liberty ships were built and trans-Atlantic seaplanes used to land. From here you face a world port. Nearer to you in the water stands a giant arch, monument to the old commercial port. Originally it served as part of a gantry crane, a machine for lifting railroad cars onto barges.

Tides also bring new residents to Canton, as well as Otterbein and Fells Point. In this part of Canton Cove you can follow the Promenade past two popular residential complexes. You may want to take time to look inside at model apartments. The first you come to is Canton Cove, condominiums replacing a tin can factory. And the second factory conversion (next to the water) is Tindeco, formerly one of the world's largest manufacturers of decorative tin containers. Just inside that building you can examine a collection of what was made. There you will find pristine Whitman Samplers and much else that collectors love to buy in high-class flea markets and antique shops. The display is well documented.

Outside the exhibit, you can drop into the Bay Café to refresh yourself. If you go on a hot summer day, you can understand why riverside beer gardens and casinos attracted sweltering city dwellers in the days before air-conditioning. "Each was a wonderland for a 6-year-old," wrote James M. Merritt in 1993, "featuring rides and games, water slides, dance pavilions and long piers extending into the bay (Bay Shore) and the Patapsco (Riverview)." At tree-shaded picnic tables Baltimoreans ate steamed crabs (75 cents a dozen). Riverview Park, located on the edge of Canton, doubtless hired Canton men as waiters.

Your return to Fells Point or the Inner Harbor can be made easily by water-taxi. Or you can walk the Harbor Promenade, of course, and return through Fells Point to the Inner Harbor (about five miles).

If you drove to Canton and are hungry, you can find restaurants in Highlandtown. *From Boston Street go north to Eastern Avenue and turn right.* Keep your eyes open for restaurant signs. For reasonably priced, authentically foreign food, go to long-established Haussner's at 3244 Eastern Avenue for an enormous German-style menu and a vast collection of art crowding the walls. In the daytime, look for Dorothea's Italian Bakery at Gough and Mount Pleasant streets. Here you can select the bread dough and additions, such as nuts or raisins, to be baked while you wait.

Like the waiters of the Spring Gardens and Curtis Bay resorts, they are free American citizens, and they seem to be eager that everyone recognize the fact and applaud it. When one of them is halted in his mad career and pauses to take an order, he does not pause long, nor does he offer respectful suggestions. The most he can be induced to say is, "Well, sport, what do you want?" . . . If you offer him a tip he takes it, but usually in a shamefaced sort of way. He wants it distinctly understood that he is the equal of any man in the house, bar none.

H. L. Mencken, *Evening Sun*
(July 12, 1910)

Phoenix foot scraper

Little Italy and Old Town

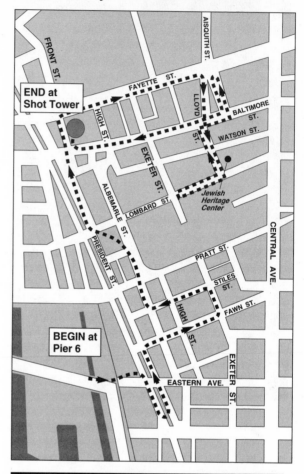

COME HERE FOR:

- Foreign accents, famous names, mostly from waves of European immigrant workers
- Sites important to author Edgar Allan Poe, musician Eubie Blake, American Zionist leader Henrietta Szold, Abraham Lincoln, and his assassin, John Wilkes Booth
- Jewish history, including Jewish Heritage Center exhibits, as well as the country's third oldest synagogue
- An eighteenth-century Quaker meetinghouse and an 1820s miniature Greek temple built to educate "indigent children without discrimination as to race or religion"
- The house where Mary Pickersgill made the original Star-Spangled Banner

- Mansion of Charles Carroll of Carrollton, signer of the Declaration of Independence and, half a century later, sponsor of the first American railroad, the B&O
- Food—Italian, French, German, and more

Looking down the hill from   81
St. Paul Street there is a
marvelous view of the
Shot Tower and the
sparkling white semi-
Palladian tower of the
church of St. Vincent de
Paul, framed by tall dark
walls. It's the sort of thing
tourists go to Bologna or
San Gimignano to see.

John Dos Passos (1973)

You can save this tour for a rainy day. The route is short, and the sights are mostly indoors. But do not wait for rain to visit these important historic buildings and museum collections. Although you will be walking a district that is only a silver dollar's throw from the Inner Harbor, the place has an exotic flavor. At the end, you can feast at an Italian restaurant, a Jewish delicatessen, a French pastry shop, or a German restaurant, with your table right next to beer-brewing vats. Also, at Baltimore City Life Museums, pick up a map of a new archaeology trail so you can extend this tour another time.

By the time you walk Old Town, you will benefit from expensive projects of the early 1990s. A great change centered on the new Shot Tower station of the Metro and proposed light rail connection. Also, Museum Row grows richer with expansion of the Baltimore City Life Museums and creation of a state-run museum of African-American history and culture. Add to that the increased eastward flow of Inner Harbor crowds to Market Place just across Jones Falls from Old Town. If you take Tour 5, you will gauge the success of Canal Walk and of Children's Museum and Children's District.

HISTORY

First, to get your bearings, look at a city map and see the Northwest Branch of the Patapsco River snaking in from the Chesapeake Bay. Imagine Harborplace facing

Baltimore, where Carroll flourished,
And the fame of Calvert grew!
Here the old defenders conquered
As their valiant swords they drew.
Here the starry banner glistened
In the sunshine of the sea,
In that dawn of golden vision
That awoke the song of Key:
Here are hearts that beat forever
For the city we adore;
Here the love of men and brothers—
Baltimore, our Baltimore!

Folger McKinsey, "Baltimore, Our Baltimore" (1916)

the snake's mouth. This walk takes you to the snake's throat. "Across the water curtain of Jones Falls from Baltimore-Town" is how an ancient guide book described where you will be walking, Old Town.

Settlement began where Jones Falls rushed into the Patapsco. First, in 1661 David Jones farmed, and then Jonathan Hanson operated a flour mill. In 1732, Edward Fell of Fells Point opened a store near where sea-going ships docked, attracted by the freshwater falls that helped wash off barnacles.

Old Town's history can be best told in cloth:

Ranking high among Old Town treasures are Baltimore Album quilts. "The most visually glorious and technically superb textiles ever made in America," says the chief curator at the Maryland Historical Society.

Old Towners transformed local sailcloth into sails of Baltimore Clippers (*Tour 1*). "Catch Me If You Can" was the challenge of Capt. Thomas Boyle's *Chasseur* and Capt. Joshua Barney's *Rossie.*

A more fragile piece of cloth, the original Star-Spangled Banner, was made on Albemarle Street by Mary Pickersgill just before the September 1814 Battle of Baltimore.

In sweatshops here immigrants sewed more clothing than any city but New York. Between 1870 and 1900 ships were funneling Europeans to work in the needle trade as well as in canneries—first the Irish and Germans, then chiefly Russian Jews and Italians.

"Who is short of food shall come inside and get it," read a Lombard Street sign in 1893 outside the headquarters of the Hebrew Relief Committee. In 1900, farther east at Central Avenue and Baltimore Street, a free public bath opened as a gift of Henry Walters (*Tour 10*). "For soap and towel: 3c - adult; 1c - child; 2½ c for laundry privileges."

Out of poor beginnings many children and grandchildren of Jewish immigrants have made their mark in the arts. One of them, filmmaker Barry Levinson, recreated their early experience in Baltimore in the film *Avalon* (1990). He shot most of the picture in authentic Baltimore settings. Other contributors to the arts include novelist Leon Uris; Ken Waissman, creator of the musical *Grease;* performer Mama Cass Elliott; poet Eli Siegel; poet Karl Shapiro; novelist Robert Kotlowitz; author Ben Herman; novelist Herman Wouk; David Jacobs, creator of the television show "Dallas"; and Larry Adler, the world's first harmonica virtuoso.

My mother came over on a freight ship. . . . All the way over they stayed in the hold of the ship and they fed them from a kettle. The hold of the ship was packed and jammed with these immigrants that were coming to America. It took them over a month to get here. When she arrived here, she didn't even know where my dad was staying.

Baltimore Neighborhood Heritage Project (1979)

African Americans, too, have a significant history here, having lived in Old Town for 200 years. "We might be spoilsports," recently wrote *Sun* columnist Wiley A. Hall 3d, "but people in *my* Baltimore [African-American citizens] can't seem to forget the struggle and the pain: Nina Simone once sang, 'Oh, Baltimore, ain't it hard just to live?'"

TOUR

Starting Point: Constellation Dock, Inner Harbor; then, Pier 6 off Pratt Street and Market Place
Length of walk: Two hours
Snacks and restrooms: Museums, Pâtisserie Poupon, Cornbeef Row, and Baltimore Brewing Company
Transportation: Water-taxi from Constellation Dock to Pier 6

Should the day turn rainy or snowy, you may want to drive. Park in these places: first, right near Pier 6 or in Little Italy near the Flag House; then, on the parking lot of the Jewish Heritage Center; finally, on Front Street next to Baltimore City Life Museums.

Begin your walk at the eastern edge of the Inner Harbor, Pier 6 (the foot of Market Place and across Pratt Street). If you take the water-taxi from Constellation Dock, debark at landing number 6 or walk along the Promenade to Pier 6.

Drivers can park in open parking lots (the nearest is on Pier 5) or in a garage on Lombard Street (entrance just left after the exit from I-83). If you wish to drive to the first center of interest, drive along East Pratt Street to Albemarle Street and turn right into Little Italy. You can park on the street there for two hours. Then walk back along Pratt Street to Pier 6, where the tour commences.

Begin walking at the bridge connecting Pier 6 with the east bank of Jones Falls. Standing on the bridge with the Inner Harbor lake behind you, look left to the distant red-brick Shot Tower and the white St. Vincent de Paul Roman Catholic Church. You will see them up close later. On your left, four smokestacks rise over the Power Plant (now planned to be converted to Sports Center USA) that once supplied electricity for streetcars (*Tour 1*).

Cross Jones Falls and walk into Old Town. Past the Power Plant, pause to examine a white statue of Christopher Columbus and six bas-relief plaques by Bigarani Anuro (1984), and look for the entrance to the Museum of Public Works and Streetscapes (opened 1982), first of its type in the country. Although looking at sewers may not appeal, you may like to explore inside. This old

Statue of Columbus

pumping station of the sewer system exhibits 2,000 artifacts from Baltimore's public services—lights, water supply, sewers, roads, garbage disposal. You can touch power mains and water pipes in a two-level re-creation of a typical understreet world. Even better, children can explore a "Construction Site," something they shouldn't—and usually can't—do.

From the museum, face the main body of water and go left to President Street and its intersection with Eastern Avenue, whose name was formerly Milk Street (an ancient street name in Nantucket still). From a Milk Street house in 1829, Edgar Allan Poe went seeking publishers and grog shops.

On the corner of Fleet and President streets stands a landmark in railroad and Civil War history: President Street Station (1850) of the Philadelphia, Wilmington & Baltimore Railroad (1837). The street name honored President George Washington.

Recently preservationists have fought to save the original western entrance of the terminal. It may be the oldest surviving big-city railroad terminal in the United States; it was one of the first public buildings to have an arched roof.

At President Street Station, travelers from the North

came face to face with slavery. "In States like Maryland," opined Charles Mackay, a Scot visiting in 1859, "slavery exists in its most repulsive form; for the owner, having no use for superabundant negroes, seems to acknowledge no duties or responsibilities towards them, but breeds them as he would cattle, that he may sell them in the best market."

On April 19, 1861, a few days after the attack on Fort Sumter, Massachusetts soldiers detrained at President Street Station en route to defend the capital, Washington, D.C. They had to pass along Pratt Street to the B&O's Camden Station, a mile west, for the last leg of the journey. On the way they were attacked with paving stones by Southern sympathizers, who were aroused by rumors of invasion.

"For God's sake don't shoot!" Mayor George W. Brown shouted at the soldiers as he led them, holding aloft an umbrella as a standard. "But it was too late," he wrote later. Sixteen people were killed, four of them soldiers. Theirs was the first blood shed in the Civil War.

A Baltimore poet living in Louisiana, James Ryder Randall soon wrote "Maryland, My Maryland," a call for Maryland secession, and later on Confederates sang it to the tune of "O, Tannenbaum":

Avenge the patriotic gore
That flecked the streets of Baltimore
And be the battle queen of yore,
Maryland, my Maryland.

In a separate attack at President Street Station that same April 19, Baltimoreans cornered troops from Pennsylvania and four more people died. For Northerners, President Street thereafter lived in infamy. Bostonians sang these words:

There's a swelling cry for vengeance on the
    counterfeits of men [Baltimoreans],
Who haunt that hold of pirates—That foul
    assassin's den!

By the time you arrive, this pre–Civil War landmark will house exhibits of that war.

From the original façade of President Street Station, cross Eastern Avenue, move left one block up President Street to Fawn Street and turn right. The name Fawn Street commemorates Americans' fighting the second war against England. In 1812, *Niles' Weekly Register* announced the arrival at Boston from Halifax of the cartel ship *Fawn* with 500 prisoners aboard. Such small success at the beginning of the War of 1812 deserved commemorating in a street name. Earlier that fall, 100 Baltimore combatants had marched into Canada and been routed.

Here in Fawn Street, you are entering Little Italy. Beginning with the Gold Rush of the 1850s, Genoese immigrants rented rooms preparing to go West. Some never left town. After those families bought houses, they mingled with Jewish residents. "Men and women lean out of the upper windows and try to breathe," said a reporter visiting Fawn Street in July 1923. "Old men who wear long beards and closely buttoned coats—and who never take off their hats—stroll along."

Today only some old Italian traditions linger. A few residents still decorate windows with religious images, plastic flowers, and seasonal trim. And restaurants reproduce Italian cuisines. Yet you may wonder how many residents would agree with what Italian-American Josephine Vacca said in 1979: "Italy I love like a mother. United States I love like my mother-in-law."

Visiting politicians love the restaurant food of Little Italy just as much as Baltimoreans do. Young Spiro Agnew had become a faithful diner at Sabatino's Italian Restaurant, 901 Fawn Street, when he and the co-owner Sabatino Luperino studied law at the University of Baltimore. Then, in 1973, Agnew sat down to Veal Français just five hours after resigning his post as vice-president of the United States at a nearby courthouse. "Can I get a job here?" was Agnew's jest.

"In every Italian restaurant in Little Italy, you will always find a member of the owning family in the kitchen," noted a reporter. That authenticity is why Maria's, 300 Albemarle Street, early on attracted such celebrities as Rocky Marciano, Max Baer, and Joan Blondell. "Gene Autry trotted down here on his horse," said Maria Allori of Maria's. "He tied that goddamn horse outside on Albemarle Street."

Pause to look around at the corner of Fawn and High streets. High Street today hiccoughs through Old Town, modern buildings intruding here and there in its progress from harbor to hills. Old Town's streets skewed to the northwest, mostly parallel to Jones Falls as it flowed down at a sharp angle to Baltimore-Town's checkerboard.

Meeting near here, talented needlewomen created Baltimore Album quilts. Our use of the city's name as a generic identification shows how special these textiles are. Not only is the needlework fine, but also the complex, appliqued "pictorial blocks depict [the women's] world with skill, naive charm, and humor," wrote quilt authority Dena S. Katzenburg. From their pre–Civil War world they portrayed B&O steam engines and city monuments. Although you may have trouble buying a quilt (the best go for five or even six figures), you can study examples at the Baltimore Museum of Art and at the Maryland Historical Society.

In addition to these unsung artists with the needle, Old Town had celebrated performing artists when in the 1830s the acting family of Booths wintered in various houses nearby. "There was something wild—and more than wild—about every member of them," said an acquaintance. One time a drunken Junius Brutus Booth pawned himself for the price of a drink and placed himself in a Baltimore pawnshop window with the price tag.

All across America Junius Booth and his son Edwin rendered Shakespeare's lines so memorably that both actors became part of popular American culture. Another actor son, John Wilkes Booth, entered our culture through a final drama at Ford's Theater on April 13, 1865—the assassination of President Lincoln. After fleeing through southern Maryland, Booth was cornered and killed across the Potomac. His bones (without a marker) now lie with other Booths in Greenmount Cemetery—about a mile and one-half north of where you walk.

From High Street, continue to walk on Fawn Street one block to Exeter Street, turn left, and go one block to the corner of Stiles and Exeter streets. The street names High and Exeter recall eighteenth-century English settlers. After the Revolution, the royal street name of Prince gave way to local Stiles. Capt. George Stiles, who held Privateer-

---

Once a year Exeter Street is in gala attire. When a great fire [in 1904] swept over Baltimore, the people around St. Leo's church were frantic at the thought of losing their homes and all of their possessions. They crowded the church, praying to St. Anthony of Padua to deliver them, for all know well that he is powerful in his aid against fire and loss of property.

Invoking his aid they promised that if their homes were spared they would honor his memory yearly with a great festival. With anxious hearts, and yet with faith, they watched the wall of fire eating steadily eastward. But St. Anthony heard them. The fire stopped at the Falls; Exeter Street was safe.

Letitia Stockett, *Baltimore: A Not Too Serious History* (1928)

ing Commission #1 in the War of 1812, later, as mayor, expanded the city to more than thirteen square miles.

On the Stiles Street corner stands St. Leo's Roman Catholic Church (1880–81), the first church built by and for Italian immigrants.

From the church, walk along Stiles Street back past High Street to Albemarle Street. Turn right and walk along Albemarle Street. From a house at 245 Albemarle Street, the D'Alesandro family has launched two Baltimore mayors and a California representative in Congress. The first of the mayors, Thomas D'Alesandro Jr., may have ruled a city of a million people and may have been driven in a chauffeured limousine, but this house was still home. The only changes were the addition of a third floor and four trunk telephone lines. One story goes that when he got off the train after touring Pittsburgh's renewed Golden Triangle, he said, "The difference between Pittsburgh and Baltimore is that they have Mellons and we have watermelons."

Cross Pratt Street to the Star-Spangled Banner Flag House (1793), 844 E. Pratt Street. Here widow Mary Young Pickersgill, known as "a lady of quality and maker of colors," sewed the flag flown at Fort McHenry during the Battle of Baltimore. Her mother had made the 1775 Grand Union flag for Gen. George Washington. By now you realize how seriously Baltimoreans commemorate the battle and the composition of "The Star-Spangled Banner." In 1931, for example, Baltimore's Mrs. Reuben Holloway—impressive in a foot-tall hat—successfully lobbied Congress to designate this Baltimore song as the official national anthem. We had none earlier.

In the summer of 1814, Maj. George Armistead, commander of Fort McHenry, was preparing for an attack by the British after they had burned Washington. "We have no suitable ensign to display over the Star Fort," was the message brought by Capt. Joshua Barney to this house, "and it is my desire that the British will have no difficulty in seeing it from a distance."

So Mrs. Pickersgill made it big—42 by 30 feet—and, of course, defiant enough for the British navy to target. The flag contained 400 yards of English bunting. Since there were fifteen states at the time, it had fifteen stripes, each two and a half feet wide, and fifteen stars, each two feet across, point to point.

At first Mrs. Pickersgill sewed in the front room of this house. Then, for the piecing together, she spread the parts on the upper floor of Claggett's Brewery malthouse two blocks away (now Brewers' Park). "I remember seeing my mother down on the floor placing the stars," recalled Pickersgill's daughter.

Both the Flag House and the 1812 Military Museum next door are open for visitors. Prized exhibits include a bedroom overmantle displaying a silk shawl printed with the Declaration of Independence, made to honor Lafayette's 1824 visit to Baltimore, and Charles Willson Peale's full-length portrait of Col. Benjamin Flower, General Washington's commissary and Mrs. Pickersgill's uncle. If you have time and interest, you may want to explore the adjacent 1812 museum.

Outside in a rose garden you can rest on a lawn and examine a stone map showing the course of the War of 1812. Overhead flies a replica of the old flag. All of this open space was once filled with small shops and work-places, along with artisans' houses. By the time you visit, Albemarle Street may be freshly framed with greenery.

After your respite in the garden, you should walk only as far as the end of the Flag House fence on Albemarle Street and turn left onto Granby Street. Like the street pattern, street names link Old Town to an English colonial origin: High Street, Exeter Street, and the royal King, Queen, Prince, and Duke streets. To these the colonists added names important to colonists, including names of English governmental officials who supported their protests against George III: Albemarle (for George Monk, Duke of Albemarle), and Granby (for John Manners, Marquess of Granby).

Walk about fifty paces to the left along Granby Street to enter Brewers' Park. Look across the park to a forty-foot timber sculpture marking the main entrance. Go in and explore where beer was brewed from 1783 to 1879. In 1983 the site of the Peters-Claggett malthouse and brewery was excavated by the Baltimore Center for Urban Archaeology. Thomas Peters began brewing strong beers for American and French troops of the Revolution.

Directly in front of you rises a cut-away re-creation of Peters's Federal-style residence. On the site, archaeologists found 22,000 household objects next to the house in an abandoned privy—bone toothbrushes, Dutch pipes, and much china of a wealthy family.

In the mid-nineteenth century, Old Town became a brewing center, because German immigrants brought their own brewers. Appropriately adjacent to this site stands a modern brewery, the Baltimore Brewing Company, bar and restaurant, 104 Albemarle Street, with entrance on Granby Street (837-5000).

Leaving Brewers' Park at Lombard Street, you have

The citizens of Baltimore! Their patriotism and valor defeated the veteran forces of their enemy, who came, saw, and fled.

A toast offered by Stephen Decatur after the Battle of Baltimore

Baltimore City Life
Museums wall

Front Street on your left. In old cities, Front streets front
on water. Baltimore's originally ran beside Jones Falls,
now covered nearby with I-83. An 1830s Front Street
Theater attracted crowds to hear the "Swedish Nightingale," Jenny Lind.

In that same theater Abraham Lincoln received his
party's 1864 nomination for a second term of office. That
event occurred only half a year before his assassination.
"Like a mountain pine high above all others, Mr. Lincoln stood in his grand simplicity and homely beauty,"
wrote Frederick Douglass at the time.

*Now cross Lombard Street and walk past the Carroll
Mansion to the Front Street entrance to Baltimore City
Life Museums' main site.* Go through the gate and enter
the restored Carroll Mansion. It remains a fine early
townhouse.

"There are sweet old Carroll houses, I believe, in
several sites [around Baltimore]," wrote Henry James of
a 1905 visit to Baltimore, "—the luckiest form perhaps
in which a flourishing family may have been moved to
write its annals." Other Carroll annals survive very well
in Mount Clare (*Tour 7*) and Homewood, now part of
Johns Hopkins University Homewood campus, thirty
blocks north of here.

"Vicissitudes" is the word for this Carroll house's

Thanks to Mr. Barnum's
["the King of Advertisers"]
foresightedness, the visit
of Jenny Lind to Baltimore
is one of the pleasantest
memories of my boyhood.
It entered his wise head
that a good way to win a
golden opinion in Balti-
more was to invite all the
high school to a free treat.
So we, who paid nothing,
thankfully went to enjoy
with those who paid
twenty or fifty or one
hundred dollars for the
same pleasure.

Jacob Frey, *Reminiscences
of Baltimore* (1893)

Charles Carroll of Carrollton: Signer

When you stand in a home of a Carroll, you can rehearse roles the Carroll family has played in the history of America, Maryland, and the District of Columbia. In 1678, Charles Carroll the Settler prospered in Maryland and bought land. On Carroll property in 1729 Baltimore-Town was laid out. The Settler's grandson, Charles Carroll of Carrollton, promoted the American Revolution and signed the Declaration of Independence.

He reminded us with very natural pride that he had signed the Declaration of Independence, and that by so doing he risked, together with his life, the most considerable fortune that there was in America. "Even after we signed," said Carroll, "we thought that Great Britain, frightened by that, would seek to get closer to us, and that we could be good friends. But the English pressed their point of view and we ours."

Alexis de Tocqueville's journal (1831)

The year before Carroll's death, Alexis de Tocqueville, French author of the classic study, *Democracy in America,* recorded in his journal that Carroll "holds himself erect, has no infirmity; his memory is rather uncertain. The whole way of life and turn of mind of Charles Carroll make him just like a European gentleman."

At 95, Carroll had outlived all other signers of the Declaration of Independence. While living in the Carroll Mansion, he held to this routine: a bath, a five-mile ride on horseback, early bed, and a diet devoid of spicy and greasy foods—"They excite the passions," he said—and two or three glasses of champagne and two or three more either of claret or madeira—or both.

When Carroll died, his body lay in state in this house. Crowds pushed in: "They went even so far as to examine the morning-gown, to touch the lifeless body, and to place their hands on the forehead," according to Carl D. Arfwedson, a visiting Englishman. Carroll left vast land holdings, including Carrollton (north of Washington, D.C.) and much of what became Howard and Carroll counties. As U.S. senator, he had been influential in choosing a site for the nation's capital. By chance, his cousin David Carroll owned much of the land in what became the District of Columbia.

history. It actually never belonged to anyone *named* Carroll, although Charles Carroll of Carrollton wintered here with his daughter and her husband, Polly and Richard Caton, and died upstairs. Built in 1804, enlarged in 1808, and again in 1812, the mansion belonged to the Catons from 1818 to 1858. During the family's stay, three footmen routinely waited in attendance during dinner. When the archbishop came to dine, reported the visiting Earl of Carlisle, he "wore his long violet robes, which I have never seen done on similar occasions, either in Ireland or in this country [England]."

After Carroll's time, the building became in turn a furniture store, the city's first vocational training school and the first recreation center, a nursery school, and finally, in 1967, a house museum. Through it all, the exterior façade retained the proportions you see, white marble belt course between the first- and second-story windows, and recessed panels between those windows. Restorers copied the original portico and reproduced interior plaster and floors. But the curving stair retains the original low risers for easy ascent.

Inside the Carroll Mansion, you will be made to feel at home and offered a self-guided tour. Throughout the house you can read comments by early visitors. Paint colors are of the period; so are furnishings. Noteworthy is a red velvet armchair in which Carroll sat for a portrait. Another family possession returned to the house is a Sheffield silver entrée dish, its lid engraved with the Caton and Carroll coats of arms.

There is much else to notice: an 1830s oil painting of "Hollingsworth's Mill on the Jones Falls" upstream from here (by Cornelius de Beet); a tin bathtub. Sometimes Carroll's favorite whist game is set up in the drawing room. Baltimore's only remaining old-style Counting House room occupies the southwest chamber to the left of the front entrance. Here Richard Caton managed business affairs of the richest man in Maryland, perhaps in America. Earlier, local gossips had regarded Caton as an English adventurer.

The Carroll Mansion introduces visitors to a complex of Baltimore City Life Museums. These museums cluster around the H. Chace Davis Jr. Courtyard, named for the successful president of the governing board (1975–90). Inside the museum complex, the 1840 House puts you in the lives of wheelwright John Hutchinson and his family—the whole round of cooking, clothing, cleaning, making do. If you take time to visit the Hutchinsons, you may get to taste such dishes as Mustering Day gingerbread baked in an open hearth.

Soon—maybe by the time you arrive—an addition will show a special face on the side facing downtown, incorporating the ornamental cast-iron front of the 1869 Fava Fruit Company Building that once stood on the site of the Baltimore Convention Center (*Tour 7*).

Another part of the City Life Museums, Baltimore Center for Urban Archaeology, lets you play detective in an exhibit called "Archaeologists as Detectives: Solving History's Mysteries." There is a life-size excavation pit, together with objects found from early Baltimore shops, industries, wharves, and residences. Look for a find from the Thomas Peters's family privy, a chamberpot with King George's seal at the bottom—"a most appropriate place to show where sympathies lay on this side of the Atlantic," said director Elizabeth Anderson Comer.

Other artifacts came from excavations at Cheapside Wharf, done when the Gallery at Harborplace was about to be built on the site (*Tour 1*). At Pratt and Calvert streets, Cheapside excavators uncovered a 200-year-old wharf of oak and pine in fine condition. In another Baltimore project, Mount Clare Plantation, archaeologists uncovered the bowling green, forecourt, "falls" garden, and orchard (*Tour 7*).

From the City Life Museums, continue walking up Front Street the rest of the block to East Baltimore Street. This part of Front Street ends as a thoroughfare, and you may treat yourself with coffee and pastry at Pâtisserie Poupon, 820 E. Baltimore Street (332-0390).

Continue walking along a path north of Baltimore Street to 9 Front Street, the early nineteenth-century dwelling (c. 1790) of Baltimore's second mayor, Thorogood Smith. Saved from demolition, this rowhouse looks lonely without its row. Just beyond it look for stone sculptures created in the 1970s.

Neighboring Phoenix Shot Tower (1828) always stood alone. Ever since it was built as the tallest structure in the nation, it has been admired as a marvelous work in brick—a million of them. From the top of the 234-foot tower, molten lead dropped through perforated pans into a "quenching tank" of cold water. "The swift passage of the lead droplets down the shaft cooled, rounded and solidified the pellets into shot" for guns, explained a newspaper columnist.

If you have driven to Little Italy, you now may drive to the next center of interest, the Jewish Heritage Center. Take Baltimore Street east (with your back to the Shot Tower) to Central Avenue, turn right, and go to Watson Street. Turn right and look for the entrance to the Jewish Heritage parking lot on the left.

If you choose to walk, leave the Shot Tower behind you, and walk along East Fayette Street for three blocks. You will be passing the main post office (1971), a large cream-

Shot Tower

colored structure on the left across the street. Sights along the way—trash, empty buildings, empty lots—are sobering.

En route, look to your left just beyond the post office at the huddle of old rowhouses. Not far north of here at 319 Forrest Street (now demolished) was the birthplace of a famous African American, composer Eubie Blake, whose parents had been born slaves.

When you reach Lloyd Street, turn right and look for the entrance to the Jewish Heritage Center on the left beyond

Eubie Blake: Ragtime pianist and composer

Although Eubie Blake's mother favored church music, by the time he was 15, Eubie was playing ragtime at Old Town bawdy houses, and then at the grander Goldfield Hotel of champion boxer Joe Gans. "Gans did things in a big way," recalled Blake. "He *spent* his money. The first Negro in Baltimore to own an automobile. So naturally, everybody in the *world* came to the Goldfield. All the sport stars, people like John L. Sullivan and Jack Johnson."

Blake sold his first composition, "Red-Hot Momma," to Sophie Tucker when she was playing at the Maryland Theater downtown. After Blake took up a career in music, he moved to New York. He went on to write ragtime and showtunes, such as "I'm Just Wild about Harry" and "Baltimore Buzz." In the road company of his show "Shuffle Along," a 15-year-old Josephine Baker danced her first steps on the way to fame at the Folies-Bergère. In his nineties, he played in recording studios and once entertained President and Mrs. Carter and guests on the South Lawn of the White House. Blake's career extended until he died at age 101, an international celebrity.

Baltimore Street. Naming a street Lloyd wouldn't have surprised eighteenth-century Marylanders because of the power of the Lloyds of Wye on the Eastern Shore. Edward Lloyd IV (all heads of the family were named Edward) represented Maryland at the Constitutional Convention of 1787, six years after his plantation house had been looted and burned by the British. After the Revolution, Lloyds, Carrolls, and other landed gentry allied themselves with Baltimore's new merchants (Pattersons, Gilmors, and more) and with new flour merchants (Ellicotts, Tysons, and others).

On your left as you proceed south on Lloyd Street, read historic markers about Lloyd Street Synagogue (1845), oldest in Maryland and third oldest in the United States. Only Touro Synagogue in Newport, Rhode Island, and Beth Elhim in Charleston, South Carolina, are older.

Here on Lloyd Street presided the first ordained rabbi to live in the United States, Rabbi Abraham Rice. Trained in Bavaria, he led the congregation here from 1840 to 1849 and again in the 1860s. His opposition to peddling on the Sabbath and other orthodox stands led some members to form Har Sinai Verein, the first lasting Reform Congregation organized in the country.

Lloyd Street Synagogue was threatened with demolition in 1960, but the Jewish Historical Society restored it. Go inside to see the original wooden pews, women's balcony, a cast-iron fence, blue and white cuspidors, ritual baths, and ovens for baking Passover bread. Today this building provides a dignified setting for lectures and concerts.

Next door to the synagogue, find the entrance to 15 Lloyd Street and rest in Freedom Park (1977), the garden of the Jewish Heritage Center (1987). It houses the largest regional Jewish historical society in America and is the only historical society maintaining two religious structures as well as a modern museum. Note the sculpture by Arthur D. Valk III.

Go inside the building for information, restrooms, and a gift shop. Next to the lobby, curators set up exhibits about the past 150 years of Jewish life in Baltimore. Today there are approximately 100,000 Jews in the Baltimore area. Many of them trace their roots to this old neighborhood and a time when Old Town made a kind of decompression chamber on the threshold of the New World for Jewish immigrants. "Stadt luft macht frei" (City air makes people free) was an old German proverb that applies here.

Leave the Center and turn left to the corner of East Lombard Street. Read the historic marker at the B'nai Israel Synagogue (1876) next to the Jewish Heritage Center. The building served the Chizuk Amuno Congregation, a group that seceded from the Baltimore Hebrew Congregation because they wanted traditional Jewish worship. Later in the century, the B'nai Israel Congregation was known as the "Russische Shule." Earlier, Irish and German immigrants had moved north of Old Town, replaced by Russians and Italians.

Many of these newcomers sewed in sweatshops. Although immigrants continued to come as late as 1912, relatively few stayed in Baltimore. In 1912, 28,357 people arrived in port, and of them 15,105 were Russian. Of that number, only 2,552 gave Baltimore as a final destination; 666 were listed as "Hebrew" and 323 "Russian."

Nearly everyone lived in rowhouses. During the 1830s and 1840s Lombard Street and small alleys had 2½-story modest rowhouses. The houses you pass had a third story added in the 1840s and 1850s. In them 400 sweatshops operated around the turn of the century.

Probably some Baltimorean will turn an old rowhouse into a Museum of Immigrants. New York City's Lower East Side now has a Tenement Museum, with two

And, wonder of wonders, there was also a bathroom that boasted a built-in flush! Two large attic rooms were on the topmost floor; these were put to practical use as more bedrooms when the family moved in. The windows in these rooms were never closed, even in the frost of winter, and often, when it snowed, a sharp breeze would blow the snowflakes across to kiss the cheeks of the young children snuggled warmly in their beds. Rarely did we suffer from colds.

Lillian Tucker, recalling her youth on East Baltimore Street, *Our Third Cousin Ceely* (1955)

privies, one water spigot, and clotheslines galore.

What sets Old Town apart from other districts in this book is the long residence of African Americans. Some descend from early Old Towners. Census figures of 1910 show that African Americans made up 31 percent and foreign-born residents 42 percent of Old Town's population. At that time Old Town received more newcomers than any other district of the city. Here, a century and more ago, descendants of slaves (as well as of free African-American men and women) formed a considerable workforce. They competed for jobs with newcoming immigrants.

Few of the current residents own homes. In 1951 a federal government pilot project replaced decayed area rowhouses with high-rise Flag-House Courts. But high-rises for families receiving public assistance has led to manifold problems and proven unpopular. Plans are afoot to replace these towers with new low-rise buildings that would lower the population density and allow each household access to outdoor space.

Just around the corner from Lloyd Street on Lombard Street, you will find several delicatessens. Try knishes at Attman's or a Baltimore combination sandwich made of corned beef, cole slaw, and Russian dressing—called "Cloak and Dagger." The delicatessens are what is left of a mid-twentieth-century "Cornbeef Row" and of a century-long marketplace. When 1010 through 1018 were demolished in 1992, old market-goers came to watch. "It's sad," said 1920s resident Moe Gordon, "Even if you saved the buildings, you can't bring it back, you can't put the pickles back in the barrels and the olives on the sidewalk and the storekeeper who would come out and stick his hand down in a barrel of herring, pull out a fat one, wrap it in old newspaper and give it to the customer for a quarter."

West of where you are walking on Lombard Street (near High Street), in October 1849, Edgar Allan Poe was found sick and dying.

After eating at a deli, return north up Lloyd Street to East Baltimore Street. Once there, move thirty paces to the right to Aisquith Street. The name is hard to spell, hard to pronounce, and hard to find without a guide. Aisquith Street squiggles through Old Town and uphill.

A few paces south of the meetinghouse, Aisquith Street passes the side of McKim Free School, which has faced Baltimore Street since 1833. A bequest of $600 annually from Quaker merchant John McKim supported a school for indigent boys and girls without any

> When young [African-American] people came up from the country . . . you always had to report to somebody that . . . your folks down in the country knew; then you came up there and stayed with them until you got a job. But of course most all domestic work then was done by colored people, practically all of them. Got $1.25 a week; if you got $2.50 a week, you was getting big money.
>
> Samuel J. Ware, Baltimore Neighborhood Heritage Project (1979)

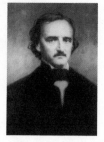

Edgar Allan Poe: Poet, critic, and innovator in fiction

In Baltimore Edgar Allan Poe found himself as a writer and was found. At the end of his teens he came to live in Old Town with his father's sister, Maria Poe Clemm, and her family. They became his mainstay through life. Before he left town seven years later, he secretly married Maria's daughter Virginia, age 13, his first cousin. He also published tales and poems that made him famous. In a middle-class apartment (now demolished) at Eastern and Central avenues, Poe received reviews of early books of poems, including *Al Aaraaf* (1829), the only one printed on Baltimore Street.

If the poem is published, succeed or not, I am "irrecoverably a poet." . . . I should add a circumstance which, tho' no justification of a failure, is yet a boast in success—mine is a poem . . . by a minor & truly written under extraordinary disadvantages [alienation from his wealthy foster father].

Edgar Allan Poe, letter written in Baltimore to Philadelphia publisher Isaac Lea (May 1829)

The final chapter of Poe's life also began in Old Town. At 40 years old the famous writer, widowed, had just become engaged to marry an old Richmond sweetheart. On his way to New York he stopped in Baltimore. His movements then are a mystery. Outside Ryan's public house on October 3, 1849, *Sun* printer Joseph W. Warner found Poe collapsed and very ill. Since Poe was ill and because he was not wearing his own clothes, scholars speculate that he had been drugged and taken to vote repeatedly from polling place to polling place.

Warner immediately called Poe's uncle and a physician friend of Poe's. They carried him to Washington Hospital, a building now part of Church Home and Hospital on Broadway at Fayette Street, "where he was tenderly nursed until the time of his death." So wrote his cousin Neilson Poe, who arranged burial in the Poe family plot in what is now Westminster Cemetery (*Tour 7*).

discrimination as to race or religion. Quakers managed the school simultaneously with their own school, founded in 1784 to give Quaker children "a guarded education," free from worldly influence.

Today a recreation center occupies McKim School. This small Greek revival temple was meant to look like the north wing of the antique Propylaea in Athens. If it perched above the Aegean Sea instead of above Baltimore Street, tourists would climb up to see it.

At the corner of Fayette Street stands a second landmark building, Old Town Friends Meeting House (1781) of time-darkened red brick. The building would be at home in an English meadow. Prominent Baltimore businessmen, such as sponsors of the B&O, belonged to this meeting or its Lombard Street offspring. Women customarily sat on one side of the bare room, and men on the other.

From the meetinghouse, come back past McKim School to Baltimore Street. Turn right there and walk back to the Shot Tower. (If you drove, retrace your route to the post office, turn left on Exeter Street, and park. From there you can take in much of history walkers are passing as they amble to Front Street and you.)

You will be following what was before World War II the Jewish main street. It had more class than Lombard Street, where butchers reigned. Here on Baltimore Street and on Aisquith Street centered intellectual life. Henrietta Szold conducted her "Russian School," for example, next to McKim at Aisquith Street.

Once residents worshiped in five synagogues close to this corner; three nearby schools were important in Jewish history. Another landmark, just behind you as you leave Aisquith Street, the Jewish Educational Alliance at 1200 E. Baltimore Street pioneered daycare with a playground on the roof.

If you walk, on your right you pass Hendler Creamery Company's headquarters and plant at 1100 E. Baltimore Street. Hendler's ice cream, advertised as "the Velvet Kind," reigned a favorite throughout the town. The company pioneered packaging ice cream in individual containers instead of dipping by hand.

At 1023 E. Baltimore Street is the Labor Lyceum (now a warehouse), headquarters of garmentmakers' unions in the early 1900s. As activists, 100 women garment workers left the lyceum for President Woodrow Wilson's inauguration in 1913, to demonstrate with middle-class suffragists for the vote and female workers' rights.

When you reach the 800 block of Baltimore Street just before Front Street, notice a spruced-up row of "shop steading," an example of how old shops can be recycled. Once again you face the choice of entering or not entering Pâtisserie Poupon, 820 E. Baltimore Street, well known for French pastries, especially lemon tarts.

At the very end of East Baltimore Street, just beyond Front Street, is a site precious to Jews for many decades. Here, next to the then-visible Jones Falls, Jews gathered on Rosh Hashana afternoon each fall to recite Tashlich prayer, symbolically casting away the sins of the old

Henrietta Szold: Humanitarian

"If I [Fiorello La Guardia], the child of poor immigrant parents, am today mayor of New York, giving you [Henrietta Szold, founder, in Old Town, of the first American night school] the Freedom of the City, it is because of you." La Guardia called night schools the "instrument of American democracy."

For new immigrants in town, Henrietta Szold, daughter of Rabbi Benjamin Szold, opened an embryonic settlement house contemporary with Jane Addams's famous Hull House in Chicago. With it Szold founded a Russian night school, opened November 1889, that charged 30 cents a month in tuition. "The curriculum consisted of English, English, and again English," she said. "The eagerness of the pupils was often painful to witness, and nothing more pathetic can be imagined than the efforts made by men well advanced in years to crook their work-stiffened fingers around a pen."

They [Jewish youngsters with several years of American life behind them] know only drudgery and grinding work. Their home life is not enticing. They have become Americans in naught but levity, shocking grammar, and the despicable smartness of the street and factory.

Henrietta Szold, letter (1889)

Henrietta Szold founded the Jewish women's organization Hadassah and became a leader of Zionism here in 1893 and later in Israel. Just before World War II she made three trips to Nazi Germany to organize the rescue of 13,000 Jewish children.

year and starting afresh. Even today some Jews rewalk this route.

At Front Street, turn right past the Shot Tower. Across Fayette Street stands a landmark of religion, St. Vincent de Paul Roman Catholic Church, 120 N. Front Street, and rectory (962-5078). The church shines all white and classical with its three-tiered tower and gold cross on top. Early pastor the Reverend John B. Gildea designed this building. Inside, clear glass windows should frame the sky the way eighteenth-century colonial church windows did (only one clear glass window remains). Completed in 1841, it was known for years for offering a "Printers' Mass" after midnight to accommodate newspapermen.

From St. Vincent de Paul Church, retrace your steps to Fayette Street, and turn right. Leave Old Town with a

final note of its eighteenth-century origins. Fayette
Street, named to honor Lafayette, then had other names
as it snaked through town—Kintamini, King Tammany,
and Wapping. This part of it, Pitt Street, honored the
eighteenth-century English Parliament's William Pitt,
First Earl of Chatham. Baltimoreans loved him because
when he was dying, he had himself carried into Parliament to protest the hated Stamp Act. "If you conquer
them [American colonists], what then?" he asked. "You
cannot make them respect you, you cannot make them
wear your cloth . . . coming from the stock they do, they
can never respect you." Loss of Pitt's name from the
street reflected declining English influence when wave
after wave of other national groups found Old Town an
open door to America.

*Go to the intersection of the Fallsway and I-83. Cross
both to continue your walk along Tour 5. Should you wish
to return to Constellation Dock, simply take the Metro at
Shot Tower Station (scheduled to open in 1995) and go to
Charles Center Station. There take the Calvert Street exit
and walk down to the harbor. You can also walk back to
Pier 6 and pick up a water-taxi for the voyage back to
Constellation Dock.*

ADDITIONAL TRIPS

Suggested forays beyond Old Town to places associated with what you have seen here include:

Edgar Allan Poe House and Museum, 203 N. Amity
    Street (396-7932)
Great Blacks in Wax Museum in Baltimore, 1601 E.
    North Avenue (563-3404)
Homewood, house museum on the Johns Hopkins
    University campus at 34th and Charles streets
    (516-5589). Its builder was the son of Charles Carroll
    of Carrollton.
Westminster Preservation Trust, Church, and Cemetery
    (Poe's grave), Fayette and Greene streets (328-7228)

Downtown, the Burnt District

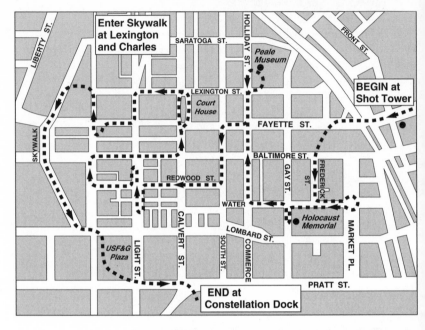

Enter Skywalk at Lexington and Charles

SARATOGA ST.

LIBERTY ST.

HOLLIDAY ST.

FRONT ST.

Peale Museum

LEXINGTON ST.

Court House

BEGIN at Shot Tower

SKYWALK

FAYETTE ST.

BALTIMORE ST.

GAY ST.

FREDERICK ST.

REDWOOD ST.

WATER

Holocaust Memorial

LOMBARD ST.

CALVERT ST.

MARKET PL.

USF&G Plaza

LIGHT ST.

SOUTH ST.

COMMERCE

PRATT ST.

END at Constellation Dock

COME HERE FOR:

- A power-generating center for politics and finance— for mayors like William Donald Schaefer and Kurt Schmoke and financiers like Johns Hopkins
- Places of importance to achievers, ranging from the country's first female portrait painter and the first American bishop of the Methodist Church to hard-boiled writers Dashiell Hammett and James M. Cain
- Building of significance to artist and museum-keeper Rembrandt Peale, the oldest structure in the Western Hemisphere built as a museum and operating today as one of the Baltimore City Life Museums
- The white-marble courthouse where ended the political career of Nixon's vice-president, Spiro Agnew (a native Baltimorean)
- The Holocaust Memorial and the earliest American monument to war dead, along with a dozen other monuments, sculptures, and fountains
- "The Block," notorious everywhere for striptease artistes like Blaze Starr
- The "Big Metropolis" look, including skyscrapers and a mixed-use redevelopment of twenty acres of Charles Center

Prepare to learn the ways of power, both political and financial, and the corruption zaniness trailing both like smoke. In the early nineteenth century, for example, Scotch-Irish merchants controlled the boomtown of Baltimore like a modern mafia.

Modern powerbrokers have left much to admire as well as regret. While Spiro Agnew's political career ended in a courthouse right next door to City Hall, Mayor William Donald Schaefer persuaded business and political leaders to create Baltimore's "Renaissance." Near City Hall, old brokerage houses like Alex. Brown nestle beside "The Block"—a fabled and fading district of bars and strip joints. And everywhere there are fountains and memorials to past greatness.

Get ready to walk old narrow byways as well as the new Skywalk. That overhead walkway passes Charles Center's offices, apartments, and the oddity of a legitimate theater disguised as a fortress. Such a military face suits this district, for war memorials and men's clubs long made downtown a male's domain. Male characters dominate the mysteries *The Glass Key* and *The Continental Op* of Dashiell Hammett, who once worked down here as a Pinkerton detective.

Do not be put off by tales of Baltimore's corruption and violence. For here virtue has triumphed, too. For instance, you will pass the birthplace of America's Methodist sect. "Reform the nation," was its first cry, "and spread scriptural holiness over these lands."

> The object of the men of property here [in Baltimore] . . . is universally wealth. Every way in the world is sought to get and save money. Landjobbers, speculators in land; little generosity to the public, little public spirit.
>
> John Adams, delegate from Massachusetts to the Continental Congress meeting in Baltimore, 1776–77

HISTORY

You will be going through the territory laid out in 1729 as Baltimore-Town, a settlement then quite distinct from Old Town and Fells Point. Unlike those two districts, eighteenth-century Baltimore-Town has disappeared, leaving only ancient street patterns and street names—*and* stories.

The original Baltimore-Town survey resembled an Indian arrowhead with its point near today's Constellation Dock. As though magnetized, that riverside point has always drawn those seeking wealth. But growth was slow. In 1775 there were only 560 houses and 6,000 people in Baltimore. That winter, when the Continental Congress fled Philadelphia for refuge here, members complained about deep mud on the main street, Baltimore Street.

The British did not occupy this city during the Revolutionary War; it was a supply center, and Baltimoreans prospered. Proceeds from exporting wheat and flour next filled their pockets. Prospects of riches lured immigrants from England, Germany, and Northern Ireland, as well as newcomers from other states.

They had the "pull-down-and-build-over-again spirit" that Walt Whitman found in American cities. More important, the Big Fire of 1904 leveled almost every building within the bounds of original Baltimore-Town. "We are doing the phoenix trick here," said prominent Johns Hopkins physician Dr. William Osler about a rapid rebuilding after the fire. Much of the re-built Burnt District remains below a high range of much newer structures—most of them banks. Those peaks resulted from a 1960–90 large-scale development in and near Charles Center and the Inner Harbor. Charles Center was the first vast demolition and replacement project. Its thirty-three acres plus $145 million remade the heart of commercial downtown.

Before Charles Center, downtown suffered from neglect. In 1958 a cure was tried. A Greater Baltimore Committee of business executives formed and proposed radical demolition and rebuilding. Some people doubted. "Baltimore is not in bad enough shape yet to support that kind of organization," protested the chairman of the Baltimore Gas & Electric Company. Later he came into line, but not until the Mercantile Bank president applied pressure. Baltimoreans, it is said, back into the future.

TOUR

Starting Point: Constellation Dock; then the Shot Tower, Old Town, where Tour 4 ends
Length of tour: Two hours
Transportation: Water-taxi; metro (when the Shot Tower Station opens)
Snacks and restrooms: Market Place public museums and restaurants; City Hall; Peale Museum; Baltimore Street fast food outlets between Light Street and Calvert Street; Harborplace

---

If you have just taken Tour 4, you are at the Shot Tower. If you skipped Tour 4, walk from Constellation Dock on the Promenade past the Aquarium to President Street, cross it, turn left, and walk three blocks to the Shot Tower. With the Shot Tower on your right, face the downtown towers to the west. On President Street, you are walking beside Jones Falls, once a major millstream (now covered by roads in this district). Upstream at Bath Street George Washington used to ford it en route north. The fact that President Street was named for President Washington proves the persistence of eighteenth-century Baltimore. So does Bath Street, which takes its name from the Earl of Bath's speaking out for the colonists. Marylanders, he said, should have the same liberties as those other English people enjoyed. You are about to leave Old Town, laid out in 1732, and enter Baltimore-Town, chartered in 1729.

Begin the walk by cautiously crossing President Street. Take Fayette Street to Frederick Street (first street on the left) and walk under the bridge of police headquarters to Baltimore Street.

Look to the right along Baltimore Street at remnants of a once bawdy, now fading and pornographic, strip called the Block. "When strip-tease still seemed vital," wrote columnist Russell Baker, "it [the Block] was one of the earth's cultural centers. Swells from uptown, from the horse country, from distant stately Washington came with their dates." In the 1940s the Two O'Clock Club, 414 E. Baltimore Street, featured striptease artist Blaze Starr, whose affair with Louisiana governor Earl Long was told in a book and a film called *Blaze*.

Proceed along Frederick Street across Baltimore Street to Water Street. There turn left. Once you reach Market Place, you will be standing in one of the town's major nineteenth-century spaces. It was then called Center Market, or Marsh Market, or Market Space, or simply the Space. People used to throng here. As recently as 1970, Market Place resembled a Roman piazza, with an old fountain and mouldering brick façades. By the time you arrive, you may think you have stumbled on a Disney World version of the old harbor. In the planning stage, this open space was called a canal walk, with shallow pools and floating food kiosks looking vaguely like historic Baltimore ships, oyster boats, banana barges. "The idea is to make this more like a Paris street, where you can eat and drink and sit at a café," said the New York designer James Wines.

But the view of harbor shipping anchors you in Baltimore. Even though the distant HarborView towers light up the night sky with the newest of lighting, there on your far left stands the two-generations-old Candler Building, named for the inventor of Coca-Cola. Inside, where Coke was produced and bottled, every doorknob retains the Coca-Cola signature name, although the building was converted to offices years ago.

From 1763 until the mid-1980s, a wholesale fish market in Market Place provided ordinary citizens with soft

Oasis Cabaret: Nothing Is Too Bad for the Best

From all walks of life we attract the best people in the world down here and nothing is too bad for them. Our show girls try their darnedest to do something, but the poor dears simply don't have it in them to perform in the accepted manner. They might sing, not good, but it's loud, and when they dance—well, let it go at that. One thing is most evident though, the doings are so terrible they're good. Prove it for yourself to-night.

1930s advertisement

crabs and oysters in season. When fishmongers moved out, a developer spent $30 million converting the building to a mall of music bars. Closed since 1989, it may be a bright nightspot when you walk past.

With your back to the Fish Market, walk to the circular A. E. Booth Fountain (1907) in the center of the square. In the 1850s you would have viewed an early structure of today: Maryland Institute College of Art (*Tour 11*). Here 6,000 Baltimoreans gathered for culture. And in this largest clear indoor space in the nation, politicians nominated Millard Fillmore, Franklin Pierce, and Henry Clay for president. In 1864 President Lincoln addressed the Sanitary Fair, a Union fundraiser for medical supplies (*Tour 11*).

From the fountain go back into Water Street. In early Virginia and Maryland, almost every port had a Water Street. When laid out in 1747, Baltimore's Water Street paralleled the curving shoreline. Its modern straightening adjusted to the city's grid pattern by jogging a few feet south at South Street. "Underneath the new Paris [read: the new Baltimore], the old Paris is distinct, like the old text beneath the lines of the new," wrote Victor Hugo.

On your left as you leave Market Place, red-brick, odd-shaped buildings thrust at you like giant sculptures: they comprise the Harbor Campus of Baltimore City Community College (1976). It carries on the area's tradition of education begun by the Maryland Institute in 1826. Now plans call for a $17-million expansion on its five acres, including a commercial hotel at the Pratt Street side, opposite Christopher Columbus Center for Marine Research and Exploration (*Tour 1*).

Walking along Water Street, on your right you pass the Brokerage, a complex of converted early twentieth-century shops and factories. Inside you may find the Eubie Blake Cultural Center, as well as the planned Children's Museum district ($30 million). "Baltimore would be the first city to designate a children's district, with a children's museum as the centerpiece," said Katrine Fitzgerald of the American Association of Museums. By the time you walk past, it will include a wellness center, counseling center, early learning and development center for infants and toddlers whose parents live or work downtown, and a latchkey program for older children who live in nearby Old Town. "The center by itself, the museum by itself—they're very exciting," said Mayor Kurt Schmoke in 1994. "But all of this together is going to be great. It starts kids out and starts families out as thinking of cities as places where you can

[In the market] O! what a quantity of superb beef, mutton, lamb, veal, and all sorts of fowls—hogsheads full of wild ducks, geese, pheasants, partridges; I must not forget to mention the loads of sweet-cakes of all sorts and fashions that covered the outside tables of the market-houses.

U.S. Attorney General William Wirt, letter from Baltimore (1822)

have fun. I think that's going to help Baltimore in the long run."

Businesses such as the Chocolate Factory, 608 Water Street, came along after the Big Fire. The fire stopped near here at Jones Falls, but not before wiping out nearby historic printshops such as Hatch and Dunning's, where in *Al Aaraaf* Edgar Allan Poe published some of his best poems.

Today, the repose of Water Street contrasts with parallel trafficky Baltimore and Lombard streets. You will cross Frederick Street, named for a prince in the House of Hanover, Britain's eighteenth-century royal family.

Just before you reach the next street, Gay Street, on your left spreads the Holocaust Memorial, designed by local architect Donald Kann and local sculptor Arthur D. Falk III. This Water Street side resembles a tomb, massive, stark, and pale. Behind this façade, and sloping to Lombard Street, an earth mound suggests the site of interment. In springtime the mound becomes a bouquet of blossoms—six rows of flowering trees commemorating the loss of six million Jews. *Walk left on Gay Street* to see trees and on the Lombard Street side a sculpture by Olin Russum. It offers a shelf on which Jews can observe the old custom of leaving stones in honor of the dead.

On the Water Street side of the memorial you may sit on hard white stone blocks to contemplate. Read the tablet near Water Street: the design represents, it says, "the intrusion of cold, dark, brutal force into a pleasant natural and inviting setting." Appropriately, the site abuts an area of 1890s Jewish sweatshops. Refugees from Russian pogroms here created half of Baltimore's mountain of clothing. Also near this memorial to victims of tyranny and injustice, a printshop first published "The Star-Spangled Banner."

Although today it leads to Route 40 East and to Johns Hopkins Hospital, Gay Street used to cross eighteen marshy acres that divided Jonestown and tiny

---

Calling to mind that we are in Baltimore, we cannot fail to note that the world moves. Looking upon these many people, assembled here, to serve, as they best may, the soldiers of the Union, it occurs at once that three years ago the same soldiers could not so much as pass through Baltimore. The change from then till now, is both great, and gratifying. Blessings on the brave men who have wrought the change, and the fair women who strive to reward them for it.

Pres. Abraham Lincoln, address to Baltimore Sanitary Fair (April 18, 1864)

Baltimore-Town. Named in 1747 for Nicholas Ruxton Gay, surveyor of those acres, it still forms a Sam Browne belt—a diagonal swathe—across the grid pattern of other streets.

At Gay Street, the editor of the *Federal Republican,* Alexander C. Hanson, created a historic test of freedom of the press: on June 22, 1812, a mob destroyed his printshop because of editorials opposing war with England. "We shall cling to the rights of freemen, both in act and opinion, till we sink with the liberties of our country or sink alone," wrote the editor.

Under orders from the Gay Street home office of the Merchants & Miners Transportation Company, ships long sailed the East Coast. "From the north came canned goods, chocolates, machinery, shoes and soap," recalled one-time stevedore J. Frederick Douty. "From the south came fruit, raw wool in big bags, lumber and stinking bundles of uncured hides." Two hundred passengers sat down to renowned full-course meals (23 cents each). "All the ships tried to get their fresh water in Baltimore (the best along the coast)."

At 40 S. Gay Street stands the U.S. Custom House, a chaste beaux-arts structure built in 1903 (962-2666). "A monumental and classical design," reads the landmark designation. "[It] symbolizes the commercial glory of America and the Port of Baltimore." This custom house doesn't lord over the harbor as did its nationally famous predecessor, Benjamin Henry Latrobe and Maximilien Godefroy's Merchant's Exchange (1816). In its ninety-foot-high domed great hall (now demolished), the body of President Lincoln was raised up so his face could be seen by mourners as a band played, "Peace, Troubled Soul."

Go inside the custom house to look at Baltimore's historic port displayed in wall murals called *The History of Navigation*. Painted by Francis Davis Millet, the ceiling canvas, "Entering Port," stretches thirty by sixty feet. It adorns the call room where ship captains used to gather (962-2666).

Come back to Water Street and cross Custom House Avenue. On your right is the Chamber of Commerce Building (1904). This Renaissance-style structure replaced the 1880 Corn and Flour Exchange, burned in the Big Fire. Today it provides a link in the Culinary Arts Institute chain of twenty-odd buildings of Baltimore International Culinary College. Creampuffs have taken the place of stock powers. Here you can join a

ninety-minute cooking class any Monday through
Thursday (752-4983).

You are walking where early nineteenth-century
financiers both lived and worked. In the 1820s, Gay Street
south of Baltimore Street became a fashionable center.
Then, unlike today, the rich lived downtown and the
poor on the outskirts. But, of course, resident tycoons
escaped heat and epidemics at country retreats perched
on nearby hills. Native Baltimorean Robert Gilmor Jr.,
for example, hired famous New Yorker A. J. Davis to
design one of the greatest American country houses,
Gothic-style Glen Ellen (c. 1820, now demolished).

"Men generally pursue their own interests without
regard to any other persons," wrote tycoon Robert
Oliver. He and his clan of rich immigrants formed a
Scotch-Irish mafia. They traded in slaves, privateered,
and dealt high-handedly in real estate. But they were not
the sole buccaneers. "The bulk of the inhabitants [of
Baltimore], collected from all quarters, are bent on the
pursuit of wealth; to get money honestly, if they can, but
at any rate to get it," noted Lt. John Harriott, former
British merchant marine officer, in 1809.

*After you cross Custom House Avenue on Water Street,
look for Commerce Street.* Survey juxtaposed architectural
styles: the sober stone building survives from the Big
Fire of 1904, rebuilding at 301 Water Street, although it
is only a shell overlapped by a shiny, modern high-rise.
Pause at the corner in silent salute to the dead of April
19, 1861—first bloodshed of the Civil War. The unmarked site—two blocks to your left, near the harbor
at Commerce and Pratt streets—is where Union volunteers were attacked by Baltimoreans sympathetic with
the South.

*Turn right down Commerce Street and watch for a
name change to Holliday Street.* Cross Fayette Street and
enter City Hall Plaza to rest and get a drink of water
from the "temperance" water fountain there (on the
wall nearest City Hall). While you sit in the plaza, you
can read about this area. The street is named for John
Holliday, sheriff in 1770. Back when boom times filled
Baltimore Street with commerce, this cross street attracted culture.

Today's leaders still deliberate in City Hall on Holliday Street. Lighted at night, it gleams like a white wedding cake (thanks to its rehabilitation in 1975). A century earlier, Baltimoreans had special reason to savor
their Louvre-like City Hall. "The total cost of the im-

posing pile, including the ground and its magnificent furniture throughout," boasted a contemporary, "has been $2,271,135.65 out of an appropriation of $2,500,000 leaving a surplus of $228,864.36."

"When I first came here [to City Hall] more than twenty years ago," said Mayor William Donald Schaefer, "it was old, dimly lit, cold in the winter and hot in the summer." Much of George Aloysius Frederick's original structure remains: look for old lighting fixtures in yellow and red brass; and interior wood shutters, now refinished, that again cut glare.

Schaefer left all that behind when he became governor. His mayoral term was filled out by City Council president Du Burns, the first African-American mayor of Baltimore. He, in turn, was succeeded by Kurt Schmoke, the first elected African-American mayor. "Formidably smart and blessed with a wry sense of humor," wrote Jonathan Yardley, "Schmoke is young, handsome, and black." Yale faculty still recall with wonder his persuasiveness as undergraduate spokesman during the Black Panther crisis in New Haven.

Go inside City Hall if only to see some of the photomurals of local landmarks, all copied from old engravings or photographs. Ask to see the rotunda. Notable are the scagliola pilasters (half columns that were hand-painted on plaster to resemble marble). From marble floor to stained glass in the dome (now specially lighted), restorers removed grime and called attention to soaring space. The city's logo of the Battle Monument dominates a stained glass dome.

When you leave City Hall, walk to the left and cross Lexington Street and then Holliday Street. Proceed along Holliday Street to the left to a red-brick building with a glass entrance vestibule. It is the oldest structure in the Western Hemisphere built expressly as a museum, the Peale Museum. Erected in 1814, it later had other uses until restored as a museum in 1930. It inaugurated the modern chain of City Life Museums (*Tour 4*). The museum's builder, prominent artist Rembrandt Peale, came to create a showplace like Philadelphia's Peale Museum, located in part of Independence Hall. He had collaborated in that project with his father, Revolutionary War painter Charles Willson Peale, a Marylander.

In 1814 Rembrandt Peale hoped to speed up development of cultural life in Baltimore, then feebly stirring. Where City Hall now stands was the Athenaeum's library and ballroom. "A meagre collection . . . not fattened by its corporators for intellectual feasts," said writer George Henry Calvert. Even the Holliday Street Theater, where was first sung "The Star-Spangled Banner," lacked high culture, whether in offerings or audience. "As is usual in the United States, the courtesans are relegated to the upper balcony, thus putting vice on display, so to speak," reported a German visitor.

By contrast, "an elegant rendezvous for taste, curiosity, and leisure" arrived when Peale opened his museum. Baltimoreans paid for art and, later, for exhibits of natural history specimens and curiosities such as "a dress made of the intestines of fishes, ornamented with porcupine quills and hair."

Rembrandt Peale
(1778–1860)

"Some of Rembrandt's best work [as a painter] was done during these years in Baltimore," says Peale scholar Lillian B. Miller. At the end of the War of 1812, city fathers commissioned Rembrandt to paint four heroes of the defense: Gen. John Stricker, Gen. Samuel Smith, Lt. Col. George Armistead, and Mayor Edward Johnson, whose subtle expression, an opponent said, "shows a political boss in firm control of the Jeffersonian party machinery." By thus inaugurating a municipal portrait gallery, Baltimore showed the way to other cities. Now you can see these heroes along with George Washington, painted from life by 17-year-old Rembrandt. "It has about it a truthful plainness," writes modern critic John Russell.

In Philadelphia brother Rubens Peale had developed gas lighting. So in 1816 Rembrandt designed and built his own apparatus for making gas to illuminate the building. Then he lighted his street, a first in America. With his sponsors he formed the first urban company to light a town, the Baltimore Gas Light Company.

In 1830 the Peales' Baltimore Museum and Gallery of the Fine Arts closed because it wasn't making money. "It is not to the credit of Baltimore that the liberal views and purposes of science should be sacrificed to a sordid calculation of short-sighted commercial avarice," wrote Rembrandt. Yet the value of having such an institution —a place for artists and arts—in a city was not lost on leaders in Boston and other cities.

Now you can visit the Peale Museum in its newest incarnation (396-1149). Ask to see a full-length portrait of Charles Calvert, fifth Lord Baltimore and lord proprietary of Maryland from 1715 to 1751. Painted by Herman Van der Myn, a fashionable Dutch artist in England, it shows the English proprietor with an Indian standing behind him. At Calvert's feet are an Indian bow and war club, symbolizing his dominion over Maryland. In the

1760s the painting had sparked young C. W. Peale's artistic ambitions; at age 82 he had the chance to own it.

Exhibited with it in the original museum—and on show now—was Charles Willson Peale's painting of the Peales' 1801 unearthing of a mastodon's skeleton. That was quite a find. Actually, the fossilized bones made up two skeletons, one of which was exhibited here. Not only had the Peales conducted the first American scientific dig, but also for the first time in history an extinct prehistoric animal's skeleton had been publicly exhibited. Baltimoreans came to marvel. And the science of zoology took a step forward.

Also on display today are portraits by Rembrandt's cousin Sarah Miriam Peale, America's first professional female portrait painter. Between 1828 and 1830 she posed her sitters in museum rooms. In the Peales' garden you should look for what may be the oldest architectural sculpture in the country—an 1807 bas-relief of Ceres and Neptune created by Augustin Chevalier for Baltimore's Union Bank.

When you leave the Peale Museum, turn left and walk to the corner of Lexington and Holliday streets. Here, on the left, you see a curious gabled tower rising above the parish house of Zion Lutheran Church. Designed in 1913, it looks as though a medieval pitched-roof house had been stranded there after a flood. The pleasant green of the roof matches greenery in flower garden and shrubbery below. You may go through the corner gate at Lexington Street to enjoy roses or whatever is in season. This garden provides a good place to sit.

The church building adjacent to the Parish House combines many eras (727-3939). After Baltimore's Lutheran Germans organized in 1755, they bought the ground. Not until fifty years later did they erect this church. Its builders had worked with French architect Maximilien Godefroy while he was building St. Mary's Chapel in Seton Hill (*Tour 9*).

In 1840 a fire destroyed everything except the walls. The restored church contains an array of art nouveau and Victorian stained glass, some from the most admired period. Tiffany Studio created light fixtures in the domes and adjoining parish house. German Kaiser Wilhelm gave a carillon, and Chancellor von Hindenburg, a German Bible. On Sundays you can still hear a service conducted in German.

When you stand again at the Lexington and Holliday streets corner of Zion Church, survey a remnant of a grandiose beaux-arts plan dating about 1910. According to the plan, this plaza would have been flanked by classic white structures such as those on the Mall in Washington, D.C. City Hall anchored the west end, and the War Memorial (1921, Laurence Hall Fowler, architect) bowed to it from the east. Inside, the memorial (396-3100) contains the most underused municipal space and some of the most elegant. Go inside to view the long rectangular hall's colored marbles—pale rose, pale yellow, and a parapet of black.

Today, instead of classic white structures, a solid wall of buildings in a variety of styles lines the sides of the square flanking the War Memorial and City Hall. Look at the five-story headquarters of Maryland's Legal Aid Bureau (1992), the last building on the left as you face the War Memorial. This private, nonprofit law firm in a recent year handled 50,000 cases for residents unable to afford private counsel in civil matters. The bureau is the largest of its kind in the country.

Stroll under the French-style double rows of linden trees shading walkways to the War Memorial building and notice how the carved horses there seem in a lather to get away. "These symbolize the marine forces of the state. Some have objected to them as incongruous or meaningless," said Letitia Stockett when the horses were new. "How absurd. They are fine spirited beasts!"

From the shaded walkways, leave the plaza at Fayette Street where you entered originally. Turn right and walk to the rear of City Hall one block to Guilford Avenue. On the way, look only at the right side of Fayette Street. There you survey pale stone buildings making a wall of the classical architecture that planners had in mind for the whole municipal district. At this point, notice how that street makes a jog to the right. Eighteenth-century settlers followed routes convenient to them and obedient to property boundaries.

When you reach Guilford Avenue, turn left. Its name comes from the site of one of Col. John Eager Howard's Revolutionary War battles in the Carolinas, Guilford Court House. If you were to turn right up Guilford Avenue, you would see railroad tracks left over from busy commuter and freight trains as well as the Calvert Street freight station, now the Downtown Athletic Club.

Where you turned onto Guilford Avenue, the street narrows and changes its name to South Street. Walk two blocks down South Street to Redwood Street. On the left, notice the curious way developers of Commerce Place (1992, RTKL Associates, architect), on the left side of South Street, tried to make amends for having demolished the

Safe Deposit Building that it replaced here. Now, the original entrance of 1876 (or maybe 1903) is stuck into the skyscraper's base. It faces a kind of elephants' graveyard of sculptured fragments saved from lost nearby buildings. The entrance had dominated a long brick front that had harmonized with adjacent low-rise, red-brick offices of Canton House and Furness House.

Furness House (1917), at 19 South Street, once gave an English image for English companies and now gives dignity to the Brown Advisory Trust Company, a division of Alex. Brown. Abundance of glass in Palladian windows upstairs lightens the façade. Seen in the crowd of heavy stone structures of the Redwood corridor, it is like a ballet dancer caught among elephants. Next to it stands its partner, Canton House. Demure in red brick, it, like Furness House, is listed on the National Register of Historic Places.

If you want to see a prize-winning rehabilitation of offices, inspect the Robert Garrett Building (1913) at 233 Redwood Street. The law firm of Gordon, Feinblatt oversaw the conversion to their use (576-4000). The former trading room, though converted to a library, remains elegant and is worth seeing.

Turn onto Redwood Street. At 206 Redwood Street the Merchants Club (now the Redwood Club) seems less elephantine than its neighbors. The original club, formed by business leaders in 1881, built its clubhouse to adjoin the Stock Exchange. What you are looking at is a replacement, built after the Big Fire.

This site juxtaposes God and mammon. A plaque on the left-hand corner of the club's façade tells of the site's significance for religious history: in a building on this site the Methodist Church in America was born. In May 1776 white and black Methodists met, including "Black Harry" Hosier, preacher and traveling companion of Francis Asbury. Then, on December 27, 1784, leading Methodists met here to organize the Methodist Episcopal Church in the United States of America and to ordain Francis Asbury its first bishop. So peripatetic and so well known was Asbury that his mail came addressed simply "America."

During World War I anti-German feelings forced city leaders to change the eighteenth-century name of German Street to Redwood, honoring the first Baltimore army officer killed in action overseas, George Redwood. Into its few short blocks crowd financial institutions. Redwood Street—what there is of it—is rather impressive in an Edwardian sort of way—heavy ornamentation

---

The members of the Baltimore Stock Exchange had a merry Christmas frolic after the close of the first call yesterday (December 24, 1883). . . . At the start there seemed to be an irrepressible desire for each young broker to make a football of some other member's hat, and different descriptions of head tiles were sent flying around the room. . . . [A] football of the largest size was next introduced. . . . To carom the ball on the bald head or gray hair of a veteran was voted good play.

The Early Eighties: Sidelights of the Baltimore of Forty Years Ago, Mercantile Trust & Deposit Company (1922)

Mercantile wall

marks buildings that loom above the narrow way.

One curiosity you might miss because it stands next to a parking meter is a kind of sculpture in front of 211. At top rests a cannonball fired by the British into Fort McHenry during their attack, September 13, 1814. According to the attached plaque, the rack in which the ball is mounted "was used to bend bar iron so that it could be advantageously loaded into the old Conestoga wagons."

As you progress along the right-hand sidewalk of Redwood Street to the Calvert Street corner, you will come to the Mercantile Safe Deposit and Trust Company Building (1885). "I've always been fascinated by this building," said a transplanted New Englander recently. "It looks like a cross between a safe and the crypt of a secret society." What distinguishes its Romanesque revival exterior are varied window shapes and carved stone ornamentation against the foil of red brick. Just around the corner, on its Calvert Street side, notice the so-called spy step built into the wall for watchmen to check inside for burglars.

Standing at the bank's corner, you can look to your right and across Calvert Street to the side of the building of prominent brokers Alex. Brown & Sons (1900). You

can detect charred marks on the brick walls, left by the
Big Fire that destroyed the buildings around it, with the
exception of the Mercantile bank.

Continue walking along Redwood Street to Light Street.
On the right for years stood the Southern Hotel, suc-
cessor to the popular eighteenth-century Fountain Inn
where Lafayette stayed and so did other patriots. "The
chief who unites all hearts" was the toast offered Gen.
George Washington here.

Loop fifty paces to your left down Light Street to find a
London-style mews with cluster of bars and outdoor
tables in summer. Here you can sit and snack at the confluence of tiny streets: Grant Street takes its name from
the proprietor of Fountain Inn; Mercer Street remembers John Mercer, a property owner in 1795; the name of
Cheapside, nearby, descends from early Cheapside
Wharf, itself a namesake of a medieval London street.
Over there, Cheapside once had one of the Eleanor
Crosses, half-timbered houses with overhanging second
stories, and an execution block. Here we lack all that.

Cross Light Street, turn right, and walk half a block
to enter the NationsBank Building (1929, Taylor and
Fisher, Smith and May, architects), with its recently
regilded top. The interior shouts "Jazz Age!" in a flamboyance of art deco. Although the exterior looked fancy
enough, the huge banking room must have been meant
to stun the depositor into wonder. Everything about the
room demands attention—mosaic floor, state flags,
painted ceiling, colored marble galore. Don't miss the
metal work of Samuel Yellin of Philadelphia—gates,
handrails, barrier screens.

*Then go out to Light Street, turn right, and proceed
downhill to Redwood Street. Turn right and proceed along
Redwood Street.* Hansa Haus (1907), on the right, en-
livens the Redwood corner at Charles Street with a half-
timbered second story, and Swiss- or German-style
dormers. The name goes back to early occupants, the
North German Lloyd Steamship Company. Note the
colorful German coats of arms in a series of shields
above the first-floor windows. With the exception of
post–World War II buildings, noted ones like this one
were designed by Baltimore architects. Parker and
Thomas did Hansa Haus, the B&O Building, and the
Savings Bank of Baltimore (now the Bank of Baltimore).

*Turn right at Charles Street and go one block north to
examine the Bank of Baltimore.* "Temple of Thrift," as it
was called when it opened in 1907, it copies the Erech-
theum on the Acropolis in Athens. Ornamentation

around the bases of columns and the lion heads along the cornice were cast from originals in Athens.

From Charles Street, turn right into Baltimore Street and walk two blocks to Calvert Street. In these blocks study on the right a row of architecturally old-fashioned shops. Outside 104, Fader's, stands a cigar-store Indian. By contrast, look across at the array of tall buildings. As a group, they make the snappiest up-to-date streetscape on this tour. The oddest, 6 St. Paul Center (designed by the Hillyer Group of Princeton, 1984), extends a needle with a flag on top. That, says a local columnist, makes "a massive digital gesture towards the stately old Maryland National Bank Building [now NationsBank] across the street. . . . It looks like something in a Batman film." Built by Merritt Commercial Savings and Loan, which failed, it became state offices for $12.2 million of tax-payers' funds.

At Calvert Street, turn left to go one block to Monument Square. Calvert Street remains the only major artery to retain its name from the original 1729 town plan. Other-wise, everything on the street is as transitory as breath. John Eager Howard's mansion Belvedere sat magnificent but doomed in the path of this street as it projected north; the house came down in 1870. A railroad station came and went on Calvert Street at Saratoga Street. Even the Sunpapers, since 1950 a giant on Calvert Street, pro-duces the most evanescent of products, the daily paper that next day carries out the garbage.

Stand at the Fayette Street end of Monument Square. On the Equitable Building (southwest corner of Monu-ment Square) a plaque marks the site of Barnum's Hotel (1825–89). Its chefs improved the flavor of diamondback terrapin by exercising the turtles in the courtyard. In 1842, Charles Dickens praised Barnum's for providing "curtains to his bed, for the first and probably the last time in America" and for having "enough water for wash-ing himself, which is not at all a common case." Here he and author Washington Irving drank through straws "a most enormous mint-julep, wreathed in flowers."

The present Equitable Building (1894) became the city's first skyscraper. Originally the building offered of-fice workers Turkish baths in the basement and a garden on the roof. You can compare it for handsomeness with One South Calvert Building (originally the Continental Trust Building, 1901) a block down Calvert Street on the far left corner (stand with your back to the monument). That structure survived the Big Fire better than the Equitable Building did. Some critics reason that its

Negro Warrior

Chicago architect, Daniel H. Burnham, knew better
how to build skyscrapers.

"Baltimore has square buildings and circular lives,"
said the best-known occupant of what was long called
the Continental Building, novelist Dashiell Hammett.
From it he moved to California and wrote. Because he
had worked for the Pinkerton Detective Agency, headquartered here, he named his first major detective the
Continental Op. Look over the door and first-floor windows at ornamental black birds. Some local readers believe that those birds inspired Hammett's famous "black
bird" of *The Maltese Falcon.*

When you enter Monument Square, you learn why
President John Quincy Adams called Baltimore the
"Monumental City." The Battle Monument was the
first war memorial erected in the country and certainly
one of the first anywhere honoring ordinary warriors,
not generals. *It is a good idea to walk completely around
the square twice. Then sit next to the monument to read
and look about.* At the Lexington Street end, you will see
the statue of a black soldier in a World War II uniform.
This sculpture (1971) by James B. Lewis of Morgan
State University commemorates all black fighters in
American wars.

Behind the statue in the center island rises the early
nineteenth-century Battle Monument. Its image is dis-

played on all Baltimore City documents as official emblem. As such it represents what city residents of 1814 saw as their finest moment—a vigorous and more or less successful encounter with the British at the Battle of North Point. It commemorates a truly popular defense. Ordinary citizens dug the ramparts and trained as soldiers in the weeks after the British army burned Washington. Luckily, British land and sea attacks caused Baltimoreans relatively few casualties. Their names appear on bands wrapping the columnar monument.

Some visitors think the design of the monument eccentric. Designed for free by the French emigré architect Maximilien Godefroy, this monument contains both Egyptian and Roman elements. The pale marble *fasces,* emblem of strength in unity, is topped by a classically robed female holding up a laurel wreath. She may be a representation of Baltimore or of peace itself. The sculptor was Antonio Capellano, an Italian invited to town by Godefroy (*Tour 8*). "This simple commemoration excites the spectator more than the proudest trophies raised to unknown thousands who fell they knew not wherefore, in a foreign land," wrote British lecturer Frances Wright, visiting Baltimore in 1818.

Before hotels intruded, Monument Square was where some of the town's powerful lawyers and bankers lived. Unhappily for them, everyone in 1834 knew where to go when the Bank of Maryland failed. Angry depositors tore down a bank director's front wall here, threw his furniture into the street, and tossed his law library into the square, and burned it. "Had they been able to catch the Obnoctious Directors of said institution," wrote Quaker witness William E. Bartlett, "they would have been altogether satisfied to have given each a coat of tar and feathers."

Walk to the west side of the square. The Baltimore Court House (1900), designed by local architects J. B. Noel Wyatt and William G. Nolting, displays an expanse of columns and classical ornament in beaux-arts style. The interior was used in a Hollywood film, *And Justice for All.* Go inside and ask to see the rich marble and mahogany in the Supreme Bench Rotunda, the Orphans Court, and the Bar Library (396-5064). Recently the structure was named for Clarence Mitchell Jr., director (1950–78) of the Washington bureau of the NAACP. A generation before, his father had waited tables at the Rennert Hotel (*Tour 8*). Politics seems to run in the family—Clarence Mitchell's brother is former Congressman Parren J. Mitchell.

Baltimoreans have built three courthouses on this site. So that Calvert Street could be extended northward, it tunneled beneath the first courthouse. "A house perched upon a great stool," recalled John H. B. Latrobe in 1850, "it straddled over a pillory, whipping post, and stocks which were sheltered under the arch, as symbols of the power that was at work upstairs."

Facing the courthouse, turn right and examine the corner building at 114 E. Lexington Street. Now headquarters of the Provident Bank of Maryland, it was originally the Federal Reserve's local headquarters (now on Sharp Street; *Tour 6*). The restored interior retains 1920s bronze and limestone decorations and a bronze enclosed guard station. Outside, a carved eagle over the entrance and elaborate bronze doors let you know how solid and substantial banking system managers thought banks were in 1928, the year before the Wall Street crash launched the Depression.

A tunnel connected this building with the stone building catercorner across Calvert Street on the east side. Originally, that building served as the second post office on the site. Now it contains city courts and a branch post office. In the basement, FBI agents in the 1930s had a practice pistol range. From 1889 to 1930, its predecessor post office and federal courthouse (1880, James Green Hill, architect) had loomed over the Battle Monument. Read the plaque on the building's entrance for the story of how, during the Big Fire, postal employees "withstood intense heat to save the building by dousing its windows with buckets of water."

Into this courthouse walked ex-governor Spiro Agnew, then vice-president of the United States, to plead nolo contendere to charges of receiving bribes. He then resigned from the vice-presidency.

After you have examined the Battle Monument, return to Lexington Street, turn left and continue uphill in the direction you were walking before you entered Monument Square. At the back of the courthouse, turn left on St. Paul Street and go to the statue of the second Lord Baltimore, Cecil Calvert (1908, Albert Weinert, sculptor) standing in front of the entrance. Legend has it that the model for the figure was a star of silent movies, Francis X. Bushman, who once lived in Baltimore County. Look on the back of the pedestal for the story of Cecil Calvert, 1606–75, "Founder of Maryland." He is here credited with establishing for the "first time in the English-speaking world freedom of religious worship according to any Christian form and separation of church and state."

For contrast, across St. Paul Street from the statue is a grove centered by a large water basin and water jet (1964). "Like a cool glass of water on a hot day" was sculptor Paul Gardescu's description. You may rest and read here. From benches in this Court Square you can examine a juxtaposition of architectural styles and materials. The slick, coppery tone structure of the Signet Tower looks as though it were made of cellophane. Across from it, at 19 E. Fayette Street, is the Georgian-style, red-brick, low-rise Bank of Baltimore. Both buildings display clocks, a rare public service downtown.

Cross Lexington Street and look to the right over Preston Gardens. Flowerbeds—especially bright tulips in April—make driving to work pleasant. Downhill from this park, the City Spring in the early 1800s provided water from a pavilion designed by John Davis (for whom Davis Street is named). "No spot in the city is more pleasant, during the hot weather," noted an 1824 visitor, William Newnham Blane, "than the public fountain which is surrounded by thick shady elms." In 1832 another visitor from England, Mrs. Frances Trollope, visited the spring and commented on groups of "Negro girls who sing in the soft rich voice peculiar to their race and all dressed with that strict attention to taste and smartness which seems the distinguishing characteristic of the Baltimore females of all ranks."

Go back down St. Paul Street past the Calvert statue to Fayette Street, turn right, and proceed one block to Charles Street. En route you will do well to look up. Much of the ornament above street level was put there in the era of walking and horse-drawn vehicles open to the sky. For instance, at 11–13 E. Fayette Street, the Macht Building (1908) exhibits so much fanciness that it is hard to take in. But two figures of females uncovered to the waist do stand out. By chance, almost opposite to them across Fayette Street stand two males with bare torsos similarly upholding heavy architecture on the Hotel Junker. They have been facing each other almost since the Big Fire.

At Charles Street, look to your left at the sculpted figures over the entrance of the B&O Building (1906). The heaviness of the figures suits that of the whole office building. But the weightiness masked the disappointment at losing out in competition to the rival Pennsylvania Railroad. Here on this corner, the B&O has left what can be thought of as a giant tombstone of Baltimore's greatest business creation.

Not even a building remains here of important events in American literary and newspaper history. Directly opposite the B&O Building, across Baltimore Street, stood the *Sun* offices and plant. During almost half of the twentieth century, writers such as H. L. Mencken helped give that newspaper a national reputation. Of one protégé who became a well-known writer, Mencken wrote, "[James M. Cain] has a great deal of talent, but manages himself very badly," meaning that he was always broke. After working as a *Sun* reporter, Cain went on to write for movies in Hollywood; he also wrote fiction. His novels *The Postman Always Rings Twice* and *Double Indemnity* led French critics to call him "a Proust in greasy overalls." Cain returned east to live out his long life in Maryland, that "churlish little state from which I fled."

Turn right on Charles Street and walk uphill past Fayette Street to Lexington Street. On your right, look for Wilkes Lane and, a few paces in, read a wall plaque that most passersby miss. Here in 1886 German immigrant Ottmar Mergenthaler invented the linotype. It revolutionized printing and loosed a flood of print a century before computers.

Beyond the plaque lies, buried under high rises, a writers' club of Poe's day, the Delphian. Poe was too poor and obscure to join, although he did satirize it in his fictional Folio Club. Members drank champagne and applauded popular songs written by member Samuel Woodworth—"The Old Oaken Bucket"—and by member John Howard Payne—"Home, Sweet Home." Even Francis Scott Key visited to read poems, although nothing as well known as his "The Star-Spangled Banner."

Members elected the scandalous English poet Lord Byron a member *in absentia.* Equally suspect in some eyes, John Wilkes, for whom the street is named, had belonged to London's Hell Fire Club. Earlier, Wilkes, a member of Parliament, had supported the American colonists: "Wilkes and Liberty!" was the toast in Boston. His name lives on in Wilkes-Barre, Pennsylvania, combined with that of Isaac Barre (*Tour 6*). Benjamin Franklin knew him and called him an outlaw "of bad personal character, and not worth a farthing." Later, his name was bestowed on John Wilkes Booth, Lincoln's assassin.

On your right above Wilkes Lane, enter the lobby of 1 N. Charles Street, the Blaustein Building (1964). There on the right stands a large sculpture by Barbara Hepworth, *Single Form.* It is her half-size copy in bronze of a sculpture in front of the United Nations in New York. A sign says that it symbolized Secretary-General Dag Hammarskjöld's "singleness of purpose in his zealous pursuit of peace." The red-brick building on the southeast corner survived the Big Fire when it stopped its northward course here. At 5 E. Lexington Street stands one of the first post-fire structures. It warrants a look because the Schloss clothing manufacturers wanted to remind customers of ties with European origins: the step-gable at the top evokes medieval Germany and the Low Countries.

Across Charles Street, at the Lexington Street northwest corner stands an old, mid-rise, stone office building, the Fidelity Building (1893). In it sits a man sometimes called "the mayor in exile," Robert C. Embry. He heads the $150-million Abell Foundation whose money goes to "focus on poor people, initiate things, and take some risks." One example: during the first two years that the contraceptive Norplant was available, the Abell Foundation invested $700,000 in advancing its use. "People's view of cities is that nothing works," says Embry. "And I think the Abell Foundation creates social change."

For contrast with his office building, look to the left at sleek One Charles Center (1962, Mies van der Rohe, architect). Its lightness soars. Look up its twenty-four-story tower along an exterior curtain wall of aluminum with a dark brown finish and gray plate glass. Then look down at the eight-sided shape, the travertine paving, and the green Tinos marble of the lobby walls.

Go right under the corner of One Charles Center. You will find two statues of Mayor Thomas D'Alesandro Jr. (1987, by Lloyd Lillie). They memorialize his political role in creating Charles Center in 1958. What do you make of the fact that there are two life-size figures of the same person, neither on a pedestal? You can sit next to the seated Tommy on a bench and have your picture taken.

On the other side of the building is the J. Jefferson Miller Fountain (1975), designed by Masao Kinoshito of Sasaki Associates. If the D'Alesandro memorial honors the political power, the Miller Fountain recalls the power of businessmen as partners in Charles Center.

Beyond the Miller Fountain, pick up the Skywalk that will carry you overhead through Charles Center. Look for a map of the Skywalk posted along its route. Below you spreads Center Plaza, said to be the only oval plaza in town and one modeled after Siena's ancient Palio. But you will witness no wild horse races here, such as Sienese enjoy. But there is a bronze horse, sculpted by Jeff Schiff (1990), bursting from a stone wall across the oval (best seen from ten paces to the right of the memorial bench).

In 1970, the space had a weekend of glory, when the

Miller Fountain and One
Charles Center

first City Fair filled it with booths celebrating Baltimore's neighborhoods. Coming shortly after the 1968
racial riots, the fair tested whether or not fears of violence would keep people away from downtown. They
did not. It attracted 250,000 peaceful people downtown.
"Baltimore had, it seemed, rediscovered the 'bread and
circuses' formula of ancient Rome," wrote Prof. David
Harvey in 1991, "to counter seething discontents, promote downtown redevelopment, and recover a sense of
civic pride and purpose."

*As you wind your way around Center Plaza and across
Fayette Street, you will see downtown Baltimore as a patch-
work quilt.* Side by side will be nineteenth and twentieth
centuries, red brick and pale stone, tall and short. Directly across traffic to your right, at 20 Park Avenue,
your eye may be drawn to a low cream and white Brewers Exchange (1896)—a lemon-meringue pie of a building. If you were to look inside, you would see that recent
restoration as offices reveals delicate plaster work and
neo-Egyptian columns, as well as crystal wall sconces
and chandeliers brought from Washington's Hay-
Adams Hotel.

*After crossing Fayette Street you will walk between two
hotels:* the newish, pale-colored Omni on the right, and
the old, red-brick Lord Baltimore Hotel (1928) on the

left. Note Renaissance-style decorations, such as the plaques you see on the wall opposite the Skywalk. Are the heads in bas-relief those of Maryland Indians and English settlers?

Across Baltimore Street the Morris Mechanic Theater (1967) confronts you on your left. "Fort Mechanic" some critics called it because its brutalist architecture made it an oddity when built; it still is. The architect, John M. Johansen, called the style "functional expressionism," meaning that the outside reflects what goes on inside. On the Skywalk, for example, you can easily see the two stair towers. Notice how the concrete walls show the image of wood forms into which the concrete was poured. "It [this theater] is anti-urban and anti-people," said architect Rich Burns recently. "It's this exposed-concrete form."

Inside the theater, by contrast, a large audience for Broadway shows gives Baltimore a good reputation in New York. "Not going to the theater," said Arthur Schopenhauer, "is like dressing without a mirror." Baltimoreans know that and have subscribed well to recent theater seasons. Soon a larger, more up-to-date performing arts center will be built in the cultural center (*Tour 11*).

With your back to the theater, make a loop to the end of the Skywalk. When you pass the twenty-four-story Mercantile Safe Deposit & Trust Company Building (1969), designed by local architects Peterson and Brickbauer, notice the stainless-steel vertical tracks used for washing windows.

Continue walking to the right on the Skywalk as far as the Arena at Hopkins Place. Descend the steps to read the historical marker attached to the stairway. In 1775–76, the Continental Congress met in Jacob Fite's tavern located near this spot. Here, in Congress Hall (as it has come to be called), delegates voted to confer "extraordinary pow-

---

Can't be done, everybody else said. Too much tension downtown. Too much hangover from the riots two years earlier. Blacks and whites mixing in public? You'll have an atmosphere of fangs. . . . And then, that September, as a city held its breath, something lovely happened. The fair opened its doors, and everybody in the world seemed to show up. Even nature helped, throwing in a minor hurricane that blew over neighborhood exhibits. Instead of killing people's enthusiasm, it brought everybody together. Strangers began helping each other put their booths back in order and, in the process, found out this wonderful thing: They had more that bound them together than pulled them apart.

Michael Olesker, looking back twenty years, *Baltimore Sun* (June 7, 1992)

Morris Mechanic Theater

ers" on George Washington as commander of the Continental Army.

Walk to the left of the plaque to look for a prize-winning sculpture by Anton Milkowski, *The Diamond* (1969). Notice its reflection in the big glass wall behind it. Also, walk to the left to read a plaque attached to the bank under the Skywalk. It marks the site of the world's first dental school (*Tour 7*).

Near here, later on, another historic incident began with a tossed cigarette. On the cold, windy morning of February 7, 1904, a fire burned eastward for three days. It swept along the harbor to Jones Falls and north to Lexington Street—almost all of the original sixty acres of Baltimore-Town. Flames lapped up much of the city's history. More fine architecture burned here than in famous fires in Chicago and San Francisco. But those towns rebuilt more gloriously.

From the plaque, move right and then left into Hopkins Plaza. This southernmost plaza in Charles Center creates an anteroom to the Inner Harbor. Some critics contend that none of these open plazas really pleases because of the absence of lively activities. Here the dominant gray Federal Building seems to forbid joy. Its exterior has been compared to a computer card. Also, visitors complain that you can go inside only by clambering up a double flight of stairs. But many habitués like the Jacob France Memorial Fountain with water shooting up as high as forty feet.

Before you leave the plaza, look around at the specially designed lights. At night the rippled molding of the shades gives prismatic effects. If you face the Federal Building, on the right you can glimpse Hopkins Place through a glass pavilion. The name of the plaza where you are standing is redundant because in 1881 the adjacent block of Sharp Street was renamed Hopkins Place. The name change honored the benefactions of the merchant Johns Hopkins (*Tour 8*). His founding a university and a hospital did more to spread the name of this city than the contribution of any other Baltimorean—except maybe H. L. Mencken and Babe Ruth.

Your tour now ends with a short stroll. When you face the Federal Building, walk to your left. Just before you go down a flight of steps, detour up to a small plaza on the right. There stands a recently erected sculpture, *Arrival of Venus,* by Jonathan Silver. Because Silver had been an art historian, he here alluded to Botticelli's painting, *The Birth of Venus.* Critics of the siting of this sculpture say the space is too great. But then a critic was once defined as someone who knows the route and can't drive.

Now descend steps from Hopkins Plaza to a terrace. It connects two black office buildings. *From the steps, turn right immediately* in order to pass on the left Sun Life Insurance Company of America Building (1966, Peterson and Brickbauer, Emery Roth and Sons, architects) at 20 S. Charles Street. Look into the glass-enclosed lobby at red marble–encased elevators and a hanging sculpture of the sun by Dmitri Hadzi.

Just at the end of Sun Life, turn left and then right in order to go along a sidewalk to the left of the second black office building, Charles Center South (1975, RTKL Associates, architects) at 36 S. Charles Street. Sometimes it is called the "Button Building," because its dark gray glass panels are attached to the structure by round, button-shaped stainless-steel pieces. The tower's hexagonal shape contrasts with its neighbors. As pointed out by local architectural historian Phoebe Stanton, this building's location makes it a kind of hinge between Charles Center and the new developments in the Inner Harbor.

Continue to the corner and look west up Lombard Street. On the right-hand side, note the Italian-looking Bromo-Seltzer Tower. On the left, glimpse a colorful

sculpture by George Sugarman at the entrance to
Edward A. Garmatz Federal Court House (*both featured
in Tour 7*).

Cross both Charles and Lombard streets to the raised
platform underneath the office tower of United States
Fidelity and Guarantee, or USF&G (1970, Vlastimil
Koubek, architect). "I like this building, the simplicity
of it," said local architect Rich Burns. "But it's isolated.
I wish it did more for the city." If a wind is blowing,
look for a rope strung diagonally across the barren platform to keep you from being blown into the harbor.
Walk across the platform to the Pratt Street side (opposite where you entered) to survey outdoor sculpture.
With the harbor on the left, look on the right at the
Charles and Pratt streets corner: you can see what was
designed by Thomas A. Todd as the Equitable Trust
Fountain (1981). You may be drawn to study its rough
stone monoliths and circle of Maryland county names
and Baltimore City up close. "The land is represented by
the granite stones," said Todd, "and the water is symbolizing the bay and the sea." On the left, a second sculpture adorns the Light and Pratt street corner: a shining
construction by Michio Ihara (1978) in front of an entrance to offices of Bell Atlantic of Maryland.

*Then, cross Light Street to explore the lobby of the new
addition to the IBM Building.* Enter fifty paces up from
the corner of Pratt Street. Its decor suggests a grand ship.

When you return to the corner of Light and Pratt
streets, you are in sight of Constellation Dock and the
beginning of your walks through Old Town and Baltimore-Town. You have seen how the west bank of Jones
Falls, Old Town, contrasts with the east: Baltimore-
Town was, and is, Downtown. You have returned to the
1729 boundary, the part of the original town plan resembling the blunt nose of an Indian arrowhead—still magical and golden.

Otterbein entrance to
residential court

Federal Hill, Little Montgomery, and Otterbein

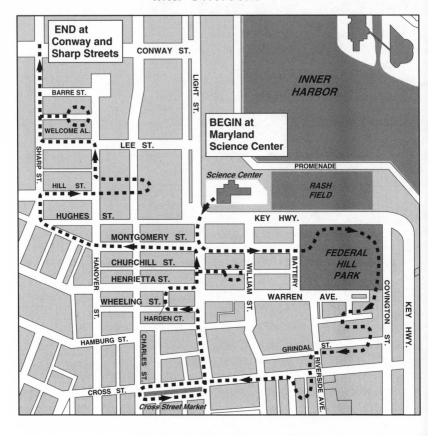

END at Conway and Sharp Streets

CONWAY ST.

BARRE ST.

WELCOME AL.

LIGHT ST.

INNER HARBOR

BEGIN at Maryland Science Center

LEE ST.

SHARP ST.

HILL ST.

HUGHES ST.

Science Center

PROMENADE

RASH FIELD

KEY HWY.

MONTGOMERY ST.

HANOVER ST.

CHURCHILL ST.

HENRIETTA ST.

WHEELING ST.

HARDEN CT.

WILLIAM ST.

BATTERY

FEDERAL HILL PARK

WARREN AVE.

COVINGTON ST.

KEY HWY.

HAMBURG ST.

CHARLES ST.

GRINDAL ST.

RIVERSIDE AVE.

CROSS ST.

Cross Street Market

COME HERE FOR:

- ◆ Sites important as sets for filmmaker Alfred Hitchcock
- ◆ Places of significance to Commodore Joshua Barney, President Lincoln, and, later, to women and children cannery workers
- ◆ "Dollar houses," a neighborhood of early rowhouses spared bulldozing and sold by lot to restorers for $1 each
- ◆ Old-fashioned blue-collar neighborhood with small stores and Cross Street Market, founded in 1842
- ◆ The Civil War site of Yankee guns trained on a city where Southern-sympathizing women flaunted disloyalty to the Union
- ◆ Water vistas down streets to the east and from Federal Hill Park

- Easy extension from this tour to the Museum of Visionary Art, Baltimore Museum of Industry, and Fort McHenry

---

In filmmaker Alfred Hitchcock's *Marnie* a shot down a rowhouse street to ships—much like Hamburg Street—ends the drama. By then the heroine has returned to the South Baltimore neighborhood you are touring.

Anyone who likes the spruced-up history at Disney World will like this tour even more because Disney's history is synthetic. In these waterside neighborhoods, you touch an earlier America. "One of the beauties of Baltimore is that it can seem caught in time," wrote a *Washington Post* reporter, "stuck in some '50s vision of things when working class people still lived in the city, where your nabe counted almost as much as your name."

You will walk a neighborhood that sharp-eyed novelist Anne Tyler used for blue-collar grittiness in *The Accidental Tourist:* "A block of row houses that gave a sense of having been skimped on." See how flat roofs and flush windows with no depth make everything look simple.

For a century or two, these houses have endured wintry blasts and tropical summers. During the 1970s the city sold many of them for a dollar apiece. Now they sell for 200,000 times that sum. Many houses offer water views, often from a new rooftop deck. You will see why sentimentalists and neighborly souls come here as determinedly as lemmings seeking the water.

To put it into perspective, Baltimore is a big, small town. It goes at a nice easy pace; it's not expensive; it's a great place to raise a family (even if you're not married). . . . [Until a recent rebirth, Baltimore] was viewed strictly as a blue collar, dusty, backward, upper-southern town situated between mature Philadelphia and sophisticated Washington.

Chip Silverman, *Diner Guys* (1990)

HISTORY

"A great red bank of clay flanking a natural harbor basin" was how John Smith described Federal Hill in 1609 when he mapped Chesapeake Bay. Almost 200 years later that hill came into its own when Baltimoreans threw a huge party there to celebrate Maryland's ratifying the Constitution.

Grand Procession at Baltimore, May 24, 1788: At nine in the morning of the first instant, the various preparations being completed, the procession, for celebrating the ratification of the Constitution by our State, consisting of about 3000 people, was formed [and marched] through the principal streets of the town amidst the acclamations of a prodigious number of spectators to Federal-Hill, where they were received by a salute of seven guns, and partook of an entertainment provided for the purpose. They were seated at a circular table of 3600 feet [presumably in circumference]. . . . The repast was elegantly disposed and consisted entirely of the productions of this country. It was closed with thirteen toasts (drunk in the excellent ale of Messrs. Peters and Company [fifteen and a half barrels]) accompanied by as many federal discharges.

The Massachusetts Centinel (May 24, 1788)

Again many street names give clues to how Baltimoreans felt in vanished times. Names chosen by landowner Col. John Eager Howard honor patriots who fought in two wars against the British, including Col. Otho Holland Williams and Commodore Joshua Barney. One successful immigrant worker left his name on a street running to his now vanished shipyard. After the War of 1812, William Easley Woodall, at 15, left Liverpool to seek his Baltimore fortune by building steamboats. "The American steamboat is superior to any other in the world," said Charles Dickens visiting Baltimore. "It is a perfectly exquisite achievement of neatness, elegance, and order."

Later on, Cannery Row would have made an apt name as well. In the late nineteenth century, canning factories spread here after inventor Thomas W. Kensett Jr. opened an oyster canning factory on the east side of Federal Hill. To be near canneries, immigrant workers lived in these modest rowhouses. No street name recalls them. Nor does a street name commemorate a Yankee fortification of the hill when the Confederacy threatened to cut off Washington from the rest of the nation.

Like most true neighborhoods, Federal Hill is only four blocks wide. Federal Hill Park forms the northern end of South Baltimore and of Federal Hill National Register Historic District (1970). Since the official district occupies the broad neck of a peninsula, the renovated blocks share many traits with adjacent South Baltimore and Locust Point (to the east).

In the early twentieth century, not everything was ideal. "[T]he district stank," reported an observer, "an unhealthy looking tumor upon the lower limb of the city, covered with mean dwellings and unsavory manufactories." Then after World War II a new generation fell in love with the water and also with old houses. "For the benefit of the Peale [Museum] we'll have a ball on Federal Hill." That 1964 proposal marked the beginning of renewing that neighborhood, according to Ellie Harvey Kelly. "It made people see the possibilities [of living] up there." With the backing of Gov. Theodore R. McKeldin and Sen. Charles Mathias, "we got a little permit to serve alcohol, arranged jitney service from parking by the station, and hired a band."

"Some structures were in deplorable shape," said pioneer rehabilitator Mary Lib McNair. "Rats, roaches, decay—sometimes things were just held in place with rope." Trips to City Hall to fight developers became routine. "New residents have no idea of the battles we

Satirical Broadside printed as a protest when the Union general forbade display of Confederate colors (red and white) in Baltimore:

On Barber's pole, and
    mint stick
He did his veto place
He swore that in his city
He'd red and white erase.

No sunrises or sunsets which exhibit such combinations [of colors] will be permitted on pain of suppression.

Anonymous

fought," continued Mrs. McNair. "We succeeded in getting an ordinance to prevent changing of roof lines. And now façades of houses must retain their original look, with no additions visible from the street."

Residents of Little Montgomery and of Otterbein tell a different story. Both were reshaped during the eager 1970s: some demolition, much upgrading, some building of infill residences. A stroll through these streets usually lures visitors to return.

TOUR

Starting Point: Constellation Dock, Inner Harbor
Length of walk: One and a half hours
Snacks and restrooms: Cross Street Market, restaurants
along Light Street and South Charles Street
Transportation: Water-taxi from Constellation Dock to the
Science Center to the beginning of the walk; or walk
past the Light Street Pavilion of Harborplace to the
Science Center

Begin your tour at Constellation Dock, and, facing the ship, walk on the brick Promenade to the right past Harborplace Amphitheater, toward the green wall of Federal Hill just across the water. Leave the Promenade at the turn in front of the Science Center and go up the steps left of the Center, cross Key Highway, and walk uphill on the left-hand sidewalk of Light Street.

You are walking in the shadow of an unbuilt network of interstate highways. In the 1950s citizens protested routing I-95 across Federal Hill to connect with I-70, I-83, and a bridge over the Inner Harbor to Fells Point. The confluence of roads would have created a permanent traffic jam.

"I say first the city is a place to live in," said a protesting witness at a public hearing about the intrusion. "They [politicians and planners] say first the city is a place to make money in. Whether I am right or they are, it makes the big difference." Archibald Rogers, first director of the Greater Baltimore Committee, saw to it that experts led by Nathaniel Owings, of nationally reputable Skidmore, Owings, and Merrill, squelched the scheme.

As you begin to go along Light Street, look on the left in the first block for a public park behind a brick wall. Go in for your first look at downtown. At the end of the first block of Light Street, turn left on East Montgomery Street.

The name of Montgomery Street honors Revolutionary War hero Gen. Richard Montgomery. For us this name and the look of the street evoke our colonial past.

John Work Garrett: President of the B&O Railroad

John Work Garrett took it upon himself to supply Lincoln with plenty of coal to heat the White House when supplies were scarce. Also, he kept Union troops supplied and moving. Garrett made the B&O one of the most successful railroads in the country by developing a mammoth transshipping port in Locust Point, South Baltimore. He employed thousands to load and unload trains and ships east of Federal Hill. Generally, the B&O paid the lowest wage of any railroad, so some residents of these districts lived at near-poverty levels. "The workers know what it is to bring up a family on ninety cents a day," recalled one of them, "to live on beans and corn meal week in and week out, and the children growing up sharp and fierce like wolves day after day because they don't get enough to eat." By contrast, Garrett prospered. He even had a Maryland county named for him.

In 1775 he almost conquered Canada for the Continental Congress. "With fewer than a thousand men, to assault in a blizzardly mid-winter night the strongest city in America, might seem a foolhardy undertaking" was a later comment. Montgomery did fail, and he was cut down by a cannonball. News of his death spread with the fame of his daring.

East Montgomery Street became a center of preservation in the 1960s when propinquity to tidal waters— even those of the dirty Inner Harbor—seemed desirable. Now every residence here is desired—even 200½, the second door from the northeast corner going toward the park. With an eighty-seven-inch frontage, it must be the narrowest rowhouse in the city. It has just room enough for the entrance and an aspidistra plant.

Notice the cobblestone paving of the 100 block. Residents of that block were once so overcome with nostalgia that they themselves physically removed smooth paving in order to expose rough stones. "It was in the middle of summer—so hot I feared the residents would have heart attacks," said Mary Lib McNair of 200. Slow down to note the garden bell at 111; the long cast-iron balcony at 114; the firehouse, converted to a residence by the director of the Baltimore Museum of Art and his wife at 125; and the wooden house at 130.

Continuing along East Montgomery Street, you will cross William Street, a thoroughfare of pristine rehabilitation. This street name honored Revolutionary War

> People call these homesteaders "the new pioneers," but like the old pioneers, they find people already living where they settle. The old pioneers wiped out the Indians with guns. Today they use the bank book—and it has the same effect as a gun.
>
> Brendan Walsh, housing counselor, St. Ambrose Housing Aid Center, *Sunday Sun* (September 4, 1977)

colonel Otho Holland Williams, superior officer of landowner Lt. Col. John Eager Howard in the Carolina campaign. "Elegant in form [six feet tall] and one of the handsomest men of that day," reported a contemporary, but with "a sternness of character which was sometimes manifested with some asperity."

At the turn of the century, some of these houses rented for $10 and $12 a month. "My Aunt Dot's house on William Street had wooden steps painted to look like marble," wrote Fulton Oursler. "And another cousin had movable steps that were taken in every night and stored in the front parlor until breakfast time . . . so that . . . every family was like a turtle with its head put away for the night." *Walk slowly to Battery Avenue in order to study architecture.*

Some of Montgomery Street's eighteenth-century houses stand at the corner of Charles Street. Walking along, you can contrast the more elaborate styles in the 200 block: Greek revival, numbers 206 and 208, and fancier Italianate in 226 through 240. Today prices range from $175,000 to $300,000.

During the War of 1812 Battery Avenue led to Six Gun Battery, now Riverside Park in South Baltimore. To fortify the city, Secretary of State James Monroe sent Capt. Sam Babcock to place earthworks and six guns, eighteen pounders, on Middle Branch behind Fort McHenry. During the British night attack, nine enemy boats slipped past that fort, but with no luck. The British force fled, "owing to the warm reception he met from the Forts Covington and Babcock," said a contemporary reporter, "whose defenders performed the duty assigned to them with admiration."

Where East Montgomery Street ends at Battery Avenue, walk up the steps leading up to the top of Federal Hill Park. If you don't want a steep climb, just walk up the slope on Battery Avenue to the right of Montgomery Street to the end of the block at Warren Avenue. Turn left into the park. Either ascent will let you circumnavigate the rim of the hill. (Vistas are described in Tour 1.) *Walk toward the downtown skyscrapers. End your stroll at a point opposite to where you entered the park.*

When earlier you looked across the Inner Harbor from Constellation Dock, you may have imagined how nice it would be to live up on the distant green height. Now that you are here in the Federal Hill Historic District, you realize that the hill slope you saw is backed by some twenty blocks of residences and shops. Some exteriors here look like pictures in a nostalgic magazine.

Brick façades haven't looked this clean since they were
erected 100 years and more ago. And doors gleam with
fresh ruby, violet, and azure paint.

Look below you. By the time you come here, an old
red-brick building at Key Highway and Covington Street
should be open as the National Museum of Visionary
Art. Visionary art is sometimes called "outsider art"
because it is done by self-taught artists. "'Outsider' art
seems bursting with emotion," said Bernard Fishman of
the American Association of Museums, "and is expressed
in a visual language much more intelligible to most
viewers than 'modern art.'" Spearheaded by Baltimorean
Rebecca Hoffberger, this museum will exhibit paintings,
sculptures, and (if space allows) whole rooms and houses,
such as a house made of beer cans.

Another museum sponsor proposes to convert 840
Key Highway, used by the Baltimore Koppers Paint
Company, as the Heritage Museum. This $15-million
project will house works by Native Americans, West
Indians, Latin Americans, and African Americans.

If you were to follow Key Highway around the base
of the hill, you would cross sites of shipyards that were
active until the 1970s. Today Key Highway carries truck
traffic to Domino Sugar and other industrial plants farther out the peninsula of Locust Point stretching to the
left. For a century and a half this waterfront has provided continental rail connections for ships of all flags.
If you took Key Highway to Fort Avenue and followed
that street, you would reach Fort McHenry at the end.
Its heavy truck traffic heads toward one of the largest
rail-sea terminals anywhere.

*When you finish walking the hill edge, you will reach
the southern side, Warren Avenue. Cross it and take a final
look at the vista downriver.* Before you leave Warren
Avenue, also look at a variety of architectural ornament
and style displayed there. Some houses are the largest on
Federal Hill. To your right at the southeast corner of
Riverside Avenue, the freshness of the Federal Park condominiums disguises an industrial past of paper milling,
industrial belt manufacturing, and furniture warehous-
ing. Any grandeur Warren Avenue wears comes from its
greater width than many other Federal Hill streets—and
also from its name.

On a hill named for the U.S. Constitution, a man
contemporaries called an aristocratic hero of the Revolutionary War, Dr. Joseph Warren, seems appropriate. In
1775 Warren sent Paul Revere on his famous ride to warn
colonists of advancing British troops.

I went strolling around
the city hardly knowing
where to stop to procure
anything to eat that I
thought would be free
from poison. . . . The
majority of the people are
malicious and not only
feel but express their hate
for us damned northern
hounds that their rebel-
lious hearts are able to
hold. Sometimes they
curse us to our faces,
sneer at us on the corners
of the streets, thrust under
our noses secession
cards to greet us with
cheers and hurrahs for
that prince of traitors
Jefferson Davis.

Philip Woodruff Holmes,
New York volunteer, diary
(1861)

Our Warren's there and bold Revere
With hands to do and words to cheer
For Liberty and laws.

So went a popular ballad following the Boston Tea Party. After the Battle of Bunker Hill, the British officer in charge of burying the dead wrote, "Doct. Warren . . . I found among the slain, and stuffed the scoundrell [*sic*] with another Rebel into one hole and there he and his seditious principles may remain."

During the Civil War crisis, Union troops set up camp around Warren Avenue. They placed sixty cannons to prevent Maryland joining the Confederacy. Pro-Southern Baltimoreans then had years of living in a city occupied longer even than Confederate New Orleans. Troops built barracks for 1,000 men, dug an eighty-foot well, and formed nine-foot breastworks. Rumors circulated that soldiers stored beer in tunnels to cool.

Go to the right and walk to the end house of the first Warren Avenue block. Turn left and go down Henry Street to Hamburg Street. As you walk away from Warren Avenue on the short block of Henry Street, you meet another Revolutionary War name, John Henry. Henry represented Maryland in the Continental Congress, served one year as governor, and was Maryland's first U.S. senator. During the Revolution, the British burned his country house and papers. Opposite Henry Street, at 337 Hamburg Street, once lived two generations of the Frazier family who, according to old accounts, said that their house was made headquarters of Gen. Benjamin Butler, the commanding officer of the Yankee occupation. He was reviled as "Beast" Butler. The house's windows were covered with iron bars, they said; inside was an iron door with a grate for passing food through, and iron rings in the floor and walls for shackling prisoners. Do not ring the doorbell—let legends sleep.

There was General Dix seated on Federal Hill with his cannon; and there beneath his artillery, were gentlemen hotly professing themselves to be secessionists, men whose sons and brothers were in the southern army, and women!—alas whose brothers would be in one army, and their sons in another. That was the part of it which was most heart-rending in this border land.

Anthony Trollope, *North America* (1862)

Just think of the ladies in the city of 'Tea,' [Boston]
Though not quite so warm and impulsive as we—
Would they walk with, or talk with, or smilingly glance
On a Southerner armed with his musket and lance,
Who took up quarters as though 'twas his right,
And staid there as long as seemed good in his sight;
   Dispensing to fathers and brothers and friends,
Such justice as suited to further his ends?

N. G. Ridgely and Nannie Lemmon, "1862, or The Volunteer Zouave in Baltimore by an Officer of the 'Guards'" (Baltimore, 1862)

Supposedly Butler's
Union headquarters

Butler, a Massachusetts politician, and his successors
at this post instituted emergency measures. They closed
the port, stationed troops along roads and telegraph
lines, garrisoned hills, and imprisoned the mayor and
civic leaders who refused to take the oath of loyalty.
Public sentiment ran against Butler and his forces.

You may not covet Butler's house, but you might give
your best eye-teeth to live at the water end of this street.
Turn left to 423–425 E. Hamburg Street. As you survey
the harbor below you, note that waterside residences are
replacing the ship repairworks of Bethlehem Steel. Today
you survey marinas of recreational sail and the high-rise
tower of HarborView. Supposedly these high-rise apartments on piers are sited to allow viewlines between them
from South Baltimore to the outer harbor. HarborView
residents pay plenty to own unimpeded views.

When you look toward the water, you are surveying
something quite different from what has stood here for a
century and more. Old-timer George Elmer tells of
going with other boys down to the shipyards where they
stripped off their clothes and dived into the harbor.
When a neighboring woman complained, twenty-five
police appeared and appropriated the clothing. The boys

were taken to Southern Police Station, scolded, and threatened with the lock-up if they repeated the crime. "But it took more than a scolding to scare us," said Elmer, "and we were back at the shipyards the next evening, but we took the precaution to put our clothes in a boat and tow it out in the river where we had the laugh on the officers."

Below you, just below the top of Federal Hill, you can see Covington Street. From the War of 1812, particularly the Battle of Baltimore, came the street names of Covington and Battery, as well as streets honoring the dead listed on the Battle Monument in Monument Square. Streets on Locust Point, a peninsula stretching from here east to Fort McHenry, bear names of warriors—Capt. James Lawrence, Capt. Stephen Decatur, Capt. Thomas Hull, and more.

The name Covington recalls the 1814 Battle of Baltimore and the repulse of the British by Fort Covington on Middle Branch upriver from Fort McHenry. The fort honored Gen. Leonard Covington, a Marylander who the year before had been mortally wounded at the Battle of Williamsburg in New York State. "Twice pierced with balls before he left his post," he was buried by "soldiers who conveyed the corpse to its honorable mansion, [and] were seen to weep." He was "not a generalissimo," reported *Niles' Register* in Baltimore.

From Hamburg Street turn right at a footpath and walk to Grindall Street. Here you get another view of a harborside being reborn. It once held bustling factories, wharves, and warehouses. Time was when the mechanic's bell rang four times each of the six working days, calling workers to attend to business or to quit.

At the foot of Grindall Street, turn right and go up to Riverside Avenue. Grindall Street is namesake of Charles Sylvester Grindall (1849–1920), who owned a number of building lots on it and along William Street. You also

---

There was something about South Baltimore I always liked. It seemed detached from the rest of the city somehow, older, of course, and it had a certain air of quiet and security. Then there was the fine hospitality at all times. On the days following Christmas a caller, even the rent collector, was asked to have a chair while cake and wine were set before him. The wines were often home-made—cherry, blackberry and the like—but excellent, and the generous slices of pound cake seem now in retrospection to have been the best ever tasted and, above all, the spirit of heartiness was genuine.

Meredith Janvier, *Baltimore in the Eighties and Nineties* (1933)

will pass Chandler's Yard, a 1970s housing renovation. "Many of these vacant and condemned houses [of Chandler's Yard] had to be virtually torn to the ground and rebuilt," wrote developer Carl William Streuver. "Work began with a 'demo' party, when neighbors gathered and 'demolished' or gutted the inside of a house, washing the dust down with a keg of beer."

As you walk Grindall Street near Riverside Avenue, you may catch a whiff of coffee. That originates in the 400 block of Grindall Street at the small roasting plant of the Pfefferkorn family. In a converted garage seven Pfefferkorns continue a business begun elsewhere almost a century ago. "The little coffee factory seems right at home in the old neighborhood," wrote *Evening Sun* columnist Jacques Kelly, "All around are a mixture of old South Baltimore families, backyard clothes lines and children playing in the street."

Turn left from Grindall Street into Riverside Avenue and walk to to Cross Street. Riverside Avenue may be the only street in Baltimore beginning and ending in a park (Federal Hill and Riverside). When you find an opening, walk to an alley behind the houses. Here, perhaps, novelist Anne Tyler found her setting for *The Accidental Tourist,* small rectangular backyards, bleak with rusted car parts and swingsets. The houses, she wrote, looked skimped on.

At Riverside Avenue, detour 100 feet to the left in order to look at a pair of tiny brick houses at 1124 and 1126. In architectural history they represent the simplest and earliest form of Baltimore rowhouses. They are said to be the only extant 1½-story brick houses of the 1800 era in the city. Each has a door and one window right on the sidewalk. Above, in a gable roof, is one central dormer window. Most residences in this area look as though the same people are living in them that lived there thirty years ago—and more.

The church you see beyond the two tiny houses is St. Mary's Star of the Sea. Since 1890 this church has shown a navigational light on the cross atop the steeple. Before being electrified, the signal was lighted every night by a man who climbed up.

Come back on Riverside Avenue to Cross Street, turn left, and walk past Battery Avenue and William Street to Cross Street Market (1842). Now you are ready for a rest, so go inside. This market is one of the handful scattered conveniently—that is, for eighteenth- and nineteenth-century market-goers. Markets like this one antedate the incorporated City of Baltimore—the first dated 1741. At

---

My father always said Fourth of July was a bad day to go out, anybody could have it at home. So every Fourth of July my father would have a party and the whole family would come. He would go over and get about six dozen crabs and my mother would have cold cuts and the boys would pitch in—I think it cost us about two-fifty per couple. . . . The party started about two in the afternoon when the shade hit the back yard at 1409 Riverside. First thing you know we had the whole 1400 block in the yard and it went on till about midnight.

Baltimore Neighborhood Heritage Project (1979)

all of them Baltimoreans count on traditional foods, such as sauerkraut that accompanies Thanksgiving turkey. Today the Saturday crowd drives from all over to market, to eat and enjoy a relatively unspoiled spot. Young people crowd the sushi bar late Friday. And Sisson's, on the north side at 36 E. Cross Street, makes beer on the premises for diners.

Rare 1½-story homes, c. 1800

You should leave the market at Light Street, where you entered. *Once outside, turn left and begin to walk along Light Street.* Right next to the market on Cross Street is a public comfort station. As you walk along Light Street, look toward the downtown skyline for an image of the 1920s boom, the NationsBank Building (*Tour 5*). Its pyramid top has gold leaf covering its ribs.

Cross Street in those days had cobblestone sides and there was always water running down there and I was one for sitting in the drain and drinking the water. My parents were always after me.

We weathered the storm, you know, we were solvent. My father owned the property and the store—he had no debts, as far as the business was concerned. And we eked out an existence. It was, you know, we didn't starve, although our neighbors did. But we worked on a low overhead; didn't employ anyone, and it was a family affair. No one received wages; just a little bit of spending money.

Baltimore Neighborhood Heritage Project (1979)

Find Hamburg Street, turn left, and go down it to Harden Court. There, turn right and walk through to Henrietta Street. This byway has an unexpectedness, hidden as it is. *At Henrietta Street, turn right and return to Light Street. Continue going north on Light Street.* On your right, look for narrow Churchill Street. Stroll along it. Churchill Street was first named Sugar Alley, and then simply Church Street. Up the hill, facing William Street and with its side on Churchill Street, stands the original structure of a Methodist congregation (now converted to apartments with parking on the ground level).

Churchill Street is as narrow as a cramped canyon. Like the rest of Federal Hill it inspires adapting ancient spaces to suit contemporary life. For example, 126 and 128 emerged from a conversion of a three-story warehouse built in the 1870s. The façade retains coarse-textured brick and unfinished mortar, evidence of a basic commercial structure. Another adaptation at 122 E. Churchill Street began with a commercial garage. The architect-owner placed a greenhouse on the roof deck. In summer, guests sit on a plant-adorned deck. It antedates rooftop decks visible from many Federal Hill streets. Henrietta Street shows some.

After looping up and back on Churchill Street, walk down Light Street to Montgomery Street. There you will turn left and walk through part of Little Montgomery Historic District. Once this small residential district was part of a large and thriving residential-industrial community with a police station, three public schools, and three churches.

You are walking along that part of Montgomery Street that is set at an angle to the regular grid of streets. On your right are houses set back and staggered like pleats; the angle of the street on which they front forced the building lines to retreat.

Since only about twenty-five houses remain out of the original twenty-four city blocks, Little Montgomery Historic District looks like an afterthought. Some streets full of houses disappeared under new highways. Other blocks gained new residences or remained vacant lots. Remaining old houses, built between 1835 and 1860, had belonged to German and Irish immigrants and free blacks. Later immigrants fled pogroms in Poland and poverty in Italy. Around 1835 the staggered houses on Montgomery Street were built as residences for freed blacks from adjacent Otterbein. They and everyone else competed for jobs in railroading and in the port. At 117

Got naace whaaht raahn
Got cooal blaahk seeed
Got biig raaaid haaaht
Jes caaaint't be beeeat
Got raid wah du mil yun
     lay-dee
All raid.

("Got nice white rind / Got coal-black seed / Got big red heart / Just can't be beat / Got red watermelon lady / All red.")

Quoted by Roland L. Freeman, *The Arabbers of Baltimore* (1989)

W. Montgomery Street stands the oldest (1820) of nine "half houses"—one room deep with a single pitched roof.

At 20–30 W. Montgomery Street pause at the Ebenezer A.M.E. Church (1865). It occupies a site of an earlier church. The present church structure is said to be the oldest standing church built by a Baltimore African-American congregation. Among the early clergy was Bishop Daniel A. Payne, a founder of Wilberforce University.

As you near the end of Montgomery Street, you will be close to the site of what was a well-known Arabbers' stable owned by Walter "Screw" Fisher. "Arabs" (pronounced A-rab, with the accent on the first syllable) sell fresh produce and oysters from horse-drawn carts in rowhouse districts. "This was one of the only jobs a colored man could do," said Arab Swayback (Mr. Elmo, also "Polecat"), "and not be hassled by white folks." "Arab," by the way, was English slang for homeless youth, and the word came to refer to a lack of fixedness.

Downtown Baltimoreans still listen for Arabbers' street cries peddling fresh strawberries. "As the Arabs dwindled, there disappeared a great variety of street cries as Baltimorean as white [marble] steps," wrote Roland L. Freeman in a 1981 photographic portrait of Arabs.

Here at the edge of Little Montgomery Historic District, you are aware of entering a Disney-type world—but authentic. The shells of most buildings date from the days of sailing ships. Otterbein Historic District consists of rehabilitated nineteenth-century houses with infill of new residences. Notice the new brick walks, period street lights, and public open spaces (along with some parking for residences). The variety of size and exterior style of houses shows how wealthy industrialists and merchants lived right next to mechanics and other working-class folk. Here you can see good examples of

---

Around the corner from Leadenhall and Henrietta streets on Peach Alley . . . dwelt in these old times "Mother" Jones. . . . She was a sort of soothsayer and herb doctor and dealt in rabbit feet and other more or less potent charms. When she was not on the lower floor, through indisposition, her husband protem, a giant of a man with gold-ringed ears, would invite me to the "throne" room above to collect the rent. Here I would find the priestess in bed. Chickens of several breeds, two crows, several rabbits (whose feet were doubtless in danger) and a parrot were all in the small space.

Meredith Janvier, *Baltimore in the Eighties and Nineties* (1933)

indigenous Baltimore rowhouse façades. Some have the Baltimoreans' favorite Flemish bond pattern (narrow end of brick alternating with long end).

Pause where Montgomery Street meets Hughes and Sharp streets, forming slices in a quartered pie. The triangle here, Hermitage Square, honored Pres. Andrew Jackson's Nashville estate, the Hermitage. The large elm tree on Sharp Street probably was not here when the square was a familiar site for political rallying. On October 24, 1878, reformer Frederick Douglass gave a speech here. You met him in Fells Point, where, as a slave boy, he had learned to read; later he escaped from slavery by train from Old Town (*Tour 2*).

In its name Hughes Street remembers the two Christopher Hugheses. Christopher Hughes, the elder: remembered first because he was Irish, then because he became a fine silversmith in an age of superior design and craftsmanship, and most of all because he owned much of Federal Hill. He even had "a frying pan house" on South Charles Street, designed for him by Benjamin Henry Latrobe, architect of the city's early and renowned cathedral (*Tour 8*). What's more, his fathering paid off: a daughter married the hero of Fort McHenry, Col. George Armistead, and a son, Christopher Jr., helped work out the peace for that war. Junior not only acted as secretary to the peace parley at Ghent that ended the War of 1812, but he also was first to bring news to President Madison of the treaty ending the war.

As landowner, Christopher Hughes gave street names to honor his son Christopher Jr.'s tenure as foreign service officer in Hamburg, Ostend, and Stockholm. Those street names and routes are still in use. And Hamburg Street still has the look of old times.

The father made money in Baltimore as a moneylender. "A crocodile, fat and dishonest" was the description by a debtor, carpenter Leonard Harbaugh, whose land Hughes had had to repossess.

Here at the meeting of Hughes Street with Montgomery Street, turn right and enter the Otterbein Historic District. You will be weaving in and out of the district. Your exploration of Otterbein begins at Sharp and Hill streets. This one, like Hill Streets everywhere, climbs a rise. And Otterbein's Hill Street rises to part of the famous homesteading district in the 1970s called, after the local church, Otterbein. From the top of Hill Street you can see the waters of the Inner Harbor. The houses look early nineteenth century outside; inside, they look brand-new. Any spirit of community there must also be new.

From Sharp Street, turn right at the first street, Hill Street, and walk to the end of the block, Hanover Street. Note 127 Hill Street for its three-star bolts securing the brick façade. *Cross Hanover Street and continue on Hill Street to Charles Street,* where a footpath takes you straight ahead into a plaza. On your right you pass Christ Lutheran Church, sponsor of Deaton Specialty Hospital and Home, whose buildings surround the plaza. At night the feeling is like being on stage: the church's lighted stained glass makes a backdrop for the Jacob France Fountain (Don M. Hidsaka, sculptor).

Walk back along Hill Street to Hanover Street and turn right. There is no accounting for the oddities in street names. Both King George Street and Queen Street disappeared from maps after the American Revolution and took more democratic names. But Hanover Street, named for the royal family of England, persisted. South Baltimoreans even pronounce it "Han-ov-er" (accenting the middle syllable as Germans do with their state of Hanover). Once Hanover Street made a dignified progress from Fayette Street down to Ferry Point on the major land route to colonial Annapolis. Now it hiccoughs along.

On the left you will be passing a number of old house façades, and on your right infill, new residences. Pause at the corner of Hanover and York streets to examine a huge metal wheel tilted on its side and serving as outdoor sculpture. Originally it functioned in the city's trolley system. You may want to duck in and out of York Street in order to see parks behind houses facing main streets. *Continue on Hanover Street to Lee Street.* Look down Lee Street to the water and smell the contrast with a century ago when the Inner Harbor, according to H. L. Mencken, "received the effluence of such sewers as existed and emitted a stench as cadaverous and unearthly as that of the canals of Venice."

At Lee Street, turn left and go one block to Sharp. As you stroll along Lee Street, notice modern touches such as fancy iron gates. Steps are of brick or white marble, with shrubbery carefully arranged between the rowhouses. Notice walkways between groups of houses, one with a vine-covered wall, another with picnic table and bench. The Joseph A. Bank & Sons chain of clothing stores in Washington and Baltimore originated nearly a century ago in a tiny tailor shop owned by Joseph Bank on the southeast corner of Sharp and Lee streets, now a residence.

That business attracted customers in days when bar-bers charged twenty-five cents, and Dr. Franklin on Lee Street charged fifty cents a visit, and that fee included medicine. Most of the houses in Lee Street date to 1830, although 129 Lee Street dates back to 1797. By 1860 this street housed a mixture of wealthy merchants and maritime laborers. By 1910 immigrants of Jewish and Italian backgrounds had moved in, and soon most houses became rental properties.

Turn right on Sharp and go past Welcome Alley. Again duck in to see manicured plantings and to note the street sign marking Pubped Walk (evidently copied from an abbreviated note on a plan for Public Pedestrian Way). *Then return to Sharp Street, turn right, and proceed to Barre Street.*

A century and a half ago, Sharp Street must have been as crowded as a convention. In its district mixed black and white, slave and free, residence and shop. Joshua Johnson, free African American and immigrant portrait painter, recently has generated interest almost as great as that of his mentors, the Peale family of artists. Like them he painted portraits of a number of wealthy Baltimoreans of the first half of the nineteenth century. Johnson lived in this neighborhood, "a self-taught genius" (in his own words). Though his house is no more, his art can be seen at the Maryland Historical Society.

Along Sharp Street you will find historical markers attached to Martini Evangelical Church (1867–1972, now Bell Tower Commons) and to School House Mews, formerly Baltimore Public School 126 (1869–1975). They stand testimony to the changes of the past twenty years here. For something new added to old houses, look at 807 and 809: a contemporary stretch of ironwork encloses a tiny flower garden and forms a balustrade up brick steps.

Gone is the old rowdiness from sidewalks fronting rehabilitated rowhouses of Otterbein Historic District. These houses have attracted many new residents. One reason is a manageable-size house—five or six rather small rooms, with no lawn to mow. If any architectural features remain, they are plain and pleasing to twentieth-century taste. The original owners, limited by working-class incomes, cut all frills. Some new owners have moved in from old suburbs such as Roland Park. "Some of [the Roland Park houses] belong to the jigsaw era," wrote rowhouse-dwelling gadfly H. L. Mencken, "others are simply preposterous, as a flirtatious fat woman is preposterous."

Opposite the row you can observe briefcase-carrying

bureaucrats attend the Federal Reserve's sedate business. For them, it may seem appropriate that the street took its name from a very proper English colonial governor, Horatio Sharpe. Other well-behaved traversers of Sharp Street include commuters taking the train to Washington and baseball fans zeroing in on the new ballpark.

Every mid-Atlantic town must have had a York Street. Baltimore has had at least two. But not every town has a Welcome Alley.

Your tour ends at Barre Street. King George III personally disliked Col. Isaac Barre, M.P. But on our side of the water, Barre's opposition to the Stamp Act in 1769 (which unfairly taxed tea) has been commemorated in Wilkes-Barre, Pennsylvania, and by this Baltimore street. Barre was an Irishman of French-Huguenot parentage, a defender of the colonists. "You have not a loom nor an Anvil but what it is stamped with America: it is the main prop of your trade," he told Parliament in 1776.

As you leave Hanover Street, you may find some of its circle of new construction overwhelming. The tallest building belongs on this city's long list of senior citizens' apartments—the one with the best view. Be sure to look at remnants of the old, such as 119 Barre Street, with its iron foot scraper shaped like a lyre and its ornamental window screen. Notice, too, the double doors in the three houses on the left just before you reach Sharp Street.

Everything is clean and cared for. Maybe the place looks the way it did in 1861 when Union troops patrolled and when English novelist Anthony Trollope visited town and wrote, "back into civilization, secession, conversation, and gastronomy."

If you have time, you can drive from Otterbein to neighboring Ridgely's Delight and Barre Circle. Both residential districts spread just beyond the new ballpark and are a treat, especially for preservationists. You might consider two other extensions of this tour:

Key Highway runs east to Fort Avenue and Fort McHenry. The fort demands a visit, but not now. Hiking out to it takes an hour from Light Street, but it certainly is well worth a drive (962-4290). Once you have parked outside the visitors' center, you can walk over acres of green park around the fortifications. There National Park Service employees give a history and tour. Go on a summer Sunday to watch the military tattoo performed by men dressed in 1812 uniforms.

Inside the fort, explore the whole story of how a Maryland lawyer, Francis Scott Key, anchored off shore, "saw the array of Baltimore's enemies as they advanced,

The cobbles [of the 1890s] were rough and uncertain, and down by the wharves the houses did lean upon one another for support, but there was color and there was flavor and there was a goodly smell . . . the tang of tar and salt water and, most potent of all, guano—that rich Baltimorean reek that delighted the hardy nostril, and made the returning excursionist know that he was nearing port. Well, we do things differently now, and not so vividly, so vigorously.

Letitia Stockett, *Baltimore: A Not Too Serious History* (1928)

saw the discomfited host of its assailants driven back in
ignominy to their ships." Key immediately wrote the
words of "The Star-Spangled Banner." Earlier he had set
other words to the same tune, an English drinking song,
"When the Warrior Returns." Also, he had earlier written the phrase "star-spangled" in a poetic line, "By the
light of the star-spangled flag of our nation."

To honor Key, admirers erected a gigantic statue (by
Charles Henry Niehans) of Orpheus, god of music, at
the entrance of the Fort McHenry National Park. A
more modest statue of Key himself stands on the Key
Monument on Bolton Hill (*Tour 12*). "Let the praise
then be given not to the writer," he commented, "but
to the inspirers of the song."

At 1415 Key Highway, to the right on the southern
shore, you can later explore the Baltimore Museum of
Industry. Here re-created workshops tell of the city's
heyday as port and manufacturing center. *Baltimore
Magazine* chose this place as the best "hands-on museum for kids"; children can operate the Kids' Cannery
and work the Children's Motorworks Assembly Line. In
1870 the building itself became part of Cannery Row,
where women and children shucked oysters for packing
in tins. Outside, see a working crane near the 1906
steam tug SS *Baltimore,* the only operating steam tug
in the country.

*Tour 7 begins on Sharp and Conway streets. So when
you come out of Barre Street, turn right and go to that
corner. Should you choose to return to the starting point
from Barre Street, just proceed to the right along Sharp
Street one block to Conway Street. There turn right and
keep going until you come to the Promenade. Head for
Constellation Dock.*

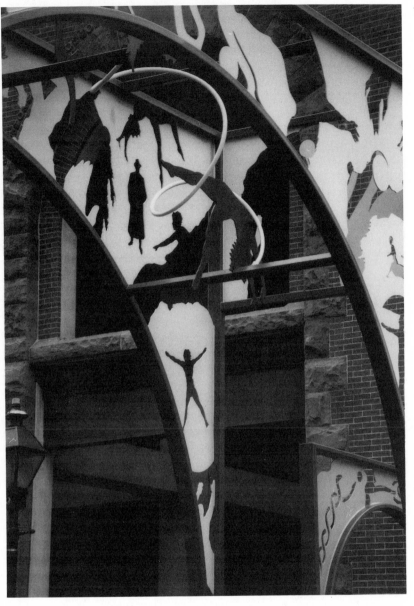

Sculpture by Linda
DePalma

Downtown, the Unburnt District

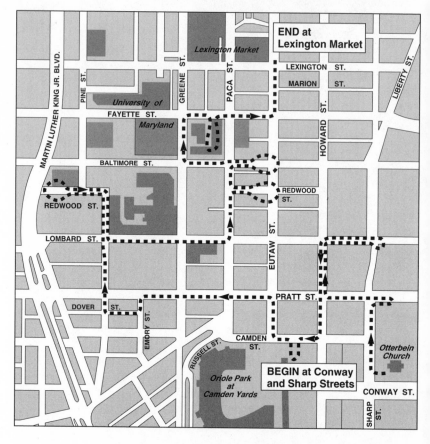

COME HERE FOR:

- House important to Babe Ruth and baseball
- Sites significant to U.S. Supreme Court Justice Thurgood Marshall and African-American history, as well as to abolitionist William Lloyd Garrison
- Places connected with thespians Mae West, the Lunts, and Helen Hayes, as well as authors Russell Baker, H. L. Mencken, and Edgar Allan Poe, and lyricist-composer Cole Porter
- Oriole Park at Camden Yards, a baseball park in a setting of historic B&O Railroad structures
- Apartments created from architecturally distinctive factory lofts
- University Center campus of the University of Maryland—including the oldest American medical

school building; new, stylish hospital structures; and the oldest tree downtown

◆ Lexington Market, the city's largest and oldest food emporium and a lively downtown daytime center

◆ An array of sculpture ranging from early nineteenth-century sphinxes in two cemeteries to a life-like modern artist painting a picture of the Otterbein Church tower rising nearby

---

[The city] is the front office of civilization, . . . drawing in [the hinterland's] money and spending it in grand and lovely ways.

H. L. Mencken

"This tottering medieval city" summed up native writer H. L. Mencken's view of Baltimore. "I am glad I was born long enough ago to remember, now [in 1926], the days when the town had genuine color, and life here was worth living." With its nineteenth-century streetscapes, this district illustrates what he had lost. Here you explore his town's special urbanism. Long ago, Baltimoreans created within a few blocks here all that is needed in a true city: residences, offices, a market, shops, churches, a sports team and place to play, theaters, a hospital or two, and cemeteries.

Your walk weaves through the downtown that escaped the Big Fire of 1904. Earlier you explored the downtown that didn't—the Burnt District (*Tour 5*). There you passed skyscrapers; here you find only one. "Let the reader who believes that we have got any value out of them [skyscrapers]," said H. L. Mencken, "go down and look at them and then retire to his praying-closet to figure out how much their splendors have set back the town in hard cash."

Here you will pass low-rise shops and loft buildings, looking much as they did in 1900. In fact, Lexington Market has been dispensing fresh provisions since 1782. Its district still draws crowds, although the make-up of the crowd is different each generation.

I have always liked the sense of sin that emanates from Baltimore. Coming from Washington with its dull clerk's respectability, its truly monumental criminal operators and its pleasing absorption in large-scale homicide, I feel that I am re-entering civilization when the car enters the yellow smog of South Baltimore and heads into the stately dilapidation clinging to the edge of downtown. There is a promise of pleasure to come. We will eat well. Conversation will be lighter, racier. Women will be more—what? Provocative. Somebody will talk about horses. What I anticipate, of course are the pleasures of sin. They seem so civilized after the vices with which Washington is concerned.

Russell Baker, *New York Times Magazine* (1973)

Cast-iron front of
Mencken factory

South of the market, baseball fans enliven summer.
And in all seasons tourists stop over from the Inner
Harbor to see Baltimore's oldest church and to explore
museums.

HISTORY

In these streets the boy H. L. Mencken played in and
about his father's cigarmaking factory. At the time he de-
voured a ton of pretzels in Ehoff's Saloon on Paca Street.
"[The human race] had a better time in the days when I
was a boy. . . . I enjoyed myself immensely, and all I try
to do [*Happy Days*] is to convey some of my joy to the
nobility and gentry of this once great and happy Republic, now only a dismal burlesque of its former self." His
books do convey that joy.

A century earlier, in 1782, John Eager Howard, Baltimore's *pater familias,* had lured development by giving
land for Lexington Market. His plan succeeded. Soon
farmers were sending wagonloads of grain and flour to

sell near the produce market. By 1790 a visitor could call
Baltimore "bustling and debonair."

Howard's choice of street names lends character: the
names of famous battles at Saratoga and Lexington tell
walkers that this district is old and important. Other
street names recall English political supporters of the
rebelling colonists: Portland, Dover, Conway, Barre,
Granby, Grafton, and Rutland.

Camden Street and Pratt Street take their eighteenth-
century names from a short, handsome, genial man who
had fine gray eyes, Charles Pratt, Lord Camden. He was
lord chancellor of England in 1766–70. An early biogra-
pher said that, in studying the classics at Eton, he
"imbibed that abhorrence of arbitrary power which
animated him through life."

Other street names honor Revolutionary War patri-
ots: Greene, Lafayette, Marion, Paca (pronounced PAY-
ka in Annapolis and PACK-a in Baltimore). At Camden,
South Carolina, American Revolutionaries with Col.
John Eager Howard distinguished themselves in battle.
Howard Street, of course, is one of three Baltimore
streets honoring him (Eager Street in Belvedere and
John Street in Bolton Hill are the other two). From
Howard's era, Baltimore ships lent street names: Dia-
mond, Sarah Ann, and Josephine.

Although this part of downtown is still lively, any
question about its being first rate is easiest answered
with historic landmarks you will pass. You can touch
the past: Davidge Hall (1812), for instance, stands as
the oldest American school structure built for training
physicians. Even before that date, the First Presbyterian
Church had established its burial ground a block north.
In it today Edgar Allan Poe's grave attracts international
pilgrims.

In addition, you will see the nation's first major
railroad station of the first chartered railroad and first
passenger line, the B&O. Near the station, later in the
nineteenth century, Jewish entrepreneurs built loft
buildings for a needle trade second only to New York
in volume of clothing produced.

Today the district perches on the edge of change.
Acres of valuable cleared land around the new ballpark
will be filled. A huge neon sign tells travelers on nearby
I-95 that over here shines University Center, location of
the University of Maryland at Baltimore. It signals a determination by Baltimoreans to retain their international
prominence in scientific—especially medical—research.

Starting Point: Just west of Inner Harbor, two blocks from
  Light Street, and the Light Street Pavilion of Harbor-
  place, at the corner of Conway and Sharp streets
Length of walk: Two and one-half to three hours
Places to rest and read (and sometimes find food and restrooms):
  University Square (South Paca Street at Redwood
  Street), Lexington Market (North Paca Street at
  Lexington Street)
Transportation (for the return): Metro or light rail
Ending point: Lexington Market

If you did not take Tour 6, you can easily reach the
starting point of this one from Constellation Dock.
*Walk between the two Harborplace pavilions to the corner
of Pratt and Light streets. There turn left on Light Street,
walk one block to the first pedestrian crossing, and cross to
Conway Street.*

If you are continuing a walk from Tour 6, you are
leaving the edge of Otterbein to go north from Barre
Street along Sharp Street. You see ahead the tower of
Otterbein United Methodist Church.

*You will first cross Conway Street, a major route on and
off I-395 that connects with I-95.*

At 112 W. Conway Street, Otterbein Church survives
as one of two eighteenth-century houses of worship in
town, and the only one still in use as a church. Even
more important, it became the mother church of the
Church of the United Brethren, a sect now merged with
Methodists. The German congregation, led by Pastor
Phillip Wilhelm Otterbein, earlier had separated from
the Lutherans. Behind the church lies Pastor Otterbein's
grave and brick parsonage (1811).

The congregation hired a Baltimore carpenter-
builder, Jacob Small Sr., to design and construct this
sturdy brick building (1785–86). It has, some people say,
a rather awkward charm. Outside, louvered openings in
the belltower repeat the rounded tops of the clear-glass
windows. Even that stylistic touch didn't prevent congre-
gational complaints about the tower's squatness. "Maybe
when you see the bill, you will find it high enough," was
the builder's answer.

If the church is open, go in to take in the bright-
ness—no gloom of stained glass windows here. Otterbein Church retains much that is original, including
some of the clear glass in the arched windows and the
bells that were cast in Germany and installed in 1789. In

the vestibule you can study a mid-nineteenth-century bird's-eye view of the city. On it you can trace your route. Begin by finding the church (located just to the left of Inner Harbor), and notice how built up this district was in 1869 and how commercial.

Outside the church, turn right along Sharp Street. As you walk on Sharp Street, you will approach the Convention Center. Although you will not be going in it, you may like to hear about it. "Light, airy and spacious," critics have said. Actually, from the street you will see mostly a series of glass canopies. The exhibition hall lies nearly underground, self-effacing. A low structure was designed to give adjacent buildings clear views to the water.

Follow Sharp Street to Pratt Street. If you are walking after September 1996, go into the Otterbein entrance lobby. There stands a human-size figure of an artist standing at an easel and painting a picture of Otterbein Church just as he sees it in the near distance. Sculptor J. Seward Johnson called the piece *Right Light.* Another Johnson work, *The Briefing,* will occupy a terrace site outdoors above Pratt Street. One bronze man is briefing another about site development.

Once you reach Pratt Street, make a loop to the right in order to view sculptor Greg Moring's untitled silvery creation. It looks rather like a windmill. In a wind it turns a full 360 degrees; it also tilts.

Cross Pratt Street to the left-hand corner of the white, modern federal courthouse. Walk to the front entrance on Lombard Street by turning right on Howard Street and right on Lombard Street; you will see a large, colorful metal sculpture, *Baltimore Federal* (1978). When the design was proposed by nationally known George Sugarman, judges protested its placement near the entrance as a hiding place for muggers. Or was there a secret reason? Maybe they didn't like bright blue, yellow, and red colors and crisp-edged metal. According to Sugarman, the design suggests not only the openness of the law, but also its continuity and protectiveness. At a public hearing, testimony favoring the work carried the day.

Return to the Pratt Street corner. On a planted berm stands a full-length statue of Supreme Court Justice Thurgood Marshall (1979, Reuben Kramer, sculptor). Marshall came to the Court as the first African American ever to sit there. The statue commands a site close to where antebellum slaves had to await sale in a "slave hotel."

Your imagination is needed now because so little

physically remains from before the Civil War. But you saw similar houses in Federal Hill, Little Montgomery, and Otterbein. Looking back, notice other strange juxtapositions. In the slave state of Maryland, for instance, Baltimore stood out as the capital of free blacks. Near Sharp Street many free African Americans resided in small alley houses behind larger houses of slaveholders, such as Edgar Allan Poe's grandparents. The writer sold his grandmother's slave when he lived in Baltimore.

Quakers at nearby Lombard Street Meeting House (now demolished) actively promoted abolition of slavery. Elizabeth Needles, for instance, organized an affiliate of the American Convention of Abolition Societies, and helped with the group's annual meeting, which alternated between Philadelphia and Baltimore.

At the time, Elizabeth's brother, Quaker cabinetmaker John Needles, wrapped abolitionist tracts around furniture he made. One Southern governor ordered all Needles's furniture burned, the tracts were so inflammatory.

Nearby, in 1829–30, young William Lloyd Garrison edited an abolitionist newspaper with Quaker Benjamin Lundy. They described slave-dealer Austin Woolfolk as "a monster in human shape." Woolfolk then accosted Lundy in the street and knocked him down. Sued by Lundy for assault, Woolfolk had to pay a fine of a dollar.

All that happened when the African Methodist Episcopal Church was being led by its founder, Daniel Coker, a Baltimorean born to a white mother and a black slave father. In this part of town, Coker established one church that is still prominent, Bethel A.M.E. Church, and taught in the school of another, Sharp Street Methodist Church. Coker taught a leading Baltimore free black, William Watkins, whose niece, Frances Ellen Watkins Harper, wrote for a national audience.

The Slave Market

The sale began—young girls were there,
Defenceless in their wretchedness,
Whose stifled sobs of deep despair
Revealed their anguish and distress.

And mothers stood with streaming eyes,
And saw their dearest children sold;
Unheeded rose their bitter cries,
While tyrants bartered them for gold.

Frances Ellen Watkins Harper

A century later, two other talented African Americans found a home in Baltimore for a time. Zora Neale Hurston recalled those days in a memoir, *Dust Tracks on a Road* (1942). Another writer and scholar, W. E. B. Du Bois, published several books during the eighteen years he lived here.

Walk to 300 Hopkins Place on the corner of Pratt Street to see the end-of-row residence of Moses Sheppard, a Quaker merchant-philanthropist. His house, purchased in 1831, has endured several changes but retains much of its original look outside. His money founded the Sheppard and Enoch Pratt Hospital for the mentally ill, established near Towson. "Put first the comfort of the patient," he instructed his trustees. Sheppard was raised in a log cabin before clerking in a Baltimore provision store and going on to make a fortune. He publicized the genius of a nearby farmer, Benjamin Banneker, an African American who had helped survey the District of Columbia and had written popular almanacs.

On your right, as you proceed along Pratt Street, rises a sleek office building by the national firm of Skidmore, Owings, and Merrill. Its giant-step shape dominates the sky here. For ballpark fans its mirror surface reflects clouds by day and the moon at night.

Cross Howard Street to examine 300 W. Pratt Street, a freshly restored achievement of nineteenth-century Baltimore industry, the façade of the old Wilkens-Robbins Building (1871) made of iron cast in ornamental forms to look like a grand palace of stone.

The old building is now flanked by two set-back wings and called by the name of the current owners, the Marsh & McLennan Building (1990). "The best of the nineteenth and twentieth centuries in Baltimore architecture" was the verdict of the American Institute of Architects jury that awarded top honors to the restoration and addition (the work of RTKL, architects). The addition marries the old by keeping the five-story height, and by a sheathing in a grid of anodized white steel struts and gray tinted glass, with a sunscreen whose slanting perforated metal panels correspond in scale to the old structure's window arches. At night the lighted façade—glowing white—catches all eyes.

Turn left on Howard Street toward the ballpark. Find a seat at the Camden Yards light rail stop in order to survey structures important to American history, and now to baseball. In this area, after the Battle of Yorktown, camped French soldiers, led by French Comte de Rochambeau. Recently an excavator for the new ballpark dug up a flintlock pistol, maybe lost by the French.

Then, within a century after Rochambeau, Camden Street lent its name to the city's main railroad station, now in front of you. Restorers have cleaned brick walls that used to be painted, and reproduced original towers, this time in aluminum, not wood. From here, nineteenth-century passengers entrained for Washington, D.C., as well as for the West. Now commuters board trains at the left rear of the station to go to Union Station, Washington, D.C.

Inside the 1855 railroad station, baseball reigns. The Babe Ruth League will probably have its hall of fame and other attractions ready for your visit. Then you can explore other facets of sports such as sportscasters and African-American baseball leagues.

You are looking at a landmark of American transportation: the B&O invented the American railroad and built the first commercial railroad. Then, as the nation's most powerful and extensive line, it dominated the city's economy for a century. In 1828 Baltimore stepped forward as the first American city to sponsor a railroad, and in 1987 it reluctantly was the last to lose one, when the line that had absorbed the B&O, CSX, moved its headquarters to Florida.

From Camden Station in late February 1861, President-elect Abraham Lincoln entrained for his inauguration. The moment was not without drama. Lincoln's Secret Service, hearing of a plot to kill him, brought him through here in the dead of night. Four years later, right after his assassination, his body was carried through this same building for public viewing.

Do not look for a historic site plaque. If there were one, it would tell about Lincoln, of course. But it should also describe the beginning here of the greatest labor uprising of America's nineteenth century, the 1877 strike against railroads. Actually it began just two miles west of this station when workers learned a 10 percent cut in wages had gone into effect. Police arrested strikers.

Then, four days later, on Friday, July 20, a crowd of 15,000 workers at Camden Station tore up train tracks and stoned the engine of a train readying to transport troops to put down the strike. "The rioters have taken possession of the Baltimore & Ohio depot," wired Gov. John Lee Carroll from inside the station, "set fire to same, & driven off all firemen who attempted to extinguish the flames."

National Guard and federal troops intervened to quell the violence. But the Sixth Regiment, attacked en

route with stones, fixed bayonets and killed ten people.
Strikes then erupted on many railroad lines. Across the
country, workers in other industries and businesses also
struck employers. In St. Louis, for instance, a general
strike brought business to a standstill. By August 5, federal forces had put down all strikes. "The late strike was
not the work of a mob nor the working of a riot," said
the *Washington Capital* a month after it ended, "but a
revolution that is making itself felt throughout the
land." Although the modern labor movement supposedly grew from the strike, B&O strikers did not win
back the wage cut.

*From the light rail stop, walk to the right past Camden
Station and the B&O freight warehouse* (1898–1905), now
converted to offices and clubs. From Conway Street,
the building looks like a freight train over a fifth of a
mile long.

*Just past Camden Station, go to the left up the Prome-
nade and look for an entrance on the left into the Camden
Club.* Inside, ask for permission to go up to the club and
look out the windows at the ballpark. Below you, after
1995, you will see a bronze statue of Babe Ruth. "Such a
tribute to Babe Ruth would accomplish the purpose,"
said Orioles president Larry Lucchino in 1993, "of telling
the world he was baseball's greatest player, an Oriole and
a Baltimore boy from humble beginnings who attained
spectacular heights." The sale price of the Orioles in
1993 also reached spectacular heights, $170 million.

*Return to Camden Street for a look through the fence at
the playing field of Oriole Park at Camden Yards.* "The
quaint splendor of Camden Yards" is how the ballpark
struck sportswriter Frank Deford. Other critics say that
the park looks like Disney World. "What saves it from
terminal cutesyness is the vast, renovated warehouse that
looms behind the right field wall," wrote the *Washington
Post* critic. "It is real, it is beautiful and it gives the park
an authenticity it would otherwise lack, a link to Baltimore's architectural heritage." Vistas from the upper-
deck concourse give "spirit-lifting views of downtown"
and "from the other side, of Baltimore's close-in neighborhoods and industries: smokestacks and steeples."

*From the ballpark, turn right and go down Eutaw
Street.* Embedded in the Eutaw Street walkway are three
five-inch baseballs marking where home runs landed
after being hit out of the ballpark in the first season.

*Go to Pratt Street. Turn left to cross Russell Street where
it becomes Paca Street.* This chief escape route to Washington and Annapolis originated as one lane leading to

the Patapsco River. Legend names the street after an
Irish immigrant of 1781, Alexander Russell, who had
twenty children. Here he ran supposedly the largest
brickworks in America. "Baltimore pressed brick enjoyed a reputation far beyond the limits of the City and
State," wrote George Frederick, architect of City Hall.
"Its bricklayers, too, were famous."

By this time you may well be arguing with Thomas
Jefferson's saying, "Walking is the best possible exercise;
habituate yourself to walk very far." On your right you
will pass a Marriott Hotel, where you may want to stop
for refreshment in the coffee shop and also for restrooms.

*Just beyond Russell Street, look for Emory Street on the
left side of Pratt Street, and turn left to 216 Emory Street,*
the Babe Ruth Birthplace and Baseball Center (727-
1539). There, at the home of maternal grandparents,
Babe Ruth was born February 6, 1895. Nearby, excavators for the new ballpark uncovered remains of his
father's saloon.

At age 7, Ruth was called "a hopeless incorrigible"
and sent to St. Mary's Industrial School (the current
Cardinal Gibbons School) to learn the shirt-making
trade. He also learned baseball. After twelve years he left
to play for the Baltimore Orioles and other teams. In
twenty-two years he played in 2,503 games with a life-
time average of .342. He hit sixty home runs in 1927
alone—not surpassed until 1961 and a longer season.
His fans loved his flamboyance and freewheeling life
that fit so well into the Jazz Age.

This twelve-foot-wide rowhouse contains memorabilia not only of Ruth (his 1914 glove, for instance), but
also of his family and of the Baltimore Orioles. That
team, managed by Edward Hanlon, is credited with in-
venting or developing base stealing, hit-and-run, place
hits, sacrifice hits, and bunts. The museum, said to be
the second-largest baseball museum in the nation, is
spreading into a nearby building. So strong is interest in
the sport that one ball autographed by Ruth recently
went for $18,500.

Now you can understand why many Baltimoreans
had wanted to name the new stadium for Babe Ruth.
Even without his name, the ballpark fills with fans. "The
Orioles do for Baltimore what the space program did for
America," said columnist George F. Will. "The team is
what all have in common."

When you emerge from the museum, you can see
to your right the edge of the historic district called
Ridgely's Delight. Its name comes from a 1721 marriage

of Charles Ridgley to Rachel Howard, heiress of the
landowning family. Not until growth of the railroading
industry nearby did the district fill with workers' houses.
Later, if you have time, stroll through the pie-shaped
neighborhood. You will find old rowhouses, intimate
scale, small parks, and much rehabilitation.

*From the museum, turn left to Dover Street. Then turn
right and walk one block to Penn Street, where you should
turn right. Cross Pratt Street and Lombard Street.* You will
pass the side of Adams Cowley Shock Trauma Center of
the Maryland Institute of Emergency Medical Services
Systems, a pioneering effort in emergency medicine.
The heliport for Medivac helicopters has helped to save
many lives.

*At the end of the first block of Penn Street after Lom-
bard Street, turn left on Redwood Street to find the entrance to St. Paul's Cemetery* (1800), one of two burial
grounds lined with tombs of early patriots. Episcopalians moved occupants here from the original graveyard next to St. Paul's Church (*Tour 8*). Here lie Charles
Carroll, Barrister (of Mount Clare), U.S. Supreme
Court Justice Samuel Chase, and landowner John Eager
Howard. Francis Scott Key lay here until removal in
1866 to Mt. Olivet Cemetery, Frederick, Maryland.
Unlike the Presbyterians' Westminster Cemetery gate
at Greene and Fayette streets, this gate is locked. Arrange to go in by phoning St. Paul's Episcopal Church
(685-5537).

*Come back down Penn Street to Lombard Street and
turn left. Go to Greene Street and turn left.* After you have
gone along Greene Street a hundred yards, turn and
look back at the corner left, 519–525 Pratt Street, converted to the Greenhouse (1892). The left portion of the
building (built separately) makes a more arresting sight
than the right side. For fifty years workers made B.V.D.s
(men's briefs) here. The initials stand for the company's
founders—Bradley, Vorhees, and Day.

The columned building above you catercornered to
the right at Greene and Lombard streets is Davidge
Hall. Facing Davidge Hall, you can see to the left at
650 W. Lombard Street the B. Olive Cole Pharmacy
Museum (727-0746). Make a jaunt over to it if you want
to see Queen Victoria's thermometer, as well as opium
pipes and a completely stocked late nineteenth-century
pharmacy. "Some of this stuff, I don't even know what it
is," said Richard Baylis, drug utilization director of the
Maryland Pharmacy Association headquartered here.

You should cross Lombard Street and climb the steps to

Oldest tree and
Davidge Hall

columned Davidge Hall and its great tree. The English
elm tree (*Ulmus campestris*), planted in 1728, probably
stands as the oldest living thing in downtown Baltimore.
Rest on a bench next to the old brick building to look
around and read. If you call ahead, you may be shown
inside (328-3100).

One of early Baltimore's most successful architects,
Robert Cary Long Sr., designed Davidge Hall, at 522 W.
Lombard Street. This classical structure makes any list of
landmarks for two reasons. First, it remains as the oldest
building (1812) in the country dedicated to medical education. Second, its rotunda with a columned porch predated by a half-dozen years Jefferson's more famous Rotunda at the University of Virginia. Inside, a wooden
dome spans sixty feet of a circular anatomical theater
and below it a round chemistry hall. On the floor of the
upper room a brass plate marks where Lafayette stood
when he received an honorary degree.

Long discreetly placed dissecting rooms between the
circular walls of the amphitheaters and the rectangular
outer walls; his concealed staircases allowed the delivery
of bodies without offending the public. When Poe lived
in town, he wrote quite a horrifying short story,
"Berenice," based on true local incidents of grave rob-
bing. In Poe's day charges of cemetery raiding led to
occasional riots—popular uprisings against science.

Davidge Hall shows how long Baltimore has been a
medical capital. In the eighteenth century, doctors here

pioneered vaccinating for smallpox. In 1807, after one antidissection mob had raided the "anatomical labora- tory" of Dr. John B. Davidge, the hall's namesake, the General Assembly incorporated the College of Medicine of Maryland. It became the first medical institution on record to give students the privilege of performing dis- sections themselves. The university, in 1823, erected its own hospital, where seniors gained practical medical experience with an intramural residency.

Look across Greene Street from Davidge portico to see the latest hospital addition, the Homer Gudelsky Tower (1993). It provides 185 beds for cardiac, neurologi- cal, and cancer patients. Its rooms surround a twelve- story atrium. Altogether, the university plans $1 billion worth of building, all aimed to make Baltimore a future high-tech center for life sciences. Near the corner, if plans go forward, rises the Health Sciences Library– Information Services Building. Its cylindrical tower juts out, giving students at the tilted window a fine view of Davidge Hall.

Over the years, graduate divisions of the University of Maryland developed around Davidge Hall. In 1840 the first dental school in the world opened in Baltimore under Dr. Horace H. Hayden. Various successors be- came part of the university in 1923. Just behind Davidge Hall on Greene Street, the National Dental Association plans to open the National Museum of Dentistry in 1996. Among exhibits will be the lower plate of George Washington's false teeth.

From Davidge Hall cross Lombard Street, turn left, and proceed to the intersection with South Paca Street. As you leave the steps, look up to the left at a loft's fading side- wall advertisement for menswear, including "night shirts." The vista beyond it to the east offers a curious- looking tower, the monument of millionaire Capt. Isaac Emerson, an imaginative chemist who developed the headache remedy Bromo-Seltzer. His tower (1911), mod- eled on that of the Palazzo Vecchio in Florence, once surmounted his factory. The four-dial gravity clock, still working, used to be the largest in the world. In place of numerals circling the clock face, Captain Emerson spelled out BROMO SELTZER. Until 1936 the tower was sur- mounted by a fifty-one-foot revolving replica of the bottle, illuminated at night with 596 lights and visible twenty miles away. Removed because of structural flaws, it could not be reproduced at the time. "Bring back the Blue Bottle!" wrote a *Sun* columnist. "Now that the Ori- oles have a spanking new stadium at Camden Yards with

Bromo-Seltzer tower
and loft

a spectacular view of the city skyline, the return of the
Blue Bottle should be an urgent urban priority."

Pause at the corner of South Paca Street, where you will
find yourself flanked by converted lofts. These buildings
deserve more than a glance because they make up the
Loft Historic District of Baltimore City. Built between
1850 and 1910, lofts made the city a center for manufacturing clothing, tobacco products, and pharmaceuticals.
In some of them women sewed for a dollar a day. In addition to such specialties as policemen's uniforms, Balti-

moreans manufactured straw hats, umbrellas, and elevator shoes. Today most of the half-dozen massive structures serve as comfortable apartments for people who
live better than the workers who most likely spent more
time here than they did at home.

On the corner of Lombard Street, Inner Harbor Lofts
display a historic marker just left of the entrance at 38 S.
Paca Street. Directly across the street rises Marlboro
Square, where Marlboro shirts were made until the mid-
1950s. A plaque posted to the left of the entrance at 410
W. Lombard Street tells the history. Go inside to look at
an unusual atrium. Notice the rhythm of brick arches
adorning buildings along Paca Street.

Long before lofts, this corner attracted crowds of
travelers on the main route to the South. And after Baltimoreans built the B&O and Camden Station, hotels
thrived. No wonder the day the cornerstone of the B&O
was laid brought out such a festive crowd.

Partly because of proximity to the B&O, early businesses spread nearby: the Knabe Piano Company began
manufacturing in 1837 and the Sachse lithography and
cartography business produced detailed bird's-eye views
of nineteenth-century American cities, including the one
you saw in Otterbein Church.

Turn left down Lombard Street into Paca Street. Right
behind Inner Harbor Lofts runs Cider Alley. Whimsical
usage had early consecrated many alleyways by name to
liquors to go with Bottle Alley: Madeira, Whisky, Wine,
Cider, even possibly Holland for Holland Gin, the drink
that almost ruined eighteenth-century England.

Loop right at Redwood Street to examine a transformed truck-delivery alley. First note five spruced-up
loft buildings, now offices and residences. Then note the
streetscape, now an urban oasis created by a collabora-

**We had a water cooler in
the cellar which was filled
only twice a day for 150
girls. . . . Our lunches we
placed on work benches
where rat poison was
thrown around and
roaches crawled up and
down continuously.**

Marion Vigneri, who worked
in the cellar of
Schoeneman's Industrial
Building, Baltimore
Neighborhood Heritage
Project (1979)

Well do I remember one delightful race I enjoyed in Margy's arms, though only four years old at
the time. It was in 1828, on the 4th of July. The corner-stone of the Baltimore and Ohio Railroad was
to be laid—the pioneer railroad of the country! . . . A grand procession, with flags flying and floats
displaying various trades, all richly adorned, and the whole animated by martial music, went up
Baltimore street. . . .

When our vantage ground was gained, corner of Eutaw street, Margy lifted me up in her arms
to behold what has never faded from my memory. . . . The printing-press float pleased me best of
all, with its attendant imps dressed as mercuries, who scattered sheets that were being printed as
the procession moved along. The last division passed, the blare of the trumpets grew faint from
a distance.

*Memoirs of Margaret Jane Blake of Baltimore, Md., and Selections in Prose and Verse by Sarah R.
Levering (1897)*

Henry Louis Mencken: Iconoclastic *genius* loci

Since Mencken has accompanied you on these walks, you may like to know that he frequented this district all his life. "He gave modern Baltimore a character," said his friend Hulbert Footner. "He represents Baltimore to the world."

At the instant I first became aware of the cosmos we all infest, Thursday, September 13, 1883, the day after my third birthday, . . . I sat on a ledge outside the second-story front windows of my father's cigar factory at 368 Baltimore Street [now 414] fenced off from space and disaster by a sign bearing the majestic legend: Aug. Mencken & Bro.

H. L. Mencken, *Happy Days* (1940)

"The great debunker from Baltimore" said *Life,* "finds the world full of fun and boobs." His friend F. Scott Fitzgerald liked his "deep belly laughs." During his life in this town, Mencken wrote more than 30 books, 200,000 letters, and decades of newspaper columns—about 3,000. In 1919, his *The American Language* set the course for linguists who ever after have had to treat our language apart from English English.

"The most naturally blessed humorist since Mark Twain," said Russell Baker. His readers in the Jazz Age heard a loud, scoffing voice in the pages of the *American Mercury* and *Baltimore Sun.* "The truth is the lie that is pleasantest to believe," wrote Mencken. "It is a sin to believe evil of others, but it is seldom a mistake." "Men have a much better time of it than women. For one thing, they marry later. For another thing, they die earlier." "Whenever *A* annoys or injures *B* on the pretense of saving or improving *X, A* is a scoundrel."

As a literary critic, Mencken all but destroyed the so-called genteel tradition. He promoted such novelists as Theodore Dreiser, Sinclair Lewis, F. Scott Fitzgerald, Dashiell Hammett, and James M. Cain. And his own memoirs, the *Days* books, gave Mencken a place in American literature. Posthumous publication of his *Diary* (1990) caused a storm when some readers accused him of anti-Semitism and racism.

To the Editors:

We wish to express our dismay at the overreaction to the *Diary* of H. L. Mencken. The *Diary* does indeed contain discourteous remarks about Jews and blacks. It also contains discourteous remarks about most races, nations and professions; in fact, Mencken's harshest words are directed at "'the only pure Anglo-Saxons left in the United States' . . . a wretchedly dirty, shiftless, stupid and rascally people." Discourtesy was Mencken's style, as it was to a considerable degree the intellectual style of the 1920s. His hyperbole did not foreclose warm friendships with Jewish publishers, writers and doctors; no white editor of the day did more to seek out and encourage black writers; no editor did more to fight for freedom of expression for all Americans.

Whatever Mencken's "prejudices"—the word he himself used to describe his essays—he was a tremendous liberating force in American culture, and should be so celebrated and remembered.

Louis Auchincloss, Ralph Ellison, John Kenneth Galbraith, John Hersey, Norman Mailer, Arthur Miller, Arthur Schlesinger Jr., William Styron, Kurt Vonnegut, *New York Review* (March 15, 1990)

Those who know Mencken only through the fierce vituperation of his newspaper articles would be astonished to discover the mildness of his proper person. Those whom he attacks afterwards become his friends. The secret is, that however furious his language, there is no rancor in it. . . .

Mencken is an inveterate bedside visitor. He knows everybody in the great world, of course; everybody who is anybody and who has the price comes to Hopkins for treatment sooner or later, and stocky, red-faced, matter-of-fact Henry is ever the ministering angel at their bedsides. He has his own notions about treating the sick; it exhausts or excites them to talk, hence they must keep quiet and Henry launches into a monologue at the foot of the bed that permits of no interruption. At the end of fifteen minutes by his watch he marches out.

Hulbert Footner, *Maryland Main and the Eastern Shore* (1942)

---

tion of artist (Baltimorean Linda DePalma) and landscape architect (Philadelphian John Collins).

DePalma's sculpture bookends the block. Her lacy, steel Redwood Arch closes off the west end. Cutouts include a coiled snake suggesting the caduceus symbolizing the nearby medical school. Among other things, pick out a swatch of ribbon with a spool and threads used in the garment industry. From this district, needle-trade workers sent out women's and men's clothing by the carload—more than any other city except New York. Do look for cutouts of the sartorially splendid Fred Astaire and Ginger Rogers dancing on high.

Near the end, on the right, read a plaque about the clothing factory formerly in the building. At the end of this block, look across Eutaw Street at another loft, the often-praised Abell Building with its bluestone, white marble, and terracotta trim. DePalma's twin columns here rise to cutouts of humans seemingly in constant movement. "It's like looking at clouds in the sky," said DePalma.

As you continue walking on Paca Street north of Redwood Street, look on the right into Napoleon Alley. Its

name probably was bestowed by the emperor's nephew
(*Tour 9*) and his descendants, although none held imperial ambitions. This narrow block looks European with
walls darkened by soot and time, and with metal fire
escapes draped overhead. Today it looks as empty of
significance as a hollow crown.

*Walk the rest of the Paca Street block to West Baltimore
Street. Go to the right there* to examine century-old cast-iron fronts like the one you saw on Pratt Street. Although
lofts were built of brick, smaller factories sported cast-iron fronts or jazzed up the ground floor façade with
ornamental—and inexpensive—cast iron. Once upon a
time, more than 100 buildings had partial or complete
façades made of cast iron. Today few remain. Those on
the streets you are walking include the following (upper
stories only): 414, 412, 409, and 407 W. Baltimore Street.
You can compare rich designs at 322 (c. 1877) with
307–309 (1866). At 414 where H. L. Mencken's father
manufactured cigars, young Henry endured a brief,
hated apprenticeship.

Return along Baltimore Street across Paca to Greene
Street. Look to your left at University Hospital (1993),
built on the site of an earlier hospital. *Go to the right
along Greene Street.* On your left peer into the plant-bedecked lobby of Veterans Hospital (1992). On your
right you pass part of the University of Maryland School
of Law. Behind a wall spreads out the old Western Burying Ground of the First Presbyterian Church.

The unplanned juxtaposing of mounds and pyramids,
tabletop gravestones and vertical slabs goes back to 1787.
An early epitaph that captures what some people call
Presbyterian gloom actually quotes from English poet
Alexander Pope, a Roman Catholic: "Mrs. Margaret
McFadon. Who Departed this Life June the 9th 1798.
In the 68th Year of Her Age. How lov'd How valued
once avails thee not. / To whom related or by whom
begot. / A heap of dust alone remains of thee. / T''is all
thou art and all Mankind shall be."

It takes its newer name, Westminster Cemetery, from
the church built over part of the graveyard. Every Halloween hundreds of the curious tour beneath the church
to peer into an early tomb and stroll among gravestones.
They hear the story of how in 1852 Presbyterians built
Westminster Church on arches over a number of graves
in compliance with a new ordinance forbidding use of
cemeteries separate from a church. Of course, the faithful were colonizing yet another Presbyterian congregation in a growing part of town.

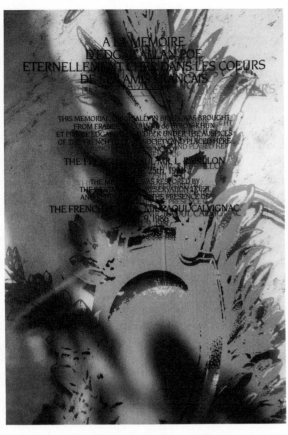

French plaque

Edgar Allan Poe's remains repose right at the entrance corner on West Fayette Street. At its dedication a book of tributes included a sonnet by French poet Stéphane Mallarmé, which has been memorized by generations of French students. Recently, when a local attorney drove French relatives past the tomb, he said his guests "almost fell out of the car" on hearing that the great Poe was buried here.

At the Tomb of Edgar Poe

Now time at last his true face has revealed.
The poet challenges with naked sword
His century, astounded that they had not heard
Triumphant death in that strange voice concealed.
The mob that heard him give a sense divine
To words their tongues had sullied and had worn
Cried out aloud his sorcery was born
From the dark dregs of poppy and of wine.
From earth and from the hostile sky, O grief
If art should fail to shape the bas-relief

With which the humble tomb of Poe must stand
 adorned.
This stone that flamed, and now is still and cold,
This granite shall forever mark the bourne
To thefts and slanders that the future yet may hold.

 Stéphane Mallarmé,
 translated by Richard Hart, Baltimore poet

Under Poe's monument lie Poe, his wife Virginia, and his mother-in-law Maria Poe Clemm. Controversy attaches itself to Poe here as everywhere in his life and posthumous career: was his body really brought here from the Poe lot at the back of the cemetery? As for the monument itself, its funding took years and gifts of pennies from Baltimore schoolchildren. "Cheap and hideous" were the words Mencken chose to describe the monument.

When you go behind the church and over to the university's fence, you will find a marker of Poe's original burial plot with his grandfather, David Poe. "A genius, and if not of the first rank, then at least near the top of the second," was Mencken's evaluation of Poe, "but a foolish, disingenuous, and often somewhat trashy man."

Just before Poe came to live with relatives in Baltimore, Maximilien Godefroy, a Frenchman married to a Baltimorean with good connections, employed the Egyptian style in designing the cemetery gates on Greene Street. He earned $5,000 for the gate and wall.

When you walk past the back of the church, turn left down a narrow passage. There you will see five vaults designed by Godefroy (or possibly Robert Mills, architect of Baltimore's Washington Monument). In fact, the rows of vaults create little houses above ground reminiscent of Baltimore's familiar rowhouses. Look for the double-lot, pyramid-shaped vault of James A. Buchanan

---

The playground at the school was a small fenced yard paved with brick. Pete [a student who was initiating the new student] flattened me on my back, straddled me and pounded my head into the brick with his fists while a hundred other boys, all strangers to me, cheered him on. [Fearing another attack] I developed the habit of knowing always who was behind me on the sidewalk and studying intersections ahead for the slightest hint of danger. Learning the same jungle moves that quarry use to avoid their predators, I was developing the reflexes necessary to survive in cities.

Russell Baker, *Growing Up* (1982)

and James Calhoun. It holds up to thirty family members spanning a half-dozen generations.

After touring Westminster Cemetery, come out the West Fayette Street gate that you had entered and turn right. You will pass Diamond Street on the left just past the ex–Poe School (Primary School for Boys is the name chiseled on it). There the national columnist Russell Baker endured part of his "growing up."

Diamond Street, like much in the neighborhood, has what Mencken called "the frowzy, unkempt, out-of-the-elbow, forlorn air of a third-rate boarding house." The street name Diamond contrasts with what you see. One letter-of-marque trader in the War of 1812 named *Diamond* took as a prize an English ship carrying 240,000 pounds of coffee from Brazil.

Pause at Paca Street to look left at the building of Baltimore General Dispensary, oldest organization in the country giving "real service free of charge to the indigent poor" both medicines and doctoring. *Now cross Paca Street and walk downhill on Fayette Street to Eutaw Street.* Explore an earlier Baltimore world simply by ringing the bell at 21 N. Eutaw Street (southeast corner of Fayette Street), the office of Baltimore Equitable Society (727-1794), the nation's third oldest fire insurance company. Displayed on fronts of insured houses, its metal plaque, called a mark, shows two clasped hands and the date of the company's founding, 1794. The Equitable remains the only fire insurer in Baltimore (or maybe in the country) still using fire marks.

The insurance company has preserved furnishings from the era when the building served as a bank. "It exudes an 1857 aura of solid, no-nonsense respectability," wrote one visitor. Other former bank buildings stand across Eutaw Street—Drovers and Mechanics is one. Downstairs at the Equitable you see dark walnut trim and long counter, twenty-one-foot-high ceiling, wire-mesh cages, and various antiques of the fire-fighting trade. There is a mahogany desk made in 1810 for the first president, Joseph Townsend.

Upstairs is a rather musty museum. In it are hundreds of marks that fire insurance companies used to place on insured buildings in order to identify them for volunteer fire companies whose services were, as they said, "subject to financial arrangements." Also, you will be able to see hand pumpers dating back to 1780, along with a collection of firemen's buckets, axes, helmets, parade hats, and cloaks. Look for the big rattles firemen used to twirl as alarms. Historians find most interesting

A bright but unsteady light has been awfully quenched. Poor Poe! he was an original and exquisite genius, poet, and one of the best prose writers in the country. . . .
I found him in Baltimore in a state of starvation. I gave him clothing, free access to my table and the use of a horse for exercise whenever he chose—in fact brought him up from the very verge of despair.

John Pendleton Kennedy, after learning of Poe's death in Baltimore (1849)

the insurance policies and records of what has been insured since 1797. Davidge Hall benefits from the oldest continuous policy—since 1823. You will see a strongbox that the guardians of those records buried during the 1814 attack on Baltimore.

On this corner you may agree with architectural critic Ada Louise Huxtable, "A rich, dense disorder makes a vital urban space." Stand outside the Equitable Building to see an array of old banks, solid and now neglected: Drovers and Mechanics National Bank, the brownstone Eutaw Savings Bank, Western National Bank. Over to the left is the Hippodrome, now for sale, a big-time vaudeville theater and the place where high-powered performers of the 1930s and 1940s appeared.

At the corner of Fayette Street, turn left and walk north along Eutaw Street. To your left up Paca Street near Baltimore Street two businesses can be investigated. "The wackiest five-and-dime you've ever been in [Mel's Corner at 226 N. Paca Street]," wrote Christopher Corbett recently in the *Washington Post*. "You can get checks cashed, you can buy bus passes, lottery tickets and money orders. You name it." There is "quite a selection of religious statuary, too."

The other curiosity is Big Boys Worldwide Food Market, 218 N. Paca Street, a kind of Third World convenience shop.

You pass Marion Street en route to Lexington Market. The name Marion Street again sets off Revolutionary War echoes because it honors the theatrical Swamp Fox, Francis Marion, fighter in Carolina swamps. To the right long stood a famous theater, Ford's (demolished). In the 1920s its stage door opened for such performers as Mae West, Helen Hayes, Houdini, Ethel Barrymore, the Lunts, and George M. Cohan. Then in the 1940s Cole Porter set his popular musical *Kiss Me Kate* in this theater. So Ford's lives on in a perennial favorite and, just possibly, Porter's greatest show.

Near this corner, landowner John Eager Howard gave a city block to friend Supreme Court Justice Samuel Chase for a residence (demolished). At the time, politics inspired Howard to offer land if the state capital would move to Baltimore from Annapolis. Rural legislators said no thanks. Today, ironically, much of the work of a state capital is performed in State Office Center just north of here (*Tour 11*).

Of course, state offices don't attract tourists away from the Inner Harbor. Fifty years ago, Baltimore didn't draw tourists at all. Other than a show at Ford's or a

It [Big Boys] included, among other things, a large palm tree, a bit of flora you don't see on Paca Street everyday. Persons from many lands trooped through the place buying such exotic products as lotus root and quail eggs. Among the many surprises at Big Boy was a frozen food case containing what I later learned was frozen bull's penis. You won't find that at the Giant.

Christopher Corbett, *Washington Post* (1993)

Rheb's Candies

drink in the Block, Baltimoreans always used to offer visitors just three places to see: Fort McHenry, the Washington Monument, and, maybe the most enjoyable, Lexington Market. As you walk toward its entrance on the left, look for the 100-foot painted mural, *E Pluribus Unum,* by Bob Hieronimus.

John Eager Howard's eighteenth-century gift of land for Lexington Market Baltimoreans still enjoy. "To a well-seasoned Maryland nose," wrote Letitia Stockett, "there is no smell on earth so delightful as the robust odor of the fish dispensary—so it was called in 1855—in Lexington Market." Long ago, the market had only blocks of disreputable sheds. Now in spacious buildings, office workers lunch here on hot pastrami. Some buy chocolates at Rheb's and Berger's cookies, also chocolate. And housewives and house husbands still select the scrapple, the crabs, and fresh lettuce for family tables.

"Faidley was great," said filmwriter and director Nora Ephron recently. "The last day we were filming on the dock at Fells Point . . . and we had just eaten forty crab cakes and softshell crabs, and I thought, I could shoot this movie forever."

From Lexington Market's Eutaw Street entrance you can easily take the Metro back to Charles Center Station. From there you have only to walk from the Calvert Street exit toward the Inner Harbor (follow the signs for the three blocks).

You may end your tour here, or you may want to drive to nearby sites that will enlarge your view of

On every side [in Lexington Market] one hears, "Oh, good morning, John," or "Well, George, where were you on Tuesday?" The purchasing is flavored with pleasant homely greetings. In this democratic atmosphere all sort and conditions of housekeepers rub shoulders. The rich accompanied by chauffeurs select lettuce with a critical finger; the moderately well-to-do carry their own purchases or adjure Charlie or Jim to put their things "in the right basket."

Letitia Stockett, *Baltimore: A Not Too Serious History* (1928)

certain aspects of Baltimore touched on in your walk.

The effect of juxtaposing of the statue of Justice Marshall with the slave market is intensified by a trip to Mount Clare (837-3262). That eighteenth-century plantation depended on slave labor. "We are going to have an opportunity to explore the emergence of the African-American culture in America," said Pamela Charshee, executive director of Carroll Park Foundation, about restoring this site a dozen blocks west.

Now the oldest house in the city—the only pre-Revolutionary plantation in a major metropolis—Mount Clare (1754–63) retains original Carroll family furnishings. A visit gives people a chance to see authentic interiors. Outside, the garden terraces ("falle garden"), orchard, and stable give a clear idea of what plantation life was like for Charles Carroll, Barrister (a distant cousin of Charles Carroll of Carrollton, the Signer) and Margaret Tilghman Carroll, his wife. Most of his time was spent as a self-described "Experiment-making Farmer," and she as an eager horticulturist who gave prize plants to furnish George and Martha Washington's orangerie at Mount Vernon.

"It's just such an extraordinary piece of good fortune that we are close to a major downtown that has so many people visiting already," said Ms. Charshee, when a $300,000 state grant aided restoration of Mount Clare as a wheat plantation and ironworks.

You can also explore what promoters call the most significant collection of railroadiana in the Western Hemisphere at the B&O Railroad Museum six blocks west at 901 W. Pratt Street (752-2490). In and around the largest circular (actually twenty-two-sided) industrial building in the world, exhibits include rolling stock ranging from 1830s steam engines to mammoth-sized diesels. On the track stands full-scale equipment used filming Walt Disney's *The Great Locomotive Chase*. You can also see a 12' × 40' HO-model layout.

From the site of the present museum there extended the first passenger railroad—"a river of iron," it was called—going over mountains to the Ohio River. Inside, you will see the first American railroad station and the spade used by Charles Carroll of Carrollton (*Tour 4*) at the laying of the first stone on the route, July 4, 1828. As you explore the forty acres of the main repair yard, you can learn how this "Railroad University of the United States" (as it was called) taught the world how to build trains and how to keep improving a rail system.

As if that weren't enough distinction, this site was

also where in 1844 the first telegraph message was received. Inventor Samuel F. B. Morse telegraphed "What hath God wrought" from the Capitol in Washington, D.C. During the Civil War, telegraph operators here used the American Morse Telegraph Code to conduct train movements for Union troops. You can take short rides along the original right of way as far as Mount Clare and, occasionally, to Ellicott City. Ask for a timetable.

An extension of this tour by car to the west along Lombard Street carries you into the literary heritage of West Baltimore. Signs direct you to the Poe House (203 N. Amity Street), where Edgar Allan Poe spent part of his apprenticeship writing stories and poems, and to the H. L. Mencken House (1524 Hollins Street), where that author lived and wrote during sixty-seven of his seventy-six years.

Other sophisticated writers in that part of town included Russell Baker, columnist and author of the Pulitzer Prize–winning memoir *Growing Up;* F. Hopkinson Smith, novelist and artist; and Dashiell Hammett, creator of *The Maltese Falcon* and the genre of hard-boiled detective stories. Not long ago, on the edge of the city northwest of here, the ashes of writer Dorothy Parker came to rest in a rose garden at the national headquarters of the NAACP. She had bequeathed her estate to that organization. It seems fitting to have that sophisticated writer at rest in a town with such a strong literary tradition. Who knows what master works she would have written had she worked here? And what might have come from two other geniuses (both born in Baltimore), Frank O'Hara and Frank Zappa, if they had stayed here?

I think Baltimore *is* a propitious place for writers because it has a distinct personality, does not seem as impersonal as many other cities, and has a heavily mixed ethnic population which, in addition to its being a large port, gives it character.

Josephine Jacobsen, Baltimore poet and short-story writer, letter to author (1984)

Cathedral Hill and Charles Street

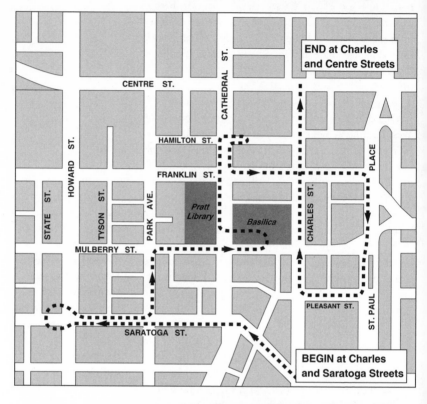

COME HERE FOR:

- Churches of significance to the widow of Stonewall Jackson, President Woodrow Wilson, and architects Benjamin Henry Latrobe, Robert Cary Long Jr., and Maximilien Godefroy
- Places connected with writers Upton Sinclair (and his Proper Baltimore mother) and Edgar Allan Poe (and his soon-to-be child bride)
- Two restaurants hallowed by time and favor
- The birthplace of major Baltimore institutions, and places where *New Yorker* writer Tony Hiss says the essence of the town is stored
- This city's one-time rival to London's Bond Street and Paris's rue de la Paix, where well-heeled women equaled the city's reputation for high fashion
- "Cardiac Hill," N Alley, and "Murder Alley"
- An eighteenth-century rectory where poets Edna St. Vincent Millay, Carl Sandburg, Robert Frost, and Amy Lowell read to the Poetry Society of Maryland

Here you can touch the first of Baltimore's golden ages, 1815–45. This age coincided with the new nation's setting its new ways in stone and brick—ways that affect everything to come. On this first hill above the Inner Harbor, the energy of a boomtown created major institutions. "Chapel Hill" was its original name. Their buildings remain even if their present offspring stretch over the region. Here, too, Edgar Allan Poe garnered his first fame. And—another achievement—these hilltop buildings gave Baltimoreans their architectural voice.

"[Rooms] where some of the sweetness that the city distilled and stored up" were recently listed by a *New Yorker* writer with Baltimore roots, Tony Hiss—the restaurant of the Woman's Industrial Exchange and the big room of the children's library in the Enoch Pratt Free Library. "'So here you are at last,' the rooms seem to be saying."

You will have time to sample several more of Baltimore's best rooms. Of all interiors to see, go inside the old cathedral—now the Basilica of the Assumption. Critics rank it near the top of America's most handsome churches. A short block from it, Old St. Paul's Rectory creates an eighteenth-century corner of serenity.

A walk down Charles Street on a fine autumn afternoon is still a romantic and stimulating adventure. To these old eyes the girls are ever pretty, and the shops are ever charming, and the gaunt monument to the northward is ever a thing of beauty. This is my home, my stamping ground, my roost. Here I can stretch my legs and feel at ease.

H. L. Mencken, *Evening Sun* (c. 1913)

177

HISTORY

Proper Baltimoreans have long wanted to escape city violence. In August 1835, for instance, rioters tore apart bankers' houses downtown, brick by brick. "The very valuable libraries of Mr. [Reverdy] Johnson and Mr. [John] Glenn were destroyed, worth many thousands of dollars," reported Col. J. Thomas Scharf. "All their stock of wine and many other valuable articles fell prey to the crowd, and were offered for sale at small prices."

For a century before that attack, Cathedral Hill had nurtured lasting institutions of the Establishment, begun in 1729 when Baltimore-Town was laid out, with lot number 19 assigned to St. Paul's Anglican parishioners. Near that church, Roman Catholic leaders built their St. Peter's. The faithful must really have wanted to go to church: the hill was so steep.

Then a brewery intruded near the churches and so did the rich, who abandoned the crowded waterside to escape malaria, yellow fever, and Baltimore mobs. Up here they lived well. In 1820, for instance, Kitty and Benjamin Cohen gave the town's first fancy-dress ball in their townhouse opposite St. Paul's. Privileged guests entered the ballroom banked with flowers from the conservatory, Mr. Cohen's pet project. Other residents

Front of cathedral

also accomplished more lasting things. In a Greek
revival mansion here, for example, Johns Hopkins
planned his gift of Johns Hopkins Hospital and Johns
Hopkins University.

For decades Cathedral Hill charmed anybody who
was anybody. Naturally, the first physician-in-chief of
Johns Hopkins Hospital, Dr. William Osler, moved here
with his wife and son and saw patients. As a doctor he
was so popular that people said he should take over
Druid Hill Park as his waiting room.

After 1900 such luminaries shed an aura on shops
and offices created in the old houses. The street attracted
the rich and almost-rich to shop or consult a fashionable
doctor or get a will made. Here brides-to-be selected
tableware from America's oldest silversmith, Kirk's. And
outside dressmakers' shops, White House chauffeurs
waited for First Ladies. Paris's rue de la Paix had a rival.

Today you are exploring a National Register historic

district. Filled with people by day, it empties at night, like so many American downtowns. Yet early builders of this district established institutions and habits of thinking still familiar in Baltimore. "The 'thereness' [Baltimore's character] had been established [by 1820]," wrote architectural historian Phoebe Stanton, with these orderly rows, church domes, and institutions.

TOUR

Starting Point: Constellation Dock, Inner Harbor; then St. Paul's Church corner, North Charles Street and Saratoga Street
Length of walk: One and three-quarters hours
Snacks and restrooms: Woman's Industrial Exchange, fast-food outlets in the 300 block of North Charles Street, Louie's Bookstore Café
Transportation: To begin, use the bus on North Charles Street (northbound) and, to return, St. Paul's Street (southbound)

Begin at Constellation Dock. You can easily walk from there to the tour's beginning: cross Light Street and walk one block to Charles Street. Turn right and proceed uphill five blocks to Saratoga Street. An alternative is to take a bus from the Charles Street corner and get off just beyond Saratoga Street.

Here at the end of the 300 block of North Charles Street, at the corner of Saratoga Street, you see a panorama of architectural styles going back 200 years. Facing the columnar Washington Monument visible in the distance, on both sides of the 300, 400, and 500 blocks of Charles Street are lines of almost uninterrupted rowhouses little changed since 1830, except for shop windows inserted a century ago.

Immediately on the left, opposite the church, you face contemporary brown-brick shops, apartment towers, and the Downtown Campus of Johns Hopkins's School of Continuing Studies.

Across Saratoga Street stands a curious, triangular-shaped building, a recycled YMCA. Called the Morris Building (1873), it retains Victorian assertiveness although no longer topped with its original turrets and towers. Its entrance of more recent date doesn't suit the building at all.

By contrast, design and decoration fit together on the exterior of an art deco office tower (301) just across Charles Street. At street level, a Jazz Age explosion of

Palladian window of old
St. Paul's rectory

zigzags, chevrons, and fans combines with vines crawling
over screens. If you glance upward, you can see greenery
overflowing a roof garden created there with a pond and
plants. Go into the lobby for 1920s excitement in marble
and bronze.

On the fourth corner, St. Paul's Episcopal Church
stands as the fourth church of that name on this site
(685-5537). Built in style of an Italian Romanesque basilica, it lacks a planned tall tower. A very recent addition
of bells fulfills a tower's purpose. An Italian antecedent
would be even more pronounced if the exterior of Baltimore red brick was painted the color of sunny Italian
stone as it was until the 1940s.

St. Paul's parish, founded in 1692, advertises as the
"Mother Church of Baltimore Episcopalians." Historical
anecdotes have attached to it like barnacles to a ship.
For instance, eighteenth-century rector William West
pleaded with the two chief leaders of the Methodists,
Thomas Coke and Francis Asbury, to give up their
defection from the established Anglican church, "a loss
accruing to each by what seemed another needless divi-

sion in the Christian Church." West failed. Now America has many more Methodists than Episcopalians.

Another curiosity centers on a homily called "Desiderata" that begins, "Go placidly amid the noise & haste, & remember what peace there may be in silence." It crops up wherever English is read and souls are worried. "Found in Old Saint Paul's Church, Baltimore; Dated 1692," says an identifying note. In fact, the piece dates only from the early twentieth century, was written by a Midwesterner, and has no tie to St. Paul's other than its having been reprinted in a church publication.

In 1854–56, architect Robert Upjohn replaced the third in a series of St. Paul's Church structures on the site. When its 1814 predecessor burned, Upjohn incorporated into the façade two salvaged bas-relief stone panels carved by Antonio Capellano. Look for them flanking the rose window above three large entrance arches. Best seen from across Charles Street, the left-hand panel exhibits Moses with the tablets of the Law and the right, Christ bearing bread.

Inside the church, Upjohn created a sense of great space with a basilica form, with clerestory windows above the nave and high overarching wooden trusses supporting the roof. Some critics think that the architect succeeded here less well than he did in the Gothic style of Trinity Church, New York. The sanctuary is a bit of a barn.

The window under the chancel's barrel vault came from Louis Comfort Tiffany's studio. "A dim religious light" from stained glass could suffuse interiors of Baltimore churches as soon as gas lights came into use. So colored glass lighted memorial services were held here on the deaths of English monarchs from Queen Victoria on, as well as for centenaries of Florence Nightingale and Gen. Robert E. Lee. Baltimoreans love looking back.

St. Paul's parish spawned educational and charitable institutions just as the Roman Catholic archdiocese did. Vestryman John Eager Howard must have helped create what Capt. Basil Hall noted in 1829, "that active desire to contribute to the wants of the wretched, which we met with in all parts of America, but in no place more conspicuously than in Baltimore." In 1799 the church established an orphanage. The vestry opened a school for boys in 1868 with "nine boarders and a few day scholars." Today both a boys' and a girls' high school (and coed elementary school) carry the St. Paul's name far out in the Green Spring Valley.

From the church, cross Charles Street and proceed west

[St. Paul's is] the aristocratic or fashionable church of the Episcopalians. . . . The congregation was very large, at least a thousand, and most fashionably and expensively dressed. . . . [The Rev. Dr. William E. Wyatt's sermon] was a fine composition, and beautifully read, with a full rich voice and great dignity of manner. . . . indeed Dr. Wyatt might pass very well for a High-Church Oxford Divine, as orthodox, gentlemanly and elegant as could be desired.

James S. Buckingham, an English author who visited Baltimore three times in 1840

on Saratoga Street a short block to where the street bends at Cathedral Street. As you pass a parking lot on the right, you are passing the site, unmarked, of Johns Hopkins's town residence. (His country house, Clifton, still dominates Clifton Park in East Baltimore.) Here he planned his world-class research university and hospital. Today they employ more people than anyone else in town.

In life, Hopkins had by then earned a reputation for being crusty, disagreeable, and vindictive. Born a Quaker in Anne Arundel County south of the city, he left his family's farm at age 17 to work in a Baltimore uncle's wholesale grocery. Family history has it that after rejection as suitor of a first cousin, he embraced money-making and never married. Neither did she.

On your right, above the corner, rises a silver historic marker (on the lawn) telling about St. Paul's Rectory. *From it, go back to 24 W. Saratoga Street and climb the entrance stone steps to the eighteenth-century rectory.*

When you approach the house, notice that the red-brick broad front centers on an unusually early rectangular transom over the door. Seen from the street, house and framing trees appear to stand on a pedestal like a rare icon in a museum display.

At the door, turn and look at the view rectors have faced: at first, harbor ships and homes of their tithing owners, and now, the business towers that flank Liberty Street below. Until recently, rectors resided in this house —living "over the shop," as it were. Their dinner talk often broke off when a troubled parishioner knocked. "But after all," wrote rector Halsey Cook in 1987, "they partly are what the church is about."

Longest residents, the Reverend Dr. Arthur Kinsolving's family, appointed a son to sit in his bedroom window with a .22-caliber rifle and shoot the rats in the backyard. "His father could never understand," wrote Cook, "that the chickens he kept there might be a contributing factor."

If you have called ahead of time for a tour, you may ring the doorbell (685-2886). Interior woodwork of about 1815 and furnishings of 1830 show how the house looked after it had been lived in for a generation. Some furniture came from a 1970s installation in the Maryland governor's residence, an effort to showcase the state's antiques. Gov. William Donald Schaefer replaced them with what critics called "Motel Modern."

Inside the entrance hall you will see the house treasure, a winding stair installed in a polygonal bay projecting out the back of a deep hall. Poet Carl Sandburg

compared it to a treble clef sign in music. He saw that
analogy when he read to the Poetry Society of Maryland
here. Edna St. Vincent Millay and other writers also
came to read when the rector's wife, poet Sally Bruce
Kinsolving, was the society's founder. "Writers are thorny
folk," wrote one of the members, "but [she] disarms any
fretful quills." One of her grandsons headed the National Gallery of Art (John Carter Brown) and another,
the National Aquarium at Baltimore (Nicholas Brown).

When you leave the rectory, pause a minute to look
at the wooden door in the stone wall. It supposedly leads
to a service tunnel for coal, champagne, and anything
else deemed unsuitable to enter the front door. From the
rectory steps you will notice four quite diverse streets
splaying out.

The view is dreary. But with imagination you can
light this corner with political as well as literary stars.
Clay Street, the narrow street leading off to the right
from the downhill slope of Liberty Street, remembers
Henry Clay of Kentucky—"Gallant Harry of the West."
In Baltimore the Whig party twice nominated him for
the presidency. He lost. The line "I would rather be right
than be president," he later said, had been applauded
beyond its merits.

Like Clay, we all love liberty as much as the patriotic
street namers did, but we love raggle-taggle Liberty
Street less. Fires and progress long ago removed significant buildings such as a German church. Because the
street paralleled the original northwest boundary of
Baltimore-Town, it angles away from the downtown
grid pattern.

Across Liberty Street from Clay Street you see a parking garage on the site of a political hotbed, the Rennert
Hotel. In the early 1900s, reforming newspapermen
attacked politically corrupt Democrats headquartered
here. "[Baltimoreans] are always, in fact, against the
newspapers," said H. L. Mencken, "and they are always
in favor of what reformers call political corruption. They
believe it keeps money in circulation, and makes for a
spacious and stimulating communal life." The hotel
starred in literary history, too. Native-born novelist
Dashiell Hammett put the hotel in his murder mystery
The Glass Key (1931) as scene of a battle between Baltimore's political bosses.

*Turning right from the rectory steps, walk along Sara-
toga Street and cross Cathedral Street.* At 106 W. Saratoga
Street, Marconi's Restaurant survives from Mencken's
lunching days. His table stood in the northeast corner of

the front dining room. You will look in vain for this restaurant's counterpart in other cities. "The floor is linoleum," wrote a *New York Times* reporter recently, "the waiters still mix drinks at the table and leave the bottle." On the stoop and along this block of Saratoga Street, notice Baltimore ornamental ironwork made from the 1830s on: for instance, 106 exhibits a wrought-iron lyre flanked by concentric diamonds, designed by German immigrant Andrew Merker in 1846.

On the right, at the end of the same block, St. Alphonsus Roman Catholic Church (837-7310) has held its corner sturdily since 1845. "A beautiful monument of German art," said the German priest-in-charge. Actually, the interior with its fan vaulting and forest of columns looks like an English abbey. "Dense, glittering exuberance [within]," wrote architectural historian Phoebe Stanton, "[St. Alphonsus] suggests the fabulous interiors Charles Barry and Pugin developed for the Houses of Parliament a few years later." A Baltimore foundry made cast-iron window tracery, vaulting ribs, and interior columns, as well as the steeple. "We are not aware of any church yet executed in this country," wrote architect Robert Cary Long Jr., "that has a ceiling so elaborately ribbed as this will be." Outside, the German-style steeple rises in stages, Long said, "like the joints of a telescope."

Further distinction comes from early pastor Father John Nepomucene Neumann (1811–60). In 1979 he was canonized as the first American male to achieve sainthood. Born in Prachatitz, Bohemia, Neumann came to America hoping to become a missionary. In 1842 he took the full vows of the Redemptorist Fathers in Baltimore's St. James's Church. As vice-provincial of the order here, he saved the African-American Oblate Sisters from dissolution (*Tour 9*).

"He rejoiced when, in 1851, he was permitted to become pastor of the unfinished church of St. Alphonsus, Baltimore," says the *Dictionary of American Biography*. Next, he reluctantly became bishop of Philadelphia. By then he had come to feel at home with Baltimoreans. "Even the bitterest Know-Nothings [anti-immigrant voters] found little to condemn in a man who could accept affronts with forgiving humility."

Cross Park Avenue and loop down and back along the block to Howard Street. For a century at least, most of the rowhouses have had shops on the street level. Recently, at 218 Saratoga Street, Maryland Art Place has been exhibiting contemporary art (962-8565). At 222 W. Saratoga Street you can see one of many substantial fire-houses built after the Big Fire of 1904. City fathers built well because earlier they had neglected to build any fire-houses at all in the district that burned. Now, converted, this firehouse serves as offices for the North Charles Street Design Organization on the first floor and the business owners' residence above.

Across Saratoga Street from the firehouse you can find the entrance to a tiny shopping arcade (219). When you reach Howard Street, look across to the southwest corner at a granite treasure chest of a building. With walls seven feet thick, it is reminiscent of the Strozzi Palazzo in Florence. In 1903 local architect Joseph Sperry designed this headquarters of Provident Savings Bank. An expansive man, Sperry had ample physical girth, wags said, paralleled by that of his bank.

Provident Bank fathered branch banking among mutual savings banks nationally. "Cultivating habits of thrift and prudence among the wage-earning classes" was Provident branch managers' goal. Earlier a Portu-guese ex-sailor originated the concept of bank branches when he was janitor at the Friends Gospel Mission in South Baltimore.

To the left of the old bank you see the northern end of what was until the 1960s a complex of department stores: Hutzler's, Hochschild Kohn's, Hecht's, and Stew-art's. Their shells remain and so do memories of happy, crowded shopping for many Baltimoreans. As far back as 1920 civil rights protesters marched here.

Straight ahead, on the left-hand side at 415 W. Sara-toga Street, G. Krug & Son carry on an iron-working foundry dating back to the eighteenth century. If you make a loop to see it on a weekday, you can step inside to hear the hammering and see part of the works.

Retrace your steps up Saratoga Street one block to Park Avenue and turn left at Park Avenue. You are walking along what survives of a once-busy Chinatown. This area has decayed mostly because officials' attention was fixed so long on the Inner Harbor, not on streets of small businesses and houses like what you are passing. Maybe you can see beneath the decay to an old beauty.

Walk one block along Park Avenue to Mulberry Street, turn right and go uphill one block to Cathedral Street. No-tice on the right three classic Baltimore rowhouses, dis-tinguished by unusual arrangement of white marble steps, ironwork, and bright colored wooden doors. They show what the whole district, rehabilitated, could look like. In 1831 Baltimore upper-class residences like these made the setting of a French novel, *Marie, or Slavery in the United States* (1835), by Gustav de Beaumont. Though now forgotten, it portrays well slavery's evil effect on Baltimoreans. The effect the author had observed when he visited with Alexis de Tocqueville, who was collecting material for his *Democracy in America* (1835). The beautiful young Marie is made a victim for having a touch of African-American blood.

At the southwest corner of Cathedral and Mulberry streets rises the modern archdiocesan headquarters of the Roman Catholic Church. In post–Civil War days, the School of Law of the University of Maryland occupied the site, its faculty consisting almost entirely of ex-Confederates, including Charles Marshall, General Lee's military secretary at Appomattox (*Tour 12*).

When you stand at this corner, you survey the site of a French encampment before the 1781 battle at Yorktown. In Baltimore, Comte de Rochambeau had worked out strategy with George Washington. The French troops' splendid uniforms contrasted with the rag-tag Americans'. For the French, adoring ladies in Philadelphia and Baltimore sewed shirts. Some of the women, we are told, wondered how men on an arduous march could be "so ruddy and handsome" and how "there could possibly be Frenchmen of so genteel an appearance."

On the front of 11 W. Mulberry Street, you will see a plaque saying that here in 1831 a committee awarded Edgar Allan Poe a $50 prize for his short story, "A Ms. Found in a Bottle." This recognition marked the beginning of his career in prose fiction. Later Poe learned that the judges had thought his "The Coliseum" the best poem in the competition, but could not bring themselves to award both fiction and poetry prizes to the same writer. So Poe went out and picked a street fight with the winning poet.

Next door to 11 Mulberry Street at 9, you see an 1835 mansion where banker John B. Morris moved when

---

[About to be married to a Frenchman in a Baltimore church, Marie was greeted by a great tumult at the door.] "The rioters!" cried an apprehensive voice. The cry flew from mouth to mouth; then a dismal silence fell below the sacred vault. The noise of a disorderly multitude could be heard without, sounding like the rumblings of an approaching storm. Driven by an impetuous wind the thundercloud sweeps on, and already the lightning is upon our heads! "Death to the colored people! To the church! To the church!" These terrible shouts re-echoed from all about; terror seized the assembled faithful; the priest grew pale, his knees failed him, the ring that was to unite us fell from his hand! Marie, paralyzed with fear, became insensible and reeled; I gave the swooning maiden the support of that arm which an instant later would have embraced my beloved wife.

Gustav de Beaumont, *Marie, or Slavery in the United States* (1835)

John Hazlehurst Boneval Latrobe: Chameleon

Latrobe, the host member of the committee that selected Poe's story, became one of Baltimore's nineteenth-century luminaries. Son of architect Benjamin Henry Latrobe, he did drafting for his father at age 15. In 1831 he designed the entrance to this, his own house, and later may have supervised adding the portico to his father's cathedral. He made a fortune as lawyer for the B&O and, in Russia, for the Baltimore Winans family, builders of the Moscow–St. Petersburg railroad.

To keep his wife from retreating to warm winters in her native Natchez, Mississippi, he designed the somewhat efficient fireplace stove popularly known as the Baltimore heater or Latrobe stove. It prefigured central heating by heating a room as well as sending warm air through a flue to the room above. "As to JHBL being ashamed of the stove," wrote his grandson Ferdinand Latrobe Jr., "he was tickled to death to make $50,000 out of it." Latrobe pushed Baltimoreans ahead as a founder of Druid Hill Park, the Maryland Historical Society, and the Maryland Institute and College of Art. His son Ferdinand served as mayor of Baltimore longer than anyone else. A sidelight on the house: in the early 1900s 11 W. Mulberry Street was rented by Dr. Adelbert J. Volck, now famous for anti-Yankee—especially anti-Lincoln—cartoons.

Of this interview, the only one had with Mr. Poe, my recollection is very distinct indeed. . . . Gentleman was written all over him. His manner was easy and quiet, and although he came to return thanks for what he regarded as deserving them, there was nothing obsequious in what he said or did.

John H. B. Latrobe, recalling an 1833 interview in an address at the unveiling of the Poe Monument in Westminster Cemetery (1875)

antibank demonstrators trashed his Monument Square house. Notice the Greek revival white marble porch and a bow window. In 1892 the Roman Catholic Archdiocese joined 9 W. Mulberry Street with 7 and added a wing to accommodate the Cathedral School. In the 1960s the Academy of Science housed its exhibits here, and in 1976 a law firm rehabilitated the building as offices.

From the Latrobe-Poe landmark, cross the street to read the historical marker attached to the cast-iron fence bounding the cathedral grounds. This cathedral—the Basilica of the Assumption (727-3564)—rises as the

Man repairing pillar

lengthened, graceful shadow of John Carroll. In 1776, he and his cousin Charles Carroll of Carrollton had journeyed to Montreal with Benjamin Franklin in a futile move to win support for the American Revolution. Then, in 1790, John Carroll became the first bishop in the Roman hierarchy of the United States. Until 1804 he held power all the way from the Canadian border to Florida and west to the Mississippi River. One of his achievements was founding Georgetown University, President Bill Clinton's alma mater.

Long ago, sailors knew they were approaching Baltimore when they saw this cathedral dome crowning its hill. Today sentimental Baltimoreans prize an 1839 engraving of that view. "The Constantinople View of Baltimore" made the new American boomtown look like the ancient Byzantine capital. Baltimore's domes and spires resemble old hilltop mosques such as Suleymaniye Mosque above the Golden Horn. Cathedral Hill floats a world above the port.

If the gate to the cathedral grounds is unlocked, walk through and follow the path to the left past a statue of James Cardinal Gibbons (1834–1921). Study his face for Irish-American amiability and political savvy. The cardinal founded Catholic University of America.

Now enter the cathedral under the portico. Here is a chance to see two monumental structures bow to each other across Cathedral Street. The old cathedral (1804), of course, doesn't really bow to anything: it wears the crown. But the twentieth-century Central Library of the Enoch Pratt Free Library does keep a discreet, yet dignified place. It sits long and low, hugging the sidewalk. By

contrast, the cathedral rises from a dais of lawns sur-
mounting a black platform created by ornamental iron
fencing painted black.

Upon entering the cathedral, you may at first be disappointed. While when it was built, it was one of the
largest structures in the country, now the interior may
seem small and plain. The scale and the plainness, of
course, create what architectural critic Nikolaus Pevsner
called the quiet directness of the architecture both inside
and out. "As one enters the great west door, the beautiful
openness of the space envelops one, and the way in
which part leads to part and the little to the big . . .
makes for one of America's truly distinguished interiors."

In 1804 Benjamin Henry Latrobe's design appeared
unconventional. The whole interior, vaulted in masonry,
struck some observers as new and daring. "The engineering needed to create a major crossing vault of 65
feet, and a double dome at the center crossing of 60
feet" was, according to Pevsner, a true test of Latrobe's
skill. The ten-foot gap between the two domes admitted
indirect light, what the French call *lumière mystérieuse.*

In 1937 Pope Pius XI elevated the cathedral to a
minor basilica. As such, it displays a papal umbrella to
the right of the altar and a papal bell to the left. When
the pontiff visits, as we hope he will, Baltimoreans are
prepared. After this structure received its new status, the
name and function of cathedral descended to the much
larger Cathedral of Mary Our Queen (1959), far to the
north. Until recently, the hats of Cardinal Gibbons and
Cardinal Shehan hung dustily up front. Now they are
put away to protect them. Earlier belief held that until
the hat disintegrated, the soul of the deceased had to
wait for heaven. Ask the guide to show the crypt beneath the archepiscopal throne. Here lie buried a number of prelates, including Archbishop John Carroll.

*After exiting the cathedral, walk on the right-hand path
around the north side of the cathedral.* Look across N
Alley to see the sculpture on the side of a garage (1991),
designed by Linda DePalma, whose cutout sculpture
you saw in University Center (*Tour 7*).

*From that view, go down the front steps and cross
Cathedral Street to the Enoch Pratt Free Library.* In 1933
this building replaced the original library structure that
Enoch Pratt had built in 1885 at the Mulberry Street end
of the present site. Together with Andrew Carnegie, he
also built branch libraries (*Tour 3*). "The general welfare
needs the gift of a man's business ability," wrote Mayor
Theodore R. McKeldin, "including his time, his

Statue of Cardinal Gibbons

thought, his personal effort, even more than it needs his money." Pratt gave his all.

Chief librarian Joseph Wheeler and architect Clyde M. Fitz broke with tradition by not making patrons ascend steps to enter, the way people always had entered such solemn places as churches, museums, and libraries. Fitz also copied department store display windows all down the block—full of books—to lure passersby inside.

Interior decoration reflects a 1920s buoyancy. Marble, bronze, and rich woods radiate wealth. Here centered a collection of books, a staff, a system of branch libraries —all admired across the country. Below the skylight in the Great Court, just past the entrance lobby, wall murals portray great printers and presses. Three early Maryland printers join the list, including eighteenth-century Baltimorean Mary Katherine Goddard, who often took over editing her brother William's newspaper.

Below those murals hang oil portraits, full length, of all six seventeenth- and eighteenth-century lords Baltimore. All but one were painted by prominent artists. Note especially on the wall to the left of the entrance, Gerard Soest's portrait of the second lord (1606–75). Responsible for the Act of Religious Toleration, he promoted emigration, as is here shown by grandson Cecil's touching a 1635 Maryland map (*Tour 5*). Notice an African-American boy standing behind young Cecil in this advertisement of the new colony.

Go straight ahead to the Reference Room and look at the ceiling there. Modeled on one in the Vatican, it is moulded and painted in elaborate designs. When you return to the main hall, turn right and look for stairs to the children's room. Walk down to discover another of Tony Hiss's choice rooms containing, you recall, some of the sweetness that the city stored up. Upon entering the room, walk to the right and look out the bow window above the fish pond to see where the boy Hiss used to enter directly from Mulberry Street. "As you descended through the terraces, the walls of the library changed texture, so that instead of walking past fluted pilasters forty feet high—as you do when approaching the main entrance—you walked next to a country-cottage wall of rough-cut fieldstone. By now, you had little doubt that you were about to enter 'a magical place.'"

Here in the sunny room children listen to stories in front of the fireplace. Its ornamental, massive fire screen and andirons came from the nearby Weisburger foundry. "You remember Hugo who ran the Peabody Bookshop on Charles Street," said Mary S. Wilkinson, a librarian, who recalled that the Weisburgers also made fireplace

---

The Cathedral . . . walls and roof are finished and a shoal of Irish labourers are busied on the interior. It is rather singular that they [church fathers] have not attempted the Gothic in this building; probably the great expense of the style may have been the cause of the Roman Doric being preferred. The principal entrances are arched, and a few pilasters carried round the walls are its principal ornament; the size and disposition of the windows [of translucent, not stained, glass], with the crossing of the transept, have been so managed as to throw into the body of the church a strong depth of shadow, the holy gloom of which will doubtless be esteemed highly conducive to genuine religious emotion, and which at least we must grant to be no way inappropriate in that ritual, of which the burning of candles forms so important a portion.

John Duncan, visiting from Scotland (1818)

equipment for the Poe Room and staff lounge of the Pratt.

Through the main entrance on Cathedral Street bookworms and others come for refuge. One of the happiest was H. L. Mencken (*Tour 7*). Today a gift of Mencken's letters, memorabilia, and books enrich the Pratt. All Menckeniana is carefully tended in the Mencken Room, open to scholars always and to the public on a Saturday nearest Mencken's September 12 birthday. The Pratt profits from publication of Mencken's treasure trove of manuscripts left in its care, including his diary. The money is welcome.

When you emerge from the Pratt Library, turn left to the corner of West Franklin Street. Across Cathedral Street you face the new home of Our Daily Bread, a 100-seat soup kitchen run by Associated Catholic Charities. Every day up to 1,000 people line up for lunch. They lunch in the Harry and Jeanette Weinberg Building, built in 1991 at a cost of over $1 million. "Many people are just one paycheck away from being homeless," said the structure's architect, Adam Gross. "They may have lost their money, but they haven't lost their dignity."

The entrance to the Weinberg is at the corner of Cathedral Street and N Alley. The N is what is left of an unimaginative alphabetizing of alleys by English surveyor Thomas Poppleton in 1816. This town offers a symphony of street names—such as Charles, Mount Royal, Baltimore, and Maryland. All of those names bring to mind spacious colonial times, unlike N Alley.

Cross Franklin Street to look at the corner brick church. Now filled by the New Psalmist Baptist Church congregation, it was built for a Scottish-American congregation and called the Franklin Street Presbyterian Church (1847). The front looks like an English Tudor gateway of the era when Presbyterianism began in Scotland. Through this church door passed such puritanical souls as Woodrow Wilson and the widow of Confederate Gen. Stonewall Jackson.

From the church cross Cathedral Street and turn left. Go to the first intersection (about 100 feet). Here turn right onto Hamilton Street.

Hamilton Street is a great street, what there is of it. Propinquity with Latrobe's cathedral and Godefroy's Unitarian Church lends enchantment. Only three blocks long, this street shelters two unprepossessing-looking clubs. For decades the two were segregated; that is, one for men, one for women. "That's a place [the women's club] where sherry is consumed," wrote one of the men, "where women bring their own bottles and mark the levels."

In recent years a few women have joined the originally all-male group. "The distinctive feature of the [14 West] Hamilton Street Club," wrote member Gerald W. Johnson, "is that it has no constitution or by-laws, no officers, no house rules, and no name, merely an address."

Each Hamilton Street organization bears the name of the street, although only the originally all-male club, at 14 West Hamilton Street, exhibits a portrait of Alexander Hamilton. That patriot's conservative politics accorded with those of the great street-namer, John Eager Howard. Political views of some present members may not be in accord. No discord over politics erupts into the street. Although quiet, neither club warrants the criticism a visitor once gave of the quiet, deadly formality in a certain London club: "A Duke's house—with the Duke lying dead upstairs."

These tiny houses at 10–16 W. Hamilton Street date from 1817 to 1824. When built, they fronted on a reservoir and had a view of the cathedral. Their architectural sophistication gives these houses a London look. If they were in that capital, the street setting would include brick walkways, ancient gas lighting, and a pub or two tucked away on a corner. This street looks unprepossessing, even scruffy.

Return to Franklin Street from Hamilton Street and there turn left. On the corner nearest Hamilton Street you pass a large building at 24 W. Franklin Street, originally built for the YMCA and now part of the Culinary Arts Institute (*Tour 5*). Go inside the lobby to examine Joseph Sperry's architectural drawing. As you proceed along the left sidewalk, notice contrasting styles of rowhouses. At 20, the entrance and the ironwork on the landing exhibit authentic 1820s Baltimore restraint.

As you walk along Franklin Street, look across the street above a parking garage entrance for a sculptured chair of the same era as the cathedral. Sculptor Linda DePalma's recent design places the chair on its side above a red ball. From seeing her art on the garage's other side, you may not be surprised at this juxtaposition.

Next, by contrast with 18 W. Franklin Street, at 16 and 14 you see examples of an 1870s eclectic style that changed the look of Baltimore rows ever after. If you are interested in styles of architecture, look carefully. Stone arches on the first story repeat Greek revival door surrounds of the 1830s. The oriel bay windows on the second stories have Gothic revival features, and the mansard roof is a simplified version of French Second Empire. In 1920, number 14 had display windows inserted in first and basement levels, and a discreet business sign hung out front. Other Cathedral Hill residences also went commercial then. This house has been tenanted, in turn, by a law bookstore, a corset shop, and an oriental porcelain shop.

Pause at the corner of Franklin and Charles streets to examine one of the city's greatest buildings. Architectural historians praise what they call the romantic classicism of the First Unitarian Church at 2–12 W. Franklin Street. "The meeting house . . . will be large and commodious," wrote pastor Jared Sparks, "and, as the architect, Mr. Godfroy [*sic*], is celebrated for his skill and taste, it will doubtless be a beautiful specimen of architecture, the most beautiful, it is said, of any in Baltimore."

So poor were the church's original 1818 acoustics, however, that sermons couldn't be heard beyond the first pew. "There has been a new church erected in our city for the dissemination of pernicious doctrines," wrote a rival clergyman, "but by the grace of God, nobody can hear what the minister has to say."

Eventually, church authorities had a ceiling constructed across the bottom of the dome to keep sounds from getting lost in the fifty-five-foot-high curve. And Unitarianism spread south and west with publication of William Ellery Channing's sermon preached at Sparks's installation. From this church Sparks went on to become chaplain of Congress, president of Harvard, and author of a popular life of Washington. He left behind as Unitarian leaders in this city philanthropists Enoch Pratt and George Peabody and artist Rembrandt Peale.

French architect Maximilien Godefroy again demonstrated, as he had in St. Mary's Chapel (*Tour 9*), that public architecture had to look different from residences. He stuccoed the brick walls and placed a large terracotta Angel of Truth, sculpted by Antonio Capellano, over the entrance. "The interior is profusely decorated," wrote John Duncan visiting from Scotland in 1820. "The ends of the pews are beautifully carved and bronzed in imitation of the antique. . . . The effect of the whole is certainly very splendid."

Outside on the corner, notice how what is left of a red-brick sidewalk next to the church runs high above the street. That present lowering of the 1820s roadway symbolizes the decline of Charles Street. That is not to say that the old prestige has died. Standing here you see marble façades above shop windows, pretentious fronts added in the early twentieth century when Charles Street rivaled the rue de la Paix. Today these shops still attract some proper Baltimoreans, although most people prefer malls.

"The cultural, social, spiritual and commercial backbone of our city" was the 1968 description of Charles Street by Isaac Lycett, president of the Charles Street Association. Even now, some of the town's favorite addresses hug Charles Street in a green wedge going north ten miles. Inside the wedge spread lawns of Roland Park, Guilford, and other preferred suburbs.

After you continue walking by crossing Charles Street, you will find other examples of the classic 1820s rowhouse at 6 (with old elaborate ironwork on two sides) and the twinned 8 and 10 E. Franklin Street.

When you reach St. Paul Place, look downhill to your left, along a nineteenth-century row that ends at Chimney House, supposedly dating from 1810 or so. It looks the way you always hope an antique house will look with its low windows and irregular shape. The whole hillside within your view would be Baltimore's match for Boston's Beacon Hill, had bulldozers stayed away.

Turn right and walk uphill on St. Paul Place. Other early houses remain, although front doors have been lowered at 330, 332, and 334 St. Paul Place. The house at 336 retains much early ornamentation, including iron grills on the first floor. That house was lived in by the Poultney family from the late 1850s to 1946.

Go right along St. Paul Place past Mulberry Street to the next corner, Pleasant Street, and turn right to go one block to Charles Street. Cardiac Hill was what this slope used to be called. Residents of this street 150 years ago must have been mountain goats, so steep is the incline. The view east down to Jones Falls, then plainly visible, resembled that down streets on Telegraph Hill in San Francisco. Below, at the corner of Davis Street, look for the tower of the Terminal Warehouse (1893–1912) built originally, said a notice, as "flour house," where flour was stored.

A fairly ancient institution survives on the right as you climb and enter Charles Street, the Woman's Industrial Exchange, a shop and restaurant (breakfast and lunch weekdays), at 333. "The cupcakes [are great]," said Nora Ephron, in town to shoot *Sleepless in Seattle.* "You can eat three or four of them and not feel bad about yourself."

Long before 1899, when the Exchange moved from across Charles Street, it purveyed chicken salad and em-

I remember meeting Mr. Poultney at Charles and Madison streets one Easter Sunday. The gala parade was passing. He had two children with him and one of them asked, "Cousin Walter, why are we standing here?" "Sir" Walter, whose raiment was particularly resplendent that Easter, replied with his charming smile, "To take the air, my dears, and to give the people pleasure."

Letitia Stockett, *Baltimore: A Not Too Serious History* (1928)

broidered baby caps. Impoverished ladies could sell their creations anonymously here, "protected," an observer said, "from a publicity which a generous nature shuns." The tearoom where you can eat breakfast and lunch displays what looks like 1950s black-and-white linoleum floor, and Naugahyde banquettes. Some waitresses recall the past, too. "All the ladies here are special," said customer Marlene Meseke, "but Marguerite [Schertle, age 90 when interviewed in 1991] has a sense of humor and she's very efficient. When you have Marguerite, you're in and out in an hour."

From the Exchange, walk to the left and cross Charles Street to Brown's Arcade at 326. In 1904 Gov. Frank Brown combined four rowhouses of 1810–20 for a European-style interior shopping mall. Eighty years later, an updating added postmodern arched doorways but retained many pressed-metal surfaces.

Across Charles Street from the Exchange, an alley once called Little Pleasant Street inspired the sobriquet of Murder Alley. Where the alley intersected Little Sharp Street, a gas lamp on an iron bracket scarcely lighted the way. "It was a dark and desperate looking place at night," wrote Meredith Janvier, "and men would scurry through on their way to the Rennert bar for a conference with 'Father' Smith, the jovial 'dispenser' at that popular café." Today you will find the spot less sinister. Walk fifty paces into the alley to see backs of houses that Poe saw when he came to one of them for his prize money.

Turn right from the Woman's Exchange and walk across Mulberry Street. Across Charles Street the corner residence of the archbishop dates from 1829, with a third floor, hyphens, and wings added in 1865. Cardinal Gibbons lived here and so did Lawrence Cardinal Shehan (whose name has been added to the street sign). This

---

One who will walk in Charles Street at the proper hour on any fine afternoon may behold a marvel—namely, the spirit of Baltimore incarnate. It is a great lady, perhaps eighty years old, but still erect, taking the air as she has taken it in good weather these sixty years. When she began the practice, Charles Street was the promenade of the fashionable, and everybody who was anybody was seen there in the afternoon.

When that small, black figure moves down Charles Street, it is as if the cathedral had suddenly started out for a stroll.

Gerald W. Johnson, *Century Magazine* (May 1930)

house connects at the back with the old cathedral of
Latrobe as it always has.

Pause at the corner of Charles and Hamilton streets
to look downhill on the right. The rowhouses you see
opposite the archbishop's residence and in adjacent
blocks date to the 1830s. Most houses now have street-
level shops. Although shops occupy first floors, you only
have to look above the shops to see the simple early Baltimore style of architecture. But behind austere brick
fronts, the original residents squandered fortunes on artifacts and decoration. They hired the Findlay brothers
of Howard Street to make and decorate chairs and tables
in Greek and Roman style. As moneyed citizens of our
early republic, they looked back to those admired civi-
lizations. "They were confident that they were doing
something great and new themselves," says *Antiques* editor Wendell Garrett. "Mushrooms of fortune" described
rich Baltimore merchants, according to a designer of
some furniture made by the Findlays, architect Benjamin Henry Latrobe.

Just as sour a view later came out in *The Jungle* and
other books of socialist Upton Sinclair. When in 1965
he visited 417 N. Charles Street (now demolished), he
couldn't say whether this or some other Baltimore
boardinghouse had been his birthplace. This address
proved proper enough for Sinclair's aristocratic Confederate lineage. But the man Upton rebelled against Baltimore's snobbishness. "I breathed that atmosphere of values based upon material possessions preserved for two
generations or more, and the longer the better," he
wrote. "Everything in my later life confirmed my resolve
never to 'sell out' to that class."

Descending the 500 block of Charles Street, you pass
Louie's, a café and bookstore. Here books compete for

The old New Mercantile [Library]—Baltimore has an odd nomenclature—was a long low room encir-
cled by a gallery. The room itself was the Victorian age in miniature. Strips of bright carpet were
stretched in convenient spots, and wicker rocking chairs were set accurately and thriftily before
each strip.

At the rear of the library there was a tiny little carpeted staircase leading to the gallery where
fame and dust contended. In summer it was a cavern of coolness and repose. In the winter when
the streets outside glittered like a jewel box, here was dusk and shadow, the atmosphere for
dreams. At length at five-thirty Miss Watkins (the shrewd, kindly, sensible librarian), bearing a large
sheet, approached the table devoted to new books, and with a motherly gesture covered them up
for the night.

Letitia Stockett, *Baltimore: A Not Too Serious History* (1928)

freshness with the food. Titles run to the arts and more advanced poetry and fiction. Out front, look up at the elaborate copper cornice. On the right farther downhill you can duck down a few steps into the Goodwill secondhand book store. Look for a new crop of old titles and phonograph records. Near it once stood the New Mercantile Library.

At the foot of the hill, you can take a breath in the park square of South Washington Place and decide whether to continue with Tour 11.

If you decide to return to the starting point in the Inner Harbor, you can walk back south along Charles Street. Or you can walk one block east from the park square on East Centre Street to St. Paul Street, where there is a bus stop thirty paces uphill to the right.

Lantern at entrance to
cathedral

Seton Hill, Park Avenue, and Antique Row

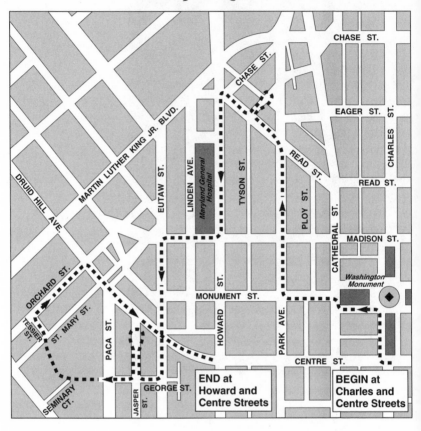

END at Howard and Centre Streets

BEGIN at Charles and Centre Streets

COME HERE FOR:

- Approaches to a saint's place—the home and chapel of the Roman Catholic Church's first American-born saint, St. Elizabeth Mother Seton
- Site important to Katharine Hepburn and Henry Fonda
- Sites important to African-American history, including recently restored Orchard Street Church and what may have been stops on the Underground Railroad
- Sites important to American education, including the first campus of Johns Hopkins University
- Five early nineteenth-century Gothic churches of architectural significance, including the chapel of America's first Roman Catholic seminary

- A feast of antiques, especially from Maryland's ample supply
- Genealogists' heaven in one of America's premier historical societies
- Unusually varied rows of eighteenth- and early nineteenth-century houses being restored

---

Seton Hill stands out as Baltimore's only official historic district named for a woman and the only one named for a saint. Moreover, Mother Elizabeth Ann Seton was the first American-born saint. You will be visiting her French-style house. There, and on several approach paths, you can (to use Henry James's phrase) "receive a deeper impression of vanished things": seminarians, riders of the Underground Railway, scholars that made Johns Hopkins University renowned, and a First Lady and a prince of the church who rallied for admission of women to the proposed Johns Hopkins Medical School.

Best of all, from this walk and talk you can examine Baltimore traits in a microcosm. For example, look for evidence of tolerance and openness to the world. That was why French Sulpician fathers built the first Roman Catholic seminary in a place known for separation of church and state and also for hospitality to diverse religious groups. For another characteristic, savor an elite elegance wherever you find it—and sophistication—as, for instance, on Park Avenue.

You also will stumble on Baltimoreans' habit of looking back. As evidence, Antique Row and the Maryland Historical Society come to mind. Although open to some innovation, Baltimoreans often practice skeptical conservatism.

HISTORY

In the eighteenth century this district gave visitors a good time. "Mr. Lux lives like a Prince," wrote John Adams of being entertained by the Lux family at their country estate, Chatsworth (now Seton Hill). A bit later, a Mr. Gray opened his formal pleasure garden modeled on London's fashionable Vauxhall. Here, for a fee, one could try escaping Maryland's steambath summer. Music and illumination by festoons of hanging lanterns inspired what advertisements promised, "a pleasing relaxation to the leisure hours."

In 1791 the district turned serious and French. Father François Charles Nagot, the superior, Father Jean Marie Tessier, and two other priests left Paris to found a branch of the French Seminary of St. Sulpice, organized in 1642.

So much modern architecture seems to be a contest to see who can produce the biggest box. No individuality. But look at these old houses and their little personal touches of decoration. The man who built them had enough feeling for them to leave his own mark on each one.

Rip Torn, *Baltimore Sun* (c. 1988)

Napoleon's anti-Church view drove them here. St.
Mary's Seminary of St. Sulpice in Baltimore opened in
the town of One Mile Tavern. That name told travelers
that they were only one mile from the harbor and still
outside city limits. This Roman Catholic seminary, the
first in the United States, sent generations of priests
throughout the nation.

Seminary buildings then filled most of what is now
St. Mary's Park. French planters and some of their slaves
fled Toussaint L'Ouverture's revolution in Haiti to settle
near St. Mary's.

In the fall of 1803 St. Mary's opened a college "open
to all without distinction of creed." For fifty-three years,
students came—3,000 in all—from Cuba, Brazil, Natchez,
Caracas, New Orleans, Charleston, and chiefly from
Baltimore. One wealthy student gave Mother Seton the
Emmitsburg, Maryland, property that became her permanent home. Today pilgrims go to her shrine there.

Somewhat later, runaway slaves heading north to
freedom found haven in so-called safe houses near the
St. Mary's seminary. At least one current resident reports
finding a hidden room in her cellar. Orchard Street
Church, originally built by and for African Americans,
supposedly served as a station on the Underground Railroad. Recent renovation retained what is called a memorial stairway leading down to where runaway slaves
might have hidden.

Other major institutions collected nearby. In 1876 the
trustees opened Johns Hopkins University on the eastern
approach to Seton Hill. The old campus, such as it was,
has vanished, and the university now has campuses on
North Charles Street, as well as in Columbia and Rock-
ville, Maryland, and Washington, D.C. Gone, too, is the
neighboring Academy of Music, where in 1876 Hopkins
worthies held inaugural ceremonies. Innovation marked
Hopkins as a new creature: no prayers or preachers appeared on the inaugural program. To give the main address, a popularizer of science, Thomas Henry Huxley,
came from England. "It was bad enough to invite Huxley," said one old-timer. "It were better to have asked
God to be present. It would have been absurd to ask
them both."

The university, in fact, imported much that was new
from abroad, especially its stated purpose "to promote
scholarship of the first order, to encourage investigators,
to develop the principle of research." As the first German-style research university in America, it soon made
its mark. Woodrow Wilson studied government here

and wrote a study of Congress. In 1879 saccharine, the first synthetic sweetening agent, came from the laboratory of Prof. Ira Remsen. Hopkins established the earliest scholarly journals and the first press in the country to carry a university's name.

The Eutaw Street Meeting House of orthodox Quakers (demolished) played a part in American higher education. Members such as Dr. James Carey Thomas led in establishing Johns Hopkins University with money bequeathed by Quaker Johns Hopkins. Another member, Martha Ellicott Tyson, invited Lucretia Mott and other prominent Quakers to plan coeducational Swarthmore College. Perhaps having twelve children of her own inspired her to think of a coed college.

One landmark that will probably have been demolished when you reach the corner of Eutaw Street and Druid Hill Avenue served as office and press of Afro-American Newspapers. Founded by John H. Murphy, who was born into slavery in 1840, it grew from its founding in 1892 into the largest African-American newspaper in the nation. "Most disputes of substance in the Negro community had a way of ending up in his editor [Carl J. Murphy's] office at the *Afro-American,* the newspaper through which he spoke from 1918 onward," said a *Sun* editorial writer.

For instance, by 1940, Pine Street had earned a reputation for the worst slum housing in the city. According to newspaper reports, the 900 block had tenants paying $3 a week, with rats galore, and an open drain. The area had produced four cases of typhus in the preceding three years. More extraordinary and terrible was a fence seven feet from the back walls of the houses that went up three stories high.

By contrast, the name Orchard Street recalls an eighteenth-century fruit orchard of landowner David Moore. He served as official flour inspector between 1781 and 1796, a position of importance when Baltimore was famous as the flour capital of the world. When he died, the *Federal Gazette* praised him as "a stranger to avarice and deception." Nearby, his namesake Moore Street has all but vanished under rerouting of commuter traffic.

Seton Hill's twentieth-century history proves that history is a holding action. For instance, although this district was placed on the National Register of Historic Places in 1975, St. Mary's Seminary's massive buildings fell to bulldozers that same year. Now many buildings along your route have been restored or rehabilitated. Many others still need "sweat equity" and cash. Luckily,

Backs of rowhouses

residents have given both. "There must be something in the city air or maybe the water," wrote Rene Parent recently in the *Sun,* "a secret compulsion to live near Chinese restaurants, an unspoken need to be within ten minutes of the Baltimore Museum of Art, an unreasonable fear of wall-to-wall carpeting, a subtle brainwashing that paralyzes the city person."

Starting Point: Constellation Dock, Inner Harbor; or the
ending point of Tour 8, South Washington Place park
square, at Charles and Centre streets

Length of tour: Two hours, including some browsing along
Antique Row

Snacks and rest stops: A McDonald's on West Franklin
Street at Greene Street; the Walters Art Gallery café;
deli on Read Street; cafe in Antique Row, 800 block
of Howard Street; Lexington Market

Transportation: To reach the beginning point at Centre
Street and Washington Place, you may simply continue from Tour 8. Or if you are starting fresh from
Constellation Dock, read directions at the beginning
of Tour 8.

---

*You will begin this tour where Tour 8 left off, at the foot of
Washington Place on Centre Street. Facing the Washington
Monument, you will be proceeding to the left and uphill.*
The tour will end with instructions on how to come
back to the starting point or, if you choose, to return to
the Inner Harbor.

If you failed to visit the Walters Art Gallery on Tour
8 or don't intend to take Tour 10, you may want to step
into the lobby (entered next to the overhead banner or
through the door facing the Washington Place park
square) to pick up a program and a floor plan. You may
decide to spend an hour here now, or you may plan to
tour when you return.

The Walters Art Gallery ranks high among Baltimore
places. Trying to tell you why in a few sentences is mad-
ness because the collections range over 5,000 years.
William T. Walters (*Tour 10*) made enough money in the
mid-nineteenth century to collect contemporary European and American sculpture and painting. His son
Henry went on to spend an average of $1 million a year
on art back when the dollar counted, during the first
third of the twentieth century.

*After you decide how to treat the Walters Art Gallery,
walk up South Washington Place, turn left at the monument, and walk west through West Mount Vernon Place to
Cathedral Street.* On the left, the Latham Hotel occupies
the site of the Garrett mansion, home in the last half of
the nineteenth century to the president of the B&O and
then to his daughter Mary Elizabeth.

En route, on your left, several classic early Baltimore
mansions remain, including a brownstone at 103 W.

Mary Elizabeth Garrett: Feminist

During the Civil War B&O president John Work Garrett sent coal to heat President Lincoln's White House and, more important, he put the B&O at the command of the Union army. After the war B&O stockholders prospered by exploitation of railroad workers. The exploitation also set off what has been called the Great Strike of 1877 (*Tour 6*).

"I have often wished . . . that Mary was a boy," her father wrote. "I know she could carry on my work after I am gone." In fact, she carried on her own work. With her inherited fortune, Mary Elizabeth influenced education for women everywhere. One project was creating, with a few other women, Baltimore's Bryn Mawr School for girls (*Tour 11*).

Mary Garrett also used money as bait to persuade the all-male board of Johns Hopkins University to admit women to the proposed medical school on an equal footing with men. As a second string attached to her crucial donation, she insisted on the highest standards of admission, including a bachelor's degree.

Osler and I sympathized with the fruitless efforts of Mr. Gilman to induce Miss Garrett to make certain comparatively slight, verbal alterations in the terms of the gift, the main change which we desired being the substitution of "equal" or "equivalent" for "same" in specifying the terms of admissions and training of women and men students, but she would not budge.

Dr. William H. Welch, recalling 1890

In May 1890 Mary Garrett formed the Women's Medical School Fund Committee. To win support she and the chief officer, First Lady Caroline Scott Harrison, gave a party in the Garrett mansion on Mount Vernon Place (now demolished) for 1,500 guests. "In a claret gown, trimmed in pearls and lace, [Mrs. Harrison] greeted guests at the Garrett house," wrote a reporter, "its Tiffany windows and carved wood walls aglow in the candle light." Cardinal Gibbons wore his scarlet robes, and "nearly every citizen of Baltimore known to society responded to the invitation." So, like her father, Mary won her point.

Monument Street that was built as a residence, became a hotel, reverted to a residence, and then was elevated to serve as the Maryland Episcopal diocesan headquarters. In 1991, when the church vacated the building, the diocese sold three Tiffany stained glass panels, each seventy-nine inches high, picturing a landscape framed by wisteria vines in lavender bloom. At auction the glass brought the highest price ever paid for an American window, $440,000. Some critics regarded the sale as vandalism since the church had removed an integral element of the residence.

Walk along West Monument Street to Park Avenue. At the corner of Park Avenue, consider exploring the Pratt House on that corner. With its Ionic portico poised above wide white marble steps, this house is as impressive, though plainer, than 1 W. Mount Vernon Place. It was built in 1847 and in 1870 enlarged with a mansard roof by Enoch Pratt. A Massachusetts man, he made a fortune selling hardware in what he called "the plain New England way."

Inside the mansion, a long parlor and a Gothic revival library show an austerity and stiff formality well suited to Victorian Mr. and Mrs. Pratt. Here the donor of the city's public circulating library locked up his own leather-bound full sets of books behind curtained glazed doors. To have a look at that room, you have to enter the main door of the Maryland Historical Society just along the block on the left at 201 W. Monument Street.

The Pratt mansion forms only part of the society's cornucopia of artifacts and memories. Four jampacked floors house classic examples of furniture, silver, china, textiles, including Baltimore Album quilts, portraits, photographs, and much more. No matter what your interests are, most likely something will catch your eye.

As you might expect, schoolchildren by the busload regularly arrive to learn Maryland history. Among other exhibits they explore the Radcliffe Maritime Museum (ship models, duck decoys); the Civil War exhibit (including uniforms from both sides, one of them bloodied); and the War of 1812 exhibit (featuring the manuscript of "The Star-Spangled Banner"). Society archives offer scholars manuscripts reaching back to seventeenth-century Calverts and Carrolls as well as a legacy from contemporary musician Eubie Blake's career (*Tour 4*).

After emerging from the society, turn right from the entrance and come back to the corner of Park Avenue. Across Monument Street from the Maryland Historical Society at 214 lived Dr. Ira Remsen, first professor of chemistry at Johns Hopkins University and its second president (1901 to 1912).

Here at the top of the 600 block, you can look downhill to survey remnants of distinguished rows. It is all right to contend with a few ghosts on a tour, providing they were all interesting people. In one of the demolished houses lived the first president of Johns Hopkins University and of Johns Hopkins Hospital, Daniel Coit

Gilman. From here his daughter Elisabeth carried forward his spirit of reform. She ran for governor on the Socialist ticket in 1945, when she was 78. "I'll frankly admit," she said, "I don't have a chance in the world of being elected. I'm running to educate the voters."

Among other ghosts in these blocks hover those of the pious sisters of Notre Dame at the Convent of the Visitation, as well as those of the great-nephew of the emperor Napoleon, Charles Joseph Bonaparte, and his wife. President Teddy Roosevelt appointed him attorney general and, later, secretary of the Navy. In those days Bonaparte's routine was to leave his Park Avenue home in time to take the 10 A.M. train to Washington, where he dispatched his Cabinet duties until lunchtime. He was ready to catch the 2 P.M. train home in time for a nap. Or so H. L. Mencken reported: "a truly fabulous compound of Sicilian brigand and Scotch blue nose, a pawky and cruel wit and yet the most humorless of men, a royalist in his every instinct and yet a professional democrat and Puritan wowser all his days long."

Here on the northeast corner of Monument Street and Park Avenue, you face a 150-year-old landmark, Grace and St. Peter's Episcopal Church. Its neat Park Avenue garden, parishioners tell us, makes an orderly Heaven, and its Monument Street garden creates a wild image of Hell. Built in 1852, this church was patterned on Philadelphia's stylish St. Mark's.

With this building, Baltimoreans pioneered the use of brownstone, "that luckless material" (as visitor Henry James called it). That stone appealed to the builder because it was easier to cut than granite or marble, and lighter to handle. The design also pioneered locally by imitating ancient English rural churches, with projecting vestibule, transepts, and a semi-detached sacristy.

Inside, the church looks suited to wealthy parishioners. For instance, the roof rests on an unusual hammer-beam construction. Look for a twelfth-century German polychrome madonna in the Lady Chapel. Mrs. Robert Garrett donated it, along with a special fund for entertaining parishioners next door in the rectory. Champagne sparkled here as late as the 1970s.

Next door, Grace and St. Peter's School educates the young. You may have noticed the playground east of the church on Monument Street. On weekdays you may glimpse youngsters in blue uniforms traipsing off to the Pratt Library or elsewhere downtown.

Go along Park Avenue past the rectory at 805 behind the church. Note the contrasting styles of rowhouses—Greek

simplicity on the left side of the street and elaborate
revival decorations on the right.

Adjacent row homes, one restored, one not

On your left as you enter the 800 block rises the dark
New Brunswick freestone mass of the First and Franklin
Street Presbyterian Church (1853–74). Maybe the impression of heaviness about the structure represents the
solid worth of the merchant class who built it. Even the
minister at the time could afford to build a stone manse
next door on Madison Street grand enough to comple-
ment the church. Ask to see the house and its graceful
curving staircase (729-5545).

On the street corner, look up to see how the church
lightens when seen against the sky. The eye is carried up
a 273-foot steeple and by a flanking 125-foot spire. Their
recent cleaning restored the look of a chocolate cathedral, crisp and ready to be displayed in a giant Easter
shop window. Interiors may surprise you with plaster
vaulting that suspends ornamental white stalactites.
Truss construction of the roof eliminates interior pillars.
Stained glass replaced plain windows one by one. When
the first window was installed at the far right, Presbyterians found it too bright. Now, three Tiffany somber-
colored glass windows, on the left just after you enter,
soothe the eyes.

Outside the church, go to the right to 205 Madison
Street, the 1880s Shirley-Madison Inn. In it still functions

Single residence

a gas-powered elevator introduced when one of many local boardinghouse keepers built the inn. Opposite, at 216 W. Madison Street, Mrs. DuBois Edgerton boarded early Hopkins professors and lecturers, such as psychologist William James and historian Herbert Baxter Adams. Here they created a salon. In another boardinghouse Thorstein Veblen got his idea of what he called conspicuous consumption for his *The Theory of the Leisure Class* (1899) from a strapped family keeping up the elaborate style of antebellum days.

Return to Park Avenue and turn left. Proceed to Read Street along the 800 block. An unusually long stretch of rowhouses juxtaposes narrow houses with pretentious

---

Birth and breeding were the dominant factors in Baltimore society during the period of Mrs. Harriet Lane Johnston's [President James Buchanan's niece and White House hostess] ascendance with the added impulse given it by the Johns Hopkins University making it receptive of all the best elements of culture when coupled with breeding. . . . Baltimore society of those [late nineteenth century] decades was yet untainted by crude wealth.

Charles Wilbur de Lyon Nicholls, a boarder at 216 W. Madison Street, *Annals of a Remarkable Salon, excerpts from my Johns Hopkins University Note Book, A Pen Picture of Baltimore Society in 1876–80* (c. 1910)

mansions. On the right at either end you find the restrained look of old Baltimore; 827, 833, and 839 are examples. In between, look for massiveness and fanciness,
as at 823, 829, and 842.

The modesty of these rowhouses contrasts with a
grandeur you see in mansions around the corner. But
whatever the scale, inside these domiciles resided people
to be reckoned with a century ago.

When you reach the corner of Read Street, look
ahead on the right to the rounded corner of the Waxter
Center for Senior Citizens at 861 Park Avenue and on
the left to the empty hulk of the Brexton, apartments
for the well-heeled in 1900. Once Wallis Warfield Simpson (later duchess of Windsor) supposedly lived here
(*Tour 11*).

*At the corner of Read Street, turn left and walk past
shops lining both sides of the 200 block.* Greenwich Village
used to spread the same air, at once tawdry and lively.
During the Jazz Age a well-known speakeasy operated
here. So did a bookmaker. During the 1960s, another
free-spirited age, Read Street Festivals filled the place
with rock music, drugs, and rowdiness. Now a more
sober street fair is held each fall.

*The first intersection, Tyson Street, offers a chance to
loop to the right down one block and back.* What makes
this narrow way worth seeing are tiny rowhouses painted
rainbow colors. A newspaperman used to publish an annual chart of the changing façade tints. After 1946, when
artist Edward Rosenfeld had moved in, other artists and
free spirits renovated houses. "Diminutive" and "flow-
ery" are words for Tyson Street. Beginning in 1956 a June
house tour brought in the curious who wanted to see
how people live in houses ten feet wide and two rooms
deep—with only handkerchief-size gardens.

These houses were built about 1820 on the farm of
Elisha Tyson. Records of a court case from an earlier
date reveal that a turnip patch covered at least part of
this street. Farmer Tyson prospered well and retired
young to devote himself to Quakerly good works such
as helping African Americans. A plaque about Tyson's
ownership in the 1790s hangs on the earliest house, just
around the corner to the left at 1115 Park Avenue. Before
the 1860s, Irish weavers made rugs in their backyards.
Rumors aside, slaves didn't live there, although African
Americans did move in after the Civil War.

*Emerging from Tyson Street, turn right up Read Street
to Howard Street, and then prepare to turn left into Antique Row, the 800 block of Howard Street.*

At the corner of Read and Howard streets, you face the State Office Center, light rail tracks, the Fifth Regiment Armory, and to your right the edge of Bolton Hill (*Tour 12*) and Mount Royal Center (*Tour 11*). Just across the intersection, next to the nearest state office building, is a plaque embedded in a stone where from 1861 to 1957 stood the Trinity African Methodist Episcopal Church.

The two blocks of Read Street you have been walking used to be called Richmond Street to go with Richmond Market at the Howard Street end.

Just after you turn left into Antique Row, glance across Howard Street to Armory Place. That spur connecting Howard Street with Linden Avenue takes its name from the Richmond Market building on the right. Here, downstairs, Richmond Market stalls dispensed fresh produce and seafood. Upstairs, troops of the Fifth Regiment drilled. The old market building has become part of Maryland General Hospital that stretches the full block.

Howard Street should by rights form the major artery of town because it is broad and because it bears the name of the man who owned most of the land bordering original Baltimore-Town. But today the street runs a blank in many of its blocks because of demolition.

Howard Street begins downtown with storage tanks for oil, and ends eighteen blocks north at Art Museum Drive with two Confederate generals on horseback facing north—Robert E. Lee and Stonewall Jackson. Later you may drive out to see their bronze mounts about to pass the peaceful Baltimore Museum of Art.

As you stroll down the east sidewalk in the 800 block of Howard Street, you pass Antique Row. Here the streetscape looks the way Howard Street always has. Back in 1800 a salesroom often doubled as workshop, with living quarters upstairs. The early nineteenth-century Irish Findlays made furniture in the style of Hepplewhite and Sheraton. Their cabinetmaking shop followed the newest craze for decorating the painted

---

In this old hall [the armory] the Confederate bazaars were held in the last years of the nineteenth century. Ah, those were the days! The Stars and Bars floated as of yore—this time quite harmlessly—and every Southern heart, and those not so Southern, thrilled at the rebel yell lustily roared by the old soldiers from the Pikesville [Confederate] home. . . . But do not imagine for a moment that these bazaars were melancholy occasions. Far from it; the youth and beauty of the land was there. Baltimore, a small and homogeneous town thronged to the Armory, and any melancholy that we felt was purely sentimental. . . . In all innocence we sang "Hurrah for the bonnie blue flag," and went home well content with the stars and stripes.

Letitia Stockett, *Baltimore: A Not Too Serious History* (1928)

surfaces with pictures of Baltimore country houses such as nearby Bolton.

As you proceed along Antique Row, you may take some time because the shops encourage browsing. You will find almost every variety of antique and almost-antique furniture, books, and possibly just what you have been looking for in silver. At 875, Harris Auction Galleries, lucky bidders have carried off such treasures as a copy of *The Postman Always Rings Twice* ($3,400) inscribed by Baltimore author James M. Cain to his mother saying that she wouldn't like the book.

When you look across Howard Street at the intersection with Madison Street, note a bank building that looks the way banks should look. First National Bank's Howard Street Branch retains ornamental window bars, a tower clock, old-fashioned tellers' cages, and much marble.

Proceed down one more block on Howard Street to Monument Street. Turn right two blocks to Eutaw Street, and then turn left. Stick to the right-hand pavement strolling down the 700 and 600 blocks of Eutaw Street. You come to George Street on the right. Turn in there and walk a half block to Jasper Street.

Take a rest on a doorstep and learn origins of street names. The seminary gave us St. Mary Street and Tessier Street for an early seminary president. George Street honors a man said to have no head for business. Perhaps George Lux did not need one, because his rich father gave him Chatsworth and he chose a bride from the prominent Philadelphia Biddle family. He named Catherine Street and Biddle Street for her. As further homage, he gave local streets Philadelphia street names —Lombard, Arch, Pine, and Penn.

By contrast, Jasper Street takes its name from an illiterate, poor, brave soldier. In 1776 Sgt. William Jasper rallied fellow soldiers at Fort Moultrie, South Carolina, by remounting their flag under heavy gunfire from British frigates. The governor of South Carolina gave the sergeant his own sword. But Jasper refused a commission because, he said, his lack of education would embarrass him as an officer. Instead, with his gift for disguising himself amazingly well, he became a successful spy.

Paca Street honors in its name William Paca, whose full-length portrait you saw in the lobby of the Maryland Historical Society. Paca served as governor and also was the only Marylander to sign both the Declaration of Independence and the Constitution.

At Jasper Street you should walk up and back the right-

hand block. Today old narrow Jasper Street—too narrow for trees—looks all dolled up. New infill residences at 618 and 607–629 harmonize with old ones. Although overhead wires remain, there are new brick sidewalks, street lamps, and granite curbstones. At the Druid Hill Avenue end, look at odd, lumpy roof shapes. When you return to George Street, look into the urban garden east of 417 before you turn right and down the half block to Paca Street. Here you may turn left for a snack at McDonald's. To find that refuge, turn right at the next corner, Franklin Street.

Where you turn, glance south three blocks on the right to 309 N. Paca Street, the tower of St. John the Baptist on the right-hand side. Inside, St. Jude Shrine contains a blaze of votive candles lit by petitioners from all over the country. "For readers living in darkness," says a brochure, "St. Jude is the patron saint of lost causes, the incurables, them as hit the bottom." He is understandably a popular figure in Baltimore.

Be sure to come back to where George Street debouches into Paca Street. You will then be ready to enter the Mother Seton House. A high point of this tour may well be Mother Seton's home and school next door to the Spiritual Center. Somewhat larger than the houses be-tween it and Franklin Street, it may have been designed by Godefroy. "[A] neat, delightful mansion, entirely new . . . in the new French style of folding windows and recesses" is how Mother Seton described it. Friendly docents will show the whole 2½-story red-brick house. The front room on the first floor retains the original floor and mantle with a tiny closet in one end. Go up a gently curving stair—also original to Mother Seton's day—to where students learned and lived. Rooms have an 1808 look. After the tour, you can ask to see St. Mary's Chapel.

Enter the chapel and take in what many people call its French exquisiteness. French priests from Paris hired French immigrant architect Maximilien Godefroy to build the chapel. Anyone interested in architectural his-tory will want to know that here was the earliest signifi-cant church of neo-Gothic design in America. Godefroy taught at St. Mary's as the first professor of architecture in the United States. His elegant plan for the chapel lost a bit because the Sulpicians had budgeted only $35,000. Elegance comes through, nevertheless, with Gothic pointed arches, flying buttresses, groined vaults.

"A little *bijou* of a thing," wrote English traveler Mrs. Frances Trollope in 1830 after visiting this chapel and

St. Mary's Chapel

"sequestered little garden." Then, her highest praise: "Holiness and quiet beauty [are] more calculated, perhaps, to generate holy thoughts than even the swelling anthem heard beneath the resounding dome of St. Peter's." Docents will show you into both upper and lower chapels. In the Lower Chapel, on the right of the altar, stands a linden-wood statue of Mother Seton, and, on the left, a statue of Sister Elizabeth Lang, who also took her vows here. Born in 1784 to a black mother and white father, she had fled Haiti and come here. (From the beginning an interracial congregation from the neighborhood worshiped in this chapel.) In 1829, she founded the first religious order of African-American women in this country, the Oblate Sisters of Providence. Theirs became the first order centered on teaching black children. Today sisters staff schools in other cities as well as St. Francis Academy here.

From the chapel you will probably want to take a breather outdoors. With your back to the main entrance of the chapel, you can see to your left the restored Franklin Court (1987). "Our concept is to expand and boost the existing retail base," said Jay French, developer of both this court and the newer Mulberry Court a

Elizabeth Ann Seton: First American saint

Paca Street hosted another "first" when New York widow Mrs. Elizabeth Ann Seton commenced a journey to sainthood in Baltimore. Already widowed and mother of five children, in 1806 she was confirmed in the Roman Catholic faith by Bishop John Carroll. Elizabeth Ann Bayley Seton took her first vows in the Lower Chapel of St. Mary's Chapel on March 25, 1809. She was a tiny woman but energetic. How impressive she must have been is evident in that in 1808 the president of St. Mary's College invited her to open a girls' school. In doing so she became the patroness of the American parochial school system. Also on Paca Street she founded the first American order of nuns, the Sisters of Charity of St. Joseph.

In 1907 Baltimore's Cardinal James Gibbons began her Informative Process of Cause for canonization, and on September 14, 1975, canonization was complete.

block south of here, "while providing affordable, quality homes in a downtown setting." All shops and apartments here were rented, French said in April 1993.

Most Seton Hill houses have high gable roofs and the simple façades of early nineteenth-century Baltimore. But you should watch for what makes each rowhouse individual. One distinguishing feature is paint. What sets these houses apart from their contemporaries in Fells Point are the rainbow colors painted on old brick. Splashes of yellow, blue, and other colors create streetscapes similar to Rainbow Row in Charleston, South Carolina.

Early Baltimore rowhouses did in fact display the same gaiety. Later Baltimoreans grew conservative: "Since the brick of the Baltimore area was porous, the fronts of all houses were painted a standard deep red," reported Cardinal Shehan, who grew up in Baltimore in the early twentieth century, "and pencilled with thin lines of white paint to resemble the mortar jointure of the bricks." Few residents go to all that trouble today.

Stand in the park or in front of St. Mary's Seminary Chapel and enjoy renewal of the old rowhouses on St. Mary Street and across the new park on Paca Street. Variety of sizes, heights, and facades makes the east side of Paca Street a lively picture. The large house at 609 contrasts with the narrow two-bay house at 631, for example.

The view provides a study in nineteenth-century

Baltimore made livable in the twentieth. Number 637
exemplifies the very small mid-nineteenth-century rowhouse, with a tiny pair of top windows through which
you can glimpse a modern skylight. By contrast, 609 has
a three-bay front, not two, and also has a passageway
through to the garden behind.

St. Mary's Park of seven acres is shaped like a diamond, but with one side uncut. When seminary buildings filled most of the land and seminarians played baseball here, sometimes passing cars caught home-run balls.
Today the park offers a gathering place for dog owners.
If you walk to the side away from traffic, you can imagine sitting in a Parisian square of quiet shade and feeling
enisled in a river of muted traffic noises.

From the park, take the exit nearest the chapel and walk
through short Tessier Street to Orchard Street. Turn right on
Orchard Street and walk to the church. Orchard Street
Methodist Church stands as an African-American landmark. (In the 1850s many African Americans lived in
Seton Hill. Today the population is about 40 percent
black and 60 percent white.) Legend has it that black
laborers built the first church on this site, by working
after hours, often by torchlight. Construction went on
from 1827 to 1837, when a congregation formed under
Truman Pratt who had been, it is said, John Eager
Howard's slave. The present Orchard Street Church, an
Italian Renaissance revival structure built in 1882, rises
above low streetscapes of renovated and new housing. It
barely escaped demolition in the early 1970s. In 1992 the
old church underwent a $4-million conversion and be-
came headquarters of the Baltimore Urban League. The
original main sanctuary soon will become an African-
American cultural arts center and museum; downstairs
and in the adjacent Sunday School Annex of 1903 there
will be a counseling center.

Conversion included all new mechanical systems and

The first time I saw the site, it looked like bombed-out Beirut, but I
knew in my heart that it was the perfect place for the Urban League to
pursue its present mission and the perfect place to preserve the rich
legacy of African Americans. Some people thought I was crazy but
having recently moved to Baltimore from Indianapolis and being the
new boy in town, I wasn't part of any establishment and was free to
take chances. It didn't take long, however, to convince the critics that
this was where the League was meant to be. So we took the plunge
and purchased the property for one dollar.

Roger Lyons, Urban League president (1993)

much replacement of old plaster. With the advice of a Morgan State University professor of architecture, work was done with 60 percent minority contractors. Funds for the conversion came one-third from gifts, one-third from government, and one-third from investors.

At the end of Orchard Street, turn right down Druid Hill Avenue. You will cross Paca Street and Eutaw Street on your way to the Centre Street stop on light rail. On your left, you will be passing near the Arena Players at 801 McCulloh Street (728-6500), home of African-American theatrical productions. North toward State Office Center look for the tower of Mount Calvary Church (Episcopal), 816 Eutaw Street (728-6140), attended by Robert E. Lee when he and his family lived nearby in a house now demolished. For seven years before the Civil War, Lee oversaw the building of Fort Carroll in Baltimore harbor for the U.S. Army.

After crossing Eutaw Street enter Howard's Park. It occupies ground where Johns Hopkins University established what passed for its first campus. Here trustees took over existing lofts and houses near the well-stocked Peabody Library (*Tour 10*). "The university was not a showplace," recalled an early graduate student.

This park is too cramped for a lacrosse field. In a small athletic cage, early Hopkins students began playing what is now the sport that gives undergraduates renown, the Indian game of lacrosse. Today next to the university's Homewood Field, 113 W. University Parkway, the Lacrosse Hall of Fame Museum exhibits photographs of early players, vintage uniforms, and equipment, as well as trophies and memorabilia. They date back to an era before athletic scholarships. "[It is] most improper for an institution of learning itself to charge admission fees for athletic contests," said early Hopkins president Joseph A. Ames.

In the middle of Howard's Park, walk to the statues of Baltimore's Revolutionary War hero Col. John Eager Howard leading his troops. Contrast this monument with Howard's equestrian gallop in Washington Place (*Tour 10*). Here the group entitled Red Brass march at ground level. "It seemed only proper," said sculptor David L. Gerlach, "to express [Howard] alongside of his fellow comrades-at-arms." Here in Howard's Park, said Gerlach, he is "more accessible to Everyman." In the 1781 battle at Eutaw Springs, South Carolina, Howard and his Maryland troops suffered heavy casualties; he was one of 351 wounded. "At Eutaw Springs the valiant

Little had been done to the old buildings [of the original Johns Hopkins University] except to cut out partitions so as to provide lecture-rooms with long tables running down the center and comfortable chairs in which the students sat with their notebooks. There was no campus.

I learned how to work, how to use books. . . . I met men who were not afraid to use their minds, not afraid of what they might find if they looked for the truth.

Frederic C. Howe, *The Confessions of a Reformer* (1925)

died," wrote poet Philip Freneau, "How many heroes are no more!"

Walk past the sculpture to examine the large red-brick building of City College (1895–99), a high school for boys. It later became Western High School for Girls, then Bay College, and now Chesapeake Commons. After a fire in the 1970s, developers spent $11 million converting the structure to nearly 100 apartments.

To your right as you face Howard Street, you will see vacant lots belonging to the estate of native Baltimorean "Honolulu Harry" Weinberg—so named from his being an absentee landlord residing in Hawaii. "In downtown Baltimore, Weinberg long stood in the way of the city's attempts to rejuvenate the Howard Street shopping district," wrote an *Evening Sun* reporter. "Nevertheless, Weinberg's wealth in real estate grew by default [proximity to properties being restored nearby, and renting to others who pump money into them]." Now the land belongs to the Harry and Jeanette Weinberg Foundation, worth almost $1 billion, one of the twenty-five largest American foundations. It gives money exclusively to help the poor (*Tour 8*). When Weinberg died, it is said, he was buried in the middle of the twenty-three burial plots he owned in Baltimore's Hebrew Cemetery.

Walk across Howard Street to the northeast corner of Centre Street to see the recently rehabilitated Greyhound Bus station, converted to offices. Designed in 1941 by a leading architect for Greyhound, William Arrasmith, its art moderne rooms once solaced soldiers leaving for war and cheered the transient. After bus traffic moved out in 1987, the building lay idle until recently converted. The first tenant was an agency set up to coordinate metropolitan Baltimore, the state-funded Baltimore Regional Council of Governments. Here, too, the Maryland Council for the Humanities has recently moved its headquarters, as has the Maryland Arts Council.

From the former bus station, look across Howard Street, down the block beyond Chesapeake Commons, to see the remaining one of three theaters. By the time you read this, that auditorium (1903) may have taken on new life as a performing and media arts center for Towson State University. As such, it becomes part of a Howard Street corridor of theaters that includes (to your right) the new performing arts center, Meyerhoff Symphony Hall, Lyric Opera House, and Theatre Project. In the old trio of theaters, rising stars played. During a run there in 1932, Henry Fonda married Margaret Sullavan.

And Katharine Hepburn recalled beginning her acting career in Baltimore. "I got two very nice notices for my little part. I was known a bit socially in Baltimore [as niece of Dr. and Mrs. Donald Hooker]. I hoped that wasn't the reason I was noticed." Today Baltimore planners think of turning Howard Street into a performing arts boulevard.

You are now perched at the Centre Street light rail stop. A ticket kiosk stands to the left as you exit the park. Board on the park side of the tracks. Get off at the Camden Yards stop nearest Pratt Street. From there you can easily stroll east on Pratt Street (away from the ballpark) toward Constellation Dock. An alternate route is to cross the tracks to Centre Street and walk past Park Avenue and Cathedral Street to Charles Street, where you began this tour. From there, turn right and walk south a half dozen blocks to the harbor and Constellation Dock.

Lion

Mount Vernon Place and Washington Place

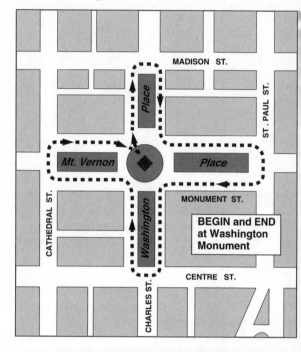

COME HERE FOR:

- Baltimore's best parlor—and the nation's
- The first major American monument erected to honor George Washington
- A master work of urban design by Robert Mills: four garden squares flanking the monument in the form of a Greek cross
- An outdoor Pantheon of statuary, including nymphs in fountains, warriors on horseback, and a great-size lion
- House and gallery important to two of America's premier art collectors
- Houses connected with two English kings, Edward VII and Edward VIII, First Lady Lou Henry Hoover, and President Woodrow Wilson
- The largest rowhouse in Baltimore, designed for the grande dame of the Establishment, Mary Frick Garrett Jacobs, by prominent national architects Stanford White and John Russell Pope
- "Culture Corner," with the Walters Art Gallery,

Peabody Conservatory of Music, and Peabody Library

◆ A fine set of views
◆ Greek revival residences where several mothers of young sons planned America's first country day school

[In Mount Vernon Place] I   223
felt . . . quite as the visitor
as yet unintroduced may
feel during some long pre-
liminary wait in a drawing-
room. He looks at the furniture, pictures, books; he
studies in these objects
the character of the house
and of his hosts.

Henry James, *The American
Scene* (1905)

You are walking into the drawing room—the best parlor —of Baltimore. As you walk here, you will learn the story of its creation—and the secret of its preservation. Also you will observe restored structures and parks—all fresh and quite distinguished.

As you stroll, note the grand scale established by the tall, pale Washington Monument. The four squares flanking it form a sculpture garden. Surrounding these garden squares, ample mansions and institutions create a Baltimore diadem.

HISTORY

In the beginning was Howard's Woods, the southern edge of John Eager Howard's eighteenth-century Belvedere estate. Here in 1809 Howard donated the city's highest ground for America's first major monument to General Washington. (Those two Revolutionary warriors had been friends.) "I know that this people [Americans] has its heroes," wrote visiting French novelist Gustav de Beaumont in 1825, "but nowhere have I seen their statues. To Washington alone are there busts, inscriptions, a column; this is because Washington, in America, is not a man but a god."

Robert Mills won the competition to design the monument and oversee construction. In 1831, after Howard's death, heirs deeded land for a unique set of four park squares abutting the monument. These rectilinear parks formed a Greek cross of greenery draped along the crown of a hill and down two sides.

This plan ranks high among urban designs of America. For its originality, Robert Mills has not received

Ascending to it [the Washington Monument], we saw this beautiful little city spread at our feet; its roofs and intermingling trees shining in the morning sun, the shipping riding in the basin, and crowded round the point; while, in the distance, the vast waters of the Chesapeake, and more near those of its tributary rivers, gleamed in broad lines of silver through the dark extent of forested plains, that stretched beyond the more cultivated precincts of the young city.

Frances Wright D'Arusmont, *Views of Society and Manners in America . . . during the Years 1818, 1819, and 1820* (1821)

Washington Monument,
c. 1930

enough praise. His thought may simply have been to give his monument a spacious setting. And the Howard family landowners must have delighted in having so many excellent building lots facing green parks. In a letter of October 1820, Mills proposed the design of a 105-foot promenade leading uphill to the monument in place of streets, and a second promenade of sixty-two feet, crossing east and west.

On drawings of proposed squares, Mills inscribed the names of America's favorite icons, Washington and Mount Vernon. Today West Mount Vernon Place flanks the monument on the hilltop; East Mount Vernon Place flanks it on the eastern hill slope. North Washington Place flanks the monument on the hilltop; South Washington Place, on the southern slope.

Next, Howard's heirs created building lots facing the squares, some for each heir. During the antebellum era generous-sized houses began to frame the parks. Clearly by then, boomtown Baltimoreans could afford the stability of Mount Vernon. Theirs became one of the best addresses south of Philadelphia.

Probably nowhere else in America can you still see so clearly the lost world of the big-city rich at their apogee. In 1851 everyone came to see the new 1 W. Mount Vernon Place, "the handsomest residence that had yet been constructed in Baltimore," wrote Latrobe Weston.

After the Civil War, residents such as John Pendleton Kennedy held the limelight as "a sort of concentrated essence of what is best in both the social and architectural spirit of the city," wrote Victorian architect J. B. Noel Wyatt. Residents have entertained First Ladies, with and without husbands present. Both President Lincoln and Robert E. Lee came, at different times, as guests. Sharing such a world stage, wealthy residents led in founding the Baltimore Museum of Art, Walters Art Gallery, Peabody Institute, and more.

For 150 years citizens have rallied to the Washington Monument to deal with anything significant. In 1835, for instance, aged Gen. Sam Smith met with a few leading citizens here. "These carrying the star-spangled banner waving over their heads marched through the streets," reported an observer, William E. Bartlett, "and thus collected a pretty considerable band" and quelled the riot after a bank failure. For a happier example, here African Americans celebrated what a contemporary printmaker called "the result of the Fifteenth Amendment and rise and progress of the African race in America and its final accomplishment and celebration."

Over the years, some owners enlarged houses and brought them up to date. Other owners sold to institutions or to developers of apartment houses. In 1900, boardinghouses menaced the special character. Since 1926, however, not much has been demolished, and nothing has been built on these four squares since the Leakin Building of the Peabody Conservatory. Every proposal to alter the frame of buildings stirs up opposition.

Today all sorts and conditions of men and women make pilgrimages to this hilltop. They come a mile inland from the Inner Harbor for history, for art, for

music, for food—and something more, something intangible: "It is continuity," said the English author G. K.
Chesterton, visiting in 1920. "It is the presence of the life
first breathed into them [Baltimoreans] and of the purpose of their being; it is the benediction of the founders
of the colonies and the fathers of the Republic."

Still, Mount Vernon is no longer the snobbish address it was before the advent of the car and the disap-
pearance of servants. Now apartments in mansions give
comfortable settings to people who like this sort of
place—people who like what local promoters call "fine
buildings and special parks of old-world character."
Students cluster here. A swank hotel and an elderhostel
bring more and more out-of-towners to discover what is
interesting in Baltimore's—and the nation's—best parlor.

TOUR

Starting Point: Constellation Dock in the Inner Harbor
Length of walk: One and one-half hours
Transportation: Bus north on North Charles Street

*Start from Constellation Dock, walk west away from the
water two blocks along Pratt Street and turn right on
Charles Street.* From that intersection you can see the top
of the Washington Monument, your destination. *You
may walk or take any bus going up Charles Street. Get off
the bus when it stops on Monument Street, to the right of
the tall column of the Washington Monument.*
You are looking at the first major monument ever
built to honor George Washington. "It's a Baltimore
treasure, a world treasure," said architectural historian
Phoebe Stanton in December 1992 when the monument
reopened after a $275,000 restoration.

As you look up to the top of the monument, you see
Washington dressed like the Roman warrior Cincinna-
tus (sculptor Enrico Causici), who also had given up his
sword for a plough. Here Washington submits his resig-
nation as commander-in-chief of the Continental Army.
Appropriately, he faces toward Annapolis, where the actual ceremony took place in 1783 before Congress in a
room preserved at the Maryland State House.

"Great Washington stands high aloft on his towering
main-mast in Baltimore," wrote Herman Melville in
Moby-Dick, "and like one of Hercules' pillars, his column marks that point of human grandeur beyond
which few mortals will go." The monument's setting
also fits that high praise. Here, close to the sky, the site
tops the central eminence (as traveler Henry James

called this hill). A circular drive of cobblestones encloses a red, white, and blue sidewalk that in turn rings a cast-iron fence. Closest in, Mills's cast-iron fence encircles the monument's base like a dignified, tributary wreath.

Find the door on the north side of the base and enter the exhibition space. Here you learn how the monument came about. The winner of a design competition, Robert Mills, described himself as "the first native American who directed his studies to architecture as a profession." He had learned from Jefferson at Monticello.

Because the original site given him far downtown was rejected by people who feared that the column might fall on valuable houses, Col. John Eager Howard gave this site to the nation. The managers slowly raised money with a lottery to pay for construction, but too few citizens gambled. So Mills eliminated ornamentation and four sculptural groups planned for the top of the grand base. The final version, a stark Tuscan column, derived from the Column of Trajan in Rome.

If your legs are good, and you like heights, climb its 228 steps for panoramic views.

Emerging from the monument and its exhibits, walk straight ahead and cross to the sidewalk next to the park. With your back to the monument, walk to your left and then turn right on to the sidewalk opposite the church. You pass 700, the Washington Apartments, an imposing structure of 1906 that almost broke the unspoken height limitation on buildings facing the park squares: nothing should be built higher than the monument. The Washington Apartments reach to within six inches of the limit of 178 feet.

Since the Washington Apartments replaced only one residence, it had to fit a long, narrow lot. Its architect stretched a beaux-arts façade along Washington Place with the entrance in the middle of the long side. He adorned the pale stone with cast-iron balconies and carved stone ornaments. Compare the relative restraint of these embellishments with the flamboyance (just across the square) of Mount Vernon Methodist Church.

Next door, the yellow Roman brick Stafford Hotel (1894) replaced the residence of Dr. William A. Moale. The hotel provided an excellent address for generations of hotel guests, including F. Scott Fitzgerald before he settled in Baltimore. Around the turn of the century, wealthy Baltimoreans wintered there, presumably because in January their country houses were unheated and dreary. Also, for decades the Stafford provided a popular haven for honeymooners spending their first night together. In 1970 bureaucrats converted the hotel to subsidized public housing for the elderly.

On the left front wall near the entrance a plaque tells us that a group met in the Stafford to create the American Psychoanalytic Association. "To further knowledge of Dr. Sigmund Freud's pioneering work" reads the citation. Members would have had their hands full if they had treated certain fashionable patrons of the Stafford. One curious case reached a crisis in the bridal suite. There Baltimorean Henry Lehr, called "King of the Gilded Age," announced to his bride that he had married her only for her money. No sex. Then, for the rest of his life, with her in tow, he jested and charmed his way to become the favorite clown of Mrs. Astor's New York and Newport. Behind him was a miserable youth and the suffering of a native-born proper Baltimorean without cash. He wiped Baltimore's staid dust from his dancing slippers.

Squashed against the Stafford, the Graham-Hughes house (1893) at 718 Washington Place belonged to one family longer than any other house in these squares—eighty years. This gray stone pile looks best from across Madison Street. Imagine a horse-drawn carriage approaching from Charles Street and seeing the full variety of turret, generous bay windows, large chimneys, and prominent portico. "The Graham-Hughes house is Baltimore's best house in the French château style of architecture," says architect Walter Schamu. "It is evidence that this city has one excellent example of every style of building produced in the past 200 years."

At the end of North Washington Place, Madison Street, turn right and go into the park square. Here you can rest your feet and survey building styles, statuary, and flowers. On this site in the early 1800s hot-blooded males dueled, as they explained, as "a symbol of prestige and distinction." More often than not, Baltimoreans, when challenged to fight, preferred to stay home.

Beside you in the park stands an equestrian statue of John Eager Howard by Emmanuel Fremiet. He seems to be dashing north on horseback up Charles Street. "A hospitable, hearty, bluff, soldierly, curt gentleman" (so a contemporary described Howard). The story goes that at the Revolutionary battle of Cowpens, he attacked Tarleton's best troops and won seven British swords. "You have done well," his commanding officer Morgan said. "Had you failed, I would have had you shot, for you charged without orders." Look on the base for a copy of the medal awarded him for valor at Cowpens.

William R. Smith having on yesterday morning made an ungentlemanly and unprovoked attack on me in the street, and having refused to give me honorable and proper satisfaction, I am compelled to declare him a coward and no gentleman. Jeremiah Hoffman.

Advertisement in *Federal Gazette and Baltimore Advertiser* (October 20, 1804)

Stroll around the flowerbed to examine the second of the two statues, that honoring U.S. Chief Justice Roger Brooke Taney (pronounced TAWN-y) in his judge's robes. Sculptor William Henry Rinehart as a youth had worked in a stone yard on the site of the Peabody Institute.

Standing here, you can appreciate the absence of high-rise buildings such as those that loom over other choice urban districts, such as Philadelphia's Rittenhouse Square. Across Madison Street from Howard's statue, the left-hand corner building incorporates one of the oldest houses and retains the original portico. On your right you see a restaurant that replaced the University Club, which, in turn, had converted a solid residence to its use.

From here you survey the whole of North Washington Place. Sightseers have not always had the freedom of these park squares; in the Gilded Age they were fenced and locked. When Mayor Ferdinand Latrobe opened the gates, "the little girls and boys rushed in," an editorial writer said, "and filled those gloomy little jail-yards with life and freshness."

Now walk down the left sidewalk toward the monument and stop at 715. The house and its two neighbors behind the church illustrate the generous scale of Mount Vernon residences. At 715 notice the vestibule entrance with its elaborate wood paneling, colored mosaics in wall and floor, and curious windows of tiny glass cubes, punctuated with bull's-eyes.

Novelist Edith Wharton's stuffiest characters would feel at ease entering these doors, as did many real Baltimoreans and their guests. "You feel that it is always afternoon here," reported the *London Daily Chronicle* in 1894. "Elegant ladies slip out of great spacious doorways into roomy family carriages driven by old colored servants in livery."

Most servants of the 1890s—African-American women and men—were doing the same menial tasks they had done as slaves or as hired free women and men.

Forty years ago my father took his son for a walk in Frederick and, stopping in front of a small house in the outskirts of the town, said: "There lived Roger B. Taney, Chief Justice of the United States, while he practiced law at the Frederick bar. He removed the government deposits from the United States Bank, which was wrong; he made the Dred Scott Decision, in which he was wrong again; but he was a great judge and a good man."

Bernard C. Steiner, *Roger Brooke Taney, Chief Justice of the U.S. Supreme Court* (1922)

[Speaking of Taney's style of address] I can answer his argument, I am not afraid of his logic, but that infernal apostolic manner of his there is no replying to.

Baltimore attorney William Pinckney

"Colored women have had many hard battles to fight to protect themselves from assault by employers, white male servants, or by white men, many times not being able to protect themselves in fear of losing their positions." So said Richard Macks, Robert Garrett's head butler in the late nineteenth century at 11 W. Mount Vernon Place.

Walking toward the monument, you will be at George Washington's back and approaching a green and red stone church. *On the way, duck into a narrow street marked East Branch Lane.* On your right, look at the backs of condominiums recently created in mansions. Turn left (behind 717 Charles Street) into Lovegrove Street. Look to the left for a two-story, cast-iron veranda. Just such a one elicited praise from the visiting Henry James, "where, above the easy open-air 'Southern' hospitality, an impression now of shafts of mild candle-light across overlaced outer galleries and of throbs of nature's voice in the dark vaster circle, the Maryland boughs, at their best, presided in the unforgettable grand manner."

When you return to Washington Place, and as you walk beside the church, look above the highest windows to a series of carved faces. They supposedly show prominent Baltimoreans of the Victorian age. No one recalls which ones.

Mount Vernon Place United Methodist Church (1872) replaced the district's earliest mansion (1829), residence of John Eager Howard's son Charles. There in 1843 the lawyer-poet Francis Scott Key died while visiting his daughter, Mrs. Charles Howard. (Read a bronze plaque attached to the church's corner.) Key's sister Anne was married to Chief Justice Taney, evidence of intermarriage in Maryland's Establishment. Another of Key's brothers-in-law, Edward Lloyd V, ruled the plantation where Frederick Douglass lived as a boy slave (*Tour 2*).

For their church's design, Methodists chose Victorian Gothic and a strange color of stone. "When there has been a heavy fall of snow, then the green serpentine stone has a lovely bloom like ripe almonds or the bright texture of pistachio nuts," wrote Letitia Stockett. Arrange to see the spacious interior, lit from high stained glass windows (685-5290). Methodists then liked designs in windows, not biblical portraits. Back at the church corner, look around you to the left. Here, at the top of a steep incline, you can understand why this hilltop served admirably for Baltimore's first balloon launching on June 3, 1784. Then no buildings, no monument, nothing

but perhaps some trees could hide the ascent from mul-
titudes below.

*Now walk past the front of the church and look at 10 E.
Mount Vernon Place,* a brownstone mansion of Italianate
Renaissance design by architects Niernsee and Neilson,
designers of half a dozen mansions hereabouts. Constructed for businessman Albert Schumacher, it required
seven servants to run it. Today, called Asbury House, it
is used by the church and can be entered if you phone
ahead of time (685-5290).

A bit less grand, number 12 has housed distinguished
people. Originally, it belonged to Col. Richard E. France
and later to the president of the Peabody Institute,
Charles J. M. Eaton. Once upon a time, when composer
Hugh Newson lived there, world-famous Polish pianist
Ignace Paderewski visited. From the 1930s into the
1970s, fashionable painter Trafford Klots had a studio in
the carriage house behind the mansion. His double portrait of the Duke and Duchess of Windsor, exhibited at
the Maryland Historical Society (*Tour 9*), memorializes a
leisure class. Wearing a yellow frock, the duchess from
Baltimore almost dominates a Palm Beach setting.

"Mount Vernon Place [about 1885] began to look a
little dingy and neglected," reported architect J. B. Noel
Wyatt in 1895, "and the statue of Washington might almost have trembled, as, from the top of his tall marble
shaft, he watched the invading army of boarding houses
fast closing around his social stronghold, heretofore held
impregnable." In 14, a Miss McConkey ran a boardinghouse.

Before Miss McConkey let rooms here, the house
belonged to Col. Charles Carroll. As a prosperous descendant of Charles Carroll of Carrollton, he could
retreat to his country property whenever he wanted to.
Of course, no one stayed here during Baltimore's subtropical summers. One of the colonel's sons fought for
the Union at the battle of Gettysburg, two sons joined
the Confederate army, and one son stayed home. That
one was an insurance policy, the colonel said, to keep
the Carroll line going. He did that, and he also went on
to become governor of Maryland.

The history of 16 E. Mount Vernon Place records
ownership by the Abell family, founders and owners
(until recently) of the *Baltimore Sun,* and by the Mount
Vernon Institute, the memory of which has grown dim.
Now it holds up-to-date apartments.

Brownstones at 18–28 E. Mount Vernon Place are

the only examples of group-house building in the four squares. They profited "the lottery king," Col. Richard E. France, just before the Civil War. A vignette of this end of the square recalls a lady of great age who retained "the keenest interest in public affairs, and also in her good looks and love of finery," wrote a friend. "If Josephine would only use silk *or* velvet, lace *or* feathers, instead of combining them all together!"

Before leaving this block, you should look at the red-brick paving on the street. Probably all streets once had the same pleasant paving instead of dull, patched asphalt. Notice adjacent Charles Street's paving of Glassphalt, shiny with smoothed glass fragments in asphalt.

At St. Paul Street, turn right and walk into the park square and look at a standing bronze statue of a lawyer and reformer, Severn Teakle Wallis, by Laurent Marqueste. In 1903 the Municipal Arts Society (created by the anticorruption Reform League in 1899) gave it in recognition of his courage and eloquence. In the 1850s Wallis had confronted the nativist Know-Nothing party as well as later political bosses.

With your back to the statue, look across St. Paul Street to a new apartment complex called Waterloo Place. Its developers won a 1991 award from the National Association of Home Builders. The name Waterloo Place recalls Waterloo Row, early nineteenth-century rowhouses in this block. The row was bulldozed in the 1960s. Now a furnished Waterloo Row parlor is on view in the Baltimore Museum of Art.

Robert Mills built Waterloo Row when he was supervising construction of his Washington Monument. Mills, a South Carolinian, moved to Baltimore in 1817 and stayed three years. In addition to working on Waterloo Row and the Washington Monument, he was president and chief engineer of the water-works company. In 1836 Mills began erecting a national Washington Monument on the capital's Mall. Completed in 1884, it topped at 555 feet, highest of human structures at the time.

Like the loss of Waterloo Row, other structures are vulnerable to demolition. Such threats run through Mount Vernon's history. For instance, the group of four houses (27–33) on your left as you walk up the park have caused trouble for the Peabody Conservatory board ever since 1962 when it proposed replacing them with a student plaza. "Because structures at the building line delineate the sides of the square and all visible adjacent streets, the central open area of the square [should remain] tightly enclosed," wrote Phoebe Stanton for the

He was a gamecock to the last feather. When one of the most murderous desperadoes of the Know-Nothing neighborhood of Fraud and Violence urged him to leave the polls (where he was a watcher) because the Know-Nothing said even he would be unable to save Wallis's life, the only reply he got was the cool, "That is your responsibility, not mine."

U.S. Senator William Cabell Bruce, *Seven Great Baltimore Lawyers* (1936)

Commission for Historical and Architectural Preservation (on which she sat). Now all you see are façades—the houses are gone. Behind are new rooms of the conservatory, including Galleria Piccola.

In the 1930s, when these houses were divided into apartments, 27 is said to have been used as a brothel. A century earlier, two of the other three houses in the group—31 and 33—had distinction, too. They were built between 1842 and 1846 by a daughter of Charles Carroll of Carrollton for investment income. She willed them to three daughters, all of them glamorous and married to English nobility. Known at the Court of St. James as the "Three American Graces," they never resided in these houses (*Tour 11*). These four houses sheltered, at various times, two governors of Maryland, two mayors of Baltimore, a congressman, a senator, and a minister to France.

Now walk up through the park to the pool. Here disports *Naiad* (1932) created by Baltimore sculptor Grace Turnbull and given by the Women's Civic League. Benches around it make a cool summer lunch spot and a place for you to rest.

Sitting in the park, look at buildings to the left of the monument; you may agree that you are looking at "strength with politeness, ornament with simplicity, beauty with majesty": such is the Peabody Institute's building (to borrow a line once said of London's famous Banqueting House). You are surveying the Peabody's original building (1860–66) and adjoining library (1876–78), both by English architect Edmund Lind. His creation in Renaissance revival style, both inside and out, continues to make a solid corner next to the monument. "Under as intelligent and faithful supervision as building ever had," said Provost Nathaniel Holmes Morison, "I do not see why it may not rival the Pantheon itself in durability and permanence."

Next, return to the sidewalk and go up the steps to the

George, who was now in the University of Maryland Medical School, was well versed in Baltimore's sexual geography. The densest concentration of available women, he said, was Mount Vernon Place, where apartments were packed with sex-crazed females. . . . We began prowling this Bohemia after dark. Girls did not pounce upon us. "Let's ring some doorbells," George said, nudging me into a dark vestibule to look for a doorbell with a feminine name beside it. It was hard to resist George. We rang doorbells. Sometimes a girl, sometimes a woman far gone in years would come to the door, and we would introduce ourselves if she looked sex-starved or say we'd rung the wrong bell if she looked too angry or too long in the tooth, and in every case the door was slammed against us.

Russell Baker, *Growing Up* (1982)

George Peabody: Philanthropist

At the top of East Mount Vernon Place, salute Peabody's statue. It was a gift from the Robert Garretts, who commissioned W. W. Story to duplicate the statue that a grateful British public had placed in London.

George Peabody (Baltimoreans say "PEA-body," New Englanders "PEA-bdy") was born in 1795 in Danvers, Massachusetts—earlier, as Salem Village, the site of the infamous witchcraft trials of 1692. Poor as a boy, he prospered during twenty years in a Baltimore dry goods firm. From here in 1837 he moved into London's financial center. He became so rich that during the Civil War he rescued the faltering credit of the embattled United States in England.

Fortunately for the world, it is the nature of people in Massachusetts to be useful. Certainly, Peabody practiced philanthropy on such a scale that he taught others like Enoch Pratt and Johns Hopkins to give generously to Baltimore. Peabody's benefactions stretched from model housing for London's poor to this cultural center; they extended from Yale's natural history museum to huge, post–Civil War grants in support of Southern education for blacks as well as whites.

In 1856 leading citizen John Pendleton Kennedy was puzzled by a letter from financier George Peabody: "I suppose you Baltimore people do not care to have an institution established among you, as I have heard nothing of the suggestion I made through Mr. Mayhew some years ago." The suggestion was to give a temple of the arts—"a library, a scholarly lecture series, and academy of music, and an art gallery." Kennedy replied that it was not want of interest but "delicacy and the want of information as to the sum." The sum turned out to be over $1 million, worth many times that figure in today's dollars.

To spotlight his institute, he insisted on building it on the most expensive site in town, right next to the Washington Monument. "I have determined, without further delay, to establish and endow an Institute in this city, which I hope, may become useful towards the improvement of the moral and intellectual culture of the inhabitants of Baltimore, and collaterally to those of the State, and also, towards the enlargement and diffusion of a taste for the Fine Arts," wrote Peabody in 1857.

When Peabody died in London, Queen Victoria ordered his body taken home to Boston with royal pomp on the newest warship. Peabody lay in state, flanked by six-foot candles in a mortuary chapel erected on the main deck. After the burial in Massachusetts, the ship's crew stopped in Baltimore.

Stack room at Peabody

main entrance. You will have to sign in. Go through the
door to the right of the sign-in desk to see a much admired cast-iron staircase. In 1861, the bill from Hayward,
Bartlett & Company was $3,378. It spirals upward rather
like a great black feather boa.

To the left of the sign-in desk you should walk into a
generously sized reading room on a well-lighted corner.
High up on the walls you see part of the institute's
painting collection.

Straight ahead of you author John Pendleton
Kennedy's eyes look right at you from a face resembling
actor Rex Harrison's. On the far right, look for a full-
length portrait of George Peabody. Photographed in
London by John Mayall and tinted by A. Arnoult, it
remains a rare example of early photography.

Walk through the door under the clock for the *pièce
de résistance,* six stories of balcony stacks, skylighted,
surrounding a marble court. Students of such matters
call it the most beautiful room in the city. That is why
the space often rents for parties. Ornamental cast-iron
balconies, their design picked out in gold, lend elegance.
Old books and exhibits give a cultured atmosphere.

On the shelves is the famous collection of 300,000 books. Provost Morison bought so well that it was "exceeded in quality as a scholar's library only by those in Washington and Cambridge" (so said his grandson, Harvard historian Samuel Eliot Morison). Among the rare items here is Diderot's famous *Encyclopédie* and Hans Holbein's 1549 *Dance of Death*.

A list of choice collections made by the Bibliographical Society of America included the fields of archaeology, architecture, art history, early science, geography, maps, ornithology, and early journals in science and engineering. Ask the current librarian about holdings in your interests. You may be shown the recently restored rare book room.

When you emerge from the library, turn left and then left again. Walk downhill on the Peabody side of Washington Place to Peabody Mews, entrance to Peabody's campus plaza. Go through the gate to a dormitory (1960) designed by Edward Durrell Stone, architect of the Kennedy Center in Washington. Notice Stone's trademark cement screens with pierced openings. In order to see exhibits in the recently created Galleria Piccola (659-8257), go through the door on the far right, enter Arthur Friedheim Library, and go one flight up. Exhibits change frequently.

From the plaza you can get permission from the guard to enter the new elderhostel, Peabody Inn, created from four mid-nineteenth-century mansions. Once you return to Charles Street, look at the continuous ornamental cast-iron balcony that unites these houses. Not part of the elderhostel, the attached first house, 609, built about 1848, has first- and second-floor verandas. It was once the home of a Bonaparte, Napoleon's nephew and son of Betsy Patterson, Jerome Napoleon Bonaparte. Now filled with Peabody offices, it could well be called Bonaparte House.

At the intersection with Centre Street, turn right and walk across the square to the original palazzo of the Walters Art Gallery. Henry Walters later willed the building with his collection to Baltimore.

Turn right along Centre Street to the entrance. Although the main entrance to the Walters is around the corner on Centre Street in a new wing, go in the old one on Charles Street to experience a museum of 1909. Every touch seems right: the portrait of the founder, and a marble staircase neither steep nor grandiose.

Go inside the Walters to the top of the stairs into a skylighted court modeled on the sixteenth-century

Palazzo del Universita (Palazzo Bianco) in Genoa. Occasionally patrons of the arts dance and drink among art treasures. In a gallery to the right of the court, artistically lighted jewelry attracts all eyes the way England's crown jewels do. Fabergé eggs displayed here once belonged to royalty.

You probably will want to come back for a real exploration of the Walters. It will take hours because the bequest of William and Henry Walters, more than 25,000 works of art, ranks as one of the greatest in American art history. Just to walk around this original set of galleries (restored in 1989) leads you past medieval Italian religious paintings, knights' armor, French Louis XIV furniture, and on and on. Both the father, William Walters (1819–94), and son, Henry Walters (1848–1931), collected French painting in Paris from contemporary artists.

When you come out of the Walters, walk to the center of the park square and look up to the monument. Early engravings and photographs make much of this view. Here almost every May since 1911 the Women's Civic League sponsored a one-day Flower Mart, the city's oldest neighborhood fair. With streets closed to traffic, people from all over bought plants and frolicked around the Washington Monument. The sun always shone on the Flower Mart.

As you wend your way up through the park square of Washington Place South, you will come to a fountain pool. In it stands a metal statue by Henry Berge Sr. of an exuberant sea urchin with arm upraised. In 1915 this pool became a centerpiece in a redesigning of these squares by the New York firm of Carrere and Hastings.

Above the pool an equestrian statue of Lafayette by Andrew O'Connor lords over this southern park square and the fountain pool next to it. When President Calvin Coolidge dedicated the pool in 1924, there was controversy about placement so close to the monument. "It looks like Washington's spitoon," said H. L. Mencken, looking at the statue and fountain basin. The statue's stone pedestal carries inscriptions from President Raymond Poincaré of France and President Woodrow Wilson.

After you climb past the alley behind the gallery, you have on your left the door to the Hackerman House. Later, you may want to enter and see the Walters' Asian art exhibited in this 1850 mansion. Just step inside to look down on a café that fills the mansion's original garden.

This mansion seems to have provided a fit place for entertaining the future king of England, Edward VII. Although the house suited the original owners, Dr. and

Some [French paintings here] are so famous as to be [the envy of major museums worldwide]. The *Odalesque with Slave* and the *Oedipus and the Sphinx* by Ingres, the *Christ on the Cross* and the *Marphise* by Delacroix, the *Goose Girl* by J. F. Millet, the *Hope* of Purvis de Chauvannes, the *At the Café* by Manet, and the *Before the Race* by Degas—all these are key events in the evolution of French painting.

John Russell, *New York Times* (May 10, 1992)

William and Henry Walters: Art patrons

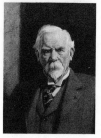

William Thompson Walters made a fortune in the Baltimore commission business before the Civil War, and afterwards knitted segments of Southern railroads into the Atlantic coastline. During the war, he and his son lived in Paris, where they collected contemporary French art. The father also became enamored with Far Eastern porcelains and caught the fever for things Japanese.

Like all children, Henry was simply climbing on the shoulders of his parent to reach a greater goal than Papa. In collecting on his own, Henry competed with J. P. Morgan and other tycoons for the best. He beat out competition to bring the first painting by Raphael to the United States. Like Morgan, he collected with what has been called "feverish enthusiasm." In his sixties, for instance, he amassed distinguished representative examples of armor. But he especially liked small, well-decorated objects that he could fondle in his pocket.

He also showed taste as well as local pride in buying works of Baltimoreans. Alfred Jacob Miller, for instance, has earned an enduring audience. Recently a Miller painting brought $150,000 at auction. Miller pioneered in sketching and painting the Grand Tetons and Indians. Afterwards he returned to Baltimore where he lived out his life, in the words of a contemporary, "a bon vivant, the epitome of the gentleman bachelor."

Mrs. John Hanson Thomas, its next owners, in 1892, Mr. and Mrs. Francis M. Jencks, made it grander. To do that, Mrs. Jencks's brother, the well-known New York architect Charles A. Platt, widened the circular staircase and inserted an oval Tiffany skylight. You can see those features, as well as some of Platt's Italian Renaissance mantles and other decorative touches. Baltimore architect Francis Jencks, who grew up here, recalls that his parents moved down from New York just so that they could live in this house. (Phone for hours and fee, 547-9000.)

On the main and second floors, Asian art exhibits include porcelain, screens, Buddhas, and changing exhibits of Chinese painting and Japanese woodblock prints. The room that was the Jenckses' library retains Elizabethan revival woodwork, including carved heads of luminaries such as Queen Elizabeth and Columbus. Now the room also displays Japanese art collected by William Walters.

As you leave Hackerman House, turn left, and at the corner of West Mount Vernon Place, turn left again. Walk past the marble portico of Hackerman House, brownstone at 3 (condominiums) and the painted brick of 5, the Walters family house. Henry Walters maintained this house, fully staffed and ready for his arrival, all during his final twenty years when he lived in Manhattan. He rarely came here.

Next to the Walters rowhouse stands the largest and most extravagant rowhouse in the United States, the brownstone at 9–13. Its prestigious New York architects Stanford White and John Russell Pope bent to the pocketbook of the owner, Mrs. Mary Frick Garrett Jacobs, to create grandeur that you now can explore when you are invited by a member of the Engineering Society, which owns this mansion. Or you can join one of the docents there in a planned tour (539-6914). The Tiffany skylight over the spiral stair alone makes the visit worthwhile.

Mary Frick Garrett Jacobs—called Mame—ruled here. When her first husband, Robert Garrett, died, she married his doctor, Henry Barton Jacobs. To envision how she lived, consider that in 1940, when the house and its contents were put up for auction, 1,210 lots of articles included 485 dinner plates, 1,147 wine glasses and finger bowls, 179 bath towels, and 100 oriental rugs and carpets. And this was just the local auction—for unimportant items. To a New York auction house went her most valuable articles, her jewelry, and her gold-plated dinner set and gold Venetian glassware. With all those possessions at the turn of the century, Mame did all she could to be the most talked about and influential social leader.

Mrs. Jacobs's architect in the rebuilding of 9–11 W. Mount Vernon Place, Stanford White, was star of the premier Gilded Age architectural firm McKim, Mead, and White. Their goal was to create the world of New York's Four Hundred in Baltimore. Following Lucullan banquets, the Jacobses gave musical evenings to scores of guests. No one dared refuse an invitation.

After the deaths of Dr. and Mrs. Jacobs, the mansion served as a Shriners' lodge. In 1962, city authorities sold it to the Engineering Society as a clubhouse. By then one Tiffany window had been lost from the vestibule. Today the Stanford White entrance gives a good idea of what lies within—elaborate oak wall panels, with shell and floral carvings, coffered ceiling in Moorish design, inglenooks flanking a fireplace, a Venetian lantern, Louis XV sconces. As you face the balcony, notice an ornamental door placed, it is said, so that Mrs. Jacobs could look down unseen at visitors and decide whether or not to receive them.

Exiting from the club, turn left and walk to the corner of Cathedral Street. You will be opposite the entrance to a hotel that recently was converted from an apartment house.

At Cathedral Street, turn right, cross the park, and then turn right again in order to walk past the final group of buildings, the even-numbered side of West Mount Vernon Place. This side of the park square shows you why Mount Vernon passes as the most European of Baltimore districts. Styles here are eclectic: the mansion at 16, for example, has a loggia on the third floor, added in 1890 to a house built in the 1850s.

At 16 W. Mount Vernon Place the steps intrude onto the sidewalk, and the landing is arranged so that residents can look down on passersby. Above, at every floor residents can walk out onto an open place and survey the park square. Many other houses on these squares give the same treat, whether from balcony or bay window.

Now look at the next mansion in the row, 14, as another illustration of conspicuous consumption. Originally a big, simple house of the 1840s, like 12 next door, this house was elaborately "Frenchified" at the turn of the century. With carved stone lions over door and window and three cast-iron lions holding up each lamp post at the entrance, the entrance looks royal. This house (now offices) belonged to one-time ambassador to Belgium Theodore Marburg. The first draft covenant of the League of Nations supposedly was drawn up at the house by President Woodrow Wilson and Ambassador Marburg working at a desk that is still here.

With its second-floor, cast-iron balcony stretching across very long drawing room windows, the mansion resembles a London townhouse of the 1840s. It is one of three Mount Vernon Place houses built by the Gordon family, more than by any other family there. "The Garretts merely *owned* more houses," said Douglas Gordon, a descendant, "and anybody can do that."

Built in 1842, 8 W. Mount Vernon Place remains the oldest house on the squares and the most frequently written about. Its colors make it look like a lemon soufflé. With its Doric portico and ample windows, it exemplifies the best Greek revival style. For permission to see the Georgian-style music room, library, and dining room upstairs, phone 837-3240. "There was extensive remodeling," wrote D. K. Este Fisher, who grew up

Chef Michel Richard [of the new Citronelle restaurant atop Latham Hotel Baltimore] looks out at the statue of George Washington atop the monument, and the church spires nearby. "When you come from Los Angeles, where everything is kind of new—this, of course, is older—it makes me feel very comfortable, because I'm from Europe. And I feel like home here."

Baltimore Sun (April 11, 1993)

in the house around the turn of the century, "including much of the elaborate woodwork, the mantels, etc., and great mahogany doors . . . said to have been salvaged from a well known house in New York."

In the 1890s a resident daughter, Sally McLane Fisher (Mrs. William Cabell Bruce), worked on plans for what is said to be America's first country day school, the Gilman Country School (1897). "The scions of their houses were playing ball in the streets or chasing cats up an alley," wrote a founder, recalling a reason for the new school. "They came home hungry from school at half-past two, the family having lunched an hour before— for Baltimoreans no longer dined at three o'clock."

That change of lunch hour happened about the time that the next-door mansion, number 6, got a new and fancy façade. You can contrast architectural styles here: the fanciness in 6's stone next to 8's austerity in painted brick. Notice especially 6's bold round bay, curving steps, and, over the entrance, intricately carved leaf designs. In the panel on the left you can spot a face peering out from the foliage. Alternating bands of cut and uncut stone help make a busy carnival of a house.

Next door you are back at the Washington Apartments on the corner. Maybe you are ready to relax in the adjacent west square, the one opposite 6 W. Mount Vernon Place. It attracts more sitters than the others because few cars pass by. Another reason for the west square's popularity is that people like seeing recently renewed flowerbeds and the reconstructed large pool and fountain. In the center of a round basin dances a bronze sculptured figure of a sprightly boy balanced on one foot and looking down at a turtle returning his glance. In 1923, when the Baltimore Museum of Art staged an outdoor show in this square, curators decided to place the boy and turtle right where you see them.

Sitting in this park square, you should look at the south row with the Walters house and the largest rowhouse in town. It probably wouldn't be intact if it hadn't been for a mid-twentieth-century fight led by Douglas H. Gordon. In 1955 all the south row of West Mount Vernon Place, except for 1, were slated to be torn down in order to add a wing to the Walters Art Gallery.

The buildings' existence today supports a kind of scientific principle that Douglas Gordon called "The Gordon Curve": a building has maximum value when it is new and again when it is 100 years old. A new house declines in value in the eyes of citizens until it reaches the age of 70. Then, old-fashioned and ugly, it faces demolition. Next, if it survives, it begins to attract favorable interest. And at age 100 it will be venerated. When Gordon propounded this theory, most of these houses were seventy years old, the dangerous age.

"During nearly fifty years he [Gordon] stopped every attempt to trashify Mount Vernon Place," recalled a long-time journalist, R. P. Harriss. "He had a strong, some thought handsome, face, forthright speech, an intimidating presence that made City Hall politicians and sleazy promoters quail when he faced them at zonal hearings or in the courtroom."

"It has about it that eighteenth century manner that one finds at old Mount Vernon, the home of General Washington," wrote a 1920s sitter. "Here on the balustrades are War and Peace, those fine Barye Bronzes. They are well placed and already at home, staining the marble with rich hues of green and copper."

By 1900 these bronzes had been added to what was becoming an outdoor sculpture garden. Amidst the greenery you have seen fountain nymphs, a chief justice, two warriors charging to battle, a pensive reformer, and a philanthropist. No local elected official and no Civil War figure made the cut. Controversy, people agreed, naturally was to be avoided in such a serene place.

At the western end of Mount Vernon Place, you end your walk. If you wish to continue walking on Tour 11, you will begin right here. Should you care to break for lunch or other refreshment, just return to the café at the Walters or go to Centre Street, where there are two sources of supply, or walk south on Charles Street to Louie's Bookstore Café (518 N. Charles Street, 962-1224) or to the Woman's Industrial Exchange (333 N. Charles Street, 685-4388).

To return to Constellation Dock on foot, retrace your steps by walking south on Charles Street. Or, with the monument behind you, walk west along the 100 and 200 blocks of West Monument Street to the central light rail line stop (heading south) on Howard Street. The destination sign will say Cromwell Station. Get off the trolley at Camden Yards and walk along Pratt Street (with the ballpark behind you).

Iron porch of local
manufacture

The Cultural Center

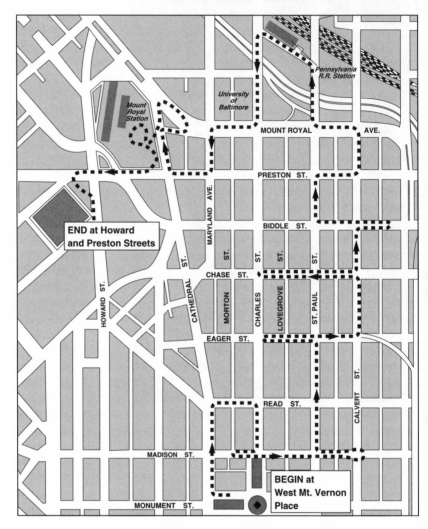

Mount Royal Station

University of Baltimore

Pennsylvania R.R. Station

MOUNT ROYAL AVE.

PRESTON ST.

END at Howard and Preston Streets

MARYLAND AVE.

BIDDLE ST.

ST.

ST.

ST.

ST.

ST.

CHASE ST.

CATHEDRAL ST.

HOWARD ST.

MORTON ST.

CHARLES ST.

LOVEGROVE ST.

ST. PAUL ST.

EAGER ST.

CALVERT ST.

READ ST.

MADISON ST.

BEGIN at West Mt. Vernon Place

MONUMENT ST.

COME HERE FOR:

- Love and stethoscopes, including two royal brides, and a quartet of pioneering Hopkins doctors
- Residences of spectacular achievers in romance, literature, and medicine—including the Duchess of Windsor, Gertrude Stein, and luminaries of Johns Hopkins Hospital
- The old Establishment's solid way of life—churches, clubs, theaters, schools (including the first college-preparatory school for girls in the nation), even a cemetery

- Free exhibit of many antique Baltimore prints and maps, including Audubon's famous view of canvas-back ducks swimming the 1830s Inner Harbor
- Four theaters, two railroad stations, two colleges, one armory, one grand hotel, and important outdoor sculpture
- Victorian architecture both solid and fanciful, including a mansion designed by Stanford White and the hotel where F. Scott Fitzgerald gave a dance for his debutante daughter Scottie and embarrassed her

On this tour you will meet luminaries of high voltage. For example, of all American cities probably only Baltimore can boast two royal marriages. "My poor, dear romance," said the Duchess of Windsor, née Wallis Warfield of 222 E. Biddle Street, Baltimore, speaking of her late husband, briefly King Edward VIII of England and Emperor of India. Earlier, Betsy Patterson of South Street, Baltimore, had married the future king of Westphalia.

In the realm of medicine, too, Baltimore has reigned supreme. "If you are a doctor in these United States," wrote historian Dr. Bertram M. Bernheim, "you have been affected by the Johns Hopkins Medical School and Hospital." Hopkins and the University of Maryland medical institutions make Baltimore a medical capital still.

Here stand the actual buildings associated with royal romance, as well as those of pioneering doctors and patrons of culture. By contrast with cities like New York and Los Angeles, Baltimoreans have preserved the entire enclave where long ago luminaries lived.

This long tour can easily be divided into two. If you are chiefly interested in people, walk the first part (up to Mount Royal). But if you want to explore the cultural district, walk the second part, which offers museums and other interiors—probably good for a rainy afternoon.

HISTORY

"Staff members [in early Johns Hopkins Hospital] sought the pleasanter surroundings and better homes across town," wrote Dr. Bernheim. Also, these physicians were looking for the cachet of fashionable Baltimore by moving to Charles Street hills. People of fashion, of course, go to hilltops everywhere, not just in Baltimore. In this guidebook, you are continuing to move up from tidewater to piedmont, from the Inner Harbor to the heights. And place names reflect elevation—Cathedral Hill, Mount Vernon, Mount Royal.

[Though] not so learned and scientific as the ladies of Boston, [the ladies of Baltimore] are more affable and more engaging. They are not so ostentatious of display as the ladies of New York, but their social qualities, their desire to gratify, and their power of pleasing is much greater.

James S. Buckingham, *America, Historical, Statistic, and Descriptive* (London, 1841)

The medical faculty [of Johns Hopkins University] despite its international contact, remained parochial in its outlook; it brought citizens of the world to Maryland and made them Baltimoreans; the hygiene faculty took people from boroughs and fields of the Americas and made them citizens of the world.

Dr. Thomas B. Turner, *Part of Medicine, Part of Me* (1980)

Topographically, this district lies within the embrace of Jones Falls flowing along the northern and eastern boundaries. The name Eager Street recalls an heiress, Ruth Eager, whose grandfather George Eager bought the land from Lord Baltimore in 1688. A century later her son, John Eager Howard, built a mansion for his bride. You will walk over the site of Howard's Belvedere, a 1784 country estate and mansion that until 1870 overlooked Jones Falls and the harbor. "One of the finest landscapes in nature," said visiting Jedidiah Morse in 1792.

Howard's heirs vetoed a proposal to create a version of New York's Central Park at Belvedere. Instead, they profited from creating a wealthy residential quarter. Then, if tycoons couldn't live on Mount Vernon Place, at least they enjoyed propinquity. So between 1850 and 1900, Queen Victoria's reign, architects created grand settings to show off the daughters of the houses.

To do that, architects abandoned the classic, restrained Baltimore rowhouse. That is why Renaissance revival and other styles make this walk a feast of expensive, late nineteenth-century streetscapes. Here well-heeled residents gave balls, enjoyed their clubs, and worshiped in elaborate churches they built. "Worldly people are such a comfort!" said a woman who grew up here. For their children, residents hired African-American or European immigrant women as nannies.

The residents supported private schools such as Bryn Mawr, Calvert, and Boys' Latin. Young children attended dancing classes, and young debutantes swirled through an elaborate ritual of being presented to society.

Mount Vernon residents even had the convenience of their own classy railroad station of their own railroad, the B&O's Mount Royal Station. One could, of course, use the Union Station of the Pennsylvania Railroad in a pinch. Finally, at death, they repaired to their own cemetery, Greenmount, just across Jones Falls and visible from the district.

In recent history, the symbols of Mount Vernon changed from stylish ostrich plumes in ladies' headdresses to stethoscopes in the hands of physicians. By World War I, most fashionable residents took advantage of the advent of the automobile and of garden suburbs such as Roland Park to move from town. Homes of Victorian high society often became doctors' offices. Later on, the northern part of the district sported new car showrooms next to old railroad yards. Today that part, called Mount Royal Center, attracts students as well as concert- and theatergoers. "We have more cultural facili-

---

Like everybody else who had a colored nanny, I was filled with Negro superstitions. Never throw your hat on a bed, never hang anything on a doorknob, never sit down thirteen at table, never start a journey on a Friday, never let a peacock feather into your house.

Wallis Warfield, Duchess of Windsor, *The Heart Has Its Reasons*

ties touching each other," said president Fred Lazarus of the Maryland Institute College of Art, "than exists in any other area of any other city in the country, and yet no one talks about this as a cultural center."

"Preserve its historic character" heralds the banner of Mount Vernon's planners today. So far it waves fitfully, what with heavy traffic, lack of parking, and a long-standing reluctance on the part of wealthy Baltimoreans to live downtown. This district's twin, Philadelphia's Rittenhouse Square, enjoys a more prosperous fate because it retains cachet for Old Guard as well as New. Still, a walk through these streets brings you close to both "dear old back-when Baltimore" and hopeful new cultural institutions very much alive.

TOUR

Starting Point: Constellation Dock, Inner Harbor; if continuing to walk from Tour 10, the western end of West Mount Vernon Place

Length of tour: Two and one-half hours; this makes a longer walk than most of the others, but there are no hills to climb and few building interiors to explore

Snacks and rest stops: A number of restaurants and delis are scattered along Charles Street; the Belvedere's Owl Bar; Pennsylvania Railroad Station; Poe's Pub in the Law Center, University of Baltimore

---

If you begin at Constellation Dock, walk west away from the water two blocks along Pratt Street and turn right on Charles Street. From that intersection you can see the top of the Washington Monument, your destination. You may walk or take any bus going up Charles Street. Get off the bus when it stops to the right of the Washington Monument.

Emerging from the park square of West Mount Vernon Place at Cathedral Street, you should turn right and proceed for two blocks to Read Street. In the 700 and 800 blocks of Cathedral Street you will be passing residences of women and a few men of character. At 702 Cathedral Street, for example, Pres. Abraham Lincoln spent a rare night away from the White House. On April 18, 1864, he was a guest there of William J. Albert, president of the Sanitary Fair, a fundraiser for medical supplies. That night, just five months after the Gettysburg Address, he delivered his famous "Liberty Speech" at the Maryland Institute in Market Place (*Tour 5*).

After the speech, Lincoln returned here for a gathering of leading Republicans, prominent citizens, and supporters of civil rights for freed slaves. Today the Albert mansion houses a Christian Science reading room and the Third Church (685-7183). Except for the addition of an auditorium and a replacement with brick of the original brownstone façade, the house is preserved as Lincoln knew it. Ask to see the dining room. Its mantel was paraded through the streets on a wagon so that downtown crowds could admire the carving.

In 1930, next door at 704 Cathedral Street, editor H. L. Mencken and his bride, Sara Haardt Mencken, set up housekeeping in their third-floor apartment. Because they could see so many church towers, Mencken said that they dwelt among the angels.

Both of them had spaces set aside for writing. She was writing fiction later collected in *Southern Album,* and he was closing out his editorship of the *American Mercury.* Since she was suffering terminal tuberculosis, he determined to make her remaining years the happiest.

Walk to the corner, where young dancers in the School for the Arts practice on the site of banker Alexander Brown's ballroom. Across Cathedral Street, at 18 W. Madison Street, Peabody provost Nathaniel Holmes Morison and his wife reared a large family on money from cannily buying Civil War Union bonds low and selling high. Morison liked this Southern city, whose Baltimore wife and local "pleasant social life," wrote grandson Samuel Eliot Morison, Harvard historian, "ameliorated his New Hampshire austerity." Across Madison Street at 816 Cathedral Street, a century and a half ago, lived Emily Caton McTavish, granddaughter of Charles Carroll of Carrollton (*Tour 4*). Unkind people said that she must have been hiding behind the door when beauty was passed out to her sisters, the "Three American Graces." In the early nineteenth century, those three belles had charmed the English court of George IV, married nobility, and never come back to Baltimore. Sister Emily married here and comforted the great old age of her grandfather, the signer of the Declaration of Independence. Her house still contributes to the dignity of Cathedral Street.

Continue walking north on Cathedral Street to 820. Just up the street, on the site of the Medical Arts Building, once lived a rival of the "Graces" for international fame, Betsy Patterson Bonaparte. Her residence possibly offered the same large scale as 820 Cathedral Street, with light flooding the second-floor drawing room through extraordinarily tall windows.

The daughter of early nineteenth-century entrepre-

It is a literal fact that I still think of Sara every day of my life, and almost every hour of the day. . . . She had a sharp intelligence, and yet she was always thoroughly feminine and Southern, and there was not the slightest trace of the bluestocking in her. Marriage is largely talk, and I still recall clearly the long palavers that we used to have.

H. L. Mencken, *The Diary of H. L. Mencken* (May 31, 1940)

neur William Patterson (*Tour 3*), Betsy at 18 had so fascinated Napoleon's brother Jerome, then only 19, that he
ignored the emperor's wishes and married her on Christmas Eve, 1803. "As to your love affair with your little
girl," wrote Napoleon, "I pay no regard to it." So he had
the marriage annulled, although Betsy had given birth
to a son. "Had I but waited," she said, "with my beauty
and my wit, I could have married an English duke, instead of which I married a Corsican blackguard."

The emperor made her ex-husband king of a German
principality, Westphalia, and Betsy later reluctantly returned to live out a long miserly life in Baltimore. Dying
at 94, she had outlived her son, whose marriage to a Baltimore heiress had dashed hope of his becoming a king.
Her son and grandson are also buried in Baltimore—but
miles away. Her epitaph: "After life's fitful fevers she
sleeps well."

Walk across Cathedral Street to the Christmas Tower
of Emmanuel Episcopal Church at 811 Cathedral Street
(685-1130). It really should be called the Epiphany Tower
because figures of the Wise Men dominate. In Emmanuel
Church Baltimoreans still conduct fashionable weddings
and funerals. One bridegroom, George C. Marshall,
later became a World War II five-star general and architect of the Marshall Plan for aiding postwar Europe.

Wars touched this building as early as the Civil War
when pro-Confederate parishioners fought with Union
sympathizers. To keep order in the narthex when
prayers ceased, the vestry hired security guards. Today
ornamental shields adorning the walls remind us of
warrior knights. Ask for the printed key explaining
shield emblems.

Right after World War I major alterations changed a
mid-Victorian sanctuary to a junior Westminster Abbey
in architectural style. To the left of the altar, carved in
Germany, the Peace Chapel is lighted through English
stained glass, signed with the artist's logo, a sheaf of
wheat in the lower left corner.

Although you should notice three Tiffany studio windows lighting the back of the main space, be sure to see
the baptistery glass, designed by Tiffany's contemporary
John Lafarge, to the right of the altar. Some experts
think it the best in Baltimore. If you go in the morning,
the blue panel behind the font will be at its brightest. Its
light falls on a white angel holding up the basin on the
font. The angel's model was sculptor Daniel Chester
French's twelve-year-old daughter, Margaret. Look at the

modeling of the angel's feet. Later French carved a statue of Lincoln for the Lincoln Memorial.

Turn right and walk along West Read Street to touch Jazz Age literature. Just behind Emmanuel Church a stable had been converted for a repertory theater company, the Vagabonds (*Tour 2*). Here in 1933 Zelda Fitzgerald's play *Scandalabra* flopped, despite doctoring by her husband F. Scott Fitzgerald.

Across the street in an apartment at 16 Read Street, perennial bachelor H. L. Mencken courted Goucher professor Sara Haardt. "The apartment was compact but comfortable—a living room, bedroom, bath and a long narrow kitchen, one end of which was called a 'butler's pantry,'" recalled later tenant Robert Chambers. "I have read somewhere that when Mencken was courting Sara and visited, she [Sara] would have a Goucher student chaperone and do her homework in the butler's pantry (thereby, no doubt, preserving Sara's reputation at Goucher)."

At the time, Mencken's fellow writer Huntington Cairns lived with his wife at 14 Read Street. They embraced the daring ways of the Jazz Age. For instance, her way of making an entrance at a party was to wave her cigar and say something shocking to men she didn't know, such as "Have you ever seen a whale copulate?" Her husband befriended pioneering writers such as Ezra Pound. Cairns got on well with H. L. Mencken, both brilliant Baltimoreans who had not gone to college. "College only addles your brain," said Mencken. Near this corner once lived many Maryland governors and Baltimore mayors. Frank Brown, for example, won nomination for governor by inviting members of the Maryland General Assembly to dinner here.

In office, Brown once secretly sent a state oyster boat to rescue four falsely accused young black men from Chestertown on the Eastern Shore, where they had been scheduled to hang for the murder of a white physician.

Today, although you may not like Charles Street's rows being broken for parking lots, you may enjoy good restaurants in flourishing converted old houses. *Turn right on Charles Street and walk toward the Washington Monument. At Madison Street make a loop to the right as far as Morton Street.* This stretch of mansions ends with a view of steeple-rich First Presbyterian Church. By contrast, back when President James Madison drove along Madison Street, he said that it wasn't such an honor having a street named for him that began at a charity school, ran past the poorhouse, and ended at the penitentiary.

Today both corners of Charles Street at Madison Street display old brick mansions adapted to new uses. They form a kind of protective gateway to the park and Washington Monument. Turn right and move along to 6 with a clown's head carved over the heavy brownstone entrance. Through this door in 1869 passed a man but recently in command of the Confederate Army, Robert E. Lee. His hosts here, the Stanley Tagarts, had been friends in Baltimore since before the war, when Lee had commanded a unit of the U.S. Army Corps of Engineers building Fort Carroll in the outer harbor. "As true a trout as ever swam!" is how Lee appeared to Baltimore-ans. So when he appeared, they cheered him.

Continue past mansions at 8 and 10 Madison Street to study examples of building styles that contrast with each other and with the Italianate 6. Notice the delicate fanlight of the colonial revival style at 8 that reflects the taste of heirs of Confederate Gen. Isaac Trimble, who led prominently in Pickett's Charge at Gettysburg and lived to tell about it.

Cross Morton Street to 12 Madison Street, home of one of the city's luminaries, John Pendleton Kennedy. His brick and brownstone mansion looks solid enough for the congressman who promoted Morse's telegraph and Perry's opening of Japan to trade. Kennedy served also as secretary of the Navy and, at the end of his life, as provost of the University of Maryland.

By becoming Edgar Allan Poe's patron he had saved Poe from suicide (*Tour 4*). As if that weren't enough, Kennedy in his *Swallow Barn* (1832) invented the myth of the "Old South" in fiction, and thus in his plantation novels wrote forerunners of *Gone with the Wind*. "He [Kennedy] had the somewhat rare excellence of being playfully earnest; and, though he had strong convictions, never made them the scourge of other men," wrote Boston editor and poet James Russell Lowell.

Turn back and walk past Charles Street to St. Paul Street. As you descend the hill below Charles Street, pause just before Lovegrove Street. Study the garden and house set back on the left. Filled with dappled light, this scene recalls old charmers in Charleston, South Carolina. The name of Lovegrove Street reaches back, too—to 1819 and James Lovegrove, a bookbinder, stationer, and bookseller.

Loop downhill to Calvert Street. There on the right stretch the old homes of Loyola College and Loyola

High School. On this corner, St. Ignatius Roman Catholic Church fathers have recently instituted a rigorous school for inner-city boys.

Farther along the block, Center Stage has built a reputation for producing a variety of plays, classical and experimental (685-3200). There are two theaters; the newest, called Head Theater, offers flexible arrangement of stage and seating. Recently the artistic director moved on to Yale's repertory theater.

The donor of the Head Theater, Baltimorean Howard Head, made money by producing a lightweight ski from aircraft materials, and later by developing an oversized tennis racquet, with a larger sweet spot that made hitting the ball easier. "It was my impatience and arrogance that if I couldn't play, it must be the equipment that was wrong."

Walk back up Madison Street. Turn right at St. Paul Street and walk the two blocks to Eager Street. Look along the 700 and 800 blocks at the long stretch of century-old red-brick façades. Although the rows may look seedy, they belong to a famous and endearing story. Just imagine the rows as a Court of Beauty: here lived several of the ten beauties chosen by bachelor Alfred Jenkins Shriver, each to be painted as she looked "at the height of her beauty" in the 1890s, when he was a young man-about-town. As he ordered, the painting hangs now in a lecture hall that he donated to his alma mater, Johns Hopkins University.

When you proceed across Read Street, look to the left. Tidy rowhouses here would make a setting for a Cleveland Amory play about Proper Baltimoreans.

As you proceed up the 900 block of St. Paul Street, you may have a hard time being enthusiastic about the present state of beauty here. Maintenance is at best

---

I was born in Baltimore in 1867, at a time of genteel and dignified serenity. The stress and strain of the war was over, and a spirit of restfulness had settled down over the charming old city. . . . I shall never forget our nursery, that warm and comfortable big room with its deep, open fire in the wide chimney, presided over by Mammy Cynthia, her white, woolly head all tied up in a bright bandanna handkerchief. . . .

Such slow motion as that of the streetcars and horse-drawn carriages and wagons did not interfere with children playing in the street, and in wintertime they made a gay scene with sleighs moving along, the horses jingling their bells, and trains of youngsters on their sleds hitched on behind or coasting downhill. Without motors or trolleys there were no suburbs, and all of our friends lived in town in the winter and in the country, the mountains or at the seashore in summer.

Lelia Symington, sister of Charles J. Symington, and quoted by him in *Skippin' the Details* to describe life at the corner of Read and Calvert streets in about 1873

Dr. William H. Welch: Statesman of medicine

"The laziest man ever heard of," wrote H. L. Mencken of Welch. "His great fame in the world was probably due mainly to his extraordinary talent for getting publicity." When Welch won the competition to bring the nation's first public health school to Hopkins, Pres. Charles W. Eliot of outmaneuvered Harvard supposedly complained, in a towering rage, "Baltimore is a provincial community compared with either Boston or New York."

Welch's larger-than-life statue stands in front of Shriver Hall, Homewood campus, Johns Hopkins University. Called "Popsy" by Hopkins medical students, bachelor Welch lived on the second floor of 937 St. Paul Street, a house overfilled with books. "When the desk got too cluttered up," wrote a colleague, "he would open a newspaper and spread it over letters and manuscripts and start fresh. I counted four such layers."

spotty in an island of what we have to call urban decay. Yet both rows are intact—no houses missing. And so the possibility for restoration exists. Look, for example, at 914 and 916 with their iron stoop decorations and fences along front gardens. Also, look on the same side for two curbside marble blocks, once used for climbing in the carriages.

Many residents subsequently abandoned St. Paul Street to live all year round out there in Hunt Cup country. Those emigrées were later criticized by local journalist Gerald W. Johnson for having the "fat-headed complacence of so many possessors of old money, who are really convinced that what Grandfather did for Baltimore in the administration of Benjamin Harrison has absolved the family forever from any further civic obligation."

Today National Landmark plaques adorn two houses. At 901 lived Samuel Shoemaker, owner of Adams Express Company, shippers in 1853 of anything throughout the South and West—gold, pianos, corpses, whatever. Immediately after the Civil War ended, the company carried relief supplies to destitute Southerners free.

The other plaque, at 937, tells us that Dr. William H. Welch, one of the "Big Four" founders of clinical services at Johns Hopkins Hospital, lived here.

Another plaque could mark 915 St. Paul Street as residence of John O'Donovan, a founder of the Maryland Hunt Cup, an annual timber race held in the Worthington Valley north of the city. In 1894 he led in setting up

Dr. Thomas S. Cullen: Civic leader

At 20 E. Eager Street, Dr. Thomas S. Cullen lived and practiced gynecology. During the early years of Hopkins Hospital, he and Dr. Howard Kelly pioneered in the field of gynecology and wrote the standard textbooks. "He worked so damned hard," wrote H. L. Mencken, "butchering all morning, seeing patients all afternoon, writing about tumors all night."

The size of his bills to patients always bore some relation to the size of the patient's bank account. "Punctual and gregarious" described Cullen. Besides medicine, Cullen addressed city-wide issues. He cozied with political bosses to gain what Baltimoreans needed. "Osler and Welch got the typhoid out of Baltimore's drinking water and Welch got the dirt out of the milk," said Huntington Williams, city health commissioner. "Cullen got politics out of the health department, and I'm not sure it wasn't the hardest job of the three."

As board president of the Enoch Pratt Free Library, he wanted to build a new central library building. To do it, he simply invited himself along on a drive with the mayor, who had opposed a necessary bond issue. That drive did it: the present central library was built. "Tom never asked for anything unreasonable, he never asked for anything for himself," said the mayor later, "and when he once started asking, he never stopped. Never."

rules that are followed to this day: it is a four-mile race without artificial jumps to be run over natural hunting country. Today several thousand spectators crowd a natural grandstand of a hillside. On the grass they spread tablecloths, lunch, chat, and flirt. Some people even cheer the race.

At Eager Street, make a loop to the left and walk to Charles Street. Both sides of this unit block retain the original residences of post–Civil War Baltimoreans, mostly unaltered. The district's commercial zoning exempted this block—one reason for its preservation, some people say. Yet William Marburg's impressive mansion at 6 E. Eager Street (1906) once provided offices for six physicians and the local American Institute of Architects. Bronze wreaths on the balconies declare victory over ordinances and time.

"Sober, discreet, and respectable" are words of a visitor describing the block. Notice that certain residences underwent a "colonializing," probably in the 1920s, with fan lights over doors at 12, 14, and 16 E. Eager Street.

At the corner of Charles Street, at 1 E. Eager Street, examine architectural details of the Eager Street façade and entrance of the Maryland Club (727-2323). From the way it holds its corner, you can say that its local archi-

tects, Baldwin and Pennington, deserve the famous epitaph proposed for English architect Van Brugh: "Lie
heavy on him, earth, because he laid many a heavy load
on thee."

On the corner take a gander north to the right at
1009 Charles Street. Since it now houses the office of
an interior decorator, Rita St. Clair, you can go in for a
look (752-1313). An 1889 bride in the Gordon family here
found "that period in Baltimore one of great elegance
and the formality very charming." Her husband expected her to pay no fewer than twenty-six calls in an
afternoon, leaving calling cards and using a cab at a
dollar an hour. At best, she made only twenty visits an
afternoon.

About another surviving mansion, an anecdote about
the Establishment comes down to us from a limerick
circulated among teenage students in private schools
of 1900. At 1016 N. Charles Street (to the right and
across Charles Street), a very respectable Mrs. William
Munnikhuysen gave a fancy-dress ball. For fun, she had
the basement transformed into "Hell" with dark corners
and demons racing about in red tights. Afterwards (as
Francis Beirne reported in *The Amiable Baltimoreans*),
these lines circulated:

There was a young lady named Nance
Who attended the Munnikhuysen dance
She went down the cellar
With a handsome young feller
And now all her sisters are aunts.

*When you loop back along Eager Street, go past St. Paul
Street to Calvert Street. Turn left and walk past the rows of
Belvedere Terrace.*

Until 1879, Belvedere, the admired country mansion
of John Eager Howard, sat doomed here in the path of
advancing Calvert Street. Once its site was cleared, one
architectural firm drew plans for houses on the east side
of Calvert Street, and a different firm built Belvedere
Terrace on the west side. Today east-side houses serve
mostly as lawyers' offices, and those on the west are split
up into apartments.

Early Hopkins researchers made this district a doctors' row. At the north end of Belvedere Terrace, with
entrance at 107 E. Chase Street, Johns Hopkins brain
surgeon Dr. Harvey Cushing and his family made
their home.

At the end of Calvert Street's 1000 block, turn left into

Dr. Hugh Hampton Young: "Diamond Jim" Brady's surgeon

At 1025 N. Calvert Street lived "the foremost genito-urinary surgeon in America." Dr. Young earned international fame for operations on malfunctioning prostates. The son of a Confederate general, he seemed "a gay young Texan" when he studied medicine at the brand-new Johns Hopkins Medical School. Later he became chief of surgery at Hopkins, and World War I chief of urology of the American Expeditionary Force.

The good doctor was adept at civic enterprise as well as with surgeon's knife. From grateful patient "Diamond Jim" Brady he extracted funds for a major urological clinic at Hopkins Hospital. Again, when Dr. Young objected to building the Baltimore Museum of Art on a small downtown lot, he wangled a large tract on the Johns Hopkins University Homewood campus—free.

"They say he made huge sums of money and lived the full life," wrote historian Dr. Bertram Bernheim, "but what of it?" In London during the summer of 1929, Young rescued seventeenth-century records of Maryland. "When I read these old documents, I was so fascinated that I decided they must go back to Maryland, and bought them." Then in 1933 he bought portraits of all the lords Baltimore. They had descended in the Calvert family and now adorn the main hall at the Pratt Library on Cathedral Street (*Tour 8*). "With a flourish and a nonchalance and a suddenness and a devil-may-care-let-the-future-go-hang [attitude] that made people literally gasp," wrote Bernheim, Young got things done.

Chase Street and walk the two blocks to Charles Street, where the Belvedere makes a large exclamation mark at the end of low rows. This street name honors a neighbor and close friend of landowner John Eager Howard, Samuel Chase, signer of the Declaration of Independence and Supreme Court justice. Not everyone shared Howard's enthusiasm for Chase: "Damned busy, restless, incendiary, ringleader of mobs, foul-mouthed and inflaming son of discord" is how the mayor of Annapolis once described him.

Chase's country retreat here neighbored Howard's Belvedere. During the Revolutionary War, when Colonel Howard was recuperating from battle wounds, he had his doctor court a Philadelphia belle, Peggy Chew, for him by letter. She succumbed to Howard's indirect charms, and afterward for forty years made Belvedere the social center of town. Once at a party, to tease her "bluff, soldierly, curt" husband, she lightly told a guest of her early "refined and highly amusing" suitor, British Maj. John Andre. "He was a damned spy, sir," interrupted Howard, "nothing but a damned spy."

Dr. Harvey W. Cushing: Pioneer brain surgeon

"I'm getting used to Baltimore," wrote the 27-year-old Dr. Cushing down from Boston, "don't mind their carelessness and slowness and unreliability now that I expect it. I wouldn't choose to dwell here however."

Dr. Cushing stayed sixteen years and here did his most important research on both the pituitary gland and brain tumors.

Consider this man Cushing, thin, medium-sized, muscular, chiseled features, snapping eyes, quick-thinking, quick-acting, short-tempered, nervous, charming, sarcastic, inconsiderate, impatient, ruthless (depending on changing moods), jealous, lovable, selfish, domineering, demanding—he had a penetrating mind, stupendous ability, and there was nothing he couldn't do and do well once he decided to have a go at it.

Dr. Bertram Bernheim, who had worked with Cushing at Hopkins, *The Story of the Johns Hopkins* (1949)

Two of Cushing's three daughters—later on all of them New York society beauties—spent childhood years in this house. Because of these sisters, this house also attaches itself to national romance. Here their mother, a Clevelander, learned from Baltimore social lionesses how to market her daughters. Betsy, Minnie, and Babe married America's notable fortunes—John Hay Whitney, Vincent Astor, and William S. Paley. "The three [Cushing sisters] had a basic sense of taste, a basic look about the bones in their faces," said New York's arbiter-of-style Diana Vreeland. "There was a moment when they were extraordinary."

Built as a luxury hotel in 1903, the present Belvedere contains apartments and public rooms. Like its contemporary Plaza Hotel in New York, it recalls a French Renaissance château, with its mansard roof, dominating site, and status for years as the social center of town.

Among early gaieties the tea dance became popular, partly because little tea was served. Instead, "frozen rye" and a famous mint julep—ambrosial concoctions—kept a man happy until bedtime. "These dancing parties were enjoyed by a number of young lawyers after what for some was a hard day's wait at the office," recalled an imbiber. "Ladies got their first experience in respectable drinking at the tea table either with the innocent looking martini, or the Pink Lady, a sickening drink made of cream and sloe gin."

At the Belvedere F. Scott Fitzgerald gave a dance for his daughter, Scottie, home for the 1935 Christmas holidays from boarding school. "Not that he grew loud or angry: he was just bleary-eyed, tottering and silly, and to make matters worse he insisted on dancing with some of the girls, who looked scared or embarrassed, while others giggled behind his back," recalled a young friend of Scottie's, Andrew Turnbull.

Now you may be ready to sit down in the Owl Bar, to the right inside the Belvedere's entrance at 1 E. Chase Street.

When you emerge, turn right and notice 14 E. Chase Street. Here lived architect Bruce Price, codesigner of Christ Church on the nearby corner of St. Paul and Chase streets. His daughter Emily Post acted as social arbiter of polite society nationally during the second quarter of the twentieth century. Her *Etiquette* sold thousands of copies. "A government official had been to see Emily Post regarding her tax papers," wrote society hostess Elizabeth Gordon Biddle Gordon. "He scrutinized the sheets carefully, then turned to her, saying, 'No woman has a right to make so much money.'"

Mrs. Post was not the lone Baltimorean in the circle of international tastemakers. "The extravagant editor-in-chief of *Vogue,* Diana Vreeland, claimed a healthy dose of Baltimore blue blood, as did Pauline de Rothschild, [an international] trendsetter of the 60s," said an observer of such matters. Decorator Billy Baldwin belongs with them, too.

On the corner you may like to examine the interior of Christ Church, now the place of worship of New Refuge Deliverance Cathedral parishioners (752-6524). *From Christ Church go back along Chase Street to Calvert Street. There turn left and walk the length of the 1100 block.* In 1983 the corner mansion on the right, 1129 N. Calvert Street, was restored as part of Government House (1127 and 1125 are included), a hospitality center for visiting dignitaries (396-3755). "Over 100 economically disadvantaged trainees under the tutelage of skilled artisans were involved in this extensive rehabilitation effort," says the official handout. Now it is furnished and decorated to look as it did in 1897, when it was bought by William Painter, who perfected the first bottlecap of the type used today.

Later the grandson of B&O president John Work Garrett, Robert Garrett, owned the house. In 1896 he had practiced discus throwing for competition in the first modern Olympics, held in Greece. Having been used to a 20-pound discus, he was chagrined to learn that he

Wallis Warfield, Duchess of Windsor: Royal wife

American names like Biddle were most peculiar, said the Prince of Wales on a 1920s visit to the States. He wasn't sure whether he had danced with a scrapple and eaten biddle for breakfast, or the other way 'round. Biddle Street later on contributed to the prince's eating scrapple and learning American social distinctions from his Baltimorean wife, Wallis Warfield. She lured him, some folks say, by preparing such famous local fare as Chicken Maryland.

Just then the door opened and Wallis rushed in, exclaiming that she was so glad to see me. She always had a marvelous way of kissing you and making you feel you were the only person in the world she wanted to meet at that particular time.

Elizabeth Gordon Biddle Gordon, *Days of Now and Then* (c. 1940)

In order to marry her, King Edward VIII had to abdicate. When they married and took the titles of Duke and Duchess of Windsor, they both expected to be addressed as "Your royal highness."

Not all Baltimoreans obliged, although one day they did give the royal pair a dignified reception. Everyone had a definite view of her climb to fortune and a royal title. The ex-king was her third husband, she having shed the first two. "His was the greatest demotion in the history of the Royal Navy," Baltimore critics said. "He fell from Lord High Admiral of the fleet to Third Mate on a tramp." Few comments were kind. "He chose the kind of woman who knows all the head waiters from Carlsbad to Biarritz," wrote columnist H. L. Mencken. "It will be, indeed, no wonder if he shoots himself before La Simpson shakes off her shackles."

Wally's bachelor uncle S. Davies Warfield, who had supported her in her youth, died in 1927 and left her $15,000 in a trust fund, the income was to cease should she remarry. Wally naturally objected since most of the $5 million estate had eluded her. Soon she appeared in the office of attorney William Marbury—a very well-dressed, handsome woman who expressed forcibly her dissatisfaction with the way the estate had been handled.

Some years later, the Duke and Duchess of Windsor attended a ball given by the Baltimore Assembly at the Belvedere Hotel. On that occasion, I introduced myself to the Duchess and reminded her of the meeting in my father's office when she had employed him in connection with her uncle's will. She seemed very much annoyed and vigorously denied that she had done anything of the kind.

William Marbury, *In the Catbird Seat* (1989)

Gertrude Stein: Trailblazer

Right across Biddle Street from the future Duchess of Windsor in 1904 lived another ambitious woman, Gertrude Stein. Born in 1874 and orphaned in her teens, she had come to stay on Reservoir Hill, Baltimore, with Aunt Fanny Bachrach. Later she said that she was "born longer in Baltimore" because her mother's family was "always there" and her father's was there but not as long. After Radcliffe College, she came to live in what she called her "white marble step house," while studying medicine at Johns Hopkins. "She was not too bored with what she was doing," she wrote later, "and besides she had quantities of pleasant relatives in Baltimore and she liked it."

After 1906 she decided against getting her M.D., established a salon in Paris, taught Hemingway, discovered Picasso, trained the Cone sisters of Baltimore to love the new art (*Tour 12*), and in general, as she boasted, was midwife to the twentieth century. "She made English easier to write," said H. L. Mencken, "and harder to read." Now her Buddha-like statue by Jo Davidson has a place of honor next to the New York Public Library's Bryant Park, not here on Biddle Street.

In Baltimore Stein had a major romance with another female medical student that she used as basis for her first novel, *Q.E.D.* Other parts of her Baltimore life got into a novel, *The Making of Americans,* and a book of short stories, *Three Lives.* "She had a servant named Lena," wrote Stein in *The Autobiography of Alice B. Toklas,* "and it is her story that Gertrude Stein afterwards wrote as the first story of the Three Lives."

would have to throw the Greek discus of 4²/₅ pounds. The result? He set a world record of 97 feet, 7 inches.

At the corner of Biddle Street, you will be rewarded if you loop to the right a hundred yards to see former homes of two ambitious and extremely successful women. See 212 E. Biddle Street, once home of author Gertrude Stein, and 215 E. Biddle Street, once home of the Duchess of Windsor.

From Stein's house walk back along Biddle Street to St. Paul Street and turn right. On your right at the corner (1201) stands the Wilkins house (1877), with unusual patterns in brick. Turn right so that you can walk past a number of architecturally elegant mansions. Some have marble façades.

At the corner on the right, 1217, you pass the mansion that Stanford White, of McKim, Mead, and White, designed in 1887 for Ross Winans, scion of a railroad family. Examine details of brick, stone, and iron, including narrow brick paving and rounded corners of the house. Gone is the old garden, except for remains of a wall fountain. Behind the parking lot, notice the Winans's carriage house, now offices. Across the street at 1114 stands another house supposedly designed by Stanford White. Both of White's houses lavish rich surface ornaments on a château-style red-brick structure.

If you look north from the Winans corner, you can see in the distance architect White's cone-topped tower on the First Methodist (Lovely Lane) Methodist Church (1882). It is worth the trip to see Tiffany windows and a domed ceiling of the main space: on it are the heavens as they appeared over the building at 3 A.M. on the dedication day, November 6, 1887.

Still facing north away from downtown, you should look to the left along the gardened house fronts of East Preston Street. By the way, this street was not named for Mayor James Preston, who brought the Democratic Convention to Baltimore in 1912 and for whom Preston Gardens is named. Rather, the name honors Col. John Eager Howard's Revolutionary War comrade-in-arms, Col. William Preston of Virginia.

Now at Preston Street, turn right and go one block to Calvert Street. There turn left and walk one block to Mount Royal Avenue.

From that vantage point, you will scan the horizon to the upper right and find a Gothic brownstone chapel marking the location of Greenmount Cemetery, Valhalla of Mount Vernon worthies for 150 years. In its way, Greenmount's tombs simply repeat the elegant rows the families inhabited when alive.

Here lie eight governors and six mayors, most of the great philanthropists of the city (including Johns Hopkins), Gen. Joseph Johnston (C.S.A.), and John Wilkes Booth. Goodness knows what the Duke and Duchess of Windsor would have had inscribed on their tombs had they ended up in Baltimore's Greenmount Cemetery, as they had once planned to do. Both, however, after negotiation, were permitted burial in Frogmore, Windsor Castle, with royalty. Managers of Greenmount then breathed more easily because it meant no security problem for them.

Move from the Calvert Street corner of Mt. Royal Avenue left to St. Paul Street (one block), and then turn right up St. Paul Street into the plaza to enter Pennsylvania Station. (Construction should be finished by the time you walk here.) Go inside to see three restored colored-glass skylights and cleaned marble walls of the main lobby. When you enter the room with train gates, look at green wall ornaments that were made in Cincinnati's Rookwood Pottery. Also, at the far end, notice the opaque glass windows, artistically designed for this space.

Instead of exiting where you came in, go to the Charles Street exit. Just outside on the right notice the sculptured metal fence (1979), designed by William Leizman as a windscreen. To the right over the bridge, the Charles Theater shows avant-garde films. A dozen blocks below it stands the original Goucher College campus, its buildings converted into offices.

From the station's entrance turn left to go south on Charles Street. Once you reach the Mount Royal Avenue corner, read the plaque on the south wall and then enter the door of the brown-beige building and go into the Academic Center of the University of Baltimore (625-3000). This university of about 6,000 students, now part of the state university system, began as a private night school for business and law (1925). Graduates include Vice-President Spiro Agnew, Gov. William Donald Schaefer, and other politicians. So much of the real estate hereabouts now belongs to the university that a cartoonist showed a sign reading "Welcome to the University of Baltimore" and then, in small print, "and the rest of Baltimore."

On the walls of the first- and second-floor corridors of the Academic Center, you see a variety of Baltimore and Maryland prints and maps. No other place open to the public and free gives you a look at so many. Other pictures in this collection hang along hallways of the Lyric Theater, which you will soon pass.

Stroll down the corridor in front of you until you find the short corridor displaying pictures of Martha Washington—and, of course, George. Note also bird's-eye views of the city, so popular in the days before air photography. Views here offer a chance to compare the city, then with now. Go up the stairs (or take the elevator) and on the second floor hunt for a series of prints showing Union military camps and hospitals in Baltimore when it was an occupied city.

For another prize on the second floor, look for the Audubon print of canvasback ducks. "In the background is a view of Baltimore [in the 1830s]," wrote Audubon, "which I have had the greatest pleasure in introducing. The generosity of its inhabitants, who, on the occasion of a quantity of my plates having been de-

stroyed by a mob during an outburst of political feeling, indemnified me for the loss."

Greek cathedral

When you return to the first floor, go back to the place you entered and turn left along that corridor to the first chance to turn left for more pictures. *At the end, leave the building. You will emerge into a student plaza.* Diagonally to the left on a corner of Mount Royal and Maryland avenues sits a bronze statue of Edgar Allan Poe (*Tour 7*). Sculpted in Rome by Moses Ezekiel, it took a long time arriving, delayed by a fire, an earthquake, and World War I. Poe is here shown in his cups, H. L. Mencken said. "General Grant was also very wet, but all his public monuments show him firmly on his legs, with his eyes to the front."

Turn left down Maryland Avenue to the next corner, Preston Street. On the right is the Greek Orthodox Cathedral of the Annunciation (1889) (727-1831). Go up the entrance steps to read the plaque on the right side of the doors. In the early 1930s developers were ready to demolish the church for a filling station. Already in the late 1920s, a Lord Baltimore gas station stood at the next corner to the south, Cathedral and Biddle streets.

In 1934 a Greek Orthodox community bought this Romanesque-style church, originally built for Congregationalists. Its Byzantine touches well suit use as a Greek Orthodox cathedral. Greek letters over an entrance arch look natural: "House of God, Gate of Heaven." Inside you still see four Tiffany stained glass windows, although the original domed ceiling has been sealed off. Every

November communicants put on a street festival with Greek food and dancing.

Turn right from Maryland Avenue and walk one block to Cathedral Street. On the near left corner is the Theatre Project; enter on West Preston Street and go upstairs. Here you can see performances by actors and dancers, some straight from the Edinburgh Festival (539-3091).

Turn left at the theater to look at the pair of large structures. 1211 Cathedral Street houses the headquarters of the Medical and Chirurgical Faculty of Maryland (539-0872). Read the historical marker here and also on the building next door, now part of the headquarters but built as the University School for Boys. Inside, exhibits of early medical instruments may interest you. Also exhibited are portraits of physicians dating back to the eighteenth century. Worth looking for is Rembrandt Peale's portrait of Dr. Horace Hayden, Peale's friend and the founder of the world's first dentistry school. Archives are open to researchers in the history of medicine.

This organization, founded by twelve physicians in 1799, retains what historian John C. French called its "quaint and old-timey name." "[The name's] special use originated in the medieval University of Paris, where graduates in medicine, by virtue of being a body exercising a liberal profession of which they had a monopoly, became the distinctive faculty." In Maryland the establishing of such a "faculty" was originally opposed by a few doctors as setting up a monopoly. Today MedChi serves as a physicians' professional and advocacy group, a component of the American Medical Association.

Across Cathedral Street, on the northwest corner of Preston Street, you see Meyerhoff Symphony Hall (783-8000). Designed by nationally known Pietro Belluschi (1982), the building depended for most of its $10.5-million cost on local developer Joseph Meyerhoff. Go inside and ask to look around. There are no straight walls—only curves—and admired acoustics. This hall holds more than 2,400 seats that are often filled by schoolchildren attending Baltimore Symphony Orchestra concerts.

Meyerhoff Symphony Hall replaced the original Bryn Mawr School for Girls (1885) on this site. That first strictly college preparatory day school for girls in the United States was founded as feeder for Bryn Mawr College, near Philadelphia. The school granted diplomas only to students who passed the college's stiff entrance examination. When parents complained to founder

Every criticism that people have about the ritual [the cotillion] is true: it is a contrived, undemocratic, and hedonistic anachronism. But, as Lenny Bruce once said about the more athletic variations of sex, as long as it's done in private and nobody's getting hurt, why worry about it?

Ann Egerton, once a debutante here (1980)

M. Carey Thomas about girls having to study Greek, the reply was, "That's so they can read Homer."

Meyerhoff Symphony Hall

From the round building you should continue your walk by walking north toward the thin column of the Revolutionary War monument (1901). At the top of a column a statue of the goddess Liberty grasps a scrolled Declaration of Independence. On plaques at the base you will find listed the many battles fought by Maryland soldiers. "The Bayonets of the Continental Army" was their sobriquet. You will be skirting Pearlstone Park with its sculptural benches and lamp posts designed by the self-described "public artist" Scott Burton. "What is important is the new public art . . . sculpture in a huge context," said Burton. At the driveway entrance note the sculpture by Stan Edmister, who is enlivening bridges over Jones Falls Expressway with rich colors. It edges the bowl that is dominated by the B&O's Mount Royal Station (1896).

Next, cross West Mount Royal Avenue to read the historical marker to the right of the entrance of the Lyric Opera House.

The Lyric Opera House holds numerous Baltimore memories since it opened in 1892 with the famous opera singer Nellie Melba on stage. In addition to music, the Lyric for generations provided a "natural grandeur" for the Bachelors' Cotillon (idiosyncratic spelling of cotillion). That was a coming-out dance for fifty 18-year-old women "of family."

"'Is it a *suitable* marriage?' was the accepted way of inquiring if one's betrothed came from a colonial—preferably Maryland—family," recalled author Susan

Barnes Watson Crosland. The way that question was asked reflects the manners of this class. "Good manners were instilled in them from birth. Whatever was happening in their lives, their [Baltimoreans'] manners were the most beautiful I have ever encountered." She was talking in 1982 about descendants of nineteenth-century Mount Vernon residents.

Now people usually go to the Lyric for road company performances of Broadway musicals. Before, the Baltimore Symphony played there, as did the Philadelphia and National symphonies. Here, too, major opera stars performed with the Metropolitan Opera. One of them, Rosa Ponselle, after a long, sterling career, married a Baltimorean. She established a reputation for musical entertainments at her Green Spring Valley estate as well as for coaching neophyte opera singers with the Baltimore Opera Company.

You are walking through Mount Royal Center, a label for a no-man's land landmarked by institutions. "Overly sterile, rigid, lacking in spontaneity," is the *Sun* critic's description. A million people come here for Artscape (*Tour 12*); 8,000 students attend either the University of Baltimore or the Maryland Institute College of Art; 6,000 bureaucrats work at Maryland State Center; 270,000 annually attend the Lyric productions, and 450,000, Meyerhoff Symphony Hall.

Now go down the steps leading to the towered old railroad station in order to study the way that structure was turned into spaces for the Maryland Institute College of Art. The institute paid $250,000 for the building and three and three-quarters of an acre and for air rights over the tracks. "Its style was somewhat Richardsonian," wrote architect Alexander S. Cochran, "but more important was its graceful, composed scale and elegance, in a word, its grandeur."

One newspaper writer was moved to comment upon the rocking chairs that the B&O Railroad authorities had placed in the waiting room:

Rock-a-bye baby, go B&O,
Wait at Mount Royal, where no whistles blow;
Rest while you wait in a fleet rocking chair
That connects with all trains—
And at no extra fare.

Evening Sun (March 10, 1961)

Walk uphill then and go back to Pearlstone Park, where you should move to the right toward a gray stone mountain, the Fifth Regiment Armory. On your left you will see a $60-million performing arts center, if it is built by the time you walk. Its larger hall seats 2,800 and the smaller 650. *Cross Howard Street and walk to the right of the armory.* The entrance to the armory faces 29th Division Street. On a monument placed near Dolphin Street, at the northeast corner of the armory, read about Maryland's 29th Division and other units linked as "the blue and gray," an epithet recalling ancestral ties North and South.

Troops landed on Omaha Beach, Normandy, D-day, June 6, 1944, and played a major part in seizing by the end of the day "a sliver of corpse-laden beach about one and a half mile wide and five miles long," wrote Gen. Omar N. Bradley, commanding general. "Every man who set foot on Omaha Beach that day is a hero." Such a result might not have seemed likely because the 29th there exposed itself to battle for the first time. Also, many soldiers had suffered from seasickness on the crossing from England. By mid-morning, things were going so badly that General Bradley considered abandoning the beach. But the soldiers then organized themselves into ad hoc units and secured the beachhead.

Go inside the armory and ask to see the Maryland National Guard Museum. Inspect its collection of flags, documents, and uniforms. At the center of one room, a World War II jeep bears a label saying that Gen. Dwight D. Eisenhower had ridden in it during a November 1944 inspection of the 29th's forward positions on the German border.

In a house on this street, about 1900, U.S. senator Arthur Pue Gorman, it is said, kept a fancy mistress near where you walk. Gorman, a political boss, may merely have caught the spirit of a town that H. L. Mencken said was very tolerant of eccentricity and sin. This street is a renamed segment of old Hoffman Street, named for nineteenth-century Daniel Hoffman, respectable merchant of onions and other country produce and real estate.

Here in the Fifth Regiment Armory a highly respectable politician and Hopkins doctor of philosophy named Woodrow Wilson was nominated for his first term as president. Wilson triumphed after forty-six ballots and a Mississippi of sweat. Baltimore's stifling heat that June, H. L. Mencken reported, ruined the tourist trade for fifty years.

*Come back to Howard Street and turn right in order to
see State Office Center.* Many Maryland State agencies
headquarter here and not in the capital, Annapolis,
where land is scarce. In 1950 neighbors to the north in
Bolton Hill lobbied furiously to persuade legislators to
choose this eighteen-acre site. Before that, much of the
site contained decayed housing and shops. Success here
encouraged "Bolton Hillers" to hold fast. Their special
neighborhood is the subject of the next tour.

*At this point your tour ends. In order to return to
Charles and Centre streets, you can choose either of two
mass transportation vehicles. Just past the Meyerhoff on
Howard Street, you can board a light rail trolley heading to
your left. Get off at the stop nearest Centre Street.*

*Or cross Howard Street and go to your left a hundred
yards or so to Preston Street. Turn right and you will soon
come to the escalator for the Metro. Take a train going to
Charles Center. Get off at the Lexington Market stop.* That
stop gives a chance to eat at Lexington Market and to
look at people.

*Should you wish to return to Mount Vernon Place, take
the exit on Eutaw Street and follow Lexington Mall downhill to Howard Street and walk along that street to the left.
Pass Saratoga, Mulberry, Franklin, and Centre streets. The
next street is Monument. Turn right to get to Mount Vernon Place.*

*To return to Constellation Dock, take the Metro to
Charles Center, exit to Calvert Street, and walk south on
Calvert toward the water and away from the Battle
Monument.*

Turn now to Baltimore society. In the old days it was extraordinarily
exclusive—not in the sense of stupid snobbishness, but in the sense
of prudent reserve. The aristocracy of the state was a sound one, for
it was firmly rooted in the land, and it looked with proper misgivings
upon all newcomers who lacked that foundation. . . . But today—God
save the mark. The old landed aristocracy, put beside the new mag-
nates and their women, seems shabby and unimportant; it has lost its
old social leadership, and it has even begun to lose its land, its traditions, and its *amour propre.*

H. L. Mencken, *The Nation* (May 3, 1922)

Entrance to turn-of-the-
century residence.

Bolton Hill

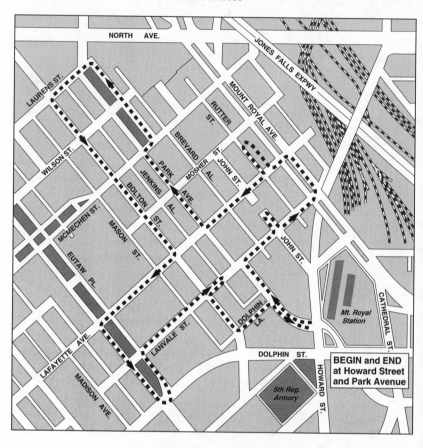

BEGIN and END at Howard Street and Park Avenue

COME HERE FOR:

- Gin and antimacassars: The 1930s "Gin Belt" and also Baltimore's attic
- House and neighborhood vital to writers F. Scott and Zelda Sayre Fitzgerald
- Sites important to McCarthy era's Alger Hiss and Whitaker Chambers
- An urban parlor district rivaling Beacon Hill in Boston and Georgetown in Washington, D.C.
- Hilly streetscapes of classic Baltimore rowhouses— red brick and white front steps—juxtaposed with more pretentious Victorian variations and all spreading under the green umbrella of Druid Hill Park
- A writers' heaven for Dr. Lewis Thomas, William Manchester, Christopher Morley, and Edith Hamilton

- Churches and shop fronts from the town's Southern past as the post–Civil War "Poor House of Virginia," to which came many widows of Confederate warriors

We Americans look to New York for the newest, Philadelphia for the first, and Boston for the best, it is said. What Baltimore offers is charm. Although that word is losing its zip, it still means "to be alluring and pleasing." Bolton Hill especially exudes "charm."

This district has bewitched architects and writers ever since it became known as the Gin Belt and Scott and Zelda Fitzgerald lived here. Before that era, the place had served as a Victorian attic of memories and antimacassars (crocheted doilies attached to chairs where macassar-oiled hair might soil upholstery). "I've lived in Bolton Hill for thirty years and know it is more than a neighborhood," wrote historian Gerald W. Johnson in 1978. "It is a state of mind."

Now visitors come to Bolton Hill just to walk around and look. They like well-preserved, post–Civil War streetscapes. Tree-lined streets open a picture book of classic brick rows. Renaissance Revival mansions, and Gothic churches. You, too, can be on the lookout for bay windows, sources of light, air, and vistas. Also poke into alleys: alley views—"Mary Ann backs," people say, balance "Queen Anne fronts."

As you walk, read handwritten notices tacked on trees alerting neighbors to backyard sales or missing tabby cats. Such notices show what a resident called "a homogeneity and friendliness not often found in large cities." They also contradict Thoreau's definition of city life as "millions of people being lonely together."

HISTORY

Bolton Hill streets sprawl over 100 acres on two hills rising from town and with views toward the Washington Monument, downtown, and the harbor. By 1800, owners of the hills had built country seats at Bolton, Mount Royal, and Rose Hill. Twenty years later, Poppleton's city plan laid out streets on the hill nearest town.

Innovation expedited development: in 1859 the first of the horse-drawn "fixed wheel" street railways opened on the western border of Bolton Hill. Those streetcars went to neighboring 600-acre Druid Hill Park. "One of the handsomest pleasurances to be found in any city," wrote a reporter from London in 1879. Here Bolton Hillers in the 1880s rode horseback before breakfast, boated, and walked. A developer named Tiffany created

"What part of the city do you live in?" he asked [in 1935]. When I told him, "Ah, Bolton street. How well do I remember it! In my time everybody who was really important in Baltimore either lived on Bolton street, or had lived there in times past, or had an uncle, son, or nephew living there, or at least had a female relative who had married a man who lived there. The boulevard to the west called Eutaw Place, was much handsomer but Bolton Street had the tone."

Gerald W. Johnson, journalist and long-time resident of 1310 Bolton Street, to the author (1978)

Baltimore is warm but pleasant. I love it more than I thought—it is so rich with memories—it is nice to look up the street and see the statue of my great uncle Francis Scott Key [actually a second cousin, three times removed] and to know Poe is buried here and that many ancestors of mine have walked in the old town by the bay. I belong here, where everything is civilized and gay and rotted and polite.

F. Scott Fitzgerald, writing from his home in the 1300 block of Park Avenue, Bolton Hill (September 9, 1935)

a grand boulevard with center garden squares, Eutaw Place, leading to that park. Johns Hopkins University's first president and early faculty added local luster.

But during two world wars greedy absentee landlords rented out single rooms to war workers, demographic patterns shifted, and property values in the neighborhood threatened to drop. While writing for the *Sun,* William Manchester had lived at 1411 Eutaw Place. He portrayed such a fear in his 1951 novel, *City of Anger.*

"A shabby-genteel fortress," said writer Murray Kempton, who had grown up here. The same year Manchester's book appeared, women garden clubbers planned their first house tour to show off the neighborhood's persistent charm. Their immediate concern was creating a name for the tour. Right away, one of the gardeners spoke a name that stuck, "Bolton Hill." It suggested bucolic pleasures and recalled Bolton Mansion (and perhaps also the aristocratic Beacon Hill in Boston). Naming the neighborhood was like pinning a fresh, fragrant gardenia on a well-preserved belle of 60. Just how the old girl is doing now will become clear as you walk. So will her struggles with urban ills.

TOUR

Starting Point: Constellation Dock, Inner Harbor

Length of walk: One and one-half hours, but longer if your pace is leisurely and if you stop for refreshment

Snacks: Two delis, one of them with tables, 1501 Bolton Street; the other at the corner of Mosher and John streets

Rest stops: Maryland Institute; Fifth Regiment Armory; Memorial Episcopal Church office, corner of West Lafayette Avenue and Bolton Street

Transportation: You can begin this tour where Tour 11 left off, in the cultural center at Howard Street

When the age of the automobile came into being, and many of you will not recall that era though *I do*, many of our Eutaw Place families of long standing moved out to the suburbs and abandoned their imposing dwellings. That fact and the event of two wars have caused the street to deteriorate. Houses that were used by a single family unit were cut up into multiple apartments and overcrowding, as you well know, has caused deterioration and blight.

Florence Hochschild Austrian, long-time resident at 1411 Eutaw Place, manuscript given to the author (1958)

Leave the Inner Harbor and walk west along Pratt Street away from the water three blocks to Howard Street and the Camden Yards light rail stop. Go north in the trolley marked Timonium to the Cultural Center stop. Cross Howard Street and turn right to Park Avenue.

On your left as you look north on Park Avenue stands a small monument (1939) honoring two local servicemen, each awarded the Congressional Medal of Honor. In World War I, Ens. Charles Hazeltine Hamman, Air Service, U.S. Navy, rescued a fellow pilot by landing a seaplane on a small body of water near Pola, Austria, and Pvt. Henry Gilbert Costin silenced an enemy machine-gun nest on the French battleground.

From the starting point you can look north uphill to a ridge of rowhouses. This is Bolton Hill itself. Between you and it, replacement of old rowhouses include high-rise Sutton Place apartments and Bolton Hill Swim and Tennis Ltd.

Behind you, Dolphin Street at Howard Street sweeps traffic away from this residential neighborhood. It also marks Bolton Hill's southern boundary. South of it the big stone Fifth Regiment Armory and newer Maryland State Office Center replace homes of early Johns Hopkins trustees. Some fled the city long ago. After the large Stewart tribe moved north of town, a reporter sourly wrote, "Anybody who lives in the Green Spring Valley has either to be a Stewart or a horse."

Turn left at Park Avenue and ascend the hill to West Lanvale Street. On your left, at Bolton Place (1965) push open the big iron gates to walk up the court to the end. Look on the left for a bas-relief owl and motto, brought here by resident author Gerald W. Johnson. *Back at Park Avenue, turn left and climb to Lanvale Street.* There, look along the left sidewalk of Park Avenue for a tall *Magnolia grandiflora*, with broad, shiny, evergreen leaves. It is a Southern tree that doesn't flourish north of Baltimore, and it suits the Southernness of Bolton Hill.

Here you find serenity. Bolton Hill is a Georgetown, D.C., without crowds, a Beacon Hill with elbow room. From this corner you should look at vistas to left and right. To the left you see the Francis Scott Key Monument and the Byzantine domes of Oheb Shalom—and behind them, the spire of old St. Peter's Church, now Bethel A.M.E. Church. When you look right, you see spires and, farther away, the medieval-looking tower of City College. When you arrive at the Park Avenue corner, you face on your left across Lanvale Street at 204 the

In my early days [1860s] there were no houses opposite [138 W. Lanvale Street] and instead we looked upon a field of green grass, where cows were picketed to pasture, and from the third story of our house could be distinguished on clear days the masts of ships in the harbor.

Latrobe Weston, "Johnny Jump-Up Hill," *Evening Sun* (July 22, 1931)

William L. Marbury Jr.: Harvard Overseer

The Marburys' son, William Jr., became another successful Baltimore lawyer who for years has been a Harvard Overseer. In his memoir *In the Catbird Seat* (1989), he recalls living next door to a boy who never let you forget that he was descended from, and named for, the founding father of the city, John Eager Howard. Later, Howard became a prominent surgeon. "His aunt Julia used to inquire of her sister, Priscilla, whether the morning papers carried news of any 'refined deaths.'" Servants in the Howard residence, listed in Howard's memoir, *Musings and Reminiscences of a Pseudo-Scientist,* included a German girl to look after his sisters, a former slave woman for the son, a house maid, a laundress, a black butler, and an Irish cook "who daily made the lightest and crispiest rolls I can recall."

Sunday-night suppers in particular were great occasions. My mother would devote several hours every Saturday to the preparation of terrapin according to a special family recipe, and on Sunday night supper always began with that dish, served with sherry and beaten biscuit.

William L. Marbury, *In the Catbird Seat* (1989)

"No American ever lives where he was born or believes what he was taught," said philosopher George Santayana. That may be true of Marbury's Bolton Hill playmates who later became prominent: Alfred Barr, director of the Museum of Modern Art; Bill Stevenson, president of Oberlin College; Hanson W. Baldwin, military columnist of the *New York Times;* Alger Hiss, the accused in the famous Hiss-Chambers case; and Savington Crampton, who, Marbury writes, was "the arbiter of Greenwich Village, New York, who could make or break literary reputations." Marbury failed to list another companion, Murray Kempton, now generally regarded as perhaps the greatest newspaperman in New York. "He kind of reminds you of the wise Episcopal bishop," said fellow Baltimorean Russell Baker.

Rolando-Thom Mansion, one of three original 1850s villas built overlooking city and harbor. Originally clergymen occupied all three. "Fine residences for the better citizens," read an advertisement for neighboring houses. The Family and Children's Services of Central Maryland occupies the mansion today.

On your immediate right, climb the steps at 159 for the historical marker. Here lived the inventor of the linotype that revolutionized printing, Ottmar Mergenthaler. Attorney William L. Marbury, with his wife, later reared a large family at 159. In 1913, when invited to sit on the U.S. Supreme Court, Marbury said he couldn't afford to give up his practice of $400,000 a year (and there was no federal income tax then).

From here you will pass rowhouses mostly of a classic Baltimore stamp. You recognize austere façades of red brick, framed with a white marble base and steps and wood cornice at the top. Doors and windows—simply holes punched into the surface—create a rhythm as groups of houses flow down and up sloping streets. "Old placid rows" was how H. L. Mencken described them.

As you walk to your right, look for good examples of this kind of house in the 100 block of West Lanvale Street on the left side. Opposite them, "the white block" of stone-fronted houses—all but one—lacks a ribbon of greenery meant to soften stiff façades.

Continue walking to your right, away from Park Avenue to John Street. These blocks housed nineteenth-century men of considerable achievement, especially ex-Confederates. At 213 Lanvale Street, Col. Charles Marshall, C.S.A., kept General Lee's farewell order as a souvenir of having witnessed Lee's surrender at Appomattox. "I have always thought that we could have had immediate restoration of peace and brotherhood among the people of these States," he later wrote.

At 150 W. Lanvale Street, former Confederate Col. Harry Gilmor reigned as city police commissioner. Tolerant Baltimoreans had forgiven his having led raiding cavalry to within five miles of downtown where they burned the governor's residence at what is now 6100 N. Charles Street. Hearing that, a Bolton Hill resident, Hugh Lennox Bond, later recalled, "I thought best to get the 'siller' [silver] out of the way, provide an extra quantity of lead [ammunition] and be ready." Luckily, the Confederates didn't ride close enough for Bond to have to shoot.

Those men were the past. From the very different world of medical scientists, Dr. Jesse Lazear lived at 127 W. Lanvale Street. In 1900 he volunteered as a human guinea pig to prove that mosquitoes carried yellow fever. Five days after having been bitten by an infected mosquito, Lazear died. "With more than the courage and devotion of the soldier, he risked and lost his life to show how a fearful pestilence is communicated and how its ravages may be prevented," said Harvard president Charles Eliot.

Turn left into John Street Park. John Street has shrunk. Once it swooped down Bolton Hill and eastward for blocks and blocks through the land of John Eager Howard, for whom it was named. In the 1950s leading residents of the 1300 block dealt with owners and city officials to tease, cajole, and bargain John Street Park

"Glory Stands beside
Our Grief"

out of the streetbed. In giving up parking in favor of
greenery, residents set an example. Nowadays pedestrian
streets like this have spread through Bolton Hill, as
you will see.

On the right, at 1303 John Street, in the 1880s a bank-
rupt former planter, Thomas Dabney, played whist with
other Southerners. "The city is full of poor Virginians,
made poor by the war," said Dabney, "and being poor
and well bred, all ostentation is tabooed, and they give
you what they have without apology." His daughter
Susan Smedes told his story in *Memorials of a Southern
Planter*—life on a thousand-acre Mississippi cotton
plantation that was worked by hundreds of slaves. The
book generally created a favorable picture of slavery, and
English Prime Minister William Gladstone praised it.

*Come back to Lanvale Street and continue past the next
corner, Rutter Street, to Mt. Royal Avenue.* Look to your
right at towers and bulky buildings of Mount Royal
Center (*Tour 11*) and the city. Its regal name came from
Mount Royal, an eighteenth-century stone mansion
overlooking Jones Falls. Running past it, the street
approached Druid Hill Park. War monuments punctu-

ated center park squares. Three remain, the one to
the Confederate dead in the 1400 block of Mt. Royal
Avenue.

*At Mt. Royal Avenue, turn left and walk past the white
Italian-style palazzo of the Maryland Institute of Art toward the more somber Gothic Corpus Christi Church.*

The church, when wet with rain, looks like an ele-
phant kneeling. Be sure to look across the parking lot
between these big buildings. Top stories of pastel rowhouses rise over a tall dark stone wall. Those tiny residences in the 1300 block of Rutter Street once may have
housed railroad workers. Eighteenth-century mill owner
Thomas Rutter gave his name to this street even though
his house and mill were downhill on Jones Falls.

Both the institute headquarters and the church recently underwent restoration. Enter the institute palazzo
by climbing the front steps or through doors under
them (to an elevator). Inside you sense that you are back
in 1910—plaster casts of classical sculpture, a patriotic
mural, and glass skylight and lighting fixtures. The stairway balustrade offers a spectacular slide—if you dared—
down to shiny brass balls at the foot.

Outside, notice above the entrance bronze portraits
of Andrew Carnegie (left), who paid for the building,
and Otto Fuchs (right), who designed the interior studio
spaces. To the right of the entrance, two large bronze
commemorative plaques rest on the lawn like tomb-
stones. No one has yet found a better place to put them.
The institute's campus sprawls along the eastern edge of
Bolton Hill. Across the street the institute trustees converted a shoe factory for exhibitions, offices, and studios,
now the Fox Building. Downhill to the south most of
the campus sprawls—student center, bookstore, the
Mount Royal Station Building (*Tour 11*). Later on your
walk northward, you will glimpse a newly built dormitory complex, with entrance on McMechen Street.

Close to the handsome Maryland Institute of Art stood (and stands) a small but beautiful Confederate war memorial, a life-size statue of a wounded and exhausted youth, supported and sheltered by
a ministering angel. . . . I witnessed the unveiling of a more recent monument [since moved to
Charles and 29th streets], much more heroic and imposing than its Confederate predecessor, repre-
senting a Union officer on a high pedestal striding forth to battle in the direction of his dying adver-
sary a few blocks away. And behind the warrior, urging him forward, is another angel, arrogant and
flamboyant by contrast with her colleague attending the dying Southerner.

Felix Morley, who grew up on the edge of Bolton Hill and later became president of Haverford College, *For
the Record* (1980)

Maryland Institute College
of Art stair

You will have to visit the Walters Art Gallery and the
Baltimore Museum of Art in order to see the institute's
Lucas collection of mostly French art: 20,000 prints, 300
paintings, 150 drawings and watercolors, 140 bronzes,
71 artists' palettes, and 70 porcelains. One appraisal
went as high as $15 to $20 million, plus the intangible
value of an intact collection preserved as the lengthened
shadow of one connoisseur.

In the mid-nineteenth century, Baltimorean George
Lucas had been so seasick on his voyage to France that
he never came back. Other people called it "a confirmed
habit of Paris." He moved in Parisian art circles, helped
Henry Walters collect art, and just generally lived well.
Lucas bequeathed the art so that art students here could
study such masters as Whistler (*Tour 7*).

Walk next door to see a bright restoration of Corpus
Christi Roman Catholic Church (1891). The Jenkins
family gave land for it as well as for the institute's
palazzo. Ask permission at the old rectory just across
Lafayette Avenue at 110 W. Lafayette Avenue (523-4161).

Inside, the church shines with imported stained glass, mosaics, and marble. Notice exterior doors with elaborate iron designs decorating the wood.

During the hottest weekend in July, Mt. Royal Avenue becomes Artscape. That festival brings thousands of Baltimoreans to eat, listen, and look.

Today, Rutter's Mill Park hides in the 1400 block of Rutter Street. *Reach the park by going from Mt. Royal Avenue left onto West Lafayette Avenue and immediately turning right into Rutter Street.* Before urban renewal days in the 1960s, the site of this passive park held a heap of tiny dwellings, quite derelict.

Return to Lafayette Avenue and walk to the corner of John Street. On your right, the large brick building—now a nursing home—was built for the Hospital for the Women of Maryland. For decades it was the lying-in hospital of Baltimore's Establishment. During the Depression it helped to anchor the neighborhood. "An extraordinary atmosphere pervaded the hospital," recalls Dr. Thomas Turner of his 1920s internship here, "a certain quiet quality contrasting sharply with the bustle of a large university hospital."

The southwest corner house, 1312 John Street, exhibits sculpture that you can see from the sidewalk. Elegant, stylized animals appear on the wall to the left of the entrance and also in hanging candelabra in bay windows. They belong to the daughter of artist Hunt Diederich, whose work was recently exhibited by the Whitney Museum in New York. A nephew of Richard Morris Hunt and son of a Prussian cavalry officer, Diederich got kicked out of the Pennsylvania Academy of Fine Arts in 1906 for "improper language used by him in a class comprised of men and women."

On the left across the street from the nursing home, you see more semi-detached houses like those facing John Street Park. Sunlight pours in from three sides of each house. Entrances are in the middle of the long side

---

This is what life in this city is all about: Saturday afternoon with rain dripping out of a leaden sky and the radio telling everybody to stay home [from Artscape] and people are dancing in the street. It starts with maybe a dozen black kids stepping lightly to music with a vaguely Caribbean beat. Now some of the spectators begin to join them. They are black and white and Asian. They slide several steps in each direction and punctuate the steps with hand claps. A man with an oil drum of a chest dances on make-believe Fred Astaire feet. Behind him is a woman with a silk skirt and an Orioles cap who's next to a toothless guy in Bermuda shorts and loafers with knee-high black socks who's alongside a pregnant woman dancing with her blond 2-year-old son.

Michael Olesker, *Evening Sun* (July 1990)

of the house, not in the narrow front facing the street. In that arrangement, the houses resemble old Charleston, South Carolina, houses. Notice a frieze of ornamental iron fence along gardens and an elaborate cast-iron balcony stretching across the two long first-floor windows of 103 W. Lafayette Avenue, the second house from the corner.

One afternoon in the 1930s a resident, Bootie Crane Royer, while riding home on a streetcar was startled to hear her old aunt, getting ready to debark, say in a loud tone, "John Street is the only respectable street left in Baltimore." That comment pretty well sums up how the Hill appeared to some residents after World War II. The place had already passed its 125th birthday.

The aunt's defiant attitude tells why the old neighborhood held fast. Some people looked down on other districts, including suburbs. Many agreed with Cyril Connolly, "Slums may be the breeding-grounds of crime, but middle-class suburbs are incubators of apathy and delirium." Some residents were too poor to move; others—with Southern roots—were too much attached to their delightful social circle.

Walk to the corner of Park and Lafayette avenues, and look up and down Park Avenue. Not far from here, downtown Park Street met and took over local Grundy Street. Evidently, the name change to Park Avenue better suited this seat of all elegance.

From this corner, turn left and make a loop into the 1300 block. Even in the Depression a Park Avenue address carried cachet. F. Scott Fitzgerald and his wife, Zelda, cynosures of all eyes in the Jazz Age, stopped off here.

Take time to look around the 1300 block of Park Avenue before descending the hill in the 1400 block. Look at 1312 because here lived Edith Hamilton, classicist and author of *The Greek Way.* "Baltimore has made a comfortable place of residence for writers of a very high rating," wrote historian Gerald W. Johnson, "from Edgar Allan Poe to John Dos Passos, Ogden Nash, and Scott Fitzgerald."

Bolton Hill's ambiance and cheap rents have lured writers: James M. Cain, Dr. Lewis Thomas, Gertrude Stein, Holmes Alexander, Hulbert Footner, Gerald W. Johnson, Christopher Morley, William Force Stead, Russell Baker, Sidney Nyburg, William Manchester, Murray Kempton.

Next door to Edith Hamilton's house at 1310 Park Avenue stands what used to be the stable of the Rolando-Thom Mansion. During the Depression, genteel ladies converted it to the Pear Tree Inn. Across the street from

F. Scott and Zelda S. Fitzgerald: Writers and cynosures of the Jazz Age

"They did both look as though they had stepped out of the sun; their youth was just so striking," said Dorothy Parker about the couple before they came to live in Baltimore. Zelda had grown up as a Southern beauty in Montgomery, Alabama, and Scott had ties with the Confederacy through his Maryland kin. When they were in their twenties, his success as a writer thrust them into sophisticated 1920s New York. He had, in fact, named the Jazz Age and described it in *The Great Gatsby*.

But by 1933 their lives were in disarray. Zelda was suffering mental illness. Scott drank too much. And his popularity and income declined. So they moved to Baltimore, where she could receive treatment and he could finish a novel he had been working on for years. Booze interfered. "The young doctors of Baltimore avoid him [Scott] as much as possible," wrote H. L. Mencken in his diary. "for he has a playful habit of calling up those he knows at 3 A.M. and demanding treatment, i.e., something to drink. How he manages to get any work done I can't imagine."

In the 1300 block of Park Avenue the Fitzgeralds, including 10-year-old daughter Scottie, made their last home together. Before leaving Baltimore in 1936, Zelda published her one novel, *Save Me the Waltz,* and Scott published *Tender Is the Night.* His flawed but classic novel portrays the downfall of a talented man with Maryland roots. The book failed to sell.

"If I have anything in common with a man [in Baltimore] intellectually our pasts seem to have been very different," Scott wrote after book sales disappointed him, "and if, on the contrary, our pasts have been the same, there is no intellectual meeting ground. I feel like the old maid . . . who 'grew less desirable and more particular.'"

Here Scott Fitzgerald also endured what he recounted in print as his "crack-up." Pacing the back porch on Park Avenue, "like a broken-stringed bow upon a throbbing fiddle—I see the real horror develop over the rooftops, and in the strident horns of night-owl taxis and the shrill monody of revelers' arrival over the way. Horror and waste."

In their Baltimore years, the Fitzgeralds paid for their Jazz Age self-indulgence, their heedlessness. Within a decade, she perished in a fire at a mental institution in Asheville, North Carolina. He died four years after leaving Baltimore to write for movies.

that property you can survey unusually varied styles of 100-year-old residences. As you return to Lafayette Avenue, you pass the office and church of Brown Memorial Presbyterians, 1316 Park Avenue, originally the parson's manse. The church (1869–70) memorialized George Brown of the Alex. Brown brokerage dynasty. To see the church, just ask the staff (523-1542).

For most of Brown Memorial's existence, proper Baltimore ladies didn't feel properly married anywhere but here. Rich donors such as the Garretts assured the church's status by buying everything first class. In particular, at least ten windows originated in Louis Comfort Tiffany's studio, more from there than in any other Baltimore church—and two of the largest Tiffany made. Today this Tiffany glass may strike you as rather lugubrious with somber colors and solemn biblical figures. But its subtle coloring may win you over.

Contrast these windows with modern versions of thirteenth-century French glass over the altar in a window memorializing U.S. Postmaster General and Mrs. James A. Gary. Several of their seven daughters married here. For one wedding President McKinley and his cabinet traveled from Washington by special train. Here Gary adorned yet another of his seven daughters with his usual gift of a diamond necklace.

When you emerge, walk across Lafayette Avenue into the 1400 block of Park Avenue. As the 1300 block of Park Avenue gives way to the 1400 block, the downhill rows are set back farther from the street on wide sidewalks. Then a much greater widening comes at Park Place (1600 and 1700 blocks), with the roadway splitting to pass center park squares. These sequential widenings make the vista ceremonial.

Architecture here adds to that effect. Most houses here are tall, and grow grander by contrast with the few regular-size rowhouses that now appear small. For instance, compare 1418 Park Avenue with 1425. On the right, at the side of 1403 appears a noteworthy cast-iron gate, one of a number of gates to look for as you go. At 1501 Park Avenue columnist Russell Baker lived with his wife, Mimi, in a basement apartment. His account of their courtship in *Growing Up* places them among the town's great romances.

At 1500 Park Avenue there once lived six Poe brothers, all of them Princeton football stars. One was named Edgar Allan Poe, though descended from a cousin that the famous writer disliked. The Poe mansion heads a row of what in the 1870s scoffers called "Frick's Folly."

Nobody, they said, would want to live so far from town. But the Fricks gave the row the high-falutin' name of Beethoven Terrace and also saw to it that a horse-car trolley came out this far. Two park squares, adjacent, created an amenity in a closely built-up city.

In a Beethoven Terrace mansion Frances and Lawrence Turnbull led artistic and literary Baltimore. Frances headed the Women's Poetry Society and, with her husband, gave receptions for Turnbull Lecturers on Poetry at Johns Hopkins University. Guests lionized literary men such as Harvard's Charles Eliot Norton, who lectured on Dante. In the 1870s the music room made a haven for Sidney Lanier, exiled Georgia poet and flutist.

Daughter Grace Turnbull became a sculptor. "I have not yet created that one supremely beautiful thing I had hoped to leave to posterity and which would have constituted my excuse for being," she said. "I have an awful suspicion that it is not from such privileged homes as ours that the most distinguished performance usually comes."

At the corner of Park Avenue and McMechen Street, make a loop to the right for a look at the Commons (1992), dormitories for Maryland Institute and College of Art students. Buildings face a grassy courtyard above the street and give students views outward over the city. Students also look directly across the street to a large, colored sculpture at School 66. "Nuts and bolts" is the description given by disapproving neighbors of James Arthur Benson's untitled work (1982).

When you return to the Park Avenue corner, walk into the 1600 and 1700 blocks, named Park Place. You can rest in the park squares on benches around either of the old fountains. Early on, the squares attracted merchant princes. Thomas O'Neill, 1733 Park Avenue, for instance, rode the streetcar down to his department store at Lexington and Charles streets every day. The story goes that, when the Big Fire was approaching, O'Neill prayerfully decided to build a new cathedral if the flames stopped short of his store. The flames did stop, and he left money to build the Cathedral of Mary Our Queen in the 5400 block of Charles Street.

Look around the Wilson Street corner to see rows of Park Place houses—no demolition, no teeth missing in the solid rows. All the residences, built between 1880 and 1910, exhibit generous proportions. Most have four or five stories and are twice as wide as the ordinary rowhouse. Here you find mansard roofs, Italianate cornices, rounded bay windows, and stone-ornamented doorways. Exteriors only hint at interior glory of stained glass skylights, brass chandeliers, gold mirrors, solid walnut doors.

"Little else but a string of stairs, with more or less extended landings," an architect complained in 1874 about such townhouses as these. "Up and down, up and down, the women folk are perpetually toiling as in a treadmill . . . in the fruitless and health-destroying labor of carrying themselves from floor to floor."

Seventy years later, in the 1950s, Bolton Hill residents worried about deteriorating houses. Particularly vulnerable to blight were large houses that had been cut up into apartments for war workers. To maintain neighborhood stability, citizens formed a private rehabilitation corporation, Bolton Hill, Inc. They bought fifteen properties with $75,000, and, after repairs, sold them. In 1959 *Look Magazine* gave this group its Community Home Achievement Award.

On the left at the corner of Wilson Street, Strawbridge Methodist Church (1884) displays stained glass windows of the best period. They glow on Christmas nights illuminated from within (669-6262). The Reverend John Goucher (for whom Goucher College was named) built the church.

Other remnants of glory you will find in poems of Elliott Coleman, creator of the renowned Writing Seminars at Johns Hopkins University. When in 1947 he rented an apartment at 1819 Park Avenue, downstairs lived physician and essayist Lewis Thomas and his wife. "Evenings, Elliott would come down to read his poetry or to ask questions about science," recalled Thomas. "My experimental rabbits later turned up, obscurely, in several of his sonnets."

When you reach the end of Park Place at Laurens Street, turn left and go past Old Friends Apartments on the left. The name comes from the building's having been built for a Quaker (Friends) meeting and schools. In the left-

---

Unconsciously the roving [gang called] Mount Royals carried on the ancient traditions of Chesapeake [Baltimore] hooligans. They were only once thoroughly routed. Aunt Bee was shopping at the North Avenue market when she saw Jeff and Skinny [her charges], unarmed, chivvied to despair by a group with hockey sticks. Rushing forth with umbrella and a head of cabbage, she hurled the vegetable like a grenade, and laid about fiercely with the other weapon. The enemy dispersed in shocked amazement.

Christopher Morley, who grew up at the edge of Bolton Hill and later became a nationally known writer and editor, *Thorofare* (1942)

hand wing, students splashed in the first indoor pool built in a Baltimore school.

Go one block to Bolton Street and turn left. Look into the right-hand block before descending the 1700 block. The sidewalk paving on the near side may well be the only gray brick walk in the city. You will see why when you walk on its bumpy surface. Compare the prettier red-brick paving at 1735 Bolton Street. "Housekeepers who took great pride in appearances used to redden their sidewalks," recalled an old-timer. "A home-brewed concoction of brick dust and water was energetically applied by young and old working together."

Just at the foot of the hill, look to the right at urban renewal projects that in the 1960s replaced a street that looked like Bolton Street. On the corner of Mason and McMechen streets once stood Harley's, where customers bought submarine sandwiches made with a special hot sauce. This shop, with its late-night crowds, irritated neighbors. Upstairs, owner Harley Brinsfield broadcast the popular jazz radio "Harley Show." Sometimes he entertained his friend Billie Holliday. Today her larger-than-life statue stands a few blocks west of here at the northwest corner of West Lafayette and Pennsylvania avenues.

On Bolton Street you will cross McMechen Street and then Mosher Street. Here you will discover what observers have called a charming village life. In front of 1501–1535 Bolton Street, a canopy of horse chestnut trees shade broad sidewalks, and a ribbon of greenery drapes around white marble steps. Across the street at 1500, the London Shop attracted First Lady Jackie Kennedy buying antiques for refurbishing the White House.

Earlier the corner store had served as a neighborhood gathering place when it was a grocery store run by Mr. John. "He acts as an informal gastronomic autocrat. . . . If a customer is worried about how to bake a cake, Mr. John will advise, at almost any hour," wrote a newcomer. "He may even make it."

At 1501 Bolton Street you have a chance to sit down and refresh yourself at a new coffee bar and delicatessen. If you sit outdoors, notice a half-dozen bay windows jutting from residences into Mosher Street sidewalks. Owners pay a special fee because these windows encroach on public sidewalks.

From the Mosher Street corner, ascend the 1400 block of Bolton Street, often considered the best example of Baltimore's classic row. Note how, in the 1400 block, round-topped entrances march downhill on the right and meet

[Billie Holliday] didn't like crowds. I'm sure she left twenty people at the club she was playing, all of 'em wanting to take her to some party, when she'd come over to my place. Billie was always bubbling over when I first knew her. [Later] she was trouble looking for a place to happen.

Harley Brinsfield

in mid-block at 1414 with the parade of those coming uphill.

At the hilltop Memorial Episcopal Church (1860) keeps its door open every day. This church fostered neighborhood revival in the 1960s and 1970s because parishioners lived nearby and because the whole community settled problems in its parish house.

The Civil War interrupted construction of the church. Go inside to see how the vestry has adapted it to modern worship. You may think the interior with its wide wooden roof rather like a barn. Look in the right transept at architect Edmund Lind's drawing of the church and its unbuilt tower. Outside, in 1968, two neighbors had a concrete terrace ripped up and a holly and magnolia planted. Here has blossomed another green corner.

At Lafayette Avenue, turn right. The street name duplicates Fayette Street. Maybe Baltimoreans forgot, or loved the French general excessively. This street runs west to the 1000 block's Lafayette Square, a park framed by mansions and churches built by devout Victorians. They cost much more than Memorial Episcopal Church and show it.

From this corner in the 1930s you couldn't throw a baseball in any direction without hitting a professional Southerner or a writer. The Reverend William Meade Dame, in the rectory, 1409 Bolton Street, wrote his reminiscences of serving as drummer boy with the Confederates at Gettysburg. Across the street at 1402, Christiana Bond wrote about dancing with Robert E. Lee. At 90 she published poetry in the *Saturday Evening Post.* Next door, at 1404 Bolton Street, Mrs. Ann Van Ness Merriam recorded *The Ghosts of Hampton,* the great Georgian Ridgley mansion near Towson. Down at Mosher Street lived Letitia Stockett, whose recollections enliven this present book.

As you walk along Lafayette Avenue, look to the right and left at 1960s and 1970s townhouses that fill the old roadbed of Linden Avenue. This oval of rowhouses replaced houses like those on adjacent streets. In one of them Alger Hiss grew up. Many Baltimoreans still feel uncomfortable when his name is mentioned. "After the accusations were first aired," wrote *Sun* editorial writer Antero Pietila in 1993, "the whole city was divided. Old friendships were broken in arguments."

Originally dubbed Garden Street, Linden Avenue gave merry parties a route to Pimlico Race Track. After

As late as 1950 the United Daughters of the Confederacy chapter was meeting in Memorial Church parish house. One day while shopping, a member noticed an unusual pin on a neighbor's dress. In answer to her inquiry, she was told that the pin commemorated a grandfather's Civil War service with New Jersey volunteers. "Oh, I didn't know they had volunteers on *that* side!"

Bolton Hill: Baltimore Classic (1978)

Wooden porches

the Maryland Jockey Club, formed in 1743, acquired the Pimlico estate in 1870, the winner of the first race was Milton H. Sanford's horse, Preakness. Afterward, the special Preakness race became the middle race of the Triple Crown, held after the Kentucky Derby and before the Belmont Stakes each May.

Continue walking to Eutaw Place. Before you reach that street, notice ranks of back verandas to right and left. The wooden one on the left is rarer than the cast-iron one on the right.

At the corner, look to your right at the Gunther Fountain, bought in 1876 from the Philadelphia Bicentennial. Recently neighbors paid to have the fountain restored and framed with Victorian plantings.

Turn left and walk one block to the Key Monument. At 1320 Eutaw Place you can tour the Lillie Carroll Jackson Museum. As a long-time leader of Maryland's NAACP, Jackson during and after World War II fought to open employment to African Americans. In 1946, her Baltimore branch had 17,000 members, largest in the country. A wall plaque tells of her role in desegregating public places.

At 1300 Eutaw Place lived the first president of the Johns Hopkins University and organizer of the Johns Hopkins Hospital, Daniel Coit Gilman. At the time he accepted the job, he was briefly president of the University of California, Berkeley, and wired his wife in Berkeley, "Chesapeake Bay oysters have a fine flavor." The Gilmans presumably served many an oyster at receptions here. A succeeding resident here, Dr. J. M. T. Finney, once turned down the presidency of Princeton University, he liked life in Baltimore so much.

From the Key Monument you can survey State Center, downtown towers, and Eutaw Place garden squares. In 1910 Theodore Marburg gave the city the Francis Scott Key monument here on what was until 1918 the highest point of land in the city. Water no longer laps against the bronze boat. City authorities drained the pool to protect wandering children from drowning. Above the water basin a bronze poet offers a bronze manuscript of his "Star-Spangled Banner" to Columbia holding the flag on high. Within sight of her, in 1949, writer William Manchester rented a basement apartment at 1411 Eutaw Place. He later wrote about the contemporary world of heroes and villains, including John F. Kennedy and Baltimore numbers runners.

Next to Key Monument rise three tiled domes of Byzantine-style belonging to Eutaw Place Temple (1893), long home of the Oheb Shalom congregation and now owned by Prince Hall Masons. Its white, rough-cut marble gleams in the sun. "[Local] Beaver Dam marble is one of the best exterior-grade marbles," says John Hardtke of Hilgartner Natural Stone Company, "that was ever quarried in this country." Quarries gave out in the 1960s.

Scott Fitzgerald also roamed here. One incident was reported by a young neighbor, Garry Moore (later a popular radio and television entertainer):

Fortunately I was driving very slowly [past the Key Monument] when Scott jumped out of the car. I got out and found Scott hiding under some bushes. "Scott," I said, "what's the matter?" He said, "Shhh! I don't want Frank to see me this way [drunk]." [The Frank referred to was Francis Scott Key, Scott's namesake.] I had to stand in front of the monument to distract "Frank" while Scott slipped by unseen.

Benjamin Szold, rabbi of this congregation from 1859 to 1892, was father of Henrietta Szold (*Tour 4*). One of eight children in the only Jewish family in his Hungarian village, he arrived in this country already trained as a rabbi. Downtown he led a conservative flock. Once during the Civil War, he failed to obtain President Lincoln's pardon for a certain deserter. "In reckless protest," we are told by a chronicler, "he held the hand of the condemned soldier while the firing squad shot to kill." Later, Szold embraced Zionism long before there was a strong Zionist movement.

If you have rested long enough, make a loop south in the 1200 block. Diagonally across from the Temple at 1210 Eutaw Place, Woodrow Wilson began his march to the White House. He occupied the third-floor back room when he began studying politics at the new Johns Hopkins University. By coincidence, within view of that house, in the Fifth Regiment Armory, Wilson was nominated for the presidency. "In all my life, I think, I have never known any one so covetous of fame as he [Wilson] was," wrote his college classmate William Cabell Bruce (later a U.S. senator), "or so confident that he would attain it."

Maybe by the time you go, the greenery will have spread downhill in a new set of planted squares right through State Center. Mansions facing the old squares, such as 1205, carry out a grand scale. Notice its garden gate dating back to 1805 when Baltimore Clippers sailed the seas. Also on the grand scale is Eutaw Place Baptist Church (1871), now City Temple Baptist, with its 190-foot tower. It marks the south end of Eutaw Place with an exclamation point. As a good Baptist, architect Thomas Ustick Walter designed the church without charge. Earlier he *had* charged for doing the capitol dome in Washington.

Other well-known men and women turned Eutaw Place into a physicians' row. Two of the so-called Big Four physicians, who first headed clinical services at Johns Hopkins Hospital, lived here. Dr. Howard A. Kelly lived at 1406 and in his hospital at the north end of the 1400 block used radium to treat cancer patients. As head of obstetrics and gynecology, he earned national fame as "a wizard in the operating room."

Of Dr. William H. Halsted, head of surgery, a colleague said that he never performed an operation in which he did not advance surgery. Before he came to Hopkins, he had become addicted to cocaine when experimenting upon himself. With addiction under control, he arrived in Baltimore to pioneer surgical procedures.

What most people remember, though, is that Halsted's romantic interest in a nurse led to the innovation of wearing surgical gloves in operating rooms: her sensitive hands suffered from washing with antiseptics. Later he married her, a daughter of Confederate Gen. Wade Hampton. "They lived a strange sequestered life in a great big house [1201 Eutaw Place, now demolished]," wrote H. L. Mencken, "where each had his own quarters and neither saw anybody."

Add to the list of eccentrics—and geniuses—Dr. Claribel Cone, who with her sister Etta collected modern art in four Eutaw Place apartments in the Marlborough, behind you at 1601 Eutaw Place. Their taste for Picassos and Matisses formed under the guidance of collector–author Gertrude Stein, a friend from Stein's years in Baltimore (*Tour 11*). Later their friendship soured: Stein had the brass to write Etta Cone trying to sell for $1,000 the typescript of *Three Lives,* a book Etta had typed for her.

Today the Cone Wing at the Baltimore Museum of Art houses everything the Cone sisters wanted—except a Picasso that proved too tall to fit their dining room (or did Etta hesitate to dine with the painting of a nude boy in the room?). It was Picasso's *Boy with a Horse,* now in the Metropolitan Museum of Art. "For my part," wrote the critic Clive Bell in 1951, "I cannot grieve to find, in an age when the emotions of artists, *amateurs,* and critics are much at the service of their theories, two ladies who bought pictures for no better reason than that they liked them."

When you feel that you have explored Eutaw Place thoroughly, turn left and walk through the street park of Lanvale Street. You will pass townhouses of the 1970s and 1980s, fountains, and three lions on pedestals (relics of a Calvert Street bridge). To left and right from this Lanvale Street Park you can make a loop into courtyards that make a center for fairly recent rowhouses. The Linden Green courtyard on the left has an unusual waterfall.

Come back to Lanvale Street and continue walking away from Key Monument. You may decide that these new courts blend in nicely with the old rows you pass just across Mason Street. This group of houses dates from the 1860s and 1870s. Count among recent residents a Hopkins classics professor; an octogenarian woman who grew up at 237, moved next door after she married, and still resides here; and André Netchaeff, a White Russian descended from a ninth-century Russian ruler,

The Misses Cone were sensitive to that shudder of anticipation that was in the air at the turn of the century, that new way of thinking and feeling which one perceives in the work of the Curies, Proust, and even Ravel.

George Boas, a friend and Hopkins professor, *The Cone Collection,* Baltimore Museum of Art (c. 1950)

Garden and entrance
to villa

who once raced his Bugatti in the 500-kilometer race at
San Sebastian, Spain.

At the corner of Bolton Street you see on your left at
232 W. Lanvale Street, behind a picket fence, the oldest
house in the neighborhood. It has always been a private
house. For forty years it was rented by Dr. William H.
Howell, an early stalwart of the Johns Hopkins medical
faculty, whose son Roger became dean of the School of
Law, University of Maryland, and whose daughter Janet
became headmistress of the Bryn Mawr School.

After World War II, Mrs. Nancy Howard DeFord
Venable moved into this villa. With her came a set of
early nineteenth-century painted furniture by the
Findlay brothers of Howard Street, now exhibited at the
Baltimore Museum of Art. Also with her came a man
she called her cousin, William Force Stead. An Oxford
poet and Anglican priest, he had officiated in 1927 at the
baptism of poet T. S. Eliot. "Walking slowly along the
edge of new housing sites [on the Hill]," a neighbor
wrote, "they resembled almost extinct sea creatures
washed up on shore." In the house they entertained
literati W. H. Auden and Tennessee Williams, among
others. Williams borrowed her name—and character?—
for *Suddenly Last Summer.*

This villa's sunny corner garden always attracts
passersby with its roses and sweet alyssum. It remains a
country house in the city's heart. "Ugly, stark, brick
structures of a later growth tower so far above it," as
novelist Sidney Nyburg described it in *The Ivory Gate,*

"as to make its low rambling outline appear almost as though it were a bit of the shrubbery itself."

From the villa stroll around the corner past the big bay window along Bolton Street's 1300 block. Here the first three houses on the left stand out in the mannerist style of ornament—stained glass, tile, and stone. And beyond them on the left look for a well-preserved second-floor wooden veranda. Across Bolton Street look for Lollipop Lane, shaped like a dog's leg. In May the lane fills with fragrant peonies. Grateful Bolton Hill children remembered with the name an endless stream of lollipops handed out by Miss Sara Monmonier.

For another stroll, make a loop into the Lanvale Street block diagonally across Bolton Street from the villa to inspect iron footscrapers. They are antique reminders of filthy walkways and streets. Look for a double phoenix bird design at 246 W. Lanvale Street. On the corner at 225 W. Lanvale Street lived Judge Hugh Lenox Bond, an ardent Union supporter. On April 18, 1864, he had addressed three full regiments of "Negro soldiers about to join Burnside" (he wrote) and then had them parade "right along [Pratt Street] where on this day three years ago the Massachusetts troops were butchered."

Once you have seen the 1300 block of Bolton Street and also the rows on Lanvale Street across Bolton Street, come back to the corner and go downhill in the 1200 block of Bolton Street to Dolphin Lane. Look straight ahead to the Fifth Regiment Armory that in 1900 replaced George Grundy's serene country house, Bolton. Supposedly Grundy named his estate for his hometown in northwest England. When he built the house in 1800, it dominated thirty acres and boasted "one of the largest ice houses in the city, brick barns and stables, sheds, a smokehouse, slave quarters, a walled garden, an orchard of peach, cherry and apple, and ten acres of rye, timothy and orchard grass." Grundy, an importer, lost the estate in 1812 when the French captured three of his ships.

The name "Bolton" appears on Poppleton's 1823 plat for an extension of the city into Baltimore County: Bolton Street is Grundy's north entrance drive transformed and extended. The street name Dolphin reminds us that we are in a sea-going town. The Baltimore privateer *Dolphin* brought in the first prize vessel in the War of 1812.

The park on the right at the end of the 1200 block displays a bronze plaque on the brick wall next to the steps. It tells of the neighborliness of two African Americans, William Gaines Contee and Edward Wilson Parrago, who were still living next to the park at its dedica-

---

The memory of the old house [Bolton] is very fragrant. It stood in the center of the grounds with a carriage drive sweeping around before the lovely entrance.... Great trees gave shade, and the lawns cut smooth and primly were dappled with shadows.... One dusky evening in the autumn I crept through the fence to examine the old place. The family had long ago departed, and the house stood tenantless, forlorn. The doorway even then retained its spacious, hospitable air, but the windows were dark and black.

Letitia Stockett, *Baltimore: A Not Too Serious History* (1928)

tion in 1971. From the park, look toward the playground across Bolton Street in order to take in urban vistas.

At the foot of the 1200 block of Bolton Street, turn left and go past Bolton Swim and Tennis Club to Park Avenue. The club came about when an ad hoc committee of Bolton Hill residents purchased cleared land that the city couldn't sell for houses. Now pool, tennis courts, and a children's playground make a neighborhood center. In 1978 the club inspired a song in a popular local musical review called "Bolton Hill Follies":

We show our legs for jogging at dawn
Tennis at two with little more on.
Grown men and women fool
Down at the swimming pool
Baring their bods for a tan.
Then at dusk we sip a martini
Wearing our trunks or stringy bikinis.

Debbie Phinney, *Bolton Hill Follies* (1978)

At Park Avenue turn right and walk to Howard Street, where you can pick up the light rail for return to downtown. Enter the southbound trolley marked Cromwell Station and get off at Camden Yards. From that stop, walk east along Pratt Street toward the water and Constellation Dock.

A Bolton Street Block Fights Back, Throws Off Blight and Regains Former Glory

Window panes were smashed. Backyards were neck deep in rubbish and back fences were burned up piecemeal for firewood. Wooden partitions were run up in beautiful old drawing rooms to make extra sleeping apartments, and rats and insects held high carnival all over the place. . . .

The sight was enough to make a stout heart quake, but instead of quaking the few residents who had held on to their homes got busy. Organizing themselves into the Neighborhood Corporation, they incorporated and bought as many additional houses as the owners could be persuaded to sell. . . .

During the past two years eight houses in the block have been restored and all but two of them by the new owners and occupants. Through the restoration some of the most charming apartments in Baltimore have come into existence and have been rented before the work of restoration has been completed.

The old families are there, too—one is represented by a great-great-nephew of Betsy Patterson, who moved in with his bride not so long ago. Newcomers from other cities who have brought along their own traditions of gentility, together with their own outlook on life, and found both compatible with the Bolton street atmosphere, contribute a certain cosmopolitanism which is an essential feature of its vitality.

Katherine Scarborough, *Baltimore Sun* (May 14, 1939)

Public market patron
and clerk

Places to Go to Indulge Special Interests

This section works in tandem with the walks. To pursue a special interest, here are notes on where to go for what. With these suggestions in hand, you can find sites by using the index, maps, and telephone numbers. And almost all suggestions have fuller notes in the regular tours. Some points of interest require driving as well as walking. All sites are accessible to the handicapped on at least one level, unless otherwise noted.

Now the city is well signed—not, as it used to be, a puzzling maze of streets. Blue-and-green signs point the way to major institutions such as colleges and museums and to such points of importance as Poe's grave and Harborplace. Downtown there are large signs over intersections naming cross streets. You will find plaques attached to historic sites.

AFRICAN AMERICANS

More than half the present population of Baltimore is African American. This group has contributed members to the city council, state assembly, U.S. Congress and Supreme Court, as well as two mayors (as of 1994).

Lillie Carroll Jackson Museum, 1312 Eutaw Place (523-1208), focuses on Jackson's years as president of the Baltimore chapter of the NAACP (1935–69). The plaque outside the door gives her birth and death dates, 1889–1975, and her words, "God opened my mouth and no man can shut it." (Not accessible.)

Enoch Pratt Free Library, Maryland Room (second floor), 400 Cathedral Street (396-5430), provides books and vertical files, and leads to other sites.

Frederick Douglass stands out as speaker and writer for change. Go to Fells Point for his sites. There you will find the only existing buildings directly related to Douglass, Douglass Terrace, rowhouses in the 600 block of Dallas Street. These he built in 1890 as rental properties.

Great Blacks in Wax Museum, 1601 E. North Avenue (563-3404), offers what is said to be the only wax museum of African-American culture and history—and the first in the nation.

U.S. Supreme Court Justice Thurgood Marshall lived at 1838 Druid Hill Avenue in 1936 (still a private residence), when he had just succeeded in having the first African American admitted to the University of Maryland Law School. A statue of Justice Marshall stands next to the federal courthouse, West Pratt Street at South Hanover Street.

ANTIQUES

Good places to see antiques include:

Mount Clare, Carroll Park, Monroe Street/Washington Boulevard (837-3262), was built by Barrister Charles Carroll in 1754. This plantation house contains original family furniture. Many furnishings remain in place where Martha Washington saw them when she visited here.

Carroll Mansion, 800 E. Lombard Street (396-3523), was the restored winter quarters of the longest-surviving signer of the Declaration of Independence, Charles Carroll of Carrollton. Now restored, the house has furnishings from the 1820s, some from Carroll himself.

In the adjacent 1840 House you can contrast the simpler interiors of a wheelwright's family.

The Star-Spangled Banner Flag House is just around the corner at 844 E. Pratt Street. Here seamstress Mary Pickersgill made the flag that flew over Fort McHenry during the 1814 Battle of Baltimore. Furnishings come from the Federal period.

The American Wing of the Baltimore Museum of Art, Art Museum Drive between Charles and 31st streets (396-7101), exhibits Maryland furniture and artifacts from the seventeenth century on. Especially prized pieces include Findlay painted furniture and recently acquired examples of eighteenth-century East Coast furniture from Dorothy Scott McIllvaine. Look for a series of authentically furnished rooms from historic Willowbrook, Waterloo Row, and Eltonhead Manor. This largest museum in Maryland owns a permanent collection of over 125,000 artworks, among which are Baltimore Album quilts. Other needlework came along with a bequest of Matisse's work and that of other major modern artists from the two Baltimore Cone sisters, who were inspired by their friend Gertrude Stein.

Maryland Historical Society, Museum and Library of Maryland History, 201 W. Monument Street (685-3750), contains furniture from all periods and one of the largest nineteenth-century silver collections in the world.

ARCHITECTURE

As a boomtown of early nineteenth-century America, Baltimore spelled money for architects. Here is a list of their remaining major structures:

Washington Monument, Mount Vernon and Washington places, the nation's first large-scale memorial to the first president, offers you a chance to climb inside stairs to a view at the top. It also contains an exhibit about its planning and construction.

Old Otterbein United Methodist Church, Sharp and Conway streets (685-4703), is the oldest church in continuous use in town (built in 1785–86) and now exhibits its history in the lobby.

Basilica of the Assumption (the old Cathedral), 400 block of Cathedral Street between Franklin and Mulberry streets, was designed by Benjamin Henry Latrobe for the first American Catholic See. It remains "North America's most beautiful church," according to architectural historian Nikolaus Pevsner. Generations have worshiped within its classical revival walls.

In the field of domestic architecture, see the indigenous rowhouse—groups of red-brick houses, with white marble steps and trim—up and down old Baltimore. Go to Bolton Hill, specifically, to study this type of house.

ART AND MONUMENTS

Art

Baltimore Museum of Art, Museum Drive between Charles and Howard Streets above 29th Street (396-7100)

Maryland Historical Society, 300 block of W. Monument Street (685-3750)

Peale Museum, 225 Holliday Street (396-1149)

Walters Art Gallery, main entrance in the 100 block of West Centre Street (547-9000)

Monuments

Battle Monument, Monument Square, Calvert Street, between Fayette and Lexington streets

Holocaust Memorial, Gay Street between Fayette and Water streets

Korean War Memorial, Canton Cove Park

The Negro Warrior, by James Lewis (next to Battle Monument)

Portrait sculpture, Mount Vernon and Washington places, and Federal Hill Park

Vietnam War Memorial, south bank of Middle Branch at Hanover Street Bridge, Waterview and Hanover streets (837-4636)

War Memorial Building, City Hall Plaza

Baltimoreans may have reached their finest hour in September 1814 when they repelled attack by seasoned British forces. The enemy's land force moved up the North Point peninsula to the east side of town. Attack by water culminated in bombardment of Fort McHenry at the entrance of the Inner Harbor. There were other river thrusts in Middle Branch at forts Covington and Babcock.

Battle Monument, Monument Square, North Calvert Street at East Fayette Street

Fort McHenry, end of Locust Point, east end of Fort Avenue (962-4290)

Francis Scott Key Monument, Eutaw Place at West Lanvale Street

Maryland Historical Society. 201 W. Monument Street (685-3750)

Peale Museum, 225 Holliday Street (396-1149)

Sites of Fort Covington and Fort Babcock (South Baltimore, near Federal Hill Park and Riverside Park, but not marked)

Star-Spangled Banner Flag House, 844 E. Pratt Street (837-1793)

CHILDREN

You can invest a day here with children—yours or the Brownie troop, or whoever. Just plan ahead, and locate restrooms and sources of food. Here are suggestions of what to do and see:

Climb Federal Hill and play on the swings and seesaws.

Go on trains at the B&O Railroad Museum, West Pratt and Poppleton streets (237-2387).

Go to the new Children's Center, The Brokerage, Market Place (if it is open by the time you visit Baltimore).

Ride antique streetcars at the Baltimore Streetcar Museum, 1901 Falls Road (547-0264).

Ride the carousel, next to the Science Center, near Rash Field and the Harbor Promenade south of Harborplace.

Tour ships docked in the Inner Harbor near Harborplace (they come and go, especially in summer); Baltimore Maritime Museum, Pier 3, East Pratt Street (396-3854).

Tour the zoo, Druid Hill Park (366-5466); more than 1,200 animals, plus a Children's Zoo .

Watch fish, dolphins, and seals at the National Aquarium (576-3800).

Work with machines (hands-on) in the Baltimore Museum of Industry, 1415 Key Highway (727-4808).

Visit the Babe Ruth Museum (his birthplace), 216 Emory Street (727-1539).

Visit the Science Center (685-5225) and Davis Planetarium (685-2370).

EUROPEAN NATIONALS

For thousands of Europeans, America began at the immigration pier on Locust Point near Fort McHenry. So many of them stayed in Baltimore that at times the town seemed inundated with foreign voices. Germans assimilated fairly quickly. Italians struck down roots in one place more permanently—now a center for Italian restaurants called Little Italy. Some of the other restaurants appear in "Information for Out-of-Towners." A drive through Canton and Highlandtown will show you ethnic churches, building and loan associations, and restaurants serving national cuisines.

FIRSTS

For a supposedly stodgy place, Baltimore has offered the world a number of innovations. These range from the first commercially successful railroad to the bottle cap, from the linotype that produced a flood of books to commercial ice cream, and from vitamin B to ouija and the motor bus.

Baltimore Museum of Industry, 1415 Key Highway
    (727-4808)
The B&O Museum, 901 W. Pratt Street (237-2387)
The Radcliffe Maritime Museum, Maryland Historical
    Society, 201 W. Monument Street (685-3750)

I-HATE-OLD-HOUSES

Some people have had it with old houses and house museums but are keen on exploring Baltimore. A good place to begin is at the Top of the World, in the World Trade Center, Inner Harbor, 401 E. Pratt Street (333-4545).

Baltimore Public Works Museum and Streetscape, Eastern and East Falls avenues (396-5565): inside the copper-roofed 1912 Eastern Avenue Sewage Pumping Station are media presentations and exhibits about the development of this city. You see also what a complex infrastructure lies beneath the streets.

Baltimore Streetcar Museum, 1901 Falls Road (547-0264) provides exhibits and a media presentation that lead to a ride in an antique streetcar along a reconstructed track next to Jones Falls.

Lovely Lane Museum, 2200 St. Paul Street (889-1512): the story of the founding of American Methodism is told through memorabilia, portraits, hymnals, and exhibits.

Peale Museum, 225 Holliday Street (396-3523): America's first museum building, and later, the first city hall, now exhibits Baltimore history as well as art of the painting Peale family.

Shot Tower, 801 E. Fayette Street (396-5894): one of the last remaining factories for making shot, this 234-foot tower dates from 1828–92.

U.S. Frigate *Constellation,* Constellation Dock, Pratt Street, Inner Harbor: a warship of 1797 gives an idea of what it was like to sail the ocean and fight.

LITERATURE

A Baltimore poet and adviser to poets and others, Richard Hart wrote, "Again and again over the years I've had conversations with a young man or woman of which the theme was, 'I've got to get out of here.'" Hart adds that Baltimore imposes its mark on writers who leave: Russell Baker, James M. Cain, Dashiell Hammett, Murray Kempton, Adrienne Rich, Karl Shapiro, and Leon Uris are examples.

Writers whose life in Baltimore affected what they wrote include John Barth, John Dos Passos, H. L. Mencken, Ogden Nash, Edgar Allan Poe, Gertrude Stein, and Anne Tyler.

H. L. Mencken House, 1524 Hollins Street (396-7997): from 1883 to 1956 (except for his married years, 1930–35) this writer lived and worked here. His full records he lodged downtown in what is now the Mencken Room of the Enoch Pratt Free Library, 400 Cathedral Street. But the furnishings he knew remain.

Peabody Library of the Johns Hopkins University, 1 E. Mount Vernon Place (659-8179): generations of scholars worked here, including Woodrow Wilson and John Dos Passos.

The Poe House and Museum, 203 N. Amity Street (396-7932): here Poe lived and wrote from 1832 to 1835.

MARITIME

Baltimore Maritime Museum, Pier 3, East Pratt Street
    (396-3854), combines the submarine USS *Torsk* with
    lightship *Chesapeake.*
Radcliffe Maritime Museum, Maryland Historical Soci-
    ety, 201 W. Monument Street (685-3750)
SS *John W. Brown,* Pier 1, Clinton Street (558-0646), re-
    stored World War II Liberty Ship built in Baltimore
    (one of the few extant)
U.S. Frigate *Constellation,* Constellation Dock, Pratt
    Street

MARKETS

Market Street (changed later to Baltimore Street)
flourished as the town's main thoroughfare. Near it,
town fathers established food markets. There people
congregated to buy, sell, and gossip. Stallkeepers came in
from farms to sell to neighborhood housewives, who
carried baskets on their arms or had them carried by servants. Now several of the old markets purvey food indoors. At lunchtime the markets are crowded, especially
on weekends. Seafood stalls thrive.

Broadway Market, entrances on the center of South
    Broadway at Lancaster Street, Aliceanna Street
    (396-9066)
Cross Street Market, 1025 S. Charles Street, entrances on
    Light Street and South Charles Street (396-3914)
Lexington Market, 400 W. Lexington Street, entrances
    on Eutaw Street, Paca Street, and Greene Street
    (685-6169)
Northeast Market, entrances on McElderry and Monu-
    ment streets (396-9024)

MEDICINE

Baltimoreans should be the healthiest folk alive because the ratio of physicians to population ranks high.

Davidge Hall, University of Maryland Medical School,
    Lombard Street at Greene Street (728-7820)
Maryland Medical and Chirurgical Society, Cathedral
    Street at Preston Street (539-0872)
National Dentistry Museum [being created in 1995]
Olive Cole Pharmacy Museum, 650 W. Lombard Street
    (727-0746)
Welch Library, Johns Hopkins Medical Institutions,
    1900 E. Monument Street (955-3413)

Two centuries ago the town's princes of finance and the princes of government could not have bowed to each other because they would have been one and the same. Today they could bow—but possibly wouldn't want to.

City Hall, War Memorial Plaza, facing Holliday Street (396-3100)

Clarence Mitchell Jr. Court House, Monument Square (333-3733)

The Law Center, University of Baltimore, Mount Royal Avenue at Maryland Avenue (837-4468)

Statue of U.S. Supreme Court Justice Thurgood Marshall, West Pratt Street at South Hanover Street

Statue of Chief Justice Roger B. Taney, North Washington Place next to the Washington Monument

Statue of Attorney Severn Teackle Wallis, East Mount Vernon Place, facing St. Paul Street

University of Maryland School of Law, 400 W. Baltimore Street. Ask to see the plaque honoring Luther Martin, who defended Aaron Burr in his trial for treason and Justice Samuel Chase at his impeachment hearing (706-7214).

PRESERVATION DISTRICTS

This past generation set up nineteen historic districts—some municipal, some federal—to preserve streetscapes. Go to the Commission on Historical and Architectural Preservation, East Fayette Street (396-4866) for maps and information.

Districts include Bancroft Park, Barre Circle, Bolton Hill, Brick Hill, Business and Government Center, Butchers Hill, Canton, Cathedral Hill, Charles Village Abell, Dickeyville, Druid Hill Park, Dundalk, Eutaw Place/Madison Avenue, Federal Hill, Fells Point, Franklin Square, Little Montgomery Street, Loft, Madison Park, Mount Royal Terrace, Historic Mount Royal, Mount Vernon, Mount Washington, Old Goucher College, Otterbein, Ridgely's Delight, Roland Park, St. Paul Street, Seton Hill, Stirling Street, Union Square, Upton's Marble Hill, Washington Hill, Waverly.

RELIGION

Victorian Baltimore must have built more churches per capita than any place since the medieval Age of Faith. Victorians also knew how to place their edifices so that spires, domes, and steeples end vistas. Here is a sampling from the dozen walks:

Jewish: Lloyd Street Synagogue, entered through the
Jewish Heritage Center, 11–27 Lloyd Street (358-9417)

Protestant: First and Franklin Street Presbyterian
Church, Park Avenue and Madison Street (728-5545)

Roman Catholic: Basilica of the Assumption, Cathedral
and Mulberry Streets (727-3564)

Other: Orchard Street Cultural Center and headquarters
of the Urban League, 516 Orchard Street, near Martin
Luther King Jr. Boulevard; Old Otterbein Methodist
Church, Conway and Sharp streets (685-4703);
Old St. Paul's Church, Charles at Saratoga streets
(685-3404); St. Jude Shrine, Paca and Saratoga streets
(685-6026); Zion Lutheran Church, 400 E. Lexington Street (727-3939)

SCIENCE

Baltimore Museum of Industry, 1415 Key Highway,
(727-4808)

Cylburn Arboretum, 4915 Greenspring Avenue
(396-0180)

Space Telescope Science Institute, edge of Johns Hopkins University, San Martin Drive (338-4700)

SPORTS

Baltimore Arena, 201 W. Baltimore Street (347-2020)

The Lacrosse Hall of Fame Museum, Johns Hopkins
University, 113 W. University Parkway (235-6882)

Oriole Park at Camden Yards, 33 Camden Street
(685-9800)

Pimlico Race Course, Hayward and Winner avenues
(542-9400)

Information for Out-of-Towners

Police/Fire/Medical Emergencies
Dial 911. University of Maryland Medical Center is
nearest the Inner Harbor; emergency department
(328-6722); physician referral service (328-0199).

Visitor Services
Baltimore Area Visitors Center, (837-4636 or 800-282-
6632). Ask for the *Guest Quick Guide* to current attractions, lodgings, and restaurants.
Downtown Partnership, 330 N. Charles Street
(244-1030)
Waxter Center for Senior Citizens (396-1341)

Airports
Baltimore-Washington International (BWI) (859-7100
or 859-7111)
Dulles (202-471-7838)
National (202-685-8000)

Auto rentals
Alamo (800-327-9633)
Avis (800-331-1212)
National (859-8860)

Accommodations
Along with the usual national chain hotels, consider
this list of bed and breakfasts, or call Amanda's Bed and
Breakfast Reservation Service at 225-0001.

Baltimore International Hostel, 17 W. Mulberry Street
(576-8880)
The Biltmore, 205 W. Madison Street (728-6550 or
800-868-5064)
Peabody Inn, Elderhostel, Peabody Mews off Washing-
ton Place South (659-8193)
Inn at Government House, 1125–1129 North Calvert
Street (539-0566)
Mr. Mole Bed and Breakfast, 1601 Bolton Street
(728-1179)
Mulberry House, 111 W. Mulberry Street (576-0111)

SHOPS

Antiques

Because early Baltimore craftsmen made names for themselves, this city offers a cornucopia of nationally famous antiques. Some are for sale.

Antique Row, 800 block of Howard Street (east side), especially Harris Auction Galleries (728-7040). During much of the nineteenth century, Baltimore provided the coastal South with stylish house furnishings. Although you probably won't find painted furniture from the early nineteenth-century Howard Street shop of the Irish Findlays, you will survey rooms full of everything else old. Ask to see silver made by the oldest American company still in business, Kirk. Now the Kirk Stieff Company, its factory store is open at Wyman Park Drive and Keswick Road (338-6080).

Colwill-McGehee Antique Decorative and Fine Arts, 1106 N. Charles Street (547-8607)

BOOKS

Apart from the usual national chain bookstores, you will find only a few shops selling new books downtown. One is Gordon's, 8 E. Baltimore Street (685-7313), and another is Louie's Bookstore Café, 518 N. Charles Street (962-1222).

For preowned books, your pickings are better, particularly in the unit block of West 25th Street. The largest and oldest in the block is Kelmscott Book Shop, 32 W. 25th Street (235-6810).

CLOTHING

With the exception of national specialty shops, women get short-changed when looking for good clothes downtown. Look in the Gallery at Harborplace.

Men fare somewhat better because there are two retail shops with some longevity to anchor them: Joseph A. Bank, corner of Light and Pratt streets (547-1700), and Eddie Jacobs, Ltd., Light Street (752-2624). Also try the Gallery at Harborplace.

GIFTS AND SOUVENIRS

Baltimore Photo Supply Co., 320 North Charles Street (752-4475)

The Dark Room, 308 North Charles Street (538-5639)

The Gallery at Harborplace, 200 E. Pratt Street (332-4191)

Harborplace, Pratt and Light Streets (332-4191)

FOOD AND DRINK

A number of places are pointed out on the walks. Here are old standbys grouped to help you choose. With the exception of the neighborhood restaurants, all these are members of the Baltimore Area Convention Visitors Association. If you want international cuisine—ranging from Afghan to Vietnamese—look in the *Guest Quick Guide* of the Visitors Center for listings.

Bertha's Dining Room, 734 South Broadway (327-5795)
Haussner's Restaurant, 3242 Eastern Avenue (327-8365)
Maison Marconi, 106 W. Saratoga Street (727-9522)
Obrycki's Crab House and Seafood Restaurant, 1727 E. Pratt Street (732-6399)
The Pavilion at the Walters, 600 North Charles Street (727-2233)
Tio Pepe Restaurante, 10 E. Franklin Street (539-4675)
Weber's On Boston, 845 South Montford Avenue (276-0800)

Of numerous long-established neighborhood places beyond downtown, here are two:

Alonso's Restaurant and Package Goods, 415 W. Cold Spring Lane (235-3433)
Frazier's Restaurant and Tap Room, 857 W. 33rd Street (889-1143)

TRANSPORTATION

By Car
Look for blue and green trailblazer signs pointing to main sites. Main streets are mostly one way.

Public Transportation
Buses provide twenty-four-hour service on main routes. The Metro runs from Owings Mills in the northwest to downtown and then northeast to Johns Hopkins Medical Institutions. Light rail service follows a north-south path from Timonium Fairgrounds to Glen Burnie. Inquire at MTA (539-5000) about hours on these last two lines.

To BWI Airport
For the BWI Airport Van Shuttle call 859-7545 or ask hotel staff. Taxi and limousine fares range from $17 to $25.

To Washington

The MARC commuter trains run weekdays from Camden and Penn stations (800-325-RAIL), and Amtrak goes every day (800-872-7245).

Taxis

Sun Cab (235-0300)
Yellow Cab (685-1212)

By Water

Al Schooner Nighthawk Cruises (327-SAIL): three-hour summer evening cruises with food, drink, and live entertainment leave from Thames Street, Fells Point.

Baltimore Defender and Guardian (685-4288): shuttle from finger pier, west shore of the Inner Harbor (Memorial Day to Labor Day)

Baltimore Patriot II and III (685-4288): narrated harbor tours, April 1–October 31

The Chesapeake Flyer (800-473-3779): high-speed ferry to Annapolis and the Eastern Shore

Clipper City (539-6277): a floating restaurant

Harbor Boating (water-taxi and paddleboat rentals) (547-0090): taxi makes fifteen stops around the Inner Harbor.

Minnie V. Skipjack (522-4214): historic Chesapeake Bay oyster boat available in summer for narrated harbor tours

Acknowledgments

Like a plum pudding stuffed with good things, this guide owes its goodness to many sources. I am grateful to everyone who contributed ingredients. Most deserving of thanks is my family, especially my unusually patient wife. Our four children pushed me into word processing, thank goodness. And Peter Fitz led me to the machine and through these pages (with assists from Debbie Kennedy and Jonathan Schorr).

Right up there for thanks are the underpaid women and men in libraries and archives. You know who you are. Readers of the manuscript in its developing phases deserve medals. Some readers slogged through the whole book, others focused on certain parts: Robert Alexander, Karen Birdsong, Barbara Bonnell, Jean Louis Bouet, John Breihan, Jennifer Bryan, Charles Carroll, Rodney Clough, Jeff Coram, H. Chace Davis Jr., Herbert A. Davis, Margaret Warner Deford, Carolyn Donkervoet, Charles B. Duff Jr., Ellen Watson Eager, Betty Lee Ellinghaus, Alan H. Fisher, Vincent Fitzpatrick III, Edward Gunts, Thomas Hallowak, Elisabeth Heyward, Margaret S. Heyward, Joan Houghton, Cindy Kelly, Ellie Kelly, Jacques Kelly, W. Boulton Kelly, Barry Kessler, Mary Lib McNair, Franklin Mason, David L. Maulsby Jr., Jay G. Merwin, Erik Olson, Garrett Power, Leonard B. Rowles Jr., Louise M. Rowles, Walter Schamu, Liz Shively, George R. Shivers, Lottchen G. Shivers, Natalie W. Shivers, Dr. Thomas B. Turner, Judy B. Waxter, William D. Waxter 3d, Christopher Weeks, and Elizabeth L. Wilkinson.

Louise Rowles had the thankless job of making the index. Nothing at all could have been done without Robert J. Brugger, my editor. I needed his gentle chivying and steady encouraging. And what would this book be like without photographs by Lisa Frances Davis? Her enthusiasm for photography and her hometown overcame all the obstacles presented by a difficult tour leader and subtropical Baltimore.

For Further Reading

Andrews, Matthew Page. *The Fountain Inn Diary* (1948).

Baker, Russell. *Growing Up* (1982).

Barth, John. *Letters* (1990).

Beirne, Francis E. *The Amiable Baltimoreans* (1951).

Brown, George William. *Baltimore and the Nineteenth of April 1861: A Study of the War* (1887).

Brugger, Robert J. *Maryland, A Middle Temperament, 1634–1980* (1988).

Dilts, James. *The Great Road: The Building of the Baltimore and Ohio, the Nation's First Railroad, 1828-1853* (1993).

Dorsey, John. *Mount Vernon Place* (1983).

Dorsey, John, and James Dilts. *The Architecture of Baltimore* (1981).

Douglass, Frederick. *The Life and Times of Frederick Douglass* (1881).

Fee, Elizabeth. *The Baltimore Book* (1992).

Fitzgerald, F. Scott. *Tender Is the Night* (1934).

———. *The Crack-Up* (1945).

Flexner, Helen Thomas. *A Quaker Childhood* (1940).

Freeman, Roland. *The Arabbers of Baltimore* (1989).

Hammett, Dashiell. *The Glass Key* (1931).

Hiss, Alger. *Recollections of a Life* (1988).

Howard, John Eager. *Musings and Reminiscences of a Pseudo-Scientist* (1985).

Janvier, Meredith. *Baltimore in the Eighties* (1933).

Johnson, Gerald W. *American Watching* (1976).

Joseph, Daniel C. *Send Me Up a Blanket! A Lawyer's Recollection* (1972).

Kelly, Jacques. *Bygone Baltimore* (1982).

Levinson, Barry. *Avalon, Tin Men, and Diner: Three Screenplays* (1990).

Lord, Walter. *The Dawn's Early Light* (1972).

Manchester, William. *City of Anger* (1953).

Marbury, William. *In the Catbird Seat* (1990).

Mencken, H. L. *Happy Days* (1940).

Mitchell, S. *A Family Lawsuit: The Story of Elizabeth Patterson and Jerome Bonaparte* (1958).

Morley, Christopher. *Thorofare* (1942).

Olson, Sherry. *Baltimore: The Building of an American City* (1980).

Reese, Lizette Woodworth. *Victorian Village* (1931).

Shivers, Frank R., Jr. *Maryland Wits and Baltimore Bards: A Literary History* (1985).

Sioussat, Annie Leakin. *Old Baltimore* (1931).

Stead, Christina. *The Man Who Loved Children* (1930).

Stockett, Letitia. *A Not Too Serious History of Baltimore* (1928).

Turner, Thomas Bourne. *Part of Medicine, Part of Me: Musings of a Johns Hopkins Dean* (1981).

Tyler, Anne. *The Accidental Tourist* (1985).

Waters, John. *Shock Value* (1981).

Index